That Others may Know and Love

Essays in Honor of
Zachary Hayes, OFM

Franciscan, Educator, Scholar

Edited by

Michael F. Cusato, OFM
and
F. Edward Coughlin, OFM

The Franciscan Institute
St. Bonaventure University
St. Bonaventure, New York

1997

©
The Franciscan Institute
St. Bonaventure University
St. Bonaventure, New York

October 3, 1997

The publication of this volume was made possible through the generous assistance of the Friars Minor of the Holy Name Province (New York), the Friars Minor of the Sacred Heart Province (St. Louis—Chicago), The Franciscan Institute (St. Bonaventure University), Siena College, and the Franciscan Federation of the Brothers and Sisters of the Third Order Regular (Washington, DC).

Cover Design
    An original water color by G. Moretti (Assisi, 1995) of the rose window of the Basilica of St. Francis is used as the background for this cover. It suggests the light which the life of St. Francis reflected onto Bonaventure's deepening understanding of the following of Christ, the Incarnate Word, the One who became for all "the Way, the Truth, and the Life." It is used with the artists permission.

ISBN: 1–57659–130–1

Printed in the USA
        Bookmasters
        Ashland, Ohio

Table of Contents

I
Zachary Hayes:
Franciscan, Educator, Scholar

II
The Franciscan Philosophical and Theological Tradition

Medieval Expressions

A Salute to Professor Zachary Hayes

While this *Festschrift* has been prepared in honor of Professor Zachary Hayes on the occasion of his sixty-fifth birthday, its publication also marks the completion of thirty years of service by him at Catholic Theological Union in Chicago.

His service has taken a variety of forms. Professor Hayes was a member of the planning team on curricular design which met for two full years before the opening of CTU. He has been a member of the Historical and Doctrinal Studies Department during all of his tenure on faculty. He has served as department chair for a number of terms and has held the position of Director of the Master of Arts Degree Program.

Professor Hayes is distinguished for his scholarship and his teaching, as this volume attests. As a colleague, his personal interest in the professional growth of other members of the faculty is without question. But, perhaps most importantly, he has been a mentor to many students, teasing out the edges of their theological thinking and always concerned that their academic life be a source for the development of their spirituality and a ground for their ministry.

On the occasion of the publication of this *Festschrift*, it is with heartfelt thanks that I join my personal congratulations to those of the faculty and administration here at Catholic Theological Union in saluting Prof. Hayes on his accomplishments as a theologian and on his service to theological education for ministry

Gary Riebe-Estrella, S.V.D.
Academic Dean
Catholic Theological Union at Chicago

June 13, 1997

"... understand that no creature has proceeded to the most high Creator except through the Eternal Word, in whom God has disposed all things, and by which Word God has produced creatures bearing not only the nature of a *vestige* but also of an *imago* so that **through knowledge and love** creatures become like God."

St. Bonaventure
On the Reduction of the Arts to Theology, #12

Zachary Hayes

Franciscan, Educator and Scholar

Gilbert Ostdiek, O.F.M.

Catholic Theological Union

There is no more apt way to begin this essay than with the words which St. Bonaventure wrote at the close of his work, *De Reductione Artium ad Theologiam*:

> And this is the fruit of all sciences, that in all, faith may be strengthened, *God may be honored*, character may be formed, and consolation may be derived from union of the Spouse with the beloved, a union which takes place through charity: a charity in which the whole purpose of sacred Scripture, and thus of every illumination descending from above, comes to rest: a charity without which all knowledge is vain because no one comes to the Son except through the Holy Spirit who teaches *all the truth, who is blessed forever. Amen.*[1]

These words express the underlying attitude which shaped the entire theological enterprise of the Seraphic Doctor. The theology of St. Bonaventure has been a central focus in the scholarly work and teaching of Fr. Zachary Hayes, O.F.M., and the spirit and wisdom of St. Bonaventure have been his constant guide.

This essay on Fr. Hayes,[2] franciscan educator and scholar, will begin with a brief chronicle of his life and educational career, review some of the influences that have shaped his development

---

[1] *On the Reduction of the Arts to Theology: Translation with Introduction and Commentary (Works of St. Bonaventure,* I), prepared by Zachary Hayes (St. Bonaventure, NY: The Franciscan Institute, 1996) 61.

[2] It gives me great pleasure to offer this essay on Zachary Hayes, franciscan educator and scholar, on the occasion of the celebration of his sixty-fifth birthday. We have been faculty colleagues for more than thirty years and franciscan confreres for even longer. I am especially grateful for all I have learned from him in those years. I also wish to thank Fr. Alcuin Coyle, O.F.M., for his careful review of this manuscript.

as a scholar and teacher, and conclude with a listing of his writings.

A Brief Biography

The essential facts of the life and educational career of Fr. Hayes are easily told. He was born in Chicago, Illinois, on September 21, 1932. He grew up in south suburban Midlothian, where he belonged to St. Christopher's, a parish served at that time by the friars of the Sacred Heart Province. He attended the parochial grade school, which was staffed by the Franciscan Sisters of Dubuque, Iowa.

In 1946 Fr. Hayes entered St. Joseph Seminary in Westmont, Illinois, a preparatory seminary run by the friars of the Sacred Heart Province. The program there included four years of high school and two years of college focused on the humanities. On July 4, 1952, he entered the Order of Friars Minor, and after a year of novitiate at Teutopolis, Illinois, he made his first profession on July 5, 1953.

He spent the years 1953-1956 doing three more years of college study at Our Lady of Angels Seminary in Cleveland, Ohio, which was affiliated with Quincy College, Quincy, Illinois. The program consisted of an extensive major in philosophy and a minor in psychology. At the conclusion of these three years, he received his B.A. from Quincy College and made his solemn profession as a friar. In 1956 he went to St. Joseph Seminary in Teutopolis, Illinois, for four years of theological studies in preparation for ordained ministry. Ordination to the presbyterate took place at the end of the third year of the program, on June 24, 1959. The summers during his years of philosophical and theological studies were taken up with the study of music. He spent the summer of 1954 studying liturgical music at St. John's University, Collegeville. During the summers of 1955-1960 he was in the program of music education a t DePaul University in Chicago and studied the pipe organ as his major instrument.

On completion of his theological studies, Fr. Hayes was assigned to serve as catholic chaplain and pastor at the U.S. Embassy in Bonn-Bad Godesberg, West Germany, and to do a doctoral program in theology in the Faculty of Catholic Theology at Friedrich Wilhelm University in Bonn. After finishing his course work and completing the writing of his doctoral thesis, he successfully passed his oral doctoral examinations in November, 1963. His thesis was written under the direction of Johann Auer and is entitled: *The General Doctrine of Creation in the Thirteenth Century, with Special Emphasis on Matthew of Aquasparta*.[3] He remained at Bonn after his examinations to see to the publication of his thesis and to take additional courses in philosophy. He was awarded the degree of Dr. Theol. on July 9, 1964.

Dr. Hayes began his career as a friar educator in the autumn of 1964. He was assigned to St. Joseph Seminary in Teutopolis, Illinois, to teach systematic theology there. Four years later, in the fall of 1968, the seminary program and faculty were merged into the newly formed Catholic Theological Union in Chicago.[4] He has been a full-time member of that faculty since that time, and in 1974 he was promoted to the rank of full professor.

In addition to his work at Catholic Theological Union, Fr. Hayes has taught at a number of schools throughout the country. He was for many years a member of the summer faculty at St. Bonaventure University, teaching in the M.A. program in Sacred Science (1966-1990) and in the Franciscan Institute (1994). He has also served as a visiting professor at St. John's Seminary in Brighton, Massachusetts, Lutheran School of Theology in Chicago, the Divinity School of the University of Chicago, the Franciscan School of Theology in Berkeley, California, the University of Notre Dame, and the Chicago Center for Religion and Science sponsored by the Lutheran School of Theology.

Finally, his educational ministry has reached out beyond the circle of schools of graduate theology. He has presented a variety of lectures, workshops, and courses in adult education, on both local and diocesan levels. He has also served in educational admini-

---

[3] Zachary Hayes, *The General Doctrine of Creation in the Thirteenth Century, with Special Emphasis on Matthew of Aquasparta* (München: Verlag Ferdinand Schöningh, 1964). Hereafter the writings of Fr. Hayes will be cited in the text by a number in brackets which corresponds to the number under which they are entered in the bibliography below.

[4] For an account of the founding of Catholic Theological Union and an indication of the role Hayes played in it, see Paul Bechtold, *Catholic Theological Union: The Founding Years, 1965-1975* (Chicago: Catholic Theological Union, 1993).

stration, on governing boards, and as an advisor to the Franciscan Institute, several franciscan colleges, and his Order on the franciscan ideal of education [20, 43, 54, 67].

Among the awards Fr. Hayes has received in recognition of his work as an educator and scholar are honorary doctorates from St. Bonaventure University (1974) and Quincy University, Quincy, Illinois (1985) and the J. C. Murray Award for Distinguished Achievement bestowed on him by the Catholic Theological Society of America in 1985. He is widely regarded as one of the leading interpreters of St. Bonaventure in this country and, indeed, throughout the world. It is proper, then, to retrace this history in order to identify some of the intellectual influences that have helped him to achieve his present stature.

The Development of His Thought

The most significant influences on the thought of Fr. Hayes, after his early educational formation, begin with his philo- sophical studies at Our Lady of the Angels Seminary in Cleveland. And so we pick up the threads there. The aim of this section is less to summarize the content of Hayes' well-known scholarly work than to trace some of the influences that have helped to direct and shape his thought.

Perhaps the single most important influence comes from a friar whom Fr. Hayes never had in class, Philotheus Boehner (1901- 1955). As providence would have it, this German friar was visiting the campus of St. Bonaventure University in 1939 at the outbreak of World War II. Marooned in this country, he joined the faculty of St. Bonaventure's and played a significant role in the early years of the Franciscan Institute.[5] Trained originally as a biologist, Dr. Boehner had developed a keen interest in philosophy, particu- larly the work of medieval franciscans. He developed this interest through his contacts and work with the French medievalist Etienne Gilson, whose work on St. Bonaventure Boehner had translated into German in 1929. His deep love of the franciscan philosophical-theological tradition, paired with his interest in

---

[5]For a detailed history of the Institute, see Conrad Harkins, "General History of the Franciscan Institute," *Franciscan Studies* 51 (1991) 7-68.

contemporary science, left a deep mark on the philosophy program in Cleveland.

Fr. Hayes never had live contact with this creative thinker, who died shortly before he was to address the philosophy students in Cleveland in the spring of 1955. However, his influence did reach Hayes through several channels. The first such channel was Boehner's writings. His history of the franciscan school was used as a class reference in Hayes' years of philosophical studies.[6] This text offered the students an alternate assessment of the franciscan tradition that varied significantly from the standard interpretation found in the handbook tradition and it introduced them to the living intellectual ferment that marked the world of the medieval universities. Boehner's works on the logic and epistemology of William Ockham were widely recognized as land-mark studies.[7] These articles opened up to the students a critical re-reading of the standard neo-scholastic approach to these foundations of the philosophical tradition. And an unpublished address of Boehner on the goal of knowledge, based on St. Bonaventure's *Collation on the Gift of Knowledge*,[8] had a great impact on the students in the philosophy program.[9] It might also be noted that Boehner's translation of St. Bonaventure's *Itinerarium Mentis in Deum*[10] was another of his works to which Fr. Hayes would later turn.

A second line of influence from Philotheus Boehner reached Fr. Hayes through several of his professors who had worked with Boehner in their graduate studies. These friars included Leonard

---

[6]Philotheus Boehner, *The History of the Franciscan School* (St. Bonaventure, NY: St. Bonaventure University, 1943).

[7]Philotheus Boehner, "Ockham's Theory of Truth," *Franciscan Studies* 5 (1945) 138-161; "Ockham's Theory of Signification," *Franciscan Studies* 6 (1946) 143-170; "Ockham's Theory of Supposition and the Notion of Truth," *Franciscan Studies* 6 (1946) 261-292. These essays were reprinted in Philotheus Boehner, *Collected Articles on Ockham* (St. Bonaventure, NY: St. Bonaventure University, 1943) 173-200, 201-232, and 232-267 respectively.

[8]*Collationes de donis Spiritus Sancti*, V, 473-479.

[9]Philotheus Boehner, untitled address, circulated internally in *Duns Scotus Philosophical Association: Report of the Sixteenth Annual Convention, March 7 & 9, 1952* (Cleveland: Our Lady of Angels Seminary, 1952; private publication).

[10]*St. Bonaventure's Itinerarium Mentis in Deum: with an Introduction, Translation and Commentary* (*Works of St. Bonaventure*, II), transl. Philotheus Boehner (St. Bonaventure, NY: Franciscan Institute, 1956).

Paskert (1910-), Matthew Menges (1913-1972), and Allan Wolter (1913-).[11] The course Hayes took in epistemology with Paskert drew from the Augustinian tradition a stress on the role of experience in our knowing and from the franciscan tradition an emphasis on the role of intuition and love in our coming to know persons and things around us in their uniqueness. From Menges' courses, Fr. Hayes gained a lasting orientation to the thought of the franciscan school. This was especially true of the course in metaphysics. Based on a text developed by Allan Wolter,[12] this course took much of its inspiration from the metaphysics of Duns Scotus and invited dialogue with contemporary thought. In effect, it was an exercise in a contemporary reconstruction of the franciscan tradition received from the past. The third mentor during these years was Allan B. Wolter. Because of his faculty duties at Catholic University of America, he was only able to teach occasionally at the seminary in Cleveland. Nevertheless his influence there was pervasive. In addition to the course in metaphysics which he had developed for the seminary students, he periodically returned to Cleveland to teach a course in cosmology which had a great impact on Fr. Hayes. Continuing in the tradition of Boehner, Wolter brought to this course his own graduate background and deep interest in both philosophy and several branches of science.[13] Built around nine great issues in the philosophy of science raised by contemporary scientific study of the cosmos, this course introduced Hayes to the question of the relationship between the medieval tradition and contemporary

---

[11]Paskert did master's work in the Franciscan Institute at St. Bonaventure's. Menges' doctoral thesis at the Pontificium Athenaeum Antonianum in Rome was entitled *The Concept of Univocity regarding the Predication of God and Creature according to William Ockham* (St. Bonaventure, NY: The Franciscan Institute, 1952). Boehner generously made all his material on Ockham available to Menges and did a thorough criticism of the manuscript for him. Wolter, while a Ph.D. candidate at the Catholic University of America, had received approval to spend time at St. Bonaventure's in order to have Boehner direct his dissertation, *The Transcendentals and Their Function in the Metaphysics of Duns Scotus* (St. Bonaventure, NY: Franciscan Institute, 1946).

[12]Allan B. Wolter, *Summula Metaphysicae* (Milwaukee: Bruce, 1958). This book is a revised version of the course text used when Hayes studied metaphysics.

[13]During his graduate studies and early teaching career, Wolter's interest in the sciences had led him to take courses in geology, physics, nuclear physics, and mathematics.

science and stirred in him an abiding interest in cosmology. He still uses Wolter's unpublished text as a reference.

Fr. Hayes thus emerged from his philosophical studies with a number of areas of interest that would continue to develop in his career as a scholar and teacher. These included the franciscan school of thought and the work of St. Bonaventure in particular, an understanding of the role of experience as the starting point for critical reflection, a franciscan approach to knowledge which sets it squarely within the more fundamental context of love, the relationship between philosophical-theological tradition and contemporary science, and the cosmic dimension of the realities dealt with in philosophy and theology. These influences continued during his years of ordination studies, when his interest in the franciscan tradition on the centrality of Christ began to take firm root.[14] Christology has occupied a central place in his scholarly work and teaching ever since. The friars named above were mentors to Hayes in another way. From their teaching and example, he discovered the intellectual tradition of the Order and a love of learning. He also came to understand that the intellectual quest has been and can still remain at the heart of franciscan spirituality and that it opens into a franciscan ministry of education.

His assignment to do doctoral studies in Bonn was providential. There he found two mentors who were able to help him build on these early foundations. The first of these was Joseph Ratzinger, who later became a bishop and then a cardinal. His published works included his thesis on the understanding of the church in St. Augustine's *De Civitate Dei*[15] and his subsequent *Habilitations-schrift* on St. Bonaventure's theology of history,[16] which was published just before Fr. Hayes arrived at the University of Bonn

---

[14]This interest was spurred by two unpublished manuscripts of Allan Wolter, "The Absolute Primacy of Christ," and "The Primacy Again," circulated in *The Scotist*, an internal publication of Duns Scotus Theological Association, St. Joseph Seminary, Teutopolis, IL. Wolter would later return to this theme in his essay, "John Duns Scotus on the Primacy and Personality of Christ," in *Franciscan Christology: Selected Texts, Translations and Introductory Essays*, ed. Damian McElrath, (St. Bonaventure, NY: The Franciscan Institute, 1980) 139-182.

[15]Joseph Ratzinger, *Volk und Haus Gottes in Augustins Lehre von der Kirche* (München: Karl Zink Verlag, 1954).

[16]Joseph Ratzinger, *Die Geschichtstheologie des Heiligen Bonaventura* (München: Verlag Schnell & Steiner, 1959).

and which he later translated into English [2]. He was Ratzinger's student in several courses in the area of fundamental theology, including questions in the philosophy of religion, God's revelation in Jesus Christ, and the doctrine of the church.

The second mentor of note at Bonn was Johann Auer. His publications included a work on the thought of Aquinas and Scotus[17] and a survey of the high scholastic teaching on grace highlighting the teaching of Matthew of Aquasparta.[18] From him Fr. Hayes took courses and seminars in the central areas of systematic theology—creation, God, Trinity, christology, grace, and sacraments— as well as a course in medieval manuscripts. Auer also served as the director for Hayes' doctoral dissertation on the general doctrine of creation in the thirteenth century, which drew heavily on the disputed questions *De productione rerum et de providentia* of Matthew of Aquasparta [1].

Under the guidance of these two mentors, Hayes was able to flesh out the theological dimensions of his earlier interests, with the addition of creation theology and the theology of history in St. Augustine and St. Bonaventure. Here too, as in his philosophical studies, he learned to situate the great medieval theologians in their own context, for example on the question of how they wrestled with the doctrine of creation within an understanding of the cosmos as they knew it. The implication to be drawn is that theology today must do the same.

This overview of some of the formative influences on Fr. Hayes cannot end without at least a brief mention of several others who have helped him to give further shape to his thought during the years of research and teaching which have followed his doctoral work. First, the works of authors such as Teilhard de Chardin and Alfred North Whitehead have reinforced his own interest in the cosmic aspects of christology and the unfinished character of creation.

---

[17]Johannes Auer, *Die menschliche Willensfreiheit in Lerhsystem des Thomas von Aquin und Johannes Duns Scotus* (München: Max Hueber Verlag, 1938).

[18]Johann Auer, *Die Entwicklung der Gnadenlehre in der Hochscholastik* (Freiburg: Verlag Herder, 1951).

Second, David Tracy's work on the critical correlation of theology and culture[19] has struck a responsive chord in Hayes. Theology of the past is not just to be reconstructed and imported as it was for use in today's world. Rather, that theology is to be brought into a mutually critical interaction with the cultural categories of the contemporary world and the experience of the church today. The medieval philosopher-theologians constructed their synthesis in interaction with the Aristotelian physics and metaphysics of their day. What happens to theology when that science and worldview change?

Third, two other scholars have served as conversation partners with Fr. Hayes on matters bonaventurian. One was Ignatius Brady (1911-1990), a friar who shared the speaker's rostrum with him on the occasion of the Seventh Centenary Celebration of the death of St. Bonaventure held at St. Bonaventure University in 1974[20] and served as a reader and guide for Hayes while he was writing *The Hidden Center* [8]. The other conversation partner is Ewert Cousins, with whom Hayes has had continuing contact not only through his writings,[21] but especially through their scholarly exchanges at the "Colloquy on the Thought of Aquinas and Bonaventure" held in 1974 under the sponsorship of the University of Chicago [22] and at the annual medieval conferences at Kalamazoo, Michigan. One particular focus of this conversation has been the relationship between metaphysics and christology in St. Bonaventure.

The fourth source of recent influence paradoxically reaches back a century and a half ago. Asked by a publisher to write a book on developments in Roman Catholic theology at the turn of the century, Fr. Hayes found, to his disappointment, that there was not much to report beyond the mainstream of the neo-scholastic revival of the time. But he did discover intriguing developments in

---

[19]David Tracy, *Blessed Rage for Order: The New Pluralism in Theology* (New York: Seabury Press, 1975); *The Analogical Imagination: Christian Theology and the Culture of Pluralism* (New York: Crossroad, 1981).

[20]Ignatius Brady, "The Opera Omnia of Saint Bonaventure Revisited," in *Proceedings of the Seventh Centenary Celebration of the Death of St. Bonaventure*, ed. Pascal Foley (St. Bonaventure, NY: The Franciscan Institute, 1975) 47-59; Ignatius Brady, "St. Bonaventure's Theology of the Imitation of Christ," in *Proceedings of the Seventh Centenary Celebration of the Death of St. Bonaventure*, 61-72.

[21]See Ewert H. Cousins, *Bonaventure and the Coincidence of Opposites* (Chicago: Franciscan Herald Press, 1978).

the Catholic Faculty of Tübingen just prior to that time. What he found there was an early attempt, especially by Johann Evangelist Von Kuhn (1806-1887), to deal with modernity by critically engaging the dominant values of nineteenth century culture in the aftermath of the enlightenment. The Tübingen School elaborated a critical epistemology as the basis for developing a fully contemporary theology.[22] Research in libraries in this country and in the archives at Tübingen led Hayes first to summarize his findings in an extensive, unpublished manuscript and then to give a series of lectures and seminar presentations on this little known development in Catholic theology. An article on Von Kuhn is forthcoming [71].

Finally, one of the most recent influences on the thought of Fr. Hayes has been his involvement in the Chicago Center for Religion and Science.[23] For the past several years the Center has offered a course on "The Epic of Creation." The staff of presenters and panelists has included experts from a variety of disciplines: astronomers, biologists, physicists, and theologians. Hayes' continuing work as one of the presenters/panelists [70] has fed his long-standing interest in a critical interaction between theology and contemporary science and led him to a deeper study of the philosophy of science.[24]

It now remains to list the writings of Fr. Hayes. They show his remarkable consistency in developing and refining the cluster of central themes that date back to his educational formation. The thought of the franciscan school and of St. Bonaventure pervade the listing, and the franciscan love of knowledge which he learned at their feet has sustained him through a fruitful career as a franciscan scholar and educator.

---

[22]An outstanding example of this kind of development can be found in Johann Evangelist Von Kuhn, *Katholische Dogmatik* (Tübingen, 1846).

[23]The Center, sponsored by the Lutheran School of Theology in Chicago, is directed by Philip Heffner, a theologian, and Thomas Gilbert, a physicist. Ralph Burhoe, longtime editor of *Zygon*, had a great part to play in its establishment.

[24]Of particular interest to him have been the works of Ian Barbour, *Religion in an Age of Science* (The Gifford Lectures 1989-1991, vol. 1) (San Francisco: Harper SanFrancisco, 1990); Arthur Peacocke, *Theology for a Scientific Age: Being and Becoming – Natural, Divine and Human* (Minneapolis: Fortress Press, 1993); and John Polkinghorne, *The Faith of a Physicist: Reflections of a Bottom-Up Thinker* (The Gifford Lectures for 1993-4) (Princeton, NJ: Princeton University Press, 1994).

A bibliography of his works

Books and Translations

1   *The General Doctrine of Creation in the Thirteenth Century, with Special Emphasis on Matthew of Aquasparta* (München: Verlag Ferdinand Schöningh, 1964).

2   Joseph Ratzinger, *The Theology of History in St. Bonaventure*, transl. Zachary Hayes (Chicago: Franciscan Herald Press, 1971).

3   *What Manner of Man? Sermons on Christ by St. Bonaventure: A Translation with Introduction and Commentary*, transl. Zachary Hayes (Chicago: Franciscan Herald Press, 1974 [reprinted 1990]).

4   *To Whom Shall We Go? Christ and the Mystery of Man* (Chicago: Franciscan Herald Press, 1975).

5   Joseph Ratzinger and Karl Lehmann, *Living with the Church*, transl. Zachary Hayes (Chicago: Franciscan Herald Press, 1978).

6   *St. Bonaventure's Disputed Questions on the Mystery of the Trinity: Introduction and Translation (Works of St. Bonaventure*, III), transl. Zachary Hayes (St. Bonaventure, NY: The Franciscan Institute, 1979).

7   *What Are They Saying about Creation?* (New York: Paulist Press, 1980).

8   *The Hidden Center: Spirituality and Speculative Christology in St. Bonaventure* (New York: Paulist Press, 1981) [reprint: St. Bonaventure, NY: The Franciscan Institute, 1992].

9   *What Are They Saying About the End of the World?* (New York: Paulist Press, 1983).

10 *Visions of a Future: A Study of Christian Eschatology* (Collegeville: M. Glazier/Liturgical Press, 1989).

11   Lothar Hardick, *"He Came to You so that You Might Come to Him": The Life and Teaching of St. Anthony of Padua,* transl. Zachary Hayes (Chicago: Franciscan Herald Press, 1989).

12   *St. Bonaventure's Disputed Questions on the Knowledge of Christ: Introduction and Translation.* (*Works of St. Bonaventure,* IV), Trans. Zachary Hayes (St. Bonaventure, NY: The Franciscan Institute, 1992).

13   *On the Reduction of the Arts to Theology: Translation with Introduction and Commentary* (*Works of St. Bonaventure,* I), prepared by Zachary Hayes (St. Bonaventure, NY: The Franciscan Institute, 1996).

14   *A Window to the Divine: A Theology of Creation* (Quincy, IL: Franciscan Press, 1996) [revised edition of entry #7 above: *What Are They Saying about Creation?*].

Articles

15   "Reflections on the Theology of Community," *Franciscan Herald* 47 (1968) 42-49.

16   "And You Are All Brothers," *The Cord* 20 (1970) 77-83.

17   "Contemporary Man and the Paschal Mystery," *Worship* 45 (1971) 151-166.

18   "The Meaning of *Convenientia* in Bonaventure," *Franciscan Studies* 34 (1974) 74-100 [abstract in *The Philosopher's Index* (1975) 266].

19   "Revelation in Christ," in *Proceedings of the Seventh Centenary Celebration of the Death of St. Bonaventure,* ed. Pascal Foley (St. Bonaventure, NY: The Franciscan Institute, 1975) 29-43 [also in *The Cord* 24 (1974) 343-355].

20   "Toward a Philosophy of Education in the Spirit of St. Bonaventure," in *Proceedings of the Seventh Centenary Celebration of the Death of St. Bonaventure,* ed. Pascal Foley (St. Bonaventure, NY: The Franciscan Institute, 1975) 9-27 [reprinted in *Spirit and Life,* vol. 2, ed. Roberta

McKelvie (St. Bonaventure, NY: The Franciscan Institute, 1992) 18-37].

21 "Incarnation and Creation in the Theology of Bonaventure," *Studies Honoring Ignatius Charles Brady Friar Minor*, ed. Romano Stephen Almagno and Conrad L. Harkins (St. Bonaventure, NY: The Franciscan Institute, 1976) 309-329.

22 "Christology and Metaphysics in the Thought of Bonaventure," in *Celebrating the Medieval Heritage: A Colloquy on the Thought of Aquinas and Bonaventure*, ed. David Tracy and published as *The Journal of Religion* 58 Supplement (1978) S82-S96.

23 "The Life and Christological Thought of St. Bonaventure," with text and translation of Bonaventure's "On the Predestination of Christ," in *Franciscan Christology* (*Franciscan Sources*, No. 1), ed. Damian McElrath (St. Bonaventure, NY: The Franciscan Institute, 1980) 59-88.

24 "Cor Inquietum in St. Augustine," in *Proceedings of the First Institute on the Augustinian Spiritual Tradition*, ed. Richard Jacobs (Tolentine Center, 1981; private publication) 1-17.

25 "Can a Catholic Believe in Evolution?" *Ligourian* 70 (March, 1982) 34-37.

26 "Doctrinal Theology in the After-Math of Vatican II," *The Serran* (1982).

27 "Visions of a Future: Symbols of Heaven and Hell," *Chicago Studies* 24 (1985) 145-165.

28 "The Plurality of Esse in Christ according to Matthew of Aquasparta," in *Essays Honoring Allan B. Wolter*, ed. William A. Frank and Girard J. Etzkorn (St. Bonaventure, NY: The Franciscan Institute, 1985) 131-152.

29 "Bonaventure, St.," in *Encyclopedia of Religion*, ed. Mircea Eliade (New York: Macmillan, 1987) I, 281-284.

30 "Beatific Vision," in *The New Dictionary of Theology*, ed. Joseph A. Komonchak, Mary Collins, and Dermot A. Lane (Collegeville: M. Glazier/Liturgical Press, 1987) 81-83.

31 "Death," in *The New Dictionary of Theology*, ed. Joseph A. Komonchak, Mary Collins, and Dermot A. Lane (Collegeville: M. Glazier/Liturgical Press, 1987) 272-273.

32 "Heaven," in *The New Dictionary of Theology*, ed. Joseph A. Komonchak, Mary Collins, and Dermot A. Lane (Collegeville: M. Glazier/Liturgical Press, 1987) 454-456.

33 "Hell," in *The New Dictionary of Theology*, ed. Joseph A. Komonchak, Mary Collins, and Dermot A. Lane (Collegeville: M. Glazier/Liturgical Press, 1987) 457-459.

34 "Last Judgment," in *The New Dictionary of Theology*, ed. Joseph A. Komonchak, Mary Collins, and Dermot A. Lane (Collegeville: M. Glazier/Liturgical Press, 1987) 565-566.

35 "Limbo," in *The New Dictionary of Theology*, ed. Joseph A. Komonchak, Mary Collins, and Dermot A. Lane (Collegeville: M. Glazier/Liturgical Press, 1987) 585-586.

36 "Purgatory," in *The New Dictionary of Theology*, ed. Joseph A. Komonchak, Mary Collins, and Dermot A. Lane (Collegeville: M. Glazier/Liturgical Press, 1987) 823-825.

37 "Parousia," in *The New Dictionary of Theology*, ed. Joseph A. Komonchak, Mary Collins, and Dermot A. Lane (Collegeville: M. Glazier/Liturgical Press, 1987) 742-744.

38 "The Charism of the Religious Life," in *Our Franciscan Charism in the World Today*, ed. Alcuin Coyle (Clifton, NJ: Franciscan Advertising and Media Enterprises, 1987; private publication) 1-12 [keynote address at the conference of Provincials of the English-Speaking Provinces of Franciscans, 1987].

39 "The Theological Image of St. Francis of Assisi in the Sermons of St. Bonaventure," in *Bonaventuriana Miscellanea in onore di Jacques Guy Bougerol, ofm* (*Bibliotheca Pontificii*

Athenaei Antoniani, 27), ed. F. Chavero Blanco (Rome: Edizioni Antonianum, 1988) 323-345.

40 "Fundamentalist Eschatology: Piety and Politics," *New Theology Review* 1/2 (May, 1988) 21-35.

41 "The Lord is Risen," *The Bible Today* 27 (May, 1989) 153-159.

42 "Bonaventure," in *Handbook of Metaphysics and Ontology*, ed. Hans Burkhardt and Barry Smith (Munich: Philosophia Verlag, 1991).

43 "Reflections on a Franciscan University," in *Spirit and Life*, vol. 2, ed. Roberta McKelvie (St. Bonaventure, NY: The Franciscan Institute, 1992) 96-109.

44 "Purgatory," in *Four Views on Hell*, ed. William Crockett (Grand Rapids, MI: Zondervan Press, 1992) 91-118.

45 "Creation," in *The New Dictionary of Catholic Spirituality*, ed. Michael Downey (Collegeville: M. Glazier/Liturgical Press, 1993) 238-242.

46 "Eschatology," in *The New Dictionary of Catholic Spirituality*, ed. Michael Downey (Collegeville: M. Glazier /Liturgical Press, 1993) 354-357.

47 "St. Bonaventure: Mystery of the Triune God," in *The History of Franciscan Theology*, ed. Kenan Osborne (St. Bonaventure, NY: The Franciscan Institute, 1994) 39-126.

48 "Eschatology," in *The New Dictionary of Catholic Social Thought*, ed. Judith A. Dwyer (Collegeville: M. Glazier /Liturgical Press, 1994) 343-348.

49 "Eschatology," in *The Modern Catholic Encyclopedia*, ed. Michael Glazier and Monica K. Hellwig (Collegeville: M. Glazier/Liturgical Press, 1994) 285-287.

50 "Heaven," in *The Modern Catholic Encyclopedia*, ed. Michael Glazier and Monica K. Hellwig (Collegeville: M. Glazier/Liturgical Press, 1994) 372.

51   "Hell," in *The Modern Catholic Encyclopedia*, ed. Michael Glazier and Monica K. Hellwig (Collegeville: M. Glazier /Liturgical Press, 1994) 374-375.

52   "Limbo," in *The Modern Catholic Encyclopedia*, ed. Michael Glazier and Monica K. Hellwig (Collegeville: M. Glazier /Liturgical Press, 1994) 511.

53   "Purgatory," in *The Modern Catholic Encyclopedia*, ed. Michael Glazier and Monica K. Hellwig (Collegeville: M. Glazier/Liturgical Press, 1994) 704--705.

54   "The Intellectual Tradition in the Franciscan Order," in *Acta Congressus Repraesentantium Sedum Studiorum OFM*, ed. S. Kremer (Rome: Secretariatus Generalis pro Formatione et Studiis, 1994) 89-108.

55   "God and Theology in an Age of Scientific Culture," *New Theology Review* 8/3 (August, 1995) 5-18.

56   "Christ, the Word of God and Exemplar of Humanity," *The Cord* 46/1 (January, 1996) 3-17.

57   "Anti-Christ," in *The Collegeville Pastoral Dictionary of Biblical Theology*, ed. Carroll Stuhlmueller (Collegeville: Liturgical Press, 1996) 35-36.

58   "Apocalyptic," in *The Collegeville Pastoral Dictionary of Biblical Theology*, ed. Carroll Stuhlmueller (Collegeville: Liturgical Press, 1996) 37-40.

59   "Death," in *The Collegeville Pastoral Dictionary of Biblical Theology*, ed. Carroll Stuhlmueller (Collegeville: Liturgical Press, 1996) 211-212.

60   "Eschatology," in *The Collegeville Pastoral Dictionary of Biblical Theology*, ed. Carroll Stuhlmueller (Collegeville: Liturgical Press, 1996) 266-268.

61   "Judgment," in *The Collegeville Pastoral Dictionary of Biblical Theology*, ed. Carroll Stuhlmueller (Collegeville: Liturgical Press, 1996) 509-510.

62 "Predestination," in *The Collegeville Pastoral Dictionary of Biblical Theology*, ed. Carroll Stuhlmueller (Collegeville: Liturgical Press, 1996) 769-771.

63 "Reign of God," in *The Collegeville Pastoral Dictionary of Biblical Theology*, ed. Carroll Stuhlmueller (Collegeville: Liturgical Press, 1996) 821-822.

64 "Resurrection," in *The Collegeville Pastoral Dictionary of Biblical Theology*, ed. Carroll Stuhlmueller (Collegeville: Liturgical Press, 1996) 839-841.

65 'Soul," in *The Collegeville Pastoral Dictionary of Biblical Theology*, ed. Carroll Stuhlmueller (Collegeville: Liturgical Press, 1996) 941-942.

Forthcoming articles

66 "Christology and Cosmology," in *Spirit and Life* (St. Bonaventure, NY: The Franciscan Institute).

67 "Franciscan Tradition as a Wisdom Tradition," in *Spirit and Life* (St. Bonaventure, NY: The Franciscan Institute).

68 "The Death of Christ in the Theology of Matthew of Aquasparta," in Festschrift in honor of Girard Etzkorn, *Franciscan Studies* (1993).

69 "The Doctrine of the Spirit in the Early Writings of St. Bonaventure," in Festschrift in honor of Ewert Cousins.

70 "Christ and the Cosmos," in *The Epic of Creation: Scientific and Religious Perspectives on Our Origins*, ed. T. Gilbert, R. Busse, W. Fuerst, J. Lesher (Chicago Center for Religion and Science).

71 "The Problem of Revelation in the Theology of J. E. Von Kuhn," *The Tübingen School and the Relevance of 19th Century Catholic Theology for the 21st Century* (proceedings of the symposium held at Boston College, September, 1996).

Book Reviews

72   Elisabeth Gössman, *Metaphysik und Heilsgeschichte: Eine theologische Untersuchung der Summa Halensis (Alexander von Hales)*, reviewed in *Speculum* 41 (1966) 134-138.

73   Jean de Fraine, *The Bible and the Origin of Man*, reviewed in *Homiletic and Pastoral Review* 68 (1967) 266-268.

74   Karl Rahner, *Theological Investigations*, III: *Theology of the Spiritual Life*, reviewed in *Homiletic and Pastoral Review* 68 (February, 1968) 450-451.

75   Higher Catechetical Institute at Nijmegen, *A New Catechism: Catholic Faith for Adults*, reviewed in *The Cord* 18 (1968) 24-25.

76   Hugo Rahner, *A Theology of Proclamation*, reviewed in *The Cord* 18 (1968) 348-349.

77   Henri de Lubac, *The Sources of Revelation*, reviewed in *Franciscan Herald* 48/6 (June, 1969) 189.

78   Stephanus Trooster, *Evolution and the Doctrine of Original Sin*, reviewed in *Franciscan Herald* 48/7 (July, 1969) 222-223.

79   Max Thurian, *The One Bread*, reviewed in *The Cord* 19 (1969) 252-254.

80   Karl Rahner, *Hearers of the Word*, reviewed in *Homiletic and Pastoral Review* 69 (July, 1969) 820-822.

81   Alice von Hildebrand, *Introduction to a Philosophy of Religion*, reviewed in *Franciscan Herald* 50/5 (May, 1971) 157-158.

82   Valentine Long, *The Angels in Religion and Art*, reviewed in *American Ecclesiastical Review* 166 (1972) 500.

83   Alcuin Coyle and Dismas Bonner, *The Church under Tension*, reviewed in *The Cord* 22 (1972) 381.

84   Ernst Stadter, *Psychologie und Metaphysik der menschlichen Freiheit: Die ideengeschichtliche Entwicklung zwischen*

Bonaventura und Duns Scotus, reviewed in *Theological Studies* 34 (1973) 323-325.

85 Wayne Hellmann, *Ordo: Untersuchung eines Grundgedankens in der Theologie Bonaventuras*, reviewed in *Theological Studies* 36 (1975) 352-354.

86 E. Randolph Daniel, *The Franciscan Concept of Mission in the High Middle Ages*, reviewed in *Theological Studies* 37 (1976) 160-161.

87 Ulrich Gottfried Leinsle, *Res et Signum: Das Verständnis zeichenhafter Wirklichkeit in der Theologie Bonaventuras*, reviewed in *Theological Studies* 37 (1976) 529-530.

88 Konrad Fischer, *De Deo Trino et Uno: Das Verhältnis von Productio und Reductio in seiner Bedeutung für die Gotteslehre Bonaventuras*, reviewed in *Theological Studies* 39 (1978) 782-784.

89 Ewert Cousins, *Bonaventure and the Coincidence of Opposites*, reviewed in *The Journal of Religion* 60 (1980) 349-351.

90 Geoffrey Wainwright, *Eucharist and Eschatology: A Systematic Theology*, reviewed in *The Journal of Religion* 64 (1984) 396-397.

91 Paul Szarmach (ed.), *An Introduction to the Medieval Mystics of Europe*, reviewed in *Emmanuel* 91 (1985) 360-361.

92 J. le Goff, *The Birth of Purgatory*, reviewed in *Theology Today* 42 (1985) 376-378.

93 D. L. d'Avray, *The Preaching of the Friars: Sermons Diffused from Paris before 1300*, reviewed in *The Journal of Religion* 66 (1986) 481.

94 David Burr, *Eucharistic Presence and Conversion in Late Thirteenth-Century Franciscan Thought*, reviewed in *The Catholic Historical Review* 73 (1987) 143-144.

95   Colm Lubheid (transl.), *Pseudo-Dionysius: The Complete Works* (*The Classics of Western Spirituality*), reviewed in *New Theology Review* 1/2 (May, 1988) 120-121.

96   Joseph Ratzinger, *Eschatology: Death and Eternal Life*, reviewed in *New Theology Review* 2/2 (May, 1989) 99-101.

97   Colleen McDannell and Bernhard Lang, *Heaven: A History*, reviewed in *Theological Studies* 50 (1989) 588-589.

98   R. Jehl, *Melancholie und Acedia: Ein Beitrag zu Anthropologie und Ethik Bonaventuras*, reviewed in *Cristianesimo nella Storia* 10 (1989) 181-183.

99   Jeffrey Burton Russel, *The Prince of Darkness: Radical Evil and the Power of Good in History*, reviewed in *New Theology Review* 2/4 (November, 1989) 106.

100   R. D. Sorrell, *St. Francis of Assisi and Nature*, reviewed in *The Journal of Religion* 70 (1990) 90-91.

101   Paul S. Fiddes, *The Creative Suffering of God*, reviewed in *New Theology Review* 3/2 (May, 1990) 101-102.

102   Adrio König, *The Eclipse of Christ in Eschatology: Toward a Christ-Centered Approach*, reviewed in *Theological Studies* 57 (1990) 377.

103   Walter Kasper, *Transcending All Understanding: The Meaning of Christian Faith Today* and *Theology and Church*, reviewed in *New Theology Today* 3/3 (August, 1990) 112-114.

104   Roger Haight, *Dynamics of Theology*, reviewed in *National Catholic Reporter* 28 (September 11, 1992) 31.

105   Joseph A. Bracken, *Society and Spirit: A Trinitarian Cosmology*, reviewed in *The Journal of Religion* 73/1 (1993) 111.

106   Emily Binns, *The World as Creation: Creation in Christ in an Evolutionary World View*, reviewed in *New Theology Review* 7/1 (February, 1994) 111-112.

107 Alan E. Bernstein, *The Formation of Hell: Death and Retribution in the Ancient and Early Christian Worlds*, reviewed in *Theological Studies* 55 (1994) 543-544.

108 Basil Studer, *Trinity and Incarnation: The Faith of the Early Church*, reviewed in *New Theology Review* 8/4 (November, 1995) 111-112.

109 Caroline Walker Bynum, *The Resurrection of the Body in Western Christianity, 200-1336*, reviewed in *Theological Studies* 57 (1996) 350-352.

Forthcoming Book Reviews

110 T. Kermit Scott, *Augustine: His Thought in Context*, reviewed for *New Theology Review*.

111 John Haught, *Religion and Science, from Conflict to Conversation*, reviewed for *Zygon*.

112 J. V. Tolan, *Medieval Christian Perception of Islam: A Book of Essays*, reviewed for *Catholic World Library*.

The Seraph in Thomas of Celano's *Vita Prima*

J.A. Wayne Hellmann, OFM Conv.
Saint Louis University

The Franciscan Institute at St. Bonaventure University recently published an English translation of Octavian Schmucki's 1963 exhaustive historical-critical study on the stigmata of St. Francis.[1] This opens for the English-speaking reader new and easier access to the texts that record the stigmata event in the life of St. Francis. This article intends to profit from the ready availability of these texts in order to illustrate and evaluate the role of the Seraph in the earliest documentation of the stigmata, especially as the image of the Seraph is utilized by Bro. Thomas of Celano in the *Vita Prima*.

In the course of this study, moving from Bro. Elias's *Encyclical Letter* through the *Parchment* in Francis's own hand and finally to Bro. Thomas's *Vita Prima*, attention will be given to the significance of the Seraph in these early texts. Also, interwoven throughout, is a critique of Father Octavian Schmucki's suppositions and approach to these texts, which he presents in the development of Chapter Three of his above mentioned work: "The Crucified Seraph and the Stigmatization."

The Earliest Accounts

The *Encyclical Letter* by Brother Elias, held to have been written by the Vicar of the Saint on October 4th, the day after Francis's

---

[1]Octavian Schmucki, "The Stigmata of St. Francis of Assisi, A Critical Investigation in the Light of Thirteenth-Century Sources," trans. by Canisius Connors (St. Bonaventure, NY: The Franciscan Institute, 1991). See Schmucki, "De Sancti Francisci Assisiensis stigmatum susceptione: Disquisitio historico-critica luce testimoniorum saeculi XIII," CF 33 (1963): 210-66, 392-422; 34 (1964): 5-62, 241-388.

passing, in announcing to the friars the death of Francis includes
the following lines:

> After having spoken about these things, I announce to you a
> great joy (Lk 2,10) and a new miracle. Such a miracle has
> not been heard of since the beginning (Jn 9,32), except in the
> Son of God, who is Christ the Lord. Not a long time before
> his death our brother and father appeared crucified,
> bearing in his body (Gal 6,17) the five wounds which are
> truly the stigmata of Christ.[2]

In the minds of some, this would be the earliest written testimony
of the stigmata. Schmucki, in his above mentioned study,[3] notes
that the absence of the Seraph in the account is due to the fact that
the purpose of the letter is the announcement of the death and the
extension of consolation to the friars who have lost their leader.
"Elias's silence about this vision can be explained by the purpose
and character of his *Encyclical Letter*."[4] However, the fact that
there are no known surviving manuscripts of the *Encyclical Letter*
and that the earliest source of this text is found in the 1620
Antwerp publication of *Speculum vitae beati Francisci et sociorium
eius*, place Bro. Elias's account on a weak foundation.[5]

  Another early text, the *Parchment* given to Bro. Leo, also
known as the *Chartula*, on its two sides preserves two of the three
extant autographs from the hand of St. Francis. This parchment
with an autograph on each side, written on Mt. La Verna shortly
after receiving the stigmata, that is, sometime during the second

---

[2]*"Epistola Encyclica De Transitu"* in *Fontes Franciscani* (Assisi: Edizioni Porziuncola,
1995) 254. Cf. English translation of this text in A. van Corstanje, *The Covenant with
God's Poor*, trans. by Gabriel Reidy. (Chicago: Franciscan Herald Press, 1966) 125-128.

[3]Schmucki, 192, 196-97.

[4]Schmucki, 197.

[5]Felice Accrocca, "Un Apocrifo la 'Lettera Enciclica di Frate Elia sul Transito di S.
Francesco'"? CF 65 (1995): 473-509. The author, following the Chronicle of Bro. Jordan
(no.50), believes Elias wrote a letter at the time of Francis's death but the text that has
come to us cannot be the original. He believes the text is composed out of a
combination of the lives of Francis by Thomas of Celano and Julian of Speyer. Also,
the suffrages requested by Elias at the end of the letter are the prescriptions found in
the Narbonne Constitutions of 1260.

half of September in 1224, was given to Bro. Leo by Francis with the request that he "guard it carefully."[6]

One side of the *Parchment* contains the blessing which St. Francis wrote for Brother Leo and the other side contains Francis's prayer, *The Praises of God*. At the top of the parchment on the side of the blessing, Brother Leo later wrote in red ink in his own hand an explanation of the occasion which prompted Francis to write the autographs:

> Two years before his death blessed Francis observed a forty-day fast on Mount La Verna . . . The hand of God touched Francis. A Seraph appeared and spoke to him. The Stigmata of Christ were impressed on his body. Afterwards, he fashioned and wrote with his own hand the praises on the opposite side of this folio, giving thanks to God for the favor conferred upon him.[7]

Important for determining the value of the above statement as an early testimony for the reality of the stigmata is the determination of the date when Bro. Leo actually added the explanation. After all, Leo continued to live for more than forty years after the death of St. Francis. Schmucki, however, writes that the remarks were added "after Francis's canonization but apparently not long after the stigmatization."[8] He adduces neither argument nor support for this statement.

Internal evidence indicates Leo's addition would have taken place after Francis's canonization and after his death, that is, "*Beatus* Franciscus duobus annis *ante* mortem suam."[9] However, it is not clear what Schmucki might mean by "not long after the stigmatization." (The canonization itself in 1228 would have been nearly four years after the stigmatization.) It seems that Schmucki wishes to date this insertion soon after the event because he later indicates that the insertion, or at least the information, predates

---

[6]Duane Lapsanski, "The Autographs on the 'Chartula' of St. Francis of Assisi," AFH 67 (1974): 18-37.

[7]Lapsanski, 35.

[8]Schmucki, 181.

[9]Lapsanski, 35.

Thomas of Celano's completion of the *Vita Prima* in 1229. Schmucki writes:

> The Parchment clearly and soberly links the origin of the Stigmata to the vision of the Seraph. Since the Poverello made known the experience of La Verna to at least Br. Leo, this must have come to the notice of Celano.[10]

An overarching thesis of Schmucki's study of the stigmata is that Francis's vision of the the Seraph and the appearance of the marks are historically connected.[11] The Seraph is the origin and the cause of the stigmata. Thus, it follows that the earlier the written insertion by Bro. Leo the better, and that the explanation of the absence of the Seraph in Elias's *Encyclical Letter* is understandable. Although Schmucki acknowledges that the later explanations of the six wings of the Seraph offered by Thomas in the *Vita Prima* (I Cel. 114), after the report on the stigmata event, have allegorical character, he sees no place for "myth or a theological interpretation" of the Seraph in Celano's actual account of the stigmata (I Cel. 94). If this is the case, then there is further reason for an early date to be attributed to Leo's insertion on the *Parchment*.

Concerning the historicity of the vision of the Seraph, Schmucki acknowledges a problem:

> it did not affect the external but only the internal senses, and therefore it neither had nor could have had true eyewitnesses, even though others were perhaps present at the time. Therefore, it is a correct inference that the Poverello had to inform his close companions about his experience."[12]

If there are no eyewitnesses somewhere or at some time, there is difficulty with historicity. If the La Verna vision, as a contemplative and mystical experience, does not affect the external

---

[10]Schmucki, 197.
[11]Schmucki, 209.
[12]Schmucki, 196.

senses, as Schmucki maintains, not even Francis, in the strictest sense, is an "eyewitness."

However, it seems Schmucki bases the historicity of the "vision of an actual Seraph" on Francis's reported communication about his experience to his companions, and especially to Brother Leo. In Schmucki's argument, it is Francis himself who is the source for the information about the vision of the Seraph. As the example of Bro. Leo indicates, there were those who had heard this from Francis. Thomas of Celano discovered this from those who had heard about Francis's vision of the Seraph. It is this received information that accounts for the presence of the Seraph in Celano's textual version of Francis's La Verna experience.

An Alternative Proposal

I wish to propose that the *Encyclical Letter* and the *Parchment* are of little or no value as sources for Thomas of Celano's report on the stigmata. Thus, they are of no value as sources for a causal relationship between a vision of the Seraph and a resulting stigmata. First of all, the lack of any manuscripts of Elias's encyclical letter makes for a weak case. Furthermore, if Bro. Elias's news that "the stigmata of Christ were impressed on his body" was promulgated throughout the Order in 1226, it is very unlikely such would not be included in the 1228 bull of canonization.[13] Indeed the stigmata is omitted not only in the bull of canonization but it is also omitted in any of the miracles read at the time of the canonization as are recorded in the Third Book of the *Vita Prima*.

Concerning the *Parchment*, a date for Bro. Leo's insertion of the explanation as after the canonization but before the 1229 publication of Thomas' *Vita Prima*, barely a year after the canonization, is a difficult conjecture. Brother Leo is not explicitly mentioned anywhere in the *Vita Prima*. The brothers Thomas mentions are Elias, Rufino, Bernard, Phillip, Giles, mostly Francis's earlier companions. During the latter years of Francis's life Thomas was in

---

[13]The text of "*Mira circa nos*" can be found in the *Bullarium Franciscanum*, vol. 1, ed. J.H. Sbaraglia (1759) 42-45. See Regis Armstrong, "*Mira Circa Nos*: Gregory IX's view of the Saint, Francis of Assisi," in *Greyfriars Review* 4. 1 (1990): 75-100.

Germany, and he would have been unfamiliar with the those who accompanied Francis during his last years.

Thus, it appears likely that Brother Thomas of Celano in his *Vita Prima* provides the first and the earliest written testimony we have for the vision of the six-winged Seraph on Mt. La Verna and the accompanying appearance of the wounds in Francis's hands, feet and side. If this is the case, unlike later *legendae*, this earliest testimony of the Seraph does not present the Seraph as an active agent in the stigmata.

Thomas does not record the Seraph as "speaking" to Francis as Bro. Leo has written. Thomas does not record the wounds as like "punctures of nails" (*quasi puncturas clavorum*) like Bro. Elias. Rather, Thomas writes of the signs of nails formed from his own flesh (*coeperunt . . . apparere signa clavorum . . . a carne elevata*). The implication of an external agent either on the part of the Seraph (as speaking) or on the part of nails (as puncturing) is not present in the Celano text. In Thomas of Celano's text, the Seraph is not a direct agent of the stigmata's appearance.

Brother Thomas of Celano's *Vita Prima*

Pope Gregory IX, issued the bull *Recolentes* on April 29, 1228, three months before the canonization itself. It provide that a burial church be built for Francis in Assisi and also commissioned Brother Thomas to write a life of the new saint. On February 25, 1229 the pope confirmed and declared official the text that came to be known as the *Vita Prima*.[14]

In three books, Thomas constructs three textual divisions of the *Vita Prima*: early conversion and mission, stigmata and death, and finally canonization and miracles. These are not only a chronological and topical division, but the three divisions are also divisions into three different treatises, each of a different nature with a different narrative and theological focus. However, the three do stand in relationship to each other. In the second book, or

---

[14]*Fontes Franciscani*, 275-424. See also *Analecta Franciscana*, 10 (1941): 1-117. The English translation is taken from "Franciscan Classics" (Santa Barbara, CA: Serra Press, 1954) 8-95.

second treatise of the *Vita Prima*, the principal tract for this study, Thomas develops the charity of the Passion and Cross as his principal theme. Within the theme of the Passion and Cross, among other events of Francis's final two years, Thomas includes the vision on Mt. La Verna. In this vision the Seraph has a role. The Seraph provides the "six wings", a central and emphasized characteristic of the vision:

> Two years before he gave back his soul to heaven, and while he was staying in a hermitage, called Alverna from the place where it stood, Francis "in a vision from God" (Ez 8,3) saw a man, who had six wings like a Seraph and who stood above him with arms extended and feet joined, fixed to a cross. Two wings were raised above the head, two were extended for flight, and two covered the whole body (ICel 94).

In the "vision of God", Francis sees a man (*virum unum*), like a Seraph (*tanquam Seraphim*) with six wings, affixed to a cross (*cruci affixum*). The Seraph is descriptive of the man affixed to the cross. Thomas continues in the narrative that Francis rejoiced at the beauty of the Seraph and at the kindly and gracious look the Seraph gave him. He also notes how the bitterness of the suffering of the one affixed to the cross stirred him to sorrow. As Francis ponders this vision "the marks of the nails begin to appear on his hands and feet, just as he had seen them a little before on the crucified man above him" (ICel 94). In Thomas's account, there is no causal nor direct relationship between the Seraph and the appearance of the "marks of the nails."

Why is the Seraph in the narrative of this earliest text? Is it because Thomas would have heard this from someone who would have heard it from Francis? This, if the above evaluation of the *Encyclical Letter* and *Parchment* has merit, can only be conjecture, without evidence. Or, does the presence of the Seraph in the narrative of a "vision of God" on Mt. La Verna, serve some other purpose in Thomas's skillful writing? To pursue this question, an examination of the thematic development of the second treatise of the *Vita Prima* is in order.

The Second Treatise: A Mysticism of the Passion and Cross

Within the flow of the second book or treatise of the *Vita Prima*, the wounds in Francis's body are of primary importance. In addition to the La Verna narrative, Thomas writes of the presence of the wounds on Francis's body in three other contexts. In the opening introduction to the first treatise, prior to the narrative of Mt. La Verna, Thomas extols Francis as a light brighter than any of the saints prior to him. He writes that Francis was "marked in the five members of his body with the signs of the Passion and the Cross, just as if he had hung on the Cross with the Son of God" (ICel 90). As the text of the treatise opens, the identity of Francis is firmly established in the identity of hanging on the cross with Christ, and this identity is the uniqueness by which Francis excels beyond all the other saints before him.

After the narrative of Mt. La Verna (1Cel 94), there follows the second context for mention of Francis's stigmata. As Thomas describes Francis's malady of the eyes, he writes that the sufferings of Christ were not yet fulfilled in him, "although he bore his marks in his body" (ICel 98). Then, after his death in the description of the mourning of the friars and the people, there is the third context for mention of Francis's wounds. In the description of the people's grief, there is consolation. Over the dead body of Francis, there is an unheard joy. Thomas writes:

> There actually appeared in him the image of the Cross and Passion, of the Immaculate Lamb who washed away the crimes of the world. The saint seemed as if he had just been taken down from a cross; his hands and feet were pierced with nails, and his right side was wounded, as if by a lance" (ICel 112).

Continuing within this same third context of mourning, Thomas again specifies another dimension of the stigmata. It brings ecclesial joy. He reports that any of the mourners present acknowledged a great gift "not only if he was permitted to kiss the sacred stigmata of Jesus Christ which Saint Francis bore in his body, but even just to look on them" (ICel 113). Finally, the whole second treatise of the *Vita Prima* concludes in number 118 with a prayer to Francis now in glory.

> O Father (Francis), show Jesus Christ, the Son of the Most High Father, those holy stigmata of His; point out the marks of the cross in your side and feet and hands, so that in mercy He may deign to show His own wounds to the Father, Who on account of them will always be truly gracious to us wretches. Amen. So be it!

The second book of the *Vita Prima,* from beginning to end, is a treatise on the passion of Christ brought to life in Francis. In the introduction to this treatise, Thomas writes that Francis excels all the saints because he is marked with the signs of the Passion and the Cross. From this introduction, the narrative recording his last two years begins with the opening of the book of the Gospels in search of God's will only to find that "the passage his eyes fell on was about the Passion of our Lord Jesus Christ" (ICel 93). From this understanding of the Gospel focused on the Passion, there immediately follows the narrative about the "vision of God" on Mt. La Verna when "there gradually appeared in his hands and feet the imprint of nails" (ICel 94). What Francis discovers in the Gospel, he sees in the vision of God.

This same suffering reality of the cross, found in the Gospel and in the "vision of God" on Mt. La Verna, continues in the physical suffering Francis endured during his last two years. The affliction of his eyes, according to Thomas, leads Francis to fulfill the sufferings of Christ within him even though already "he bore His marks in his body" (ICel 98). Finally, all is confirmed in his death. Again similiar to the introductory identity, it seemed in his death "he had just been taken down from a cross" (ICel 112); and, to witness the wounds Francis bore in his body, the people experienced the greatest of gifts (ICel 113).

Finally, at the very end of the treatise, as given in the prayer cited above, Thomas prays to God that the wounds of Francis be shown to Christ that Christ may show His own wounds to the Father on whose account God's mercy might be shown to us. The stigmata of Francis is not only what marks him as the greatest of saints in his hearing the Gospel, in his vision on La Verna, in his physical affliction, in his death, and after his death. The stigmata also marks Francis as the one who reveals the wounds of Christ in the glory of heaven as participation in the act of offering intimate intercession with Christ to the Father on our behalf and for our salvation. It is almost as though the wounded Christ of glory takes identity from the wounds of Francis. At the very least, in the stigmata, there is unfathomable intimacy of particpation not only of Francis with Christ but of Christ with Francis. In this incredible mutuality, no wonder Francis excells all the other saints.

In the second book of the *Vita Prima*, Thomas has no doubt about Francis's stigmata. It was seen by many, both before and after his death. Thomas acknowledges these wounds and interprets them as key to Francis's identity rooted in the passion of Christ on the cross. At the opening and again at the end of the treatise, Francis is presented as one who hung on the cross with Christ. In the Word of the Gospel, in his "vision of God", in his experience of human suffering, in his death and after his death, and in the glory of heaven, there is one thread identifying Francis. It is the wounds of Christ's Passion and Cross. Thus, finally in seeing Francis, as the above prayer implores, Christ sees his own wounds and finds in Francis his own crucified identity before the Father.

This is a Christ-mysticism of the highest order. This earliest Franciscan Christ-mysticism focused on the humanity and incarnation of Christ. More importantly, it focused on the identity of Francis with Christ in the wounds of the Passion and Cross. Thomas even takes these wounds of Francis to be the very self revelation of Christ unto Himself before the Father. And, this is written more than thirty years prior to the *Legenda Maior* by St. Bonaventure.

The Seraph: Tool and Symbol

In all of the events of Francis's life narrated within Celano's christological development of the second treatise of the *Vita Prima*, the Seraph plays a relatively minor role. Only in the event of the La Verna vision is the Seraph mentioned, and this is not in any direct connection with the wounds that appear in his flesh.

Rather, Francis becomes what he sees in the crucified man. In none of the other narratives concerning the wounds of Francis, nor in the final prayer, are there any illusions to the Seraph.

Is the Seraph mentioned again in the text of the treatise, apart from these narratives? As the treatise concludes, Thomas praises the great gift of the stigmata: "O gift unique, and token of special love. . ." (ICel 114). It is here that he invites the reader to move toward the same reward. The key toward reception of this "gift unique" is found in following the example of Francis, according to the teachings learned from the six different wings of the Seraph.

The allegory of the six wings of the Seraph is the device and the manner of invitation for all to share in Francis's experience of the "charity of the Passion." Just as treatise one concludes with the Greccio event of celebrating the "humility of the Incarnation" with Francis "inviting everyone to heavenly rewards" (I Cel 86), so the treatise on the Passion concludes with a similiar invitation:

> We too can certainly win the same reward, if we extend two wings over our heads, as the Seraph did; that is to say, by having a pure intention and conducting ourselves uprightly, after the example of Blessed Francis. . . . The feathers of these wings are the love of the Father, Who in His mercy bestows salvation and 'the fear of the Lord' (Eccles. 1,11). . . . With two wings also, they must fly, in order to fulfill the twofold duty of charity to their neighbor, namely of refreshing his soul with the word of God (Luke 4,4), and of relieving his bodily needs with material assistance. . . The feathers of these wings are the different works that must be done to guide and to help one's neighbor. . . . And finally, the body, destitute of merits, is to be covered with two wings. This is properly done when it is clothed again with innocence by contrition and confession, as often as it has been stripped by sin. The feathers of these wings are the various sentiments which are engendered by the detestation of sin and by the desire of sanctifying grace.
>
> (I Cel 114)

The above text near the conclusion of treatise two in Thomas' *Vita Prima* is of no little significance. The six wings provide a spiritual pedagogical device for an instruction and invitation to the reader "to win the same reward." The invitation to participation at the conclusion of both treatises one and two is important for the rhetorical and hagiographical nature of the text. Thomas writes not only to communicate information but to invite the response of the reader to participate in the mystery. He could not be more explicit about this. In the introduction of treatise two, as he begins to write about the signs of the Passion, in Francis's body, Thomas dramatically states: "*Sacramentum hoc magnum est*" (I Cel 90).

In this invitation to sacramental participation in the Passion and Cross, use of the six wings of the Seraph is more developed and more important for Thomas' overall purposes than the mention of the Seraph in the vision narration of Mt. La Verna. Brother Thomas uses the Seraph in his text primarily because the six wings of angelic nature provide opportunity to invite the reader to become a sharer in the "gift unique." The three-fold double wings invite the following three-fold double responses: "pure intention and conducting ourselves uprightly; . . . twofold duty of charity to neighbor, namely refreshing his soul with the word of God and of relieving his bodily needs; . . . clothing the body with innocence by contrition and confession" (ICel 114).

Thomas continues: "The most blessed Francis carried out all these practices most perfectly. He bore the image and likeness of the Seraph, and as he persevered on the cross, he merited to fly away to the sublime order of the spirits" (I Cel 115). It is not from the vision of the Seraph that Francis bore the image and likeness of the Seraph, but from following the practices allegorically taught by the six wings of the Seraph. It is in these practices, as he perseveres on the cross and fulfills the will of God, that Francis takes on the angelic nature of a Seraph. He acquires the six wings to "fly away" to a "sublime order." The reader and those who follow Francis are invited to do the same. The six wings have a distinct purpose, which is to draw others to participate in this great sacrament, a marvellous gift of grace.

In the employment of the "six wings" as a practical teaching device for the spiritual journey, Brother Thomas was in good company. Alan of Lille (d. 1202), who completed his life as a

Cistercian, used the same device in a similar way. In his short practical manual, *De sex alis cherubim*,[15] Alan descibed each of the six wings in specific ways, such as purity of intention, love of neighbor, confession and contrition. On each of the wings, the feathers specify the dispositions and virtues proper for each goal. The similarity between Alan's use of six wings and Thomas use of the six wings is remarkable.[16]

As a more practically minded author, Alan of Lille, uses the device of six wings as a schema for transforming virtue. Richard of St. Victor (d. 1173), a more speculatively minded writer on the nature of contemplation, also uses the same six wings. He develops them as symbolic of the way of the six degrees of contemplation: "Everyone who desires to arrive at the peak of knowledge must know these six kinds of contemplation familiarly. Certainly we are suspended above the earth and raised to heavens by these six wings of contemplation."[17] The six wings, in this case, are focused on understanding progressive development in the contemplative experience. Contemplatives are formed by these six wings of the degrees of contemplation: "Without doubt, it is fitting that he who desires and strives to fly up to the secrets of the third heaven and the hidden things of Divinity have all those six wings of contemplation."[18]

Steven Chase in his recent work, *Angelic Wisdom*, points out the tropological nature of Richard's use of the angelic form. Wisdom is to be imitated. He writes: "When imitation takes the form of wisdom, described by Richard as the goal and method of his work, the human soul clothes itself in angelic form."[19] The soul is to take on spiritual wings. Thus, not only in the practical order of virtue, but also in the speculative order of contemplative vision the

---

[15]See, PL 210: 266-80, esp. 267-68.

[16]A reading of Alan's text shows many comparisons to Thomas of Celano's use of the six wings. However, a closer and more careful analysis, which would go beyond the scope of this study, deserves to be done.

[17]Richard of St. Victor, *The Mystical Ark*, I, x, trans. by Grover Zinn (New York/Mahwah, NJ: Paulist Press, 1979) 168.

[18]Richard of St. Victor, *Mystical Ark*, I, x, 170.

[19]Steven Chase, *Angelic Wisdom: The Cherubim and the Grace of Contemplation in Richard of St. Victor* (ND, Indiana: University of Notre Dame Press, 1995) 79.

use of six wings clothing the soul in angelic form draws the soul into spiritual heights. Thomas likewise writes that as Francis carried out in his life the same instruction of the six wings offered to the reader he took on angelic form and was raised to the heights: "He bore the likeness and image of the Seraph, and as he persevered upon the cross, he merited to fly away to the ranks of those exalted spirits" (I Cel 115).

In Celano's conclusion of the second treatise, it appears that elements of both Alan of Lille's and of Richard of St. Victor's thinking on the image of six wings are operative although further study of this point would be needed. In the first, the six wings are a tool for teaching the practical order of virtue. In the second, the six wings are used as a symbol of the transformative nature of the contemplative experience, the clothing of an angelic similitude, and of the movement toward proximity with the Divine. In view of the contemplative, Francis becomes like the angelic form of the Seraph (that is, flying away to their realms), after following the teaching of the wings of the Seraph. It seems appropriate then that Francis sees those same six wings of the Seraph in his La Verna experience of the "vision of God." In placing a six–winged Seraph in the vision of Mt. La Verna, Thomas skillfully sets up the reader for what is to follow at the end of the treatise.

Why did Thomas use the six wings of a Seraph rather than the six wings of a Cherub, as did both Alan of Lille and Richard of St. Victor? First of all, it is to be remembered that in the *Celestial Hierarchy* Dionysius the Areopagite wrote that the Seraphim, Cherubim, and Thrones are situated within the first and most intimate group "forever around God. . . . permanently united with him ahead of any of the others and with no intermediary."[20] However, each specify a type of proximity to God. In commenting on the Dionysian tradition, Steven Chasen points out that, while both Seraphim and Cherubim signify immediate proximity to the divine, the Seraphim signify an "affective proximity to the divine." The Cherubim signify an "intellective proximity to the

---

[20]Dionysius the Areopagite, *Celestial Hierarchy* VI, ii (New York/Mahwah, NJ: Paulist Press, 1987) 160.

divine."[21] However, although the Cherubim which "signifies the power to know and to see God"[22] serve the intellective purposes of Richard and Alan, the Seraphim as identified by Dionysius as "firemakers" and "carriers of warmth"[23] is more appropriate for Thomas's purposes.

Thomas describes the "gift unique" of Francis's stigmata, a gift of intimacy with the Cross and Passion of Christ, as a "token of special love" (I Cel 114). It is the result of Christ's love for Francis: "He loved you much, Who has adorned you thus magnificently." Finally, in this same portion of text, Thomas concludes that the stigmata is a reward for fidelity in total love:

> The true "Father of mercies" [2 Cor. 1,3] wished to show how great a reward he deserved who strove to love Him with all his heart, namely to receive a place among the higher rank of supercelestial spirits, the ones closest to Himself (I Cel 114).

The image of the Seraph is much more appropiate than the image of the Cherubim to identify the experience of Mt. La Verna as an experience of love. Thus, to illustrate that the virtue taught by the six wings is to lead one into the mystery of intimate love, the wings are appropriately placed on a Seraph rather than on a Cherub, as done earlier by both Alan and Richard. As indicated above, the Dionysian and Victorine traditions employ the Seraph as "burning love." Having been educated at Monte Cassino, however, the monastic tradition is more immediate and familiar to Thomas. He undoubtedly would have been familiar with the image in the homilies of Gregory the Great and Bernard of Clairvaux. Gregory, for example, teaches that the Seraph are the ones "who are inflamed by the torch of heavenly contemplation."[24] In his *Song of Songs* Bernard describes the Seraph in the following manner:

---

[21]Chasen, 72.

[22]Chasen, 73.

[23]Dionysius the Areopagite, *Celestial Hierarchy*, VII, i, 161.

[24]St. Gregory the Great, *Homilia 34 in Evangelica*, PL 76:1246-59, 1252-53.

. . .for God, Who is love, has so drawn and assimilated
them to Himself, so filled them with the ardor of affection
that burns in Himself, that they seem to be one spirit with
God. . . The Cherubim's bent is to contemplate God's infinite
knowledge, the Seraphim adhere to the love that never
ends. . . the name Cherub denotes one filled with
knowledge, the name Seraph one inflamed with or inciting
to love.[25]

If the six wings lead to participation in the "gift unique" which is
"special love," Thomas in this case, rightly places them on the
Seraph.[26]

With the symbol of the Seraph and the gracious look of the
Seraph upon Francis, Thomas contextualizes the stigmata as
revealing a great love. Indeed, in this manner, he connects Francis's
wounds—participating in the Cross and Passion of Christ—with
the burning, firemaking love found in the Dionysian tradition. The
rich image of the Seraph allows Thomas to stir the affections of
his readers to desire the same "token of special love." It facilitates
his later move to identify the wounds as the adornment of a
magnificent love (cf. I Cel 114), and it sets the stage for the
christological intimacy of the final prayer to Francis in glory.

Thus, the passages at the conclusion of the second treatise,
where Thomas develops the images of the "six wings" and of the
"Seraph" is much more than "a pious commentary on the event" of
the vision of the stigmata, as Schmucki argues.[27] These final
passages invite us to participation in the great sacrament of
Christ's Passion and Cross that has just been proclaimed. These
passages are key to the ultimate purpose and nature of the text;
both the "six wings" and the "Seraph" are used first as a spiritual
pedagogical device toward communion with Francis on the cross

[25]Bernard of Clairvaux, *Sermo 19 Super Cantica Canticorum*, S. Bernardi Opera
Omnia, eds. J. Leclercq et al. (Rome: 1957) 1: 108-13, 111; see also "On the Song of
Songs I," in *The Works of Bernard of Clairvaux*, 2, n 5, trans. K. Walsh, (Kalamazoo,
Mich., 1976) 143.

[26]See Wayne Hellmann, "The Seraph in the Legends of Thomas of Celano and
St. Bonaventure: The Victorine Transition," in *Bonaventuriana*, ed. Francesco Chavero
Blanco (Rome: Edizione Antonianum, 1988): 347-356.

[27]Schmucki, 209.

with Christ in a great mystery of the power of contemplative love. This use of the Seraph is of more significance toward the development of Thomas' purposes in the second treatise than the use of a six-winged Seraph as descriptive of the man affixed to a cross. To place the Seraph in Francis's "vision of God" identifies the event not only with the angelic but also with intimate and burning love. Explicit description of the six wings on a Seraph invite the reader to the teaching those six wings embody. These can likewise draw the reader into angelic contemplation, conform the reader to the image and likeness of the Seraph, enabling perseverance on the cross and flight into loving intimacy with God.

The Seraph in the *Vita Prima*: A Conclusion

Having reviewed the *Encyclical Letter* and the explanation of Bro. Leo found on the *Parchment*, it would seem that Brother Thomas' *Vita Prima* is the earliest available written account of the stigmata. Thomas frames the last two years of Francis's life within a treatise characterized by emphasis on the Passion and the Cross of Christ. He introduces this consideration of the wounds of Christ in Francis's body as a hymn of Francis's great intimacy with Christ on the cross. This is identified as *sacramentum hoc magnum est*. In Thomas's mind, there is no doubt as to the veracity and reality of the wounds in Francis's body. There are witnesses before and after his death. These wounds are clearly the key visible sign and pointed hemeneutic for understanding Francis's mystical experience and union with Christ. According to Thomas's vision of Francis, these wounds bind together Francis's understanding of the Gospel, his mystical vision of God, his endurance of physical suffering, his death and ultimately his passing into glory into one splendid package of intimate union with Christ.

It is in view of interpreting the significance of the wounds and participation in that significance that the image of the six–winged Seraph is employed. The strongest use of the Seraph in Thomas' second treatise of the *Vita Prima* is in the practical invitation of all to participate in Francis's "gift unique." Just as Thomas concludes the first book with Francis preaching on the Incarnation in the Greccio story, *cunctos invitans ad praemia summa* (I Cel 86), he also concludes the second book on the Passion with the assurance that we, without doubt, can also attain the same burning intimacy with Christ: *Quod utique indubitanter adipisci poterimus, si more Seraphim duas alas extenderimus supra caput. . .* (I Cel 114).

It is not surprising, then, that Thomas employs the image of the Seraph in the vision of Mt. La Verna, although in a secondary role. Primary is the fact that Francis *vidit virum unum . . . cruci affixum*. What, however, is of practical import about the Seraph in that vision, following which the wounds appear in Francis body, are the six wings. These six wings are key to understanding our approach and manner of participation in the the Passion and Cross of Christ.

Unlike Schmucki, in interpreting the texts which he carefully gathered and organized, I would propose that Francis is not the source for the Seraph in the Mt. Alverna experience, but that Thomas is. Thomas was educated in the monastic tradition at Monte Cassino. He would have known something of the Dionysian tradition of the *Celestial Hierarchy*, the pedagogical device of the "six wings" as illustrated in the work of Alan of Lille, and the angelic nature of contemplation according to Richard of St. Victor. From Gregory and Bernard, he would have heard more specifically about the Seraph "whose flame is love." If not, Thomas nevertheless uses the two images of the six wings and of the Seraph for what is foremost among his purposes in writing the *Vita Prima*, namely, participation and communion in the great sacrament of intimate burning love, the Passion and Cross of Christ.

If indeed Brother Thomas of Celano's *Vita Prima* is the earliest text to treat the stigmata of St. Francis, as I propose, it is an exceptionally important text. This would make him the first to use the six-winged Seraph in relation to the event of the stigmata. What does he intend to do? As a text on the occasion of canonization, its ecclesial character for the enrichment of the life of the Church cannot be overlooked. Toward this end, he draws on two things, the practical device of the six wings for the teaching of virtue and the import of the six wings for understanding the angelic nature of contemplation pertinent to the vision of God. Thomas places the six wings more appropriately on the Seraph to illustrate that this is participation in a great sacrament of intimate love with Christ on the Cross. This is how we are to participate in the "gift unique" of love.

Thus it is appropriate that Francis would have seen a six–winged Seraph as he received these wounds of Christ. All of this is for the purpose of entering into mystical union with Christ and to hang on the cross with him. Thomas is exceptionally creative as he connects the beautiful images of the angelic with the bitter wounds of a man affixed to the cross. He must have himself found this combination to be both strange and wonderful. He brings forward the Dionysian, Victorine and monastic traditions of the angelic in contemplation, and then he focuses them into a powerful mysticism of wounds effected by the Passion and Cross of Christ.

Subsequent thirteenth–century biographers who employ the image of the six–winged Seraph of Thomas' *Vita Prima* to write further on the life of Francis often miss the point. For them, the six–winged Seraph frequently becomes more central to the vision and and also an active agent on Francis (that is, speaking to him). Later authors do not remain content to let the Seraph remain a symbolic interpretative aid for the contemplative-affective understanding of the "vision of God" and a practical guide for participation in the mystery. However, none of this was missed by St. Bonaventure. He finds before him a new and rich christological mysticism developed within the angel images of the earlier tradition. Thirty years later, Bonaventure brings his broader and richer knowledge of that tradition to bear on his writing of the *Legenda Maior*. However, in his use of angel imagery in connection with the Passion and Cross, Bonaventure takes his lead from Thomas. Without Thomas' interpretative insight into a six–winged Seraph, would Bonaventure ever have become known as the "Seraphic" Doctor?

THE MORAL REFLECTION
OF
SAINT FRANCIS AND SAINT BONAVENTURE

Jacques–Guy Bougerol

Translated from the French by
Michael Cusato, OFM with Girard Etzkorn

Saint Francis of Assisi

"All powerful, eternal, just and merciful God, grant us in our misery, that we may **do** for your sake alone what we know you want us to do, and always want what pleases you." In this prayer which concludes the letter written to the whole Order, the moral reflection of Francis of Assisi finds its meaning and takes on all its force.[1]

If the moral reflection of Bonaventure is fairly easy to present, that of Francis of Assisi seems *a priori* almost impossible. Perhaps it would be necessary to turn the terms of the problem around and to ask oneself whether the moral conduct of Francis was the source of moral reflection among those who were captivated by his personality. It would thus be a matter of following the development of that which we readily call his conversion. As Louis Lavelle has said, "Franciscan spirituality is a return to a state of simplicity and confidence where the very struggle against evil is nothing more that the presence of God experienced more directly and rendered always closer and more active."[2]

Son of a well-established cloth merchant, Peter Bernardone, Francis is naturally destined to enter into the trade which, as we know, opened the way to the rush for the gold of capitalism at the beginning of this 13th century. He has only that schooling which was necessary to succeed in business. The business of his father is

---

[1] Francis of Assisi, *EpOrd*, 263. All citations of the writings of Francis are from Kajetan Esser, *Die Opuscula des hl. Franziskus von Assisi. Neue textkritische Edition* (Grottaferrata, 1976).

[2] Louis Lavelle, *Quatre saints* (Paris, 1951) 60.

flourishing and Francis often takes his father's place when he went on the road to the great French fairs to purchase high quality cloth. He showed himself an excellent businessman, foresighted, "straightforward when he sold, careful when he bought", mindful of his accounts, courteous towards his clients, good to the poor who came to beg alms for the love of God.

However, at this same time, tension was mounting between the prosperous merchants and the great landowning nobles. Francis dreams of knighthood and glory. He lacks having been born noble; no matter, he enlists in the army of count Gentile who was making a token appearance in Apulia as a representative of pope Innocent III. He enlisted not from desire of gain, but of glory. But at Spoleto, he is invited in a dream to go back home to accomplish his destiny.[3] He then substitutes for the privilege of birth that of manners, he wastes his money on feasts, dresses up in luxurious clothing, organizes lavish banquets to the point of being elected king of the golden youth of Assisi. His parents and especially his father, eager for gain, reproach him for his crazy acts, but deep down they are happy to see their son elevating the social status of the family in the heart of the little town.

A significant event occurs which clarifies his intention. The bourgeoisie and the people raise a small army to go and attack the nobles who had taken refuge in Perugia. Unfortunately, this army suffers a heavy defeat at Collestrada and Francis is taken prisoner. But while his companions give themselves over to discouragement and sadness, he does not cease exulting and singing. To their reproaches, he responds: "I am joyful, but why? I have in mind something quite different than what you are thinking. I rejoice because one day I am going to be venerated the world over." The reflection of Francis shows that the affective source of his emotional state goes beyond the moment, namely that it is surely subservient to a more realistic ambition, but also one which is more solid.

The conditions of the detention at Perugia had to be rather difficult. Francis fell ill and he was set free. The biographers speak of a long trying illness which unsettled within himself the

---

[3]Raoul Manselli, *St. Francis of Assisi* (Chicago, 1988) 47-48.

values to which he was attached. Questions begin to stir within him about whether he was really interested in returning to work in his father's shop and in resuming his evenings out with his carefree young friends which he had somewhat forgotten. The first steps in his plan are, for him, like a visit to familiar people and things. But his perspective is not the same, he feels his strength come back to him and still something is lacking. He vaguely anticipates from an encounter or an event the signal for a new beginning. This is when the kiss of the leper occurred. Travelling a pathway on horseback in the countryside, he suddenly sees before him a leper. *Un leper*! The world of outcasts who are forbidden from entering the city. The poor! There were many in the streets of Assisi and Francis never failed to give generously to them. But lepers! Never had he ever encountered them. Then this man, who is there in front of him! Francis gets off his horse, puts a generous alms in his outstretched hand and gives him a kiss. He then galops away, at the same time joyous and resolved, without however realizing the meaning of his action. A light is suddenly lit in his conscience which is no longer going to be extinguished. It is going to prompt in Francis a complete reversal of **values**.

This conversion — which is what this moral journey ought rightly to be called — is going to take some time. A beginning has been made. He needs silence and prayer. The world of his father, that of business and money, glory and knighthood, the frivolities of *"la dolce vita"* no longer carry any weight. He feels himself irresistably drawn to the world of outcasts. Even before seeing more clearly, he knows in a confused manner, yet firmly, that this was going to be his path.

Such a radical change of **values** is for Francis like the passage from an ideal to a passion. The ideal, that of yesterday, was human glory. From now on, a passion is going to consume his whole life and prompt in him the quest for the One who is the origin of that passion. When, after days and nights of prayer directed towards the light, he comes into the chapel of San Damiano, looks at the crucifix hanging in front of him and feels the glance of Christ invade him and his lips open. The mystery of this encounter will never be disclosed by him, probably because he will perceive its depth only slowly in eliminating the gap between glance and action. Francis intends to put on the Christ of the Passion which the leper had made rise up in him: Christ will always be for him the crucified, the poor, the excluded. He will never take his eyes off the Christ of San Damiano up to the day when he will receive from him the stigmata on Mount La Verna.

Twenty years later, while dictating his *Testament*, Francis will recall only the endpoint of his conversion:

> This is how the Lord inspired me, brother Francis, to begin to do penance. When I was in sin, the sight of lepers was extremely bitter to me; but then the Lord himself led me into their company and I had mercy on them. And when I left them, that which had seemed bitter to me was changed into sweetness of soul and body. And after that, I did not wait long before leaving the world.[4]

The interior change which Francis experienced and pursued manifests itself outwardly. In going through the streets of the city and in begging his food, he finds himself exposed to the shock of the people and soon to their scorn. His father, furious for having thus been made a fool of in the person of his son summons him to court. But the bishop takes him under his protection and it is in front of him that father and son encounter each other. Throwing the money which he still had left and all his clothing at the feet of Peter Bernardone, Francis declares: "Everyone listen to me and understand. Up to now, it is Peter Bernardone whom I have called my father; but from this point forward I will say "Our Father who art in heaven". And he left, completely naked. The past is now gone forever. A naked Francis follows the naked Christ, according to the phrase of Saint Jerome. But he did not intend for all that to leave Christian society; he wanted to find his own unique way by living among the people. The Incarnation of Christ is, in fact, the link between the two contradictory sides of his conversion: a way of being radically opposed to the way of the world and, at the same time, an acceptance of what is the present world.[5]

Conquered by a living person, Jesus Christ, for whom he had been searching for four years, he burst into joy, since this discovery

---

[4] Francis of Assisi, *Test*, 428.

[5] Giovanni Miccoli, *Francesco d'Assisi* (Turin, 1991) 56-58.

is such that he no longer has need of anyone else. He remembered this while dictating his *Testament*: "No one showed me what I should do, but the Most High himself revealed to me that I should live according to the form of the holy gospel."[6] The chain of historical factors leading up to the conversion of Francis allows us to glimpse in him a movement forward which is combined with a continuous interiorization — since Gregory of Nyssa, we tend to identify the *apex mentis* with the *principale cordis*. — This interiorization led him to recognize in the Crucifix of San Damiano the person whom he had been seeking, without yet having found him all that clearly. One understands then that the joy of Francis would be simple and total. He found what he was looking for. He wants at last to live for Jesus Christ. And his joy is like an expansion of that same life: "for me, to live is Christ", as St. Paul says.

Thomas of Celano tells us that Francis, after having restored the Church of San Damiano, went to the Portiuncula in order to repair the chapel which was in pitiful shape. He put on a new habit, that of hermits, with a leather belt, a walking stick and shoes on his feet.

> But when on a certain day the Gospel was read in that church, how the Lord sent his disciples out to preach, the holy man of God, who was present there, understood somewhat the meaning of the passage; after Mass, he humbly asked the priest to explain the Gospel to him more fully. When he had set forth for him point by point all these things, the holy Francis, hearing that the disciples of Christ should possess neither gold nor silver nor money; nor carry along the way neither purse nor sack nor bread nor walking staff; and that they should have neither shoes nor two tunics but that they should preach the kingdom of God and penance: transported by the joy of the Holy Spirit, he immediately cried out: "This is what I want, this is what I seek, this is what I long to do with all my heart." Then the holy father, overflowing with joy, hastened to fulfill that saving counsel and he suffered no delay in putting into practice that which he had just heard. He immediately

---

[6]Francis of Assisi, *Test*, 438.

put off the shoes from his feet, put aside the walking staff
from his hands, kept only one tunic and exchanged his
leather belt for a small cord. He fashioned for himself a
habit that bore the likeness of a cross, that by means of it
he might chase away all temptations of the devil; and he
made a very rough tunic in order to thereby crucify the
flesh with all its vices and sins; he made it very poor and
crude, incapable of inspiring any envy whatsoever of the
world.[7]

This event took place either on 12 October 1208, on the feast of
Saint Luke, according to Gratien,[8] or on the feast of Saint Matthew,
24 February 1209, according to the Bollandistes.[9]

The moral reflection of Francis is thus lived more than something thought out. It is a passion more than the search for
righteousness. That is why he no longer judges himself and sings
the praises of the Lord, without the illness he suffered being able
to put an end to his interior song. One evening, Francis, in Rieti for
treatment of his eyes, asked one the friars who had learned to play
the zither when he was in the world, to borrow one and to play
some beautiful music: "My body is afflicted with very heavy
suffering; I would like by this means to even change the physical
pain into joy and spiritual consolation." The brother excused himself. "Then let's speak no more of this," responded Francis. But the
following night, not being able to sleep, Francis heard the exquisite
song of a zither and was filled with extreme joy.[10]

The chronicler Richer of Sens reports that one day Francis on a
journey with his brothers, stopped in a town to preach there. But
the people, seeing this man dressed like a tramp, chased him from
town, while treating him like a crazy man. Later in the
countryside, Francis, seeing many birds gathered there, began to
speak to them. Immediately the birds grouped themselves around

---

[7] 1 Cel 22.

[8] Gratien de Paris, "Essai sur sa vie et son oeuvre d'après les derniers travaux
critiques," Études franciscaines, 18 (1907) 388.

[9] Paul Sabatier, Life of St. Francis of Assisi, trans. Louise Seymour Houghton (New
York, 1930) 68-69, and esp. 69, n. 1.

[10] 2 Cel 126.

him and listened to him until he blessed them and told them to fly away. The townspeople learned this and came in their turn.[11]

At the beginning of the Order, the friars were staying at Rivotorto, poor in every way. They went to beg their alms and Francis heard them coming back singing on the road. In the middle of the night, a brother cried out for help: "I'm dying." Francis got up and asked him: "What's the matter, brother? What are you dying of?" "I'm dying of hunger". Immediately, Francis had a meal prepared and awakened all the friars; he desired that all eat with the famished brother and everything ended in joy.[12]

For Francis, the world is like the face of God: poverty, suffering, tribulation, even death itself come to life like living persons: Lady Poverty, sister suffering, brother fire, sister bodily death. Of course the simplicity of this joy is located at the end of a difficult purification. Having renounced every desire to live for oneself, to be concerned with the self, he put himself into every action with such faith, such decisiveness and such a joy that he accepts everything because he is certain, with the Lord, to surpass all and transform all.

In the spiritual experience attained at the point where the visible and invisible become one in a living unity, Francis thus attains a total presence to God and, as Louis Lavelle has written with insight, "the spiritual life, according to Saint Francis, is a kind of permanent miracle."[13] Coming down from La Verna where he had received the visit of the crucified Seraph which marked him in his hands and feet with nail marks and, in his side, with a deep wound always open, he sings a canticle whose song is wholly made from pain and suffering but from which one hears only joy.

The secret of this permanent miracle, of the exaltation of absolute poverty, of the song of joy in the midst of suffering, of the smile in the midst of insults, this secret surely resides in the value previously discovered and lived intensely. But it also equally resides in the strength of a movement toward the total unity of the self in love, which never allows a trace of personal effort to appear. Is this not the sign of a refound freedom?

---

[11]1 Cel 58.
[12]2 Cel 22.
[13]Lavelle, 60.

It is thus not surprising to find in the *Admonitions* of Francis
the witness of what he personally lived. In *Admonition 3*, he says
what perfect obedience is:

> The Lord says in the Gospel: "The one who has not
> renounced all that he possesses cannot be my disciple"; and
> "the one who wants to save his soul will lose it." That
> person abandons all that he possesses and loses his body
> who surrenders his whole self completely to obedience into
> the hands of his superior. And whatever he does and says
> which he knows is not contrary to his superior's will,
> provided that what he does is good, is true obedience. And
> should the subject sometimes see that some things might be
> better and more useful for his soul than what the superior
> may command him, let him willingly offer such things up
> to God as a sacrifice; and instead, earnestly try to fulfill
> the wishes of the superior . . . But if the superior should
> order something contrary to his conscience, although he
> may not obey him, still he should not abandon him. And if,
> because of that, he suffers persecution from others, let him
> love them even more for the sake of God. For whoever
> chooses to endure persecution rather than wanting to be
> separated from his brothers truly remains in perfect
> obedience, since he surrenders his soul for his brothers . . .
> There are, indeed, many religious who, under the pretext of
> seeking something better than what the superior
> commands, are looking back and are "returning to the
> vomit" of their own will; such are murderers who cause
> many souls to be lost because of their bad example.[14]

Commenting on the *Our Father*, Francis expresses what he
lives:

> "Let your will be done on earth as it is in heaven," that we
> may love you with our whole heart by always thinking of
> you; with our whole mind by directing our whole intention
> towards you and seeking your glory in everything; and with
> our whole strength by spending all our energies and the

---

[14]Francis of Assisi, *Adm* 3, 108.

affections of our soul and body in the service of your love and nothing else.[15]

In the first rule which Francis dictated, he reiterated his intention: "But now that we have left the world, we have nothing else to do than to follow the will of the Lord and to please him."[16]

One day, a little after his conversion, while he was passing near the castle of Montefelto with some brothers, he entered into the courtyard where many nobles and knights were gathered together. Having climbed onto a wall, he then spoke to them on the theme of *courtoisie*: *"Tanto è quel bene ch'io aspetto che ogni pena m'è diletto"* — "Such is the good which I aspire to, that all pain is a pleasure to me."[17] The whole Francis is contained in this one phrase: the whole meaning of his joy and the whole meaning of the prayer cited at the beginning:

> All powerful, eternal, just and merciful God, grant to us in our misery, that we may do for your sake alone what we know you want us to do, and to always want what pleases you.[18]

Saint Bonaventure

The moral reflection of Saint Bonaventure presents itself from a very different perspective than the one which we highlighted in Francis of Assisi. Bonaventure is aware of what he owes his blessed father in the search for peace and Christian wisdom.

> Regarding the itinerary to follow, it is none other than the most ardent love of the Crucified, that love which snatched Paul up into the third heaven and which so thoroughly transformed him in Jesus Christ that he could say: "with Christ I am nailed to the cross. I live, or rather it is no longer I who live but Christ who lives in me."[19]

---

[15] Francis of Assisi, *ExpPat*, 292.

[16] Francis of Assisi, *RNB*, 395-96.

[17] *Actus beati Francisci et sociorum ejus*, ed. Paul Sabatier, Collection d'Études et de Documents, 4 (Paris, 1902) 31.

[18] Francis of Assisi, *EpOrd*, 263.

[19] Bonaventure, *Itinerarium*, prol. 3.

Master in theology, seventh successor of Francis at the head of the Franciscan Order, Bonaventure intends to conduct his reflection first by detailing the specific function of the free will, then by describing what is the moral rectitude implanted by God in the creation of the human person, and, finally, by discussing the moral illumination whose root and ultimate end is, at the same time, charity.

A. Free will.

Our moral life is simultaneously one of seeking and satisfaction. From the moment that we open ourselves through the truth of things to the discovery of the truth of God, we experience the need to raise ourselves towards his goodness by imitating the love which he is supremely. The moral teaching of Bonaventure profoundly modified Aristotelian metaphysics in its claim to uniformly account for all the activities of the universe. On the one hand, Bonaventure relies upon the Augustinian heritage of intellectual illumination in order to present a solution of continuity between the principles which govern the activity of matter and those which preside over the activity of the mind. On the other hand, by adopting the morality of Saint Anselm and his notion of rectitude willed for itself as the essential function of free will, he rejects a finalistic determinism ruling over the universal order of secondary causes by founding it instead in the free finality of the voluntary act.

Moreover, whereas the appetitive will is tied to the determined order of natural tendencies and whereas it inspires necessary acts, free will is self-determining in the order of free decisions; its acts are essentially contingent. And in order to free oneself of the metaphysical slavery of the determinism of the appetitive will, free will is raised to the level of grace. It is with the aid of grace that the function of free will becomes specifically moral with its own motives. The influence of Saint Anselm is thus capital. It reveals itself in the structure attributed to free will in as much as it is the organ of the search of the good for the good. It is revealed also in the moral function of free will which finds in the supernatural order its full perfection. Charity will be the instrument which permits the free will to find its definitive consecration in the beatific vision.

Free will is thus a specific function of the human person: "Without any doubt, free will is found only in rational beings, as much under the aspect of freedom as under the aspect of decision."[20] Under the aspect of freedom, it is not tied to any desirable object, i t can desire all desirable objects and reject all objects to be avoided. Whether it is a question of the delectable good, of the useful good, or of the honest good, free will is the master. Animals desire the delectable and the useful. Only the human person desires the honest good. Liberty also consists in the complete mastery over acts. We can freely move our hands or our feet or our whole body, we can hate that which we have up to then loved, or the contrary. As John Damascene says, animals are rather acted upon than self-activating.[21] Human beings, by contrast, are masters of their actions and decisions.

For under the aspect of decision, free will signifies more than a judgement:

> Free will is the same as judgement by which all other powers are moved and which [all other powers] obey. The complete notion of judging consists in distinguishing between what is just and unjust, what is one's own and someone else's. No other power knows what is just and what is unjust: only that power which functions reasonably and is capable of knowing supreme justice, from which stems every rule of law.[22]

Free will thus signifies a free decision. For Bonaventure, it is really more than the rational appetite of Aristotle whose

---

[20]Bonaventure, *II Sent., d. 25, p. 1, a. un., q. 1*, in II, 593: *Absque dubio liberum arbitrium reperitur in solis substantiis rationalibus. Et ratio huius sumitur tum ex parte libertatis, tum ex parte arbitrationis.*

[21]John Damascene, *De fide orthodoxa* (version of Burgundio de Pisa, c. 41): *"Bestia aguntur plus quam agunt."*

[22]Bonaventure, *II Sent., d. 25, p. 1, a. un., q. 1, concl.,* in II, 593: *Arbitrium enim idem est quod iudicium, ad cuius nutum ceterae virtutes moventur et obediunt. Iudicare autem illius est secundum rationem completam, cuius est discernere inter iustum et iniustum et inter proprium et alienum. Nulla autem potentia novit quid iustum et quid iniustum nisi illa sola quae est particeps rationis et nata est cognoscere summam iustitiam, a qua est regula omnis iuris.*

determinism stops at the threshold of the willing of the good. Further, we are in the domain of the illumination which breaks the metaphysical continuity of the universe of the Philosopher. Free will is thus a specialized function which is not differentiated from the reason and the will. Its constituitive elements are reason, self-reflection, and voluntary decision. The reason is the faculty of moral judgement which goes beyond the appetite-will. Self-reflection is the reflected knowledge by which both the reason as much as the will have the power to know themselves and move themselves. This is the power of moral reflection:

> It is the power of commanding the reason and the will and of governing and moving both of them. The first act of this power [of moral reflection] is not one of distinguishing and willing, but an act of reflecting on these two and of moving and ruling over them. It is that act whereby one is said to will to distinguish and to will to will.[23]

The third element is voluntary decision. Thereby freedom thus has its source in the reason and the will. It begins in the one and is completed in the other: "Freedom of the will or the faculty called 'free will' begins in the reason and is consummated in the will."[24] Free will is thus the power of the final moral and irrevocably free specification stemming from the will.

Regarding all its objects, from the natural moral good to the moral good of supernatural virtues up to the object of the beatific vision, free will is called upon to determine the act conformed to rectitude and in the specifically moral intention of rectitude. But according to Bonaventure, who follows Augustine in this matter, the privilege of free will is less to be able to choose between good and evil than to be able to choose the good for the sake of the good. It is there the object par excellence of self-determination, the essential and inalienable object of our freedom. Bonaventure thus joins moral justice as defined by Saint Anselm to the honest good,

---

[23]Bonaventure, *II Sent., d. 25, p. 1, a. un., q. 2,* in II, 595: *Est virtus imperans rationi et volontati et utramque regens et movens, cuius actus primus non est discernere et velle, sed actus reflexus super haec duo et haec duo movens et regens, ille videlicet quo dicitur quis velle discernere et velle se velle.*

[24]Bonaventure, *II Sent., d. 25, p. 1, a. un., q. 6, concl.,* II, 605: *Libertas arbitrii sive facultas quae dicitur liberum arbitrium in ratione inchoatur et in voluntate consummatur.*

the object of Aristotelian morality. He does it by distinguishing the appetite-will and the free will, the natural will and the elective will. "He thereby intends to distinguish clearly between the universal and necessary finality in which the human person participates by its nature and the specifically moral finality which the human person is called to freely pursue."[25] The two wills proceed from the same power, but they differ by their motives: the natural desire of happiness which is necessary, and the willing of virtue which is contingent. They differ also by their objects: the good *"ratione commodi"* (as useful) and the good *"ratione honesti"* (as honest).

The moral function of free will consists therefore in making us pursue our final end through a willing of honesty, in elevating us through the moral use of our freedom to a level higher than that of the natural appetite for happiness. In the intention of the will as deliberative, the glory of God is substituted for happiness as first moral end. It becomes the proper object of the essentially distinterested moral will, identified with the love of kindness and friendship. Perfect charity thus has a primacy in the morality of Bonaventure.

B. Moral Rectitude

In the *prooemium* to his *lectio* in II Sententiarum (II, 4-6), Bonaventure lays out in a very concentrated manner the condition of the human person, on the basis of Ecclesiastes (7,30): "God made the human person upright, but he has entangled himself in an infinity of questions." God made the human person upright, that is creation and righteousness come from God. Ecclesiasticus 17,1-2 explains the human condition. God created the human person from the earth, with respect to the body; he made that person in his image, with respect to the nature of the soul; he gave human beings the power to turn themselves toward him, with respect to the overflowing grace which turns the soul towards God through the virtues; that is why he adds: "Like himself, he has clothed them in strength." God has not only given to human beings the possibility

---

[25]J. Rohmer, *La finalité moral chez les théologiens de saint Augustin à Duns Scot*, (Paris, 1939) 196.

of righteousness by conferring on them his image and likeness; he has made them upright by turning them towards him. Thus human beings are upright when their intelligence attains the sovereign truth through knowledge, when their will is conformed to the sovereign goodness through love, when their strength continues the sovereign power through action. The human person is wholly turned towards God.

> Consequently, the human being is first of all upright when the intelligence is consonant with highest truth. By "consonant" I do not mean that the human being is thereby all-knowing, but only by way of a certain imitation. If as Anselm says: "Truth is rectitude perceptible only by the mind", and only what is upright is consonant with rectitude, then when our intellect is consonant with truth, it is necessarily rectified. It is rendered consonant with the truth only when it actually turns toward the truth. Actual truth is defined as an agreement between a thing and the intellect. Once our intelligence is turned to the truth, it is "made true" and consequently consonant with the truth, and when consonant with rectitude, it is rectified. Thus, without truth no one judges rightly, as is said in the book *De vera religione*, and the one who looks to the truth judges rightly, as the Lord said to Simon: *You have judged rightly* (Lk 7).[26]

Bonaventure then continues:

> Similarly, the human person is rectified when the will is in conformity with the highest goodness. Highest goodness is highest equity of justice. A person is better to the extent that he or she is more just. As Anselm says: "Justice is the

---

[26]Bonaventure, *II Sent., prooemium,* 4: *Primo igitur homo rectus est, cum intelligentia summae veritati aequatur; aequari autem dico non per omnimodam impletionem, sed per quamdam imitationem. Si enim 'veritas, ut dicit Anselmus, est rectitudo sola mente perceptibilis', et rectitudini non potest aequari nisi rectum; cum intellectus noster aequatur veritati, necessario rectificatur. Tunc autem aequatur, quando actualiter se convertit ad veritatem. Veritas enim in actu definitur, quod est adaequatio rei et intellectus. Intelligentia autem nostra ad veritatem conversa verificatur, ac per hoc veritati aequatur, et dum aequatur rectitudini, rectificatur; unde 'sine veritate nullus recte iudicat', ut dicitur in libro 'De vera religione', et qui aspicit ad veritatem iudicat recte, secundum quod Dominus dicit Simoni, Lucae septimo: 'Recte iudicasti'.*

rectitude of the will".[27] However, only what is upright is in conformity with rectitude. As long as the will is in conformity with the highest goodness and equity, it is necessarily made upright. However, that will is conformed when it is turned towards it by loving. Thus Hugh of St. Victor: "Know, O my soul, that somehow by the assocation of love you are transformed to the likeness of the very one to whom you are joined by affection".[28] The one who loves goodness is made upright. And this is what is said in the book of the Song of Songs 1,3: *"The upright love you"*. The upright are turned to your goodness and your goodness bends down to them. The soul experiencing this exclaims and says: *"How good God is to the upright"* (Ps 72,1). And because only the upright experience this, therefore: *"Praise from the upright is fitting"* (Ps 32,1).[29]

The Seraphic Doctor then continues:

Moreover, the human person is made upright when its powers are conjoined to the highest power. The upright is a mean between extremes. The extremes are the first and the last, the alpha and the omega. The mean between these is action whereby the agent attains his goal. Hence, a virtue is upright whose action comes from the first principle and tends toward the final goal. Since therefore divine power does everything and does so on account of God, this is why the divine power is most righteous in acting. Nothing is conjoined to the highest power, they are undoubtedly rectified. This is why the human person is not only upright, but ruler and king, as is intimated in Deuteronomy 33,5: *"And he became king of his darling, when the chiefs of the*

---

[27] Anselm, *Dialog. de lib. arbitr., c. 3*, in PL 158, 494.

[28] Hugh of St. Victor, *De arrha animae*, in PL 176, 954.

[29] Bonaventure, *II Sent., prooemium, 4: Similiter homo rectificatur, dum voluntas summae bonitati conformatur. Summa enim bonitas est summa aequitas sive iustitia; tanto enim quis melior, quanto iustior. Sed, ut dicit Anselmus, 'iustitia est rectitudo voluntatis': nihil autem conformatur rectitudini nisi rectum. Dum ergo voluntas bonitati summae et aequitati conformatur, necessario rectificatur. Tunc autem conformatur, cum ad ipsam convertitur diligendo. Unde Hugo: 'Scio, anima mea, quod, dum aliquid diligis, in eius similitudinem transformaris'. Qui enim diligit bonitatem rectus est. Et hoc est quod dicitur Canticorum primo: 'Recti diligunt te'; recti enim ad tuam bonitatem sunt conversi, et tua bonitas ad eos inclinatur. Unde anima experta clamat et dicit: 'Quam bonus Israel Deus his qui recto sunt corde'. Et quia soli recti experiuntur, ideo 'rectos decet collaudatio'.*

people assembled and the tribes of Israel came together".
This will happen in heaven when our powers will be
conjoined to the divine power. Then we will be in full
control of our powers, as God is of his. And thus all are
kings and all are promised the kingdom of heaven.[30]

Moreover:

God has thus made the human person upright when he
made him [or her] to be turned towards Himself. In this
turning to God, the human person was not only made
rectified with respect to what is above, but also with
respect to what is below. For the human person stands in
the middle, and as long as he [or she] is turned toward God
and subject to Him, then all other things are subject to the
human being. Thus God subjected every created truth to be
judged by the human intellect, every good to its affections
to be used, and every power to its power to be governed.[31]

Furthermore, the intelligence turned towards the divine truth,
adds Bonaventure:

. . . lays claim to that wisdom through which one judges all
things according to what is said in Wisdom 7,17-21: "For he
gave me sound knowledge of existing things, that I might
know the organization of the universe and the force of its
elements. The beginning and the end and the midpoint of
times, the changes in the sun's course and the variations of

---

[30]Bonaventure, *II Sent., prooemium, 4: Nihilominus homo rectificatur, dum virtus summae potestati continuatur. Rectum enim est cuius medium non exit ab extremis. Extrema sunt primum et ultimum, alpha et omega, principium et finis. Medium inter haec est operatio, per quam efficiens pervenit in finem. Illa ergo virtus recta est, cuius operatio est a principio primo et ad finem ultimum. Quoniam ergo divina virtus omnia operatur et propter Deum, hinc est, quod rectissima est in operando. Nihil autem continuatur recto nisi rectum; cum ergo virtus nostra summae potestati continuatur, absque dubio rectificatur; et ex hoc homo non solum rectus, sed etiam rector et rex efficitur, Deuteronomii penultimo: 'Et erit apud rectissimum rex congregatis principibus populi cum tribubus Israel'. Hoc erit in gloria, quando virtus nostra continuabitur divinae virtuti; tunc erimus omnipotentes voluntatis nostrae, sicut et Deus suae, et ideo omnes reges; et ideo omnibus promittitur regnum caelorum.*

[31]Bonaventure, *II Sent., prooemium, 5: Fecit igitur Deus hominem rectum, dum ipsum fecit ad se conversum. In conversione enim hominis ad Deum non tantum rectificabitur ad id quod sursum, sed etiam ad id quod deorsum. Homo enim in medio constitutus, dum factus est ad Deum conversus et subiectus, cetera sunt ei subiecta, ita quod Deus omnem veritatem creatam subiecerat eius intellectui ad diiudicandum, omnem bonitatem eius affectui. Ad utendum, omnem virtutem eius potestati ad gubernandum.*

the seasons. Cycles of years, positions of the stars, natures of animals, tempers of beasts. Powers of the winds and thoughts of men and women, uses of plants and virtues of roots — such things as are hidden I learned, and such as are plain". That is why Adam gave all things their names (Gen 2,20).[32]

He then concludes:

God subjected all things to the will of human beings so that he might use them, and that he might convert all to his use and utility, thus Psalm 8,8: *"You have put all things under his feet"*. Likewise the Apostle, now converted to God, in 1 Corinthians 3,22: *"All things are yours"*. God also subjected everything to human governance, as Genesis 1,28: *"Subject the earth and have dominion over the fish of the sea and the birds of the sky."* The fact that the human person was created upright, both with regard to what is above him and what is below him, is alluded to in that passage [Gen 1,26]: *"Let us make the human person in our image, according to our likeness, etc."* Therefore God made the human person upright; and as long as he [or she] turned toward God, that person became like Him; and thereby human beings were given rulership over all things. Thus the upright condition of humanity is obvious.[33]

---

[32]Bonaventure, *II Sent.*, *prooemium*, 5: . . . *vindicat sapientiam per omnia diudicat, secundum quod dicitur Sapientiae septimo: 'Ipsa dedit mihi omnium quae sunt scientiam, ut sciam dispositionem orbis terrarum et virtutes elementorum: initium et consummationem, et medietatem temporum, vicissitudinum permutationes et commutationes temporum, anni cursus et stellarum dispositiones, naturas animalium et iras bestiarum, vim ventorum et cogitationes hominum, differentias virgultorum, et virtutes radicum, et quaecumque sunt absconsa et improvisa'. Unde et Adam omnibus nomina imposuit.*

[33]Bonaventure, *II Sent.*, *prooemium*, 5: *Subiecit nihilominus voluntati omnia ad utendum, ut possit omnia in usum et utilitatem suam convertere. Unde in Psalmo: 'Omnia subiecisti sub pedibus eius'. Unde Apostolus ad Deum conversis, primae ad Corinthios tertio: 'Omnia vestra sunt'. Subiecit etiam virtuti omnia ad gubernandum, Genesis primo: 'Subiicite eam, et dominamini piscibus maris et volatilibus caeli'. Ista autem recta hominis condition quantum ad superius et inferius simul tangitur in illo verbo: 'Faciamus hominem ad imaginem et similitudinem nostram, et praesit' etc. Fecit igitur Deus hominem rectum, dum ad se convertendo sibi eum assimilavit, et per hoc omnibus praeposuit; et sic patet recta hominis conditio.*

C. Moral Illumination

Charity which, for Bonaventure, is the consummation of the moral function of free will, embraces the two loves that Saint Anselm talks about: the love of concupiscence, source of the natural appetite, and the love of kindness, source of free will, because grace simulatenously informs these two loves and brings them to consummation in the possession of God. But the ultimate determination which renders the will capable of effectively willing the good and realizing it, is virtue. Thus is posed, in the order of the good, the problem which is posed in the order of the true. Human beings, for Bonaventure, are incapable of grasping the true by their own efforts. Are they capable of doing the good without the help of God? This is the capital problem of the Bonaventurian morality:

> I say that the eternal light is the exemplar of all things, and that the mind, once lifted up as was the mind of the most noble ancient philosophers, is able to reach it. And in this light, the first thing to come to the mind is the exemplars of the virtues. As Plotinus says, "it is indeed absurd that the exemplars of other things be in God and not the exemplars of the virtues".[34]

The divine archetypes act on our soul both in the order of action and in the order of knowledge:

> These virtues are impressed on the soul by this exemplary light and they go down into the cognitive faculty, the affective faculty, and the operative faculty. From the sublimity of purity is imprinted the purity of temperance; from the beauty of clarity, the serenity of prudence; from the strength of power, the stability of constance; from the rectitude of distribution, the sweetness of justice. Such are the four exemplary virtues with which the Sacred

---

[34]Bonaventure, *Hexaemeron, coll. 6, n. 6*, in V, 361: *Dico ergo, quod illa lux aeterna est exemplar omnium, et quod mens elevata, ut mens aliorum nobilium philosophorum antiquorum, ad hoc pervenit. In illa ergo primo occurrunt animae exemplaria virtutum. 'Absurdum enim est, ut dicit Plotinus, quod exemplaria aliarum rerum sint in Deo, et non exemplaria virtutum'.*

Scriptures are concerned, of which Aristotle knew nothing, but which the finest ancient philosophers did know.[35]

We now know the origin of the virtues. How are they established in our soul? All the philosophers agree in this: that the soul bears at birth natural faculties or aptitudes from which the virtues emerge; these aptitudes are developed through exercise. The soul is thus rendered capable of acting according to what one's conscience tells one. Like a mark left by God on his work, our will possesses the seeds of moral virtues. To the extent that it develops them through exercise, it is made upright and God comes to gather up the seeds and to transfigure them by the free gift of the theological virtues.[36] The moral virtues, such as the philosophers define them, are attached to our soul by a natural root, the innate rectitude of the will which confers on us a more or less imperfect aptitude to accomplish the good. This innate disposition is then developed thanks to the exercise and the repetition of its acts, from which come the cardinal virtues. But it can then happen that, if the grace introduced in us by the three theological virtues comes to inform our soul, these same natural cardinal virtues are found confirmed, fully developed, and led to their perfection by this divine gift.

> This semi-fulfilled capability does not achieve fulfillment automatically, but is also assisted by grace. For grace enhances what was pre-existing and confirms what has been so enhanced. Political power can be fulfilled by both [that is, the natural and supernatural], namely when the assistance of divine grace concurs with the practice of good customs and, because of these two, cardinal virtue achieves full perfection. And so cardinal virtue, as political, has its origin in nature, and is aided by supernatural grace, but it is

---

[35] Bonaventure, *Hexaemeron, coll. 6, n. 10,* in V, 362: *Haec imprimuntur in anima per illam lucem exemplarem et descendunt in cognitivam, in affectivam, in operativam. Ex celsitudine puritatis imprimitur sinceritas temperantiae; ex pulchritudine claritatis serenitas prudentiae; ex fortitudine virtutis stabilitas constantiae; ex rectitudine diffusionis suavitas iustitiae. Hae sunt quatuor virtutes exemplares, de quibus tota sacra Scriptura agit; et Aristoteles nihil de his sensit; sed antiqui et nobiles philosophi.*

[36] Bonaventure, *II Sent., d. 25, p. 1, dub. 1,* in II, 607.

led to perfection by both causes working together, namely grace and habitual activity.[37]

Grace is thus capable of making them arise where their natural root alone exists and where their *habitus* are still completely lacking. Indeed, as Bonaventure states elsewhere:

> The infusion of grace and virtues can be compared to the rain and a seeded field, just as the virtues informed by grace [may be compared] to light and color. If rain should fall on a field planted with various seeds which have not yet germinated, it [the rain] would cause them to germinate and produce various plants according to the diversity of seeds. If, however, it has caused others to germinate, but for lack of water the plants have already withered, a second rain will make them grow again.[38]

Bonaventure has nicely condensed his position in the *Breviloquium*:

> Charity, itself is the root, form and end of the virtues; joining all with the ultimate end and binding all together at once and in order. Hence charity is itself the weight of every ordered inclination and the bond of perfect union, preserving order in the various things that ought to be loved, as regards what is loved and what is achieved; and possessing a unity in the infused virtue in having but one end and one unique and primary beloved, which constitutes the reason to love all other objects which, by the bond of love, are made to be reunited in Christ alone, head and

---

[37] Bonaventure, *III Sent.*, d. 33, a. un., q. 5, concl., in III, 723: *Nec solum ex assuefactione ducitur haec habilitas semiplena ad complementum, sed etiam par gratiae adjutorium. Nam cum qualemcumque prius existentem amplificat et amplificando confirmat. Ex utraque etiam causa virtus politica potest suscipere complementum, videlicet quando concurrit divinae gratiae adjutorium et bonae consuetudinis exercitium, per quae duo virtus cardinalis radicata in natura ducitur ad complementum perfectum. Et sic virtus cardinalis, in quantum est politica, ortum habens a natura, ducitur ex gratia superveniente, sed ad perfectum complementum ducitur ex utraque causa concurrente, videlicet gratia et assuefactione.*

[38] Bonaventure, *III Sent.*, d. 23, a. 2, q. 5, ad 6, in III, 500: *Potest autem accipi simile de infusione gratiae et virtutum in pluvia et terra seminata, sicut de informatione virtutum a gratia accipitur in lumine et colore. Si enim una pluvia adveniat in terram in qua sunt plantata diversa semina quae non germinaverunt, facit illam germinare et secundum diversitatem seminum diversas plantas producere. Si vero iam alias germinavit, sed propter defectum aquae iam arefactae sunt plantae, tunc pluvia denuo veniens facit illas plantas virescere.*

body, who contains in Himself the totality of those to be saved.[39]

Étienne Gilson gives us our conclusion:

Thus God continually fulfills nature as nature. The soul is thus open to God. In discovering its original fragility, i t simultaneously discovers the presence of God, and in being joined to him, it attains perfection in the operations which it carries out.[40]

Primary Sources

Bonaventure:

> II Liber Sententiarum, in *Opera omnia, II* (Quaracchi, 1885).
>
> III Liber Sententiarum, in *Opera omnia, III* (Quaracchi, 1887).
>
> Itinerarium mentis in Deum, in *Opera omnia, V* (Quaracchi, 1891).
>
> Breviloquium, in *Opera omnia, V* (Quaracchi, 1891).
>
> Hexaemeron, in *Opera omnia, V* (Quaracchi, 1891).

Francis of Assisi:

> Kajetan Esser, *Die Opuscula des hl. Franziskus von Assisi. Neue textkritische Edition* (Grottaferrata, 1976).

Thomas of Celano:

> Vita prima (= 1 Cel), in *Analecta franciscana, X* (Ad Claras Aquas, 1926-41).
>
> Vita secunda (= 2 Cel), in *Analecta franciscana, X* (Ad Claras Aquas, 1926-41).

---

[39] Bonaventure, *Breviloquium*, p. 5, c. 8, n. 5, in V, 194: *Caritas ipsa est radix, forma et finis virtutum, iungens omnes cum ultimo fine et ligans omnia ad invicem simul et ordinate; ideo ipsa est pondus inclinationis ordinatae et vinculum colligationis perfectae, ordinem quidem servans respectu diligendorum diversorum quantum ad affectum pariter et effectum, unitatem autem habens in habitu quantum ad unum finem et unum principale dilectum, quod est ratio diligendi respectu omnium aliorum, quae par amoris vinculum nata sunt colligari in unum Christum quantum ad caput et corpus, quod universitatem in se continet salvandorum.*

[40] Étienne Gilson, *La philosophie de saint Bonaventure*, 2 ed. (Paris, 1943) 346.

Bonaventure's Use of
'The Divine Word' in Academic Theology

Dominic V. Monti, O.F.M., Ph.D.

Washington Theological Union

Sometime in the early years of his tenure as regent master of the Franciscan school of theology at Paris (1254-57), Bonaventure penned a response to a young teacher of arts who was concerned about the validity of the friars' way of life. In it, he both testifies to the remarkable transformation that had occurred to a itinerant band of lay penitents in a few short decades and provides a defense of his own vocation as a professor of theology.

> Hear me now on what I have to say about books and other tools. The Rule states in no uncertain terms that the brothers have the right and duty of preaching, something that, to my knowledge, is found in no other religious rule. Now, if they are not to preach fables but the divine Word, which they cannot know unless they read, nor read unless they have books, then it is perfectly clear that it is totally in harmony with the perfection of the Rule for them to have books. . . .

> [Indeed], who are better fit to teach the Gospel than those who profess and observe it? . . . Surely it is right that the brothers, like *clean animals*, should learn the divine words and *chew them over* [cf. Lev. 11:3]. And so, if the brothers are able to supply themselves with teachers, who would be so foolish as to say that the doctrine which befits them to observe and teach they must like beggars get from those who do not carry it out? . . . Yes, I praise the studious

brother, since I believe the authority to teach the Gospel of
Christ belongs to him more than anyone else.[1]

These two short paragraphs positioned the young Franciscan
Order at the heart of what has been called a "pastoral revolution"
within the thirteenth-century church, which permanently
transformed both the exercise of priestly ministry and theological
education. Responding to a hitherto unparalleled thirst for
hearing the Word of God among the townspeople of Western Europe
and spurred on by the challenge of suspect—even heretical—
unauthorized preachers, the leadership of the church was forced to
move to address the situation.[2] Building on scattered local
initiatives, the Fourth Lateran Council in 1215 mandated bishops
to "commission suitable men. . . powerful in word and work" to
assist them in supplying the "nourishment of God's Word" to the
Christian people.[3] However, it is important to underline the fact
that the emphasis of the Council "was not simply upon more
preaching, but upon more preaching of the proper sort. The church
considered fervor in a preacher an unacceptable substitute for
learning and orthodoxy."[4] Therefore the Council had also
prescribed the appointment of lectors "to teach Scripture to priests
and others, and especially to instruct them in matters which are
recognized as pertaining to the cure of souls."[5] The issue was
properly equipping men for the preaching ministry; for this a solid
grounding in Christian doctrine was absolutely essential.

---

[1] *Epis. de tribus quaest.*, nn. 6, 11 (V, 332-33, 335). Translation from my edition of
the *Works of St. Bonaventure, Volume V: Writings Concerning the Franciscan Order* (St.
Bonaventure, NY: The Franciscan Institute, 1994) 46, 51-52.

[2] The best general history of these developments is Colin Morris, *The Papal
Monarchy: The Western Church from 1050 to 1250* (Oxford: Clarendon Press, 1989) 287-
386, 417-526. Many insights are provided by the classic study of M. D. Chenu, *Nature,
Man, and Society in the Twelfth Century*, ed. Jerome Taylor and Lester K. Little (Chicago:
University of Chicago Press, 1968) 202-69; and the fine chapter "The New Emphasis
on Preaching," in Richard H. Rouse and Mary A. Rouse, *Preachers, Florilegia, and
Sermons: Studies on the 'Manipulus Florum' of Thomas of Ireland* (Toronto: Pontifical
Institute of Mediaeval Studies, 1979) 43-64.

[3] *Decrees of the Ecumenical Councils*, hereafter *DEC*, ed. Norman P. Tanner
(Washington: Georgetown University Press, 1990) 240-41.

[4] Rouse and Rouse, 57.

[5] *DEC*, p. 241.

The first Friars Minor, one of the contemporary movements of apostolic life among the laity, had been authorized by Innocent III a few years previously to preach "penance and conversion of life" to the people, avoiding any discussion of "the faith and the sacraments of the church." But both the enthusiastic response to the new brotherhood by their audience and its rapid growth, both numerically and geographically, soon propelled the Franciscans into becoming prominent agents of the pastoral reform agenda of Lateran IV.[6]

Very quickly, theological education became a major activity of the friars, as they attempted to provide the necessary training for their members to respond effectively to the contemporary needs of the church.[7] That need was specified in a special way: producing ministers who could provide "the nourishment of God's Word." Bonaventure, as a teacher in the Franciscan school, saw his own task within that perspective: enabling his students to preach "not fables, but the divine Word," on the basis of a thorough understanding of Biblical doctrine. In what sense then, we might ask, was his teaching of theology actually founded on and intended to serve the Word of God?

Zachary Hayes has observed that "there is a sense in which, for Bonaventure, theology is but an appropriate way of reading the Scriptures."[8] Yet little has been done to study the ways in which Scripture actually functions as a resource for Bonaventure as he goes about his work as a professional theologian. Part of this is due to the fact that Bonaventure himself does not bring this question up for systematic consideration in the writings which are the product

---

[6] The fundamental study of these developments remains Lawrence C. Landini, *The Causes of the Clericalization of the Order of Friars Minor* 1209-1260 (Chicago: Franciscan Herald Press, 1968).

[7] There has not been a modern general study to replace Hilarin Felder, *Geschichte der wissenshaftlichen Studien im Franziskanerorden bis um die Mitte des 13. Jahrhunderts* (Freiburg-im-Breisgau, 1904). There is a good background of the educational situation in the mendicant schools in M. D. Chenu, *Towards Understanding St. Thomas*, trans. Albert Landry and Dominic Hughes (Chicago: Henry Regnery Co., 1964) 11-199, and Jacques-Guy Bougerol, *Introduction to the Works of St. Bonaventure*, trans., José de Vinck (Paterson, N. J., St. Anthony Guild Press, 1964) 13-90.

[8] "Bonaventure: Mystery of the Triune God," in *The History of Franciscan Theology*, edited by Kenan B. Osborne (St. Bonaventure, NY: The Franciscan Institute, 1994) 46.

of his classroom lectures at the Franciscan school of theology in
Paris, either in his *Commentary on the Sentences* or his series of
Disputed Questions. Here he differs from his contemporary,
Thomas Aquinas, who on three different occasions, developed such
a consideration.[9] This lack is unfortunate, because it has led to a
somewhat distorted perception of Bonaventure's understanding of
the role Scripture plays in the theological task. It is certainly true
that on several occasions Bonaventure did offer a very rich
appreciation of the absolute importance and many-faceted richness
of the Bible for Christian faith, most notably in the prologue to his
Breviloquium, but again in the *Collations on the Hexaemeron* and
in the little treatise, *On Reducing the Arts to Theology*. However,
in none of these treatments does Bonaventure pose the specific
question of the way Biblical texts should be employed in the task
of systematic theology.[10] The most important of these, the prologue
to the *Breviloquium*,—which is itself a brilliant summary of his
own theology—is really framed as a university sermon; its style is
radically different from the remainder of the work, and in any
case, what it offers is more of an introduction to the study of
Scripture as a whole, a general hermeneutical theory, for the
incipient theologian.[11] The *Collations on the Hexaemeron*, also in
sermon form, was composed over fifteen years after he left the
classroom, and is organized around the differing stages of insight
through which the soul comes to a perception of truth. The *On
Reducing the Arts to Theology* briefly attempts to place theology

---

[9] Thomas raises this issue in his *Commentary on the Sentences*, Book I, prol., q.1, a.5;
Quodlibetal Questions VII, q.6, a.14-16; *Summa Theologiae*, I, q.1, a.9-10. See Maximino
Arias Reyero, *Thomas von Aquin als Exeget* (Einsiedeln, 1971) 31-153.

[10] As George Tavard observed: "Medieval theologians give but rare accounts of
their method. St. Bonaventure is as reserved as could be. Nevertheless, it is possible to
isolate a few statements of his which, altogether, form a summary of hermeneutics."
Transciency and Permanence: The Nature of Theology according to St. Bonaventure (St.
Bonaventure, NY: The Franciscan Institute, 1954) 196. The issue is, does "isolating a
few statements" really give an accurate portrayal of this hermeneutic in practice
rather than in theory?

[11] *Breviloquium*, introduction and translation by J. G. Bougerol, *Prologue* (Paris: Ed.
franciscaines, 1966) 22, 67-68, 78-79; Camille Bérubé, *De la philosophie à la sagesse*
(Rome: Istituto storico dei cappuccini, 1976) 117-130; P.M. Bordoy-Torrents, "Tecnicas
divergentes en la redacción del Breviloquio de S. Bonaventura," *Ciencia Tomistica* 59
(1940): 442-51.

within the total map of the sciences. None of these discusses—except indirectly—actual theological methodology. As these works offer Bonaventure's only extended discussion of Scripture, modern studies have relied on them for determining his understanding of the Bible,[12] resulting in a consequent emphasis on the importance of the spiritual senses. These works have two defects: first, they tend to assume a unified Bonaventurean theological "system," and they do not actually examine the ways in which he actually interprets Biblical texts in practice. Those scholars who have made the effort to examine Bonaventure's commentaries on Scripture in any depth have arrived at a very different conclusion: that, in fact, he tends to emphasize the literal sense of Scripture, indeed, that he should be counted among the foremost thirteenth century exegetes moving in this direction.[13] My goal in this present essay is to continue this discussion, but examining his works of systematic theology, or in Bonaventure's own term, "theology properly so called."[14] I believe that they will reveal that, without explicitly raising the questions which Thomas Aquinas does, Bonaventure answers them in a way very similar to his Dominican colleague.

Bonaventure defines the subject matter of systematic theological reflection as "the object of belief insofar as it is made understandable to the mind, and this by adding reasons. . . for our faith," thus differentiating it from Sacred Scripture, which

---

[12] Primarily Tavard, 40-55; Henri de Lubac, *Exégèse médiévale, seconde partie* (Paris: Aubier, 1961-64), 1:10-14; 2:264-72; Hans Merker, *Schriftauslegung als Weltauslegung* (Munich: Verlag Ferdinand Schöningh, 1971), esp. 16-37; Hans Joseph Klauck, "Theorie der Exegese bei Bonaventura," *S. Bonaventura 1274-1974*, ed. J. G. Bougerol, Vol. IV (Grottaferrata: Collegio S. Bonaventura, 1974) 71-128.

[13] The great pioneer here was Beryl Smalley: "Some Thirteenth Century Commentaries on the Sapiential Books," *Dominican Studies* 3 (1950): 41-77; *The Study of the Bible in the Middle Ages*, 3rd ed. (Oxford: Blackwell, 1983) 264-355 passim; *The Gospels in the Schools* (London: Hambleton Press, 1985) 201-213. My own work, "Bonaventure's Interpretation of Scripture in his Exegetical Writings" (unpublished Ph.D. thesis, University of Chicago, 1979), attempted to provide a general overview of Bonaventure as a Biblical commentator.

[14] *Itinerarium* 1.7 (V, 298). This text distinguishes theology "properly-so-called" from the symbolic and mystical modes of theology. As Fr. Zachary served as a perceptive reader of my Ph.D. thesis on Bonaventure's Biblical commentaries, this article provides an opportunity for me to revisit the topic of Biblical interpretation, but this time in the area of his own systematic theological concerns.

presents "the object of belief as such," clothed with the authority
of God's own self-revelation.[15] This distinction clarified the
respective roles of Scripture and systematic theology for the
medieval theologian: the former is the authoritative witness and
norm of faith; the latter, an attempt to make that faith
understandable, but which all the time presupposes and is
radically grounded in Biblical authority. This distinction made by
Bonaventure, lying at the very roots of the Scholastic method, had
become much more explicit and pronounced as it had been refined
over the course of a century of use.

Scholastic theology had arisen, as did every other field of
medieval science, from the classroom situation in which a teacher
commented on an authoritative text, in this case the Bible, for the
purpose of eliciting a stable body of knowledge.[16] This Scholastic
method led to systematic commentaries on the Bible, as the teacher
meticulously divided and subdivided his text, breaking it up into
smaller sense units, in the process resolving problems generated by
the attempt to grasp its meaning. This ultimately led the way to
the systematic raising of "questions," which resolved apparent
contradictions and cleared up ambiguities in the Bible through a
method of verbal and logical analysis based on Aristotelian
techniques.

---

[15] *I Sent.*, proem., q.1 (I, 7-8). The same distinction is made in the *Breviloquium*,
where Bonaventure distinguishes between the canonical Scriptures, which contain
"the object of belief as such," and the works of expositors, which deal with "the
object of belief as intelligible" (*Brevil.* 1.1 [V, 210]. On this, see John F. Quinn, *The
Historical Constitution of St. Bonaventure's Philosophy* (Toronto: Pontifical Institute of
Mediaeval Studies, 1973) 672-704.

[16] "It is important to recognize that, although the Bible alone among texts was
credited with complete inerrancy, all authoritative texts in all subjects were thought
to have this quality in a high degree. This was the reason for their acceptance as
textbooks. . . . they were authoritative because they could be depended on to be
exceptionally free from error and to express truths which were true in all
circumstances and for all time." R. W. Southern, *Scholastic Humanism and the
Unification of Europe, Volume I: Foundations* (Oxford: Blackwell, 1995) 106-107. The
chapter from which this quotation is taken, "The Sovereign Textbook of the Schools:
the Bible" (102-33), is an excellent introduction to the background of this essay. For a
good discussion of the relation of the terms "author" and "authority" in the Scholastic
method, see A. J. Minnis, *Medieval Theory of Authorship*, 2nd ed. (Philadelphia:
University of Pennsylvania Press, 1988) 10-15.

By the mid-thirteenth century, when Bonaventure embarked on his own studies, this Biblically-based method of theological education had become much more sophisticated; while some classes continued to be devoted to commenting on the Biblical text,[17] others no longer were organized around a presentation of Scripture as such. For example, one increasingly standard course offered a systematic overview of the whole of theology, using as a text the *Four Books of Sentences* composed in the preceding century by the Paris master, Peter Lombard.[18] Another development was a type of 'graduate course' offered by the masters in theology, which was not organized around a textbook at all, but simply consisted in the systematic resolution of disputed questions on a determined theological topic.[19] Thus the question arises: granted the changing focus of theological education away from commentary on the Biblical text to what we would call systematic theology, how does Bonaventure employ the Bible as a resource in constructing his own theology? In other words, how can we say that his systematic theology continues to be Scripturally-based?

To begin to answer this question, we must place Scripture within the whole context of the method Bonaventure uses in constructing his theology, that is, the "investigative mode" of posing questions, "seeking reasons to demonstrate the object of belief." As was noted above, Scripture is absolutely foundational for this enterprise, as in it the theologian possesses the object of

---

[17] These Bible courses in the theology school at Paris were on two different levels: entering theology students began with a "cursory reading" of the entire Bible offered by a Biblical bachelor, which lasted two years; advanced students attended 'graduate courses' on particular Biblical books offered by masters in theology. The product of Bonaventure's specialized magisterial lectures on the Bible (1254-57) were his commentaries on the Gospel of John and the Book of Ecclesiastes. The Commentary on Luke seems to be a later re-working and expansion of his introductory "cursory" lectures (1248-50) on that book.

[18] Alexander of Hales was the first master of theology at Paris to introduce the Sentences as a classroom text sometime during the 1220's; the practice had spread to Oxford by 1240. Bonaventure's *Commentary on the Sentences* is based on his classroom teaching at this level, during the 1250-52 academic years.

[19] Bonaventure's three series of *Disputed Questions: On Evangelical Perfection, On the Mystery of the Trinity*, and *On the Knowledge of Christ*, are such products of his teaching as master of theology (1254-57).

belief proposed to the mind with the authority of God himself.[20] Scripture thus grounds and provides a norm for all theological reflection. Even though Bonaventure may no longer have had the Scripture before him as a textbook while lecturing on the *Sentences* or disputing questions, Scripture continues to function as a governing horizon, an 'inspired text' to which his own work functioned simply as a commentary.

Here Bonaventure followed the Scholastic method utilized in every science of the time, which presupposed the authority of certain foundational texts. These were understood as containing an integrated and compete body of doctrine, even though it was recognized that there might be both gaps and contradictions within them. Furthermore, one could seek the relationship between the truths discovered though the different sciences. Thus the Scholastic method was inherently "dialectical," that is, it sought the reconciliation of opposites. It began with "questions" arising from an authoritative text about which commentators might differ, ultimately seeking to resolve the issue. So Bonaventure first proposes a *quaestio*; this is followed by a *propositio* stating authorities and reasons in support of one answer, followed by an *oppositio*, marshaling authorities and reasons for the contrary view, and ending with a *solutio* (*conclusio*), in which he shows either that the reasons given in the *oppositio* are not persuasive or that the *propositio* must be qualified or abandoned in light of the *oppositio*.

This is the procedure which Bonaventure invariably follows in his *Commentary on the Sentences* and his *Disputed Questions*. As one analyzes Bonaventure's arguments *pro* and *con* a certain position, those based on authority are distinguished, many times explicitly, from the arguments based on reason. These "authorities" may be Biblical texts, patristic authors (*sancti*), other scholastic commentators (*magistri*), or philosophical texts. Among these Biblical authority holds a unique position. Despite his inbuilt medieval deference to any and all proven "authorities," Bonaventure recognizes that at times they can be mistaken. This is certainly often the case with pagan philosophers, who did not

---

[20] *1 Sent.*, proem., qq.1-2 (I, 6-11).

have the benefit of Christian revelation to aid their thinking, but the *magistri* and even the *sancti* have erred on occasion as well.[21] The Bible, however, stands on a different level; it is infallible in principle, because it is the inspired Word of God: "the authority of the Holy Scripture is the authority of the Holy Spirit."[22] This is the characteristic which separates the Bible from every other source of theology: its absolute truth, based upon its divinely-guaranteed inerrancy. Again and again in the course of his theological argumentation, this principle of the absolute authority of Scripture is upheld by Bonaventure:

> The Holy Scripture was composed by the uncreated Word himself and the Holy Spirit. Whoever contradicts it contradicts the Highest Truth.[23]

> The doctrine of faith has been handed down in a much truer way than philosophical science, because it is the Holy Spirit and Christ himself. . . who have taught the truth of faith and of Holy Scripture, which says nothing false and in which can be reprehended in nothing.[24]

> Scripture contains nothing superfluous or useless.[25]

This unshakable authority of Scripture is the controlling factor of Bonaventure's theological methodology and is the basis of his conception of theology as a "subalternate" or subordinate science. The theologian's work must always be subject to Biblical authority and serve it. For one must always keep in mind that there is a great difference in the certainty which can be reached by means of these two sciences. Systematic theology relies on human reasoning procedures in its attempts to penetrate the truths of faith, but by this very fact it has a tendency to draw the mind away from the

---

[21] When Bonaventure deals with the question of the discrepancy that can be found among Catholic interpreters of Scripture, he underlines the fact that these differences sometimes are due to their reliance on human reasoning, "in which people are frequently deceived." 2 *Sent.*, d.15, dub. 3 (II, 389-90).

[22] 4 *Sent.*, d.43, a.1, q.4 (IV, 889).

[23] 3 *Sent.*, d.24, a.1, q.2, ad 4 (III, 513).

[24] 3 *Sent.*, d. 23, a. 1, q.4 (III, 482).

[25] 3 *Sent.*, d.36, dub. 5 (III, 809).

foundations of that faith: God's own self-revelation. No human reasoning can ever be totally certain; mistakes can be made at every step of the way. Theological science must continually have recourse to its superior science, the knowledge revealed in Scripture whose truth is guaranteed by God.[26] Therefore, no merely human testimony—no matter how venerable the source or how convincing the argumentation—can be admitted by the theologian if it contradicts the explicit testimony of the Biblical text. This point is specifically made by Bonaventure on a number of occasions in his theological works.

Perhaps the clearest instance of where this notion of theology as a subordinate science comes into play is a passage in *The Sentences Commentary*, where Bonaventure raises the question of whether the world was created at once, in a state of perfect actualization, or whether its forms were perfected over the course of time.[27] At root, this involved a case of Biblical interpretation. Augustine's *De Genesi ad litteram* had proposed that the "six days" of the creation account in Genesis had only figurative significance, whereas other authoritative commentators had taken them literally as referring to a period of time. Bonaventure first offers the arguments in favor of Augustine's argument for an instantaneous creation, advancing three Biblical texts cited by the bishop of Hippo supporting his position;[28] these authorities are then followed by logical arguments.

Then, Bonaventure proceeds to develop the contrary position. The first of these is based on the "text of Genesis," which explicitly states that it was over the course of six days that "the Lord completed the work he had begun." For Bonaventure, this point is decisive. Using one of Augustine's own principles—"the authority of this Scripture is greater than all the cleverness of

---

[26] "The certitude of Sacred Scripture exceeds any certitude of human reasoning." *1 Sent.*, proem., q.2, ad 4 (I, 11). Thomas Aquinas advances the same concept of 'subalternate science' in *Summa theologiae*, Ia, q.1, a.2. For a general discussion, see M.-D. Chenu, *La théologie comme science au XIIIe siècle*, 3rd. ed., (Paris: J. Vrin, 1967) 71-85; Ulrich Köpf, *Die Anfänge der theologischen Wissenshaftstheorie im 13. Jahrhundert* (Tübingen: J. C. B. Mohr, 1974) 145-49, 168-71.

[27] *2 Sent.*, d.12, a.1, q.2 (II, 295-98).

[28] "The most important of these was Sirach 18:1, which in the Vulgate read: "He who lives forever created all things together [*simul*].

human insight," Bonaventure turns it against its author, arguing that the explicit statement of Genesis must be preferred to the "human persuasiveness" of Augustine. What is especially important here is that Bonaventure argues for a literal interpretation of the Genesis account over a figurative one precisely on the basis of the intention of its human author: "Moses knew very well that unlettered people would understand his words literally; thus if he had meant them merely as figures he would have knowingly intended to lead people astray. It is obvious, therefore, that he meant what he said." Although Bonaventure goes on to advance five more arguments in his *oppositio*, one from the "common authority of the doctors" and four from reason, it is clear from his conclusion that it is the Genesis text that is decisive:

> There are two basic ways in which the saints have approached this question. Some have mainly followed a theological method, which draws reason to the things of faith. Some others, however, of whom Augustine is the most noteworthy, have mainly followed a philosophical method, which begins by affirming what seems most consistent with reason, and then tries to understand Scripture in a way that will confirm and attest to it. . . Although this procedure is reasonable and very attractive, because it leads the understanding away from Scripture it seems both sounder and more meritorious to instead make our understanding and reasoning completely submissive to Holy Scripture, than to lead it away in any fashion. That is what the other doctors—both those who proceeded Augustine and those who followed him—commonly understood and taught, just as the literal meaning of the text of Genesis is seen to say.[29]

What is interesting here is that Bonaventure does not simply cite a Biblical text, but emphasizes what he considers its literal meaning, the intention of its human author. Bonaventure does not deny that the creation account has other, spiritual senses: in fact, he goes on in the same passage to expound the moral, allegorical,

---

[29] *2 Sent.*, d.12, a.1, q.2, concl. (II, 296).

and anagogic significance of the six days.[30] But these spiritual interpretations are based on the literal meaning; they do not supersede it. While valid and useful, they are not the principal intention of the human author. This alone may be accepted as the basis of theological argumentation.

Bonaventure's line of reasoning in this revealing passage demonstrates that he shares the methodological position explicitly enunciated by Thomas Aquinas, who distinguished three purposes for which Scripture is useful: "the destruction of error, the instruction of morals, and the contemplation of truth." Scripture's historical or literal sense may alone be used for the first purpose, whereas the moral or tropological interpretation is particularly appropriate for the second, and the allegorical and anagogical sense for the third. Systematic theology as a scientific discipline, following an "argumentative procedure," must be based in the literal sense: "for the destruction of error, we may proceed only on the basis of the literal sense; the other senses have to be understood as metaphors, and logical argumentation may not be based on metaphorical speech."[31] Thirteenth century Scholastics were coming to recognize more and more that the spiritual senses were the wax nose of Scripture; they could be twisted to point in any direction. While this feature might make them very useful for preaching purposes,[32] it precisely ruled them out as 'authorities' for systematic theological argumentation. The spiritual senses might still be used as ornamental buttressing arguments in theology, but

---

[30] In fact, his allegorical and anagogical interpretations of this text are those which Augustine had offered as the primary meaning in his *De Genesi ad litteram*—the six days standing for the six ages of the world and as the six stages of knowledge in the spiritual creation; the latter of which Bonaventure himself would use as the architectonic of his *Collations on the Hexaemeron*.

[31] Thomas Aquinas, *1 Sent.*, prol., q.1, a.5 [(Parma, 1856), 7: 8-9). Bonaventure enumerates these same reasons in his own prologue to studying the *Sentences*: systematic theology attempts "to promote the faith by an inquisitive mode of proceeding. . . to confound heretics, to strengthen the weak, and delight the perfect" by finding "reasons" for that faith. *1 Sent.*, proem., q.2 (I, 10).

[32] Gregory the Great had emphasized this pastoral 'stretching' of texts to fit the audience: "He that treats of Sacred Writ should follow the way of a river. . .so that if, in discussing any subject, he should chance to find at hand any occasion of seasonable edification, he should, as it were, force the streams of discourse towards the adjacent valley." *Praef. in Job*, as quoted in Smalley, *Study of the Bible*, 33.

they could not provide a sure foundation for building a logical faith structure. As A. J. Minnis has described this position, increasingly taken by thirteenth century Scholastics: "Nothing necessary to faith is conveyed through the spiritual senses which is not conveyed elsewhere in Scripture, clearly and openly, through the literal sense. . . . allegory [thus] becomes at worse redundant and a t best a pleasing (and persuasive) optional extra."[33]

The passage we just examined is not an exceptional occurrence in Bonaventure's theology. Although he does not go into the same amount of detail for his reasoning, we find him following the same pattern over and over again in his theological argumentation: h e favors what he considers the literal meaning of Biblical texts over both earlier spiritual interpretations or the claims of reasoning. For example, on another occasion Bonaventure is forced to depart from Augustine's interpretation of protology. When he comes to the question of the creation of light, he again advances the different positions which had been taken on the problem. According to Augustine's interpretation, the light created on the first day referred to the spiritual nature of the angels. Although Bonaventure admits that this view is in harmony with both faith and reason, he recognizes that other commentators have taken a different position, holding that the work of the first day consisted in the formation of an actual corporeal light. The latter position should be followed as "more solid and useful," Bonaventure argues, since it "follows more closely the text of Scripture."[34] He proceeds in a similar manner in resolving questions on the divine infinity,[35] the knowledge of angels,[36] and the motive for the Incarnation.[37]

---

[33] *Medieval Literary Theory and Criticism c.1100-c.1375: The Commentary Tradition,* ed. A. J. Minnis and A. B. Scott (Oxford: The Clarendon Press, 1988) 204, from a chapter, "Scriptural Science and Signification: from Alexander's Sum of Theology to Nicholas of Lyre" [197-212], which offers an excellent overview of these trends. As Minnis points out here, Bonaventure's own rules of Biblical interpretation in the *Breviloquium* state that one should judge obscure passages of Scripture with reference to other parts of the Bible where things are explained clearly in a literal sense.

[34] *2 Sent.,* d.13, a.1, q.1 (II, 311-13).

[35] *1 Sent.,* d.43, un., q.2 (I, 768-70).

[36] *2 Sent.,* d.3, p.2, a.1, q.1 (II, 117-21).

[37] *3 Sent.,* d.1, a.2, q.2 (III, 23-28). Bonaventure does not ask whether the Word would have become Incarnate if Adam had not sinned. This question rather seeks the

In several other cases, Bonaventure had to deal with theological arguments utilizing appeals to Biblical texts on the basis of
spiritualizing interpretations of those texts by patristic authors.
One of these was in regards to the question of whether it is
necessary for the penitent to differentiate specifically between
types of mortal sin when confessing them to the priest.[38]
Bonaventure maintains the affirmative position here, basing
himself on the requirements of the famous decree *Omnis utriusque
sexus* of Lateran IV which had mandated yearly confession.
However, opponents were able to cite a passage from the book of
Wisdom as interpreted by both John Chrysostom and Augustine.
Bonaventure disposes of this quotation, however, stating that the
Fathers in question had used the passage in a context of loose
appropriation, not according to its literal meaning.

But in another case, Bonaventure was able to salvage the
opinion of one of his favorite authorities, the Pseudo-Dionysius,
even though his teaching seemed to be in direct contradiction to a
Biblical text. This was in the context of the question of whether all
the angels are sent on mission by God.[39] On this issue Dionysius was
the major authority in favor of the negative opinion, as he had
stated that it was only the angels in the narrower sense of the
word, those who comprised the lowest level of the celestial
hierarchy, who had a mission to human beings. However,
Bonaventure had to admit that this interpretation seemed to be
contrary to the obvious sense of a Biblical text, Hebrews 1:14: "are
not all the angels spirits in the divine service, sent to serve for the
sake of those who are to inherit salvation?" It seemed clear to him
that "the intention of the Apostle here" was to include all angels,
as he wished to show that Christ was superior to all angelic
creatures, both the superior and inferior. This would mean that
Dionysius was in error. However, Bonaventure believes that it

---

ratio praecipua of the Incarnation; looking at our actual historical situation,
Bonaventure believes it "more in accord with piety" to see the work of human
redemption as this principal reason. This is due to the fact that it is attested to by the
"authority of the Holy Scriptures. . . of both the Old and the New Testaments." Cf.
Zachary Hayes, *The Hidden Center* (New York: Paulist Press, 1981) 187-91.

[38] 4 *Sent.*, d.17, p.3, a.2, q.2 (IV, 459-61).

[39] 2 *Sent.*, d.10, a.1, q.2 (II, 261-62).

might be possible to reconcile both texts if we distinguish a direct
mission to human beings, exercised only by the lowest rank of
angels, and a mission exercised to other angels by the superior
ranks, although ultimately for the sake of human beings. Here we
see a favorite tack of the Scholastic method: reconciling
differences in authoritative texts through a method of making
distinctions by verbal and logical analysis.[40]

We can also see in Bonaventure's theology the authoritative
"letter" of Scripture coming into tension not only with allegorizing
patristic interpretations but contemporary theological developments. In one particularly poignant example, Bonaventure's profound Marian piety came into conflict with Biblical authority.
This was the question increasingly raised by thirteenth century
theologians as to whether the soul of Mary was sanctified prior to
any contraction of original sin. In summarizing the arguments in
favor of an Immaculate Conception, Bonaventure finds several
attractive theological opinions, as well as a number of typological
Biblical interpretations, but he is reluctantly forced to adhere to
the traditional opinion that Mary in fact was conceived in original
sin as "more reasonable and secure," for he sees no way around the
explicit authority of the Apostle Paul in two different texts: "all
have sinned and fallen short of the glory of God," and "death
spread to all because in him all have sinned" (Rom 3:23, 5:12).[41]
Reasoning on the basis of Biblical typologies must submit to a clear
literal textual authority. Interestingly enough, the following
question: whether Mary was sanctified in her womb before her
birth, is answered by Bonaventure in the affirmative. Although
there is no direct reference in Scripture to this having occurred, we
do discover there that both Jeremiah and John the Baptist were
sanctified in their mothers' wombs. Bonaventure therefore believes
that it is reasonable to deduce that a privilege granted to others
would not have been denied to Mary, especially since such would do
no violence to Scripture.[42] These two questions thus illustrate an

---

[40] See Southern, 125-31.

[41] 3 *Sent.*, d.3, p.1, a, 1, q.2 (III, 65-69). We again see here a case of the literal
meaning of a Biblical text taking precedence over several others offered in a spiritual
sense.

[42] 3 *Sent.*, d.3, p.1, a.1, q.3 (III, 70-72).

important procedure for Bonaventure: he believes that theological
insights may reasonably advance beyond what has been directly
revealed in Scripture through a process of logical argumentation, as
long as one does not contradict any other, more explicit Biblical
authority.[43]

Perhaps this examination of the absolute priority of the
literal sense of Scripture in Bonaventure's theological argumentation should conclude with a question particularly dear to
Bonaventure's heart: whether or not the renunciation of property,
in common as well as by individuals—pertains to true evangelical
perfection. This question is contained in one of his most sophisticated Scholastic works, the *Disputed Questions on Evangelical
Perfection*.[44] In constructing his argument in favor of the
affirmative answer to this question Bonaventure begins by citing
"the authority of Christ himself," going on to adduce six New
Testament references. He then goes on to enumerate eight quotations
from the works of saints who refer explicitly to "the example of
Christ" in this regard in the context of expounding other Gospel
texts; eleven other theological authorities; and seven arguments
from reason. For the contrary position, Bonaventure assembles two
Biblical texts, two theological authorities [both cited in the *Glossa
ordinaria*], and twelve arguments from reason. After examining the
case for both positions, Bonaventure concludes that the "reasons,
examples, and authorities [for the affirmative answer] must be
conceded," going on to make the following point: "Indeed, for this
conclusion, it would be sufficient to rely on just one explicit
authority from the mouth of Christ—for even if all the other
arguments could be dismissed, this alone would be more than
sufficient, even if many sayings of the Glosses and expositors and
teachers might seem contrary to it."[45] Even the most venerable
received theological tradition must stand before the judgment seat
of the inspired Word of God.

Having emphasized that Bonaventure bases himself firmly on
the literal sense in his theological arguments, it must also be

---

[43] This principle is in fact explicitly enunciated by Bonaventure on several
occasions, e.g. *1 Sent.*, d.11, dub.2 (I, 217); *2 Sent.*, d.27, p.1, art. un., q.4 (II, 478).

[44] *De perf. ev.*, a.1, q.2 (V, 125-34).

[45] *De perf. ev.*, a.1, q.2 (V, 130).

pointed out he is no fundamentalist, but uses the best of contemporary literary criticism to determine the intention of the human author. Scripture is the Word of God expressed in human words, and so it is not only appropriate but imperative to understand the artful manner an inspired author may have employed. For example, the Inspired Word may involve figures of speech. Dealing with the question of whether Christ assumed a rational soul, Bonaventure is faced with an objection based on the text of the Johannine prologue: "The Word became flesh." In his response, he makes it clear that "this is said by way of synecdoche: 'flesh is taken here for the whole of human nature. And if you ask why did the evangelist use this figure of speech, it was because in this passage he wanted to emphasize the bodily nature."[46] Likewise, dealing with a situation in which God seems to have commanded evil, Bonaventure indicates that the imperative mood in Scripture functions many times in a permissive rather than truly imperative fashion.[47]

The question of the literal meaning involving figures of speech is particularly evident in Bonaventure's discussion of protology. Here he tends to assume the validity of scientific explanations of the cosmos, and resolves apparent contradictions with Scripture by emphasizing that the inspired author had used figurative language. For example, Bonaventure asks whether heaven is in the form of an orb. The arguments for the affirmative are all based on reason, largely dependent on Aristotle. For the negative position, he is able to cite a Biblical authority: a descriptive passage in the Psalms: "you spread out the heavens like a cloak." If this Scripture be literally true, Bonaventure admits, then heaven is at best semi-circular. Although in resolving this question he admits that it is easy for our minds to agree with Aristotle, we must ask why we do not submit to the authority of Scripture. The reason is that the Psalmist here did not intend to be taken literally but was using poetic imagery: "Condescending to human simplicity, Scripture often uses vulgar images; thus, when speaking of heaven, it speaks

---

[46] 3 *Sent.*, d.2, q.2, q.2 (III, 46-47). This figure of speech is also utilized by Bonaventure in 2 *Sent.*, d.22, a.1, q.2 (II, 519).

[47] 2 *Sent.*, d.37, a.2, q.1 (II, 869-70).

of it as it appears to our senses."[48] He resolves the question of
whether the firmament possesses the same nature as material fire
in the same way.[49]

A more troublesome issue Scripture creates for the theologian is
due to the fact the same word can have two or more significations.
In these cases Bonaventure's Scholastic logical abilities are
employed to the utmost. He accepts the fact that a word, like any
sign, may be capable of more than one meaning. He also accepts the
fundamental law of logic that two true statements cannot contradict
one another. Finally, he believes that everything said in Scripture
is absolutely true. Therefore, if the Bible seems to contradict itself,
any conflict must be apparent, not real. A true contradiction must lie
in re as well as in word. So the theologian must resolve the seeming
contradictions in Scripture by going beneath the surface of
conflicting words to the underlying realities they signify. On this
level, the varying meanings of words becomes apparent. A good
deal of Bonaventure's attention is devoted to such cases, attempting
to determine in fact what his Biblical authorities really mean. A
good example of this is his discussion of the four meanings of "time"
in Scripture, ranging from a common, loose definition to one which
is strictly proper.[50] As a resource here Bonaventure could use the
ever-more-popular collections of Biblical 'distinctions,'[51] which
enumerated the various ways a word was used in Scripture. All of
this effort it is to determine the literal meaning of Biblical
passages, because it is that which has to provide the building
blocks of theological reasoning.

Yet, having said all of this, it is also clear that Bonaventure at
times does utilize the spiritual interpretation of Biblical passages
in constructing his theological arguments. Upon closer examination
of their context, however, it is evident that these play a part in
his discussion because they were already part of the received
theological tradition. I was not able to find an example where

---

[48] *2 Sent.*, d.14, p.1, a.2, q.1 (II, 341-42).

[49] *2 Sent.*, d.14, p.1, a.1, q.2 (II, 338-41).

[50] *2 Sent.*, d.2, p.1, a.2, q.1 (II, 64-65). Two questions later, Bonaventure examines
the various senses of the word "before" (*2 Sent.*, d.2, p.1, a.2, q.3 [II, 66]).

[51] See R. H. and M. A. Rouse, "Biblical Distinctions in the Thirteenth Century,"
Archives d'histoire doctrinale et littéraire du Moyen Age 41 (1974): 27-37.

Bonaventure creates such a reading on his own. But on the other hand, he had a treasure-trove of varying Biblical interpretations from patristic and earlier medieval authors to employ as reinforcing authorities whenever he felt the need or desire to do so. That Scripture could be legitimately used in different ways in different contexts Bonaventure had no doubt. In the critical discussion of the meaning of the six days of creation cited above, although he clearly disagreed with Augustine's interpretation of the literal meaning of Genesis, Bonaventure still happily accepted his reading as a perfectly valid allegory, citing with approval Augustine's own reasoning in the twelfth chapter of the *Confessions* that "one and the same Scripture can be understood in multiple ways, and in all these senses truthfully."[52] As Bonaventure expands this position further on, he emphasizes that although the Fathers may differ in their interpretation of a Scriptural text, they are not in basic disagreement:

> for they do not say what in fact actually happened [the literal sense], but what could be congruent with it; nor do they say what the Legislator, namely Moses, understood in a certain passage, but more importantly what the Holy Spirit intended, who inspired him. . . For the Holy Spirit understands many things simultaneously in the same text and so lets the expositors understand many things.[53]

Thus, although there is one "principal and literal understanding" of a text, there can be many others in an adapted or spiritual sense.[54] All of these various meanings which past Christian authors have seen in texts can be adduced as congruent reasons in theological argumentation.

Bonaventure admits a multiple interpretation of a Biblical text precisely because it had been interpreted in a variety of ways in the past tradition which he wishes to affirm; he does so by trying to show that they were all valid within their own perspective. In one particularly elaborate discussion, he confronts the widely

---

[52] *2 Sent.*, d.12, a.1, q.2 (II, 297).

[53] *2 Sent.*, d.15, dub. 3 (II, 390).

[54] *4 Sent.*, d.21, dub. 1 (IV, 558). See also *3 Sent.*, d.38, dub. 4 (III, 857) and *1 Sent.*, d.34, dub. 2 (I, 595).

divergent opinions of ancient authors on how precisely the ten
commandments of the Law were divided into two tables.[55] Josephus
had stated that there were five in the first and five in the second;
since he was a historian concerned with the way things actually
were, Bonaventure believes this is the literal sense of the passage.
But he goes on to say that the Fathers, chiefly Origen and
Augustine, had proposed other divisions which were also valid in
light of their own purposes; their interpretations do not contradict
the literal reading, but are true on a spiritual or applied level.

Virtually all of the spiritual interpretations brought into the
arguments in Bonaventure's systematic theology would have been
already familiar to his students, as they were contained in the
Glossa ordinaria, which they had studied in their introductory
theology course, the cursory reading of Scripture. In this sense, his
use of them is simply an affirmation of the received theological
tradition. I have identified only eight cases in the *Sentences
Commentary* where Bonaventure uses what is clearly a spiritual
reading of a Biblical text as an authority in constructing a theological argument, and every one of them is actually a citation of a
patristic or earlier medieval use of the text which had been
canonized in the Gloss.[56] For example, in answering the question of
whether human beings had grace before the fall, Bonaventure cites
as an authority for the affirmative response the text of Luke 10:30,
for "saints and the Gloss" had interpreted this sentence in the
parable of the Good Samaritan as part of an extended allegory.
Here the thieves signified the devil who had "stripped" the
traveler [the human race] of the "gratuitous gifts" of grace and
"wounded" its natural endowments.[57] In his *Commentary on Luke*,
Bonaventure relegates this to the end of his lengthy literal
interpretation of the parable as a derived mystical meaning.[58] Yet
he feels he can use it here in the *Sentences Commentary* as an

---

[55] *3 Sent.*, d.37, a.2, q.2 (III, 827-29).

[56] Besides the two cases I will cite in the text, the other instances are in *3 Sent.*,
d.25, a.1, q.3 (III, 543); *3 Sent.*, d.26, a.2, q.3 (III, 573); *3 Sent.*, d.23, art. un., q.4 (III,
719); *3 Sent.*, d. 24, p.1, a.1, q.1 (III, 735); *3 Sent.*, d.24, p.1, a.2, q.1 (III, 743), and *4 Sent.*,
d.4, p.1, a.1, q.1 (IV, 94).

[57] *2 Sent.*, d.29, a.2, q.1 (II, 700-01).

[58] *Comm. in Luc* .10:30 (VII, 271).

authority for his resolving this question—especially since there is no explicit Scriptural text used in defending the contrary position. In another instance, Bonaventure supports the argument for why there are only nine choirs of angels by a reference to the parable of the woman with the ten coins in Luke 15. The *Gloss* on this passage contained a reference from Bede, derived from Gregory the Great, that the lost coin signified the human race, whereas the other nine stood for the angelic choirs. But Bonaventure concludes that such an interpretation is "only from congruity; there are no express Biblical authorities on this matter."[59]

The question of the use of Old Testament "types" is a different, more ambiguous matter. Unlike spiritual interpretations, which have drawn out of the text—legitimately—by the saints, types arise because the Biblical message must be viewed as a whole. Bonaventure is working within a long Christian tradition which saw the ultimate meaning of the Jewish Law to have reached its fulfillment in the New Law of Christ. Thus the various ritual elements of the Old Law had only a provisional truth; their truly lasting significance lay in their being a kind of "predictive allegory" of Christian rites. The Old Testament does not simply foreshadow the New; in some way it already contains it.[60] Thus, Bonaventure does not view his use of types in the same light as strictly "spiritual" interpretations, for in some way the Spirit had included them as part of the actual 'base' meaning of these Old Testament passages. But once again, Bonaventure himself does construct these types; he utilizes those which were already commonplaces. His use of types in the construction of theological arguments is not surprisingly concentrated in the Fourth Book of *the Sentences Commentary*, which deals with the sacraments.

How much can Old Testament types be used as argumentation for the Christian? There is no consistent answer on this for

---

[59] *2 Sent.*, d.9, a. un., q.7 (II, 253-54). Unlike the previous example, Bonaventure believes that Jesus intended this parable as an allegory: the woman standing for divine Wisdom, and the coins for rational creatures stamped with the divine image. *Comm. in Luc.* 15:15-20 (VII, 387-89).

[60] See *4 Sent.*, d.24, p.1, a.1, q.3, where Bonaventure argues that the "New Law is in the Old, as the Truth is in the Figure" (IV, 618). Cf. *Brevil.*, prol. 6.2 (V, 208) for his general principles regarding such Old Testament texts.

Bonaventure. For example, the question arises whether we should abstain from the Eucharist because of bodily uncleanness.[61] One might answer yes, on the basis of reasoning that if such was the case in regards to the figure, how much more so in the case of the reality! However, Bonaventure dismisses this reasoning, arguing that precisely since the ritual laws were given as a figure of the New, the physical uncleanness they prohibited must be understood for us only as images of spiritual uncleanness. This alone is what prohibits a person from receiving the Eucharist. On the other hand, when it comes to the question of whether only priests can confect the Eucharist, Bonaventure reasons that since in the Old Testament only priests could offer the sacrifices in the temple and since the truth should correspond to the figure, therefore in the New Testament such a role should be limited to priests.[62]

A real conflict of possible Old Testament types is seen in the question of whether or not the reception of clerical tonsure implies the renunciation of temporal goods. For the affirmative position, Psalm 15 and Deuteronomy 18.8 are utilized to argue that if the priests of the Old Law "had no inheritance in Israel," how much more those of the New! But for the other side, the case of Jeremiah is cited, who although a priest, speaks of purchasing a field. Bonaventure resolves this quandary by going to another type. Since the priesthood of Christ was prefigured not so much by the levitical priesthood, but by that of Melchisidek, who was both priest and king, therefore "the Holy Spirit has disposed that the church have temporalities because of its human weakness."[63] In another example, the question of whether or not there should be orders in the church, Bonaventure opposes some egalitarian Pauline texts and the dominical sayings against lordship among the disciples with an interesting combination of logical reasoning from other Biblical texts. He feels that both the Pauline mystical body

---

[61] 4 Sent., d.12, p.2, a.1, q. 2 (IV, 297-98).

[62] 4 Sent., d.13, a.1, q.2 (IV, 304-05). Bonaventure makes it clear that he does not cite this as a proof from authority, but as one from reason—that is, by rational argumentation on the basis of Biblical types.

[63] 4 Sent., d.24, p.1, a.1, q.3 (IV, 611-12). Bonaventure goes on to emphasize that the Apostles themselves made such a renunciation and that this is the path of perfection.

analogy and lay military offices (citing a text here from the Song of Songs!) demand that the church should have offices and ranks. However, the most interesting of the Scriptural references in this arsenal of texts are his combining of Exodus 25:40 and Hebrews 9:23 to argue that the earthly church should imitate its celestial exemplar, which is hierarchical in nature.[64] It is interesting to note, however, that Bonaventure's general procedure is not to simply quote such texts as authorities in themselves; instead he uses them as starting points to draw conclusions on the basis of reasoning from a general typological principle: that since the New Law is already contained in the Old, the latter somehow speaks of its ultimate reference.

This brief review of Bonaventure's use of Scripture in constructing his systematic theology leads to several important conclusions. First of all, for him the literal sense of Scripture is decisive—and by this he does not mean simply what the words in a passage literally say, but what the inspired author intended to communicate through them, considering both their context and literary form. This literal meaning is the only way Scripture may be used as an 'authority' to ground theological arguments. Spiritual or mystical interpretations do continue to have a role in Bonaventure's method, but only a supporting one. They may offer congruent arguments, but are not probative in themselves. And certainly a text which is being interpreted spiritually carries no weight when another passage of Scripture explicitly supports the opposite side of an argument.

This does not mean that the spiritual senses of Scripture do not play an important role in Bonaventure's over-all theology if one uses that term in the broader sense of 'God-talk'—attempting to put the experience of God into words. When they speak of God, the preacher and contemplative rightly use Scripture in a different way than the systematic theologian. Indeed, tropological and anagogical readings may be especially useful at these levels. As Robert Southern points out, the very fact that the scholastic method of analysis diminished the role of symbolism in the schools made doctrines more abstract and difficult to convey in common

---

[64] *4 Sent.*, d.24, p.1, a.2, q.1 (IV, 612-15).

language, thus paradoxically increasing the need "for symbols, images, and anecdotes as channels of communications with the unlettered world."[65] Bonaventure's Biblical commentaries still show this dual concern: studying the text of Scripture itself both unveils God's saving truth and provides helpful *exempla* for future preachers. But in his works of *theologia propria*, he has one overriding purpose: to help the future preacher think through the faith of the church in a systematic fashion and so arrive at a solid doctrinal foundation for his ministry. To be able to preach the Word of God, one must first understand its saving message. And to accomplish this, one must rely on those parts of Scripture which in "plain words, signify and express all that concerns our redemption in terms of faith and morals."[66]

---

[65]Southern, p. 121.

[66]*Brevil.*, prol. 6.2 (V, 207).

A prospectus for

Ascending and Descending Christologies:
The Unity of Christ According to Bonaventure and His Franciscan Predecessors

Walter Principe, CSB †[1]

The papal condemnation of the statement that Christ as man is not *aliquid* channeled Christological discussions into debates about the unity of Christ. If Christ is divine and also *aliquid* as man, is he one or two? And is his union, however conceived, the greatest of unions by comparison with other unions?

The first opinion (the 'Assumptus–Homo' theory), a type of ascending Christology that started conceptually from the 'assumed man' who began to be God in the union, held that Christ, although one person, is nevertheless two, having a divine *aliquid* and a human *aliquid*. The second opinion (the 'Subsistence–Theory'), a type of descending Christology that began with the divine Word who subsisted in human nature, while holding that Christ had two natures and a human *aliquid*, wished to maintain that Christ was one; it insisted that the union in Christ was the greatest of all unions or unities after that of the three persons of the Trinity in one nature.

William of Auxerre, a secular master, posed the problems clearly in the early thirteenth century, and it was taken up by theologians who came after him. This essay will examine the positions of the following Franciscan masters between him and Bonaventure and then of Bonaventure himself: Alexander of Hales

---

[1] *Fr. Walter Principe, CSB died suddenly in March 1996 before completing the paper he proposed to write. In honor of his memory and his long asscociation with Fr. Zachary the prospectus he submitted February 26, 1996 has been included in this publication.*

in his authentic *Glossa* and *Quaestiones*, the author of book 3 of the *Summa Fratris Alexandri* (generally recognized as John of La Rochelle), Odo Rigaldi, the teacher of Bonaventure, and Bonaventure. With the exception of Odo, the necessary texts are available in good editions; quotations from Odo will be from an edition I shall make from four manuscripts (Bruges, MS. Bibl. Publ. de la Ville 208; Brussels, MS. Bibliothèque Royale 1542 [11614j; Troyes, MS. Bibliothèque Municipale 824; Vatican City, MS. Vat. Latin 5982).

This essay, I think, will show that whereas his predecessors struggled with some aspects of the question, Bonaventure contributed clarity and precision to the question through his careful analysis of supposit (or hypostasis) in relation to nature, individual, and person, and by his notion of substance and 'substantification' of the human *aliquid* in the person of the Word. This allowed him to assert the perfect unity of Christ while maintaining his full humanity and *aliquid*.

The Presence of Grace
Outside Evangelization, Baptism and Church in Thomas Aquinas' Theology

Thomas F. O'Meara, O.P.

University of Notre Dame

Are there narrow limits to the supernatural order predestined by the Triune God for the human race? Is there access to grace for those who, because of the moment or place of birth, have without any culpability not encountered the means of salvation stated by Scripture and by church practice as ordinary: being a Jew, believing in Christ, receiving baptism, or belonging to the church? The following pages pursue this question in the theology of Thomas Aquinas.

The persons who are the subject of the following essay on the extent of grace are not damned angels, heretics, or schismatics; nor are they individuals convinced of the truth of the Gospel who at some point freely and knowingly reject it. They are people— Aquinas sometimes referred to them poetically as *gentes*[1]—who live in geographical, cultural, and religious worlds which the preaching of the Gospel has not reached; they inhabit countries where the word of God in Christ is universally, generally or efficaciously absent. They do not know or believe in the Gospel, are not baptized, and do not belong to the church.

There is no question here of Aquinas comparing or evaluating the doctrines and rituals of other religions: he had little information about religions and such an enterprise was foreign to him. To ask, however, about the extent of God's "indwelling by grace" (I, 43, 6) and about the contact of human beings with the "grace of the

---

[1] Y. Congar, "'Gentilis' et 'Judaeus' au moyen age," *Recherches de théologie ancienne et médiévale* 36 (1969) 222ff. ". . . The faith of Christ flourished particularly among the peoples of the West, for in the North there are still many gentiles and in the East there are many schismatics and infidels." *In Psalmos* 48:1, *Opera Omnia* 14 (Parma edition) (New York, 1949) 335.

Spirit interiorly bestowed" (I-II, 106, 2) is an issue within Christian theology. It explores the Christian belief in God's reign on earth. What is the extent of that new "way of existing" (I, 43, 3) beyond God's creation and sustenance of the degrees of being? Is that reality, often called "grace," severely limited? How does God plan to save our tellurian race as it exists diversely in space and time and within culture and history? Did Aquinas even address these questions?

Salvation for people who had not heard of the Gospel did not attract much interest from the theologians of the thirteenth century. The following essay offers some approaches and motifs drawn from Aquinas' theology. Introductory observations look at developments in the thirteenth century which might have expanded the horizons of his theology, and at his theology of salvation as grace received by the faculties of the personality. Initially, it might appear that Aquinas wrote only random observations on this topic. We do not find a disputation by Thomas on this topic; neither of his large *summae* has a question or even an article which considers directly other contemporary religious groups (the title of the *Summa contra gentiles* would imply a formal treatment of other religions, but there is none).[2] Nevertheless, there are about a dozen articles in the *Summa theologiae* (*ST*) which touch our question, and observations about this problem in other works can be included. There are five areas where his thinking did treat this issue: (1) the ecclesiastical axiom about the limits of salvation, (2) the modes of that faith required by the Scripture, (3) baptism which Scripture and tradition locate as the normal entrance for grace, (4) the corporate leadership of Christ, and (5) the psychology of an individual's initial meeting with grace.

I

It is discovery, contact with peoples, which raises the issue of other religions. The thirteenth century, far from being a closed and

---

[2]In 3 *Sent.*, d. 25, q. 2, a. 2. Here Aquinas spoke generally of people living "before the written law being helped by grace" (a. 2).

introspective Christendom, had contacts with peoples beyond Europe. Early in the century the world of human peoples seemed to Europeans circumscribed: it was a geographical entity reaching from southern Spain to Prussia and Poland. A passage Thomas wrote around 1260 indicates a cultural geography not far removed from legend: "In particularly frigid places we find peoples dwelling who are full of animosity, but rather empty of understanding and of the arts."[3] However, as the German scholar Otto Pesch puts it, "Thomas was born at the moment when this perception of living in a closed world where the Gospel had been clearly preached collapsed."[4] Through the crusades and other exploratory journeys Europeans, as the thirteenth century progressed, met new peoples and religions outside of Christendom. Southern Spain and Sicily offered cultural contacts with Islam across the Mediterranean, and Frederick II drew to his court and new university in Palermo a variety of scholars. In the Emperor's army Europeans perhaps saw for the first time a number of North and Sub-Saharan Africans; Thomas' brother Aimo fought with Frederick in the Fifth Crusade in 1232, while another brother Rinaldo was the Emperor's page in 1240, his soldier in 1245, and in 1246 his failed assassin (for which he was executed).[5]

The Franciscans pioneered those cultural and religious contacts. The first general chapter of the Franciscans in 1217 urged missions to the East, and Francis of Assisi journeyed to the Islamic world two

---

[3]*De Regimine Principum*, c. 2.

[4]O. Pesch, *Thomas von Aquin*, (Mainz, 1988) 55.

[5]J. Weisheipl, *Friar Thomas d'Aquino. His Life, Thought and Work* (New York, 1974) 7 and M. D. Chenu, *Toward Understanding Saint Thomas* (Chicago, 1964), pp. 11f. R. Martin presents some information on theologians in the twelfth century describing implicit faith with roots in natural law and knowledge of God in "La Necessité de croire au mystère de l'Incarnation," *Revue Thomiste* 25 (1920), 273ff. On Aquinas' theology, E. Sauras, "The Members of the Church," *The Thomist* 27 (1963) 78ff.; P. Blazquez, "Bases tomistas para la teología de cristianismo anonimo," Tommaso d'Aquino nel suo settimo centenario 4, *Problemi di Teologia* (Naples, 1974) 289ff.; J. Quigley, *Salvific Faith and the Non-Evangelized: An Appraisal of Aquinas' Theology Implicit Faith* (Rome, 1984); critical of Aquinas' openness in light of the encyclical Mediator Dei of Pius XII was A. Mitterer, *Geheimnisvolle Leib Christi nach St. Thomas von Aquin und Papst Pius XII* (Vienna, 1950).

years later.[6] In 1241 the Mongol armies had reached Poland, Silesia and Hungary, and reports of their power and terror frightened the Europeans. Innocent IV introduced the Mongol problem for discussion at the Council of Lyons in 1245, and after the Council three missions of Franciscans left to gain information about the Mongol court. Some of these groups of friars, arriving in Mongol lands after a journey of two years, found not only Asian religion but Gothic Christians in the Crimea and Nestorian Christians at the Mongol court; they reported, however, little possibility of Mongol conversions. John del Piano Carpini returned to the curia in 1247 with a haughty reply from the Khan Guyuk. After a second Franciscan expedition, the friars, del Piano Carpini and William of Rubruck, wrote up reports on their missions, but these gave little information on Mongol religion.[7] Innocent IV in 1246 appointed a Franciscan to be bishop of Marrakech, and in 1307 there was an archbishop at what is today Beijing, China.

Several groups of Dominicans in the decade after 1237 had reached the Alan country beyond the Don. Louis IX sent a Dominican friar to the Mongols in 1248, and Innocent IV sent Dominicans to Georgia in 1254. Raymond of Penafort, distinguished professor of law at Bologna but also a scholar in Semitic languages, obtained permission from the general chapter of the Dominicans at Toledo in 1250 to select twenty friars for specialization in Arabic and to open a studium in Tunis; to this was added centers in Barcelona and Murcia in the 1260s. There were Dominicans knowledgeable not just in the philosophical theology but in the religious forms of Islam. William of Tripoli was born in 1270 in the Middle East and entered the Friars Preachers at St. John of Acre. He had been a diplomatic legate of Louis IX in Egypt and had been to Armenia. His *De statu Saracenorum et Mahumeto pseudo-*

---

[6]D. Berg, "Kreuzzugsbewegung und Propagatio Fidei. Das Problem der Franziskanermission im 13. Jahrhundert und das Bild von der islamischen Welt in der zeitgenössischen Ordenshistoriographie," *Orientalische Kultur und Europäisches Mittelalter* (Berlin, 1985) 59ff.; M. Baldwin, "Missions to the East in the Thirteenth and Fourteenth Centuries," on *The Impact of the Crusades on the Near East, A History of the Crusades,* Kenneth Setton, ed., (Madison, 1985) gives an overview of the missions to Islam, Asia, and eastern Christians by the friars in the thirteenth century.

[7]R. H. Davis, "Epilogue: the Mongols," *A History of Medieval Europe. From Constantine to St. Louis* (New York, 1988) 386ff.

propheta et eorum lege et fide of 1273 became the main text for those who wished to learn about Islam. He emphasized similarities to Christianity, spoke of Muslim sincerity and virtue, and advocated evangelizing Muslims through the example of life and through an attractive preaching about God without philosophical arguments or military arms.[8]

The emotionally titled papal bull, *Cum hora undecima*, was issued in March of 1247 to list the various races and nations needing evangelization. The rhetoric of the Franciscan Roger Bacon illustrates what must have been a disburging as well as new perspective on this world when he wrote around 1268: "There are few Christians; the whole breadth of the world is occupied by unbelievers, and there is no one to show them the truth."[9] A change in worldview had taken place in the decades after 1230.

So the existence of large populations to the south and to the east, peoples who could have had little contact with the preached Gospel, was hardly unknown after the middle of the thirteenth century. Marshall Baldwin writes of the Dominicans and Franciscans:

> The impact of these two men Francis and Dominic and their followers on the civilization of Europe is too well known to require elaboration here, but no discussion of the thirteenth-century missions can fail to emphasize two points. First, the type of organization adopted by the Franciscans and Dominicans was admirably suited to the furthering of distant ventures. Second, as the friars injected into the religious life of western Europe a new spirit and vitality, so they gave to a movement as old as Christianity evangelization, though languishing in the central Middle Ages, a new élan and direction.[10]

---

[8]See B. Altaner, *Die Dominikanermissionen des 13. Jahrhunderts* (Habelschwerdt, 1924); P. Damboriena, *La salvacion en las religiones no cristianas* (Madrid, 1973) 75ff.; G. Zananiri, "L'Esprit dominicain," *L'Église et l'Islam* (Paris, 1969) 189ff.; M. Voerzio, *Fra Guigliemo da Tripoli, orientalista domenicano del sec. XIII, precursore di Fra Riccoldo di Monte Croce* (Florence, 1955).

[9]*Opus Majus*, J. H. Bridge, ed. (Oxford, 1900) vol. 3, 122; see R. W. Southern *Western Views of Islam in the Middle Ages* (Cambridge, 1962) 62ff.; J. Abu-Lughod, *Before European Hegemony: the World System, A. D. 1250–1350* (New York, 1989).

[10]Baldwin, 453. The provincials of the friars preachers were concerned with theologial preparation and education in languages. General chapters from the 1240s

Thomas Aquinas would have known something of the pastoral and intellectual challenges facing some of his Dominican brothers in contact with these worlds to the south and east. M. D. Chenu observed: "We cannot read the work of St. Thomas or understand him without entering into the climate of the time, politically anguishing, evangelically exciting . . . . Thomas did not go to Morocco nor to the land of the Mongols, and he says nothing about the crusades, but he always had on his desk the works of the great Mussulman philosophers. He saw the limits of a Christianity which, having stayed within the geographical and cultural forms of the Roman Empire, was in his time conscious of having touched only a part of humanity and which was discovering the immense secular resources of the cosmos."[11] Max Seckler has noted the importance of this topic after Peter Lombard, and the special place Aquinas holds among his contemporaries by giving it an extra-ecclesial treatment.[12] In the young Aquinas one can see brevity and abstractness; yet, to this is joined a curiosity about how Christ was prefigured in pagan and Jewish texts and how revelation came to

---

on discussed evangelization in those new situations, and after Thomas' death founded an auxiliary movement for this work, the *Societas fratrum peregrinantium*. See Baldwin, 482ff. and essays by Altaner like "Sprachstudien und Sprachkenntnisse im Dienste der Mission des 13. und 14. Jahrhunderts," and "Die fremdsprachliche Ausbildung der Dominikanermissionare während des 13. und 14. Jahrhunderts," *Zeitschrift für Missionswissenschaft und Religionswissenschaft* 21 (1931) 113ff.; 23 (1933) 233ff.

[11]M. D. Chenu, *St. Thomas d'Aquin et la théologie* (Paris, 1959) 93. Aquinas appreciated the speculation of Muslim scholars, but his incorporation of their thought did not address directly the issue of what he thought about the mediation of a saving truth in their faith and theology. The audience of the *Summa contra Gentiles* remains disputed; see M. Corbin, *Le Chemin de la théologie chez Thomas d'Aquin* (Paris, 1972), 478ff. Louis Gardet thought that Aquinas knew the *Explanatio fidei* of his confrere Raymond Martin discussing and evaluating Muslim philosophical and religious texts: "But it is necessarily not the Islamic world as such in its historical and socio-cultural dimensions which entered the research and intellectual sympathy of Thomas. . .but only some of the major works which presented it." "La connaissance que Thomas d'Aquin put avoir du monde islamique," *Aquinas and the Problems of His Time*, G. Verbeke, ed. (Leuven, 1976) 148. Aquinas' views on what correct metaphysical knowledge pagan philosophers had of God contributes little to our topic; salvation comes not through some correct ontology but from the response of the personality to grace.

[12]M. Seckler, "Das Haupt aller Menschen," *Virtus Politica* (Stuttgart, 1974) 107f.

people raised in isolation. As Aquinas' theological career unfolded, he brought a deeper perspective and a wider context to this topic.

Scholars from Louis Caperan to Chenu and Pesch see the experience of a wider world by Europeans in the thirteenth century reflected in a progression in Aquinas' theology. Like most theologians of the twelfth and the early thirteenth century, the young Aquinas found his first example of human isolation from the Gospel in a bizarre individual raised alone in the woods by animals. What Pesch calls the "routine response"[13] of the Middle Ages is the sending to that individual by God of a missionary, an angel, or an inspiration and that theology is found in early works like the *Scriptum super Libros Sententiarum* (1252-56) and the *De Veritate* (1256-59). One desires only that which one knows, and so God will send an extraordinary missionary to the person isolated from society. But the theology of these early works was itself modified in the direction of interior religious orientation: in both the commentary on Peter Lombard and the disputed questions on truth there is more than the quick solution of miraculous contact by God. The commentary on the Sentences explained:

> In those things which are necessary for salvation God is or never was absent to the human being seeking salvation, unless something might remain from that person's own fault. So the presentation of those things which are necessary for salvation either would be provided for a person by God through a preacher of faith (as with Cornelius) or by revelation. Having presupposed this, it then lies in the power of free will for one to enter into an act of faith.[14]

The disputed questions *On Truth* sketched a theology of degrees of explicit faith and a diversity of historical periods and then concluded that everyone in every age is bound explicitly to believe that God exists and exercises providence over human affairs; then it faced the exceptions.

---

[13]Pesch, *Thomas von Aquin*, 53. Retelling this incident is the recent novel by J. Walsh, *Knowledge of Angels* (New York, 1994).

[14]In *3 Sent.*, d. 25, q. 2, a. 1, ad 1; the principle is offered: "Before the law was written, God helped with grace." In *3 Sent.*, d. 25, q. 2, a. 2, ad 4.

Granted that everyone is bound to believe something
explicitly, no unsuitability follows even if someone ended
up growing up among animals or alone in the woods. For i t
pertains to divine providence to furnish everyone with
what is necessary for salvation, provided that on the
person's part there is no hindrance. Thus if someone so
brought up followed the direction of natural reason desiring
good and fleeing evil, it is most certain that God either
would reveal through internal inspiration those things
necessarily to be believed or would direct a preacher there
(as Peter is sent to Cornelius).[15]

Here the principle being applied to the unusual case is providence
providing for a species, humanity; secondly we learn that the
divine inspiration need not be miraculous. Each individual can flee
evil and in this orientation comes offered internal help.

The *Commentary on Romans*, whose text is from around 1269
(after the ST has been begun) but whose ideas may be from the
previous decade, still curiously offers an example of isolated
forest-folk.

Those who have not heard one speaking of the Lord either
through the Lord himself or through his disciples are
excused from the sin of infidelity; still they have not
attained the benefit of God (forgiveness of original or
mortal sins). . . . If, however, any of them do what lies
within them, the Lord would provide from his mercy by
sending them a preacher. . . . But still, the fact that they do
what lies within them, by converting themselves to God, is
itself from God moving their hearts to good.[16]

---

[15]*De Veritate*, 14, 11, ad 1.

[16]*Super Epistolas S. Pauli Lectura* I, *Ad Romanos* (10:18) (Turin, 1953) 158. On
the shift around 1272 from this early perspective to the view in the ST, see Pesch,
"Besinnung. . .," 281f. and L. Caperan, *Le Problème du salut des infidèles* (Toulouse,
1934) vol. 1, 198f. and vol. 2, 62ff.; on the dating of the commentary on Romans, see
Pesch, 87; Weisheipl does not accept an earlier dating from Mandonnet and others
(pp. 372f.). The venerable axiom, *fecissent quod in se est* which lies behind this
exegesis is treated explicit in *ST* I-II, 109, 6; in Thomas' theology this "doing"
presumes a prevenient grace.

It should be noted that the context in this theology is the teaching of the Gospel to an individual separated from Christian society and not the presence of revelation and grace in newly found nations; the extraordinary sending of a preacher is mentioned but the last word touches interior direction and God's assistance. Later, commenting on the tenth chapter, Aquinas explained the passage (in its Vulgate translation) affirming that peoples living apart from the Jewish law were saved *naturaliter*.

> But when he (Paul) says "naturally," a doubt arises: it seems to favor the Pelagians who said that a person can through natural powers keep all the precepts of the law. But "naturally" must be interpreted as meaning through nature reformed by grace. He spoke of gentiles converted to faith who have begun to keep the moral precepts of the law through the help of grace. Or, this "naturally" can be understood as the natural law showing what is to be done (according to Psalm 4:7), which is the light of natural reason in which is the image of God. And yet, this does not exclude grace being necessary to move affectivity.[17]

These early works offer the principle that God would provide the means of salvation, if not external then internal. In the commentary on Lombard, the disputed question, and the biblical commentary theology does not stay with an exceptional vehicle of salvation but moves on to personal contact between God and the human being who aided by grace responds in a basic moral orientation which is described in general terms as a rejection of evil and a conversion to good. In this theology access to grace comes from doing what lies within the horizon of the active personality and not from external conditions of birth or religious initiation.

The ST (1266–1273) omits completely the sylvan orphan (*nutritus in silva*). Perhaps with other Europeans and through the friars Aquinas had become aware of large national groupings of infidels. Many designated missionaries would make the miraculous too frequent and ordinary, something repugnant to Aquinas' theology of God and creation. At any rate, his theology moves away from an extraordinary individual receiving an unusual

---

[17]*Ad Romanos* (2:14) 39f.

revelation to grace amid human desires and moral actions. The personal orientation of a moral life and an intellectual response to God's presence are born by and are responsive to grace.

II

What is salvation? Our topic is the salvation of men and women who have never known (and could not have known culturally or personally) about God's plan of salvation for them as it is centered in Christ. For Aquinas, theology is a "sacred teaching" about *salus* (I, 1, 1), a Latin word which can mean both human health and religious salvation. This "health" is a mode of life made known by revelation and the Gospel; it is incarnate in Jesus Christ and the church's sacraments (I, 2, 1; III, 60) and reaches people as new modes of the Trinity's presence (I, 43, 5). Salvation is not religious ideas meriting a paradise or a transitory divine power warding off a devil but a special destiny for human life joined appropriately to a new mode of existence (I, 43, 6). The divine plan (predestination) and presence (mission) unfold an ordo. An ordo was of significant interest to medieval culture: there is order in the universe and a further order of grace. It belonged to the university professor or the wise person to see and to unfold the realms which make up the world and life.[18] Aquinas prized the ability of the human mind to reach reality, to find through outward and inward exploration the forms of each being in lucid patterns. Order only enhanced diversity. Far more than a pattern or a superstructure, this real arrangement of realities flowing from a principle sets forth a fundamental plan for and constitution of the human race.

---

[18]M. D. Chenu wrote: ". . . Thomas extols the virtue of wisdom. Sapientis est ordinare ('The task of wisdom is to give order.'): the philosopher seeks to penetrate to the ultimate sources of reality, to understand the why and wherefore, and to rest only when necessity has been found. The word intelligere, Aquinas likes to think, is derived form intus legere (to read within). The world is for him intelligible; let it then render an account of itself." *Toward Understanding.* . ., 46; see B. Coffey, "The Notion of Order according to St. Thomas Aquinas," *The Modern Schoolman* 27 (1949) 1ff.

The medieval Dominican expressed this basic principle in this way:

> It is not suitable that God provide more for creatures being led by divíne love to a natural good than for those creatures to which that love offers a supernatural good. For natural creatures God provides generously . . . kinds of forms and powers which are principle of acts so that they are inclined to activity through their own beings. . . . Even more for those moved to reach an eternal supernatural good he infuses certain forms or qualities of the supernatural order according to which easily and enthusiastically they are moved by God to attain that good which is eternal. And so the gift of grace is a kind of quality (I-II, 110, 2).

"Knowing" for the medieval university professor meant knowing *"per causas"*, and the ST investigates the modes of divine causality among creatures and Christians. Destiny *(finis)* bespeaks a nature's activity capable of reaching its goals, and that activity flows from an inner principle and active grace. The ST is developed along the lines that human life is a journey whose dynamic principles are an individual human personality and the gracious help of God moving interiorly and intimately. This help is what Thomas describes as divine revelation (I, 1, 1), missions (I, 43, 3), and grace (I-II, 109, 1).

What is grace? In Christianity religious law becomes divine presence. "That, however, which is most powerful in the law of the New Testament and in which its entire power consists is the grace of the Holy Spirit which is given by faith in Christ" (I-II, 106, 1). This participation in deeper levels of God's life is born of a divine love and plan for us.[19] Only God, "a supernatural principle moving one interiorly" (II-II, 6, 1), can be the true cause of a divine life

---

[19]"Grace is that creative presence of the eternal love of God in the midst of the human personality who thereby is drawn out of the limitations of nature and brought to a shared life with God." O. Pesch, *Einführung in die Lehre von Gnade und Rechtfertigung* (Darmstadt, 1981), 89. Not only Pesch but other theologians have seen grace as an underlying motif in the *Summa theologiae*: L. Hödl, "'Lumen gratiae.' Ein Leitgedanke der Gnadentheologie des Thomas von Aquinas," Mysterium der Gnade (Regensburg, 1975), 238ff.; T. O'Meara, "Grace As a Theological Structure in the Summa theologiae of Thomas Aquinas," *Recherches de théologie ancienne et médiévale* 55 (1988) 130ff.

which becomes our life. The indwelling missions of the Trinity find their term in a love of friendship between the graced individual and God. Aquinas described the gift of grace as "a kind of quality" or a "quasi-form."[20] In this theology salvation-history is expressed in perspectives psychological and metaphysical. Goal and action-to-goal follow upon nature, and so grace as a form indicates a kind of new nature by which men and women act in the higher predestined order not as strangers or aliens but as heirs and offspring. Grace comes to a person as a perduring reality enabling persons to become true secondary causes not of grace but of their Christian lives in which grace is active (I-II, 114). "The grace of God is the sufficient cause of a person's salvation. Now God bestows grace upon people in the manner appropriate to them" (III, 61, 1, 2). Now let us turn to the five areas in which Aquinas touched on this topic.

III

A. Tradition's Ecclesial Axiom: *Extra ecclesiam nulla salus*

Five times Aquinas' writings referred in passing to the axiom, *extra ecclesiam nulla salus*. One passage in the ST along with two in other writings apply this principle to the Eucharist: "the reality of this sacrament is the unity of the mystical body without which there can be no salvation" (III, 73, 3). A fourth mentions faith, and a fifth censures acts which prompt excommunication. Apparently Aquinas interpreted the axiom not as an arbitrary decree about *gentes* (they are never mentioned) but as an ecclesiastical direction touching upon faith and the sacraments. The contexts in which this principle appears are sacramental, eucharistic and anti-heretical. Aquinas' usage of this ancient formula was intra-ecclesial: it censored church members who had separated or were considering separation from unity. In no citation is any application made to groups outside Christendom.[21]

---

[20] *De Veritate*, 27, 1; I-II, 110, 1–4.

[21] In 3 *Sent.*, d. 25, q. 2., a. 2; *Super Primam Decretalem*, #683 (This was the decretal Firmiter of the Fourth Lateran Council in 1215); *Super Evangelium S. Joannis Lectura* 6:7; In *Symbolum Apostolorum*, a. 9; *ST* III 73, 3. For a history of the

B. Scripture's Teaching: The Necessity of Faith

At the opening of his questions on faith in the ST Aquinas cited words from Paul's *Letter to the Hebrews*: "without faith no one can please God" (11:6).[22] Since faith is necessary for salvation, Aquinas was pleased to find in Hebrews a biblical definition: "Faith is the substance of things to be hoped for, the evidence of things that appear not" (11:1). Grace as a principle of new life grounds faith which is its cognitive facet giving some intimation of a special destiny for knowing and willing. Faith gives now "the very beginnings" (II-II, 4, 1) of what hope finds in the future; faith directs the intentions, actions and virtues of an individual life within the "ordo" of grace. Theologically faith is a stable form emerging from grace (II-II, 6, 1, 3), a supernatural *habitus*, located in the mind where the will, moved by grace, leads the intellect to assent to that which lies above the structures of nature and psyche (I, 12, 3; II-II, 4, 1). Hearing about Christ and human free will are not fully adequate causes of faith. "The cause of faith is much more the one who makes the believer agree to what is said, and this comes not through compelling the reason but through the will . . . . God . . . causes faith in the believer in that he inclines the will and illumines the understanding . . . ."[23]

In the ST's second question on faith, Aquinas raised three times the issue of its necessity. Does one need some faith? Does one need faith in the Incarnation, or faith in the Trinity? The first issue is not a command to believe something religious, but the need for faith as a knowledge directing life and setting up human destiny

---

axiom, see J. Theisen, *The Ultimate Church and the Promise of Salvation* (Collegeville, 1976) 1ff; Y. Congar, "No Salvation outside the Church?," *Wide World My Parish* (Baltimore, 1961) 93ff; F. Sullivan, *Salvation outside the Church? Tracing the History of the Catholic Response* (New York, 1992). Lateran IV in 1215 had used the axiom (Denzinger-Schönmetzer, *Enchiridion symbolorum et definitionum* (Barcelona, 1963), #802), and Aquinas' comment on a decretal is connected to this conciliar text; but the council's issue is the necessity of all the sacraments, and its context seems to be sects denying the necessity of ecclesial and sacramental life after baptism. Especially helpful is the treatment of G. Sabra, *Thomas Aquinas' Vision of the Church* (Mainz, 1987) 158ff.

[22]Scripture passages are translated from Aquinas' Latin text.
[23]*De Veritate*, 27, 3, 12.

(this view begins the entire ST I, 1, 1). Faith is important not because it fulfills the command of a strict God or initiates us into gnostic mysteries, but because knowing directs human nature and knowledge moves activities. Actions compose a life, and acts are the metaphorical "way" by which men and women move to God's destiny by means of the new life principle enabling participation in God's plan. So learning about our true destiny from God is essential: thus faith embraces salvation in the act of knowledge.

Jesus Christ is certainly central to faith's object. And yet, Thomas Aquinas had a modest theology of history in which Christ touches people through faith according to different historical stages. "Consequently the mystery of Christ's Incarnation was to be believed in all ages and by all peoples in some fashion but in ways differing with the differences of times and peoples" (II-II, 2, 7). Adam and Eve before sin had explicit faith as a facet of their high state of grace. After the fall and later in history, Hebrew faith touched the realities of salvation-history, as Messianic faith anticipated the passion of Christ in beliefs and rituals.

Is not the mission of the Logos incarnate in Jesus a climax in the history of grace? "After the time of grace all are bound to have an explicit faith in the mysteries of Christ" (II-II 2, 7). But at once an objection appears in the ST questioning this conclusion by introducing human beings in other religions who could not have heard of the Gospel. Those who did not receive a special revelation had "neither explicit nor implicit faith in Christ." Aquinas replied not by expanding the number of special revelations, like Job or the Sibyl mentioned in earlier works,[24] but by introducing the distinction between "implicit" and "explicit" faith.

> If they, however, were saved to whom revelation was not given (in this special way), they were not saved without faith in a mediator. Because even if they did not have an explicit faith, they had an implicit faith in divine providence and believed God to be the liberator of people according to ways which pleased him, and according to which he had revealed himself to some knowing the truth" (II-II, 2, 7, 3).

---

[24] As was presented in *3 Sent.*, d. 25, q. 2 a. 2, ad 3.

Implicit faith had appeared earlier in the questions on grace (I-II, 106, 1, 3), but Aquinas left the mode and extent of implicit faith after Christ vague. The perspective here of his theology of exceptions to explicit faith (similar to the subsequent articles on the Trinity) does seem to be that of the past: "After the time of grace revealed, insightful as well as ordinary people (*majores* and *minores*) are obligated to have explicit faith in the mysteries of Christ, particularly with regards to those things which are solemnized in the church and publicly proposed" (II-II, 2, 7). Nevertheless, this passage seems to refer, first, to a problem mainly before Christ and possibly also to the contrast between educated and uneducated people in appreciating Christian dogma. Nevertheless, such a theology in its principles calls for a broader application.

A third article asks if faith in the Trinity is necessary: it is inquiring not into a secret dogma for the human race but into a revelation connected to the Incarnation. In the "time of grace"[25] we are bound to believe this revelation of God's life, while before Christ the reality of the triune God was hidden, even in "the faith of the majores." In the responses to two objections, however, the medieval Dominican clearly was discussing the conditions of Christians and of those personally contacted by evangelization— not millions of human beings of other times, ignorant of explicit revelation. In the first objection we learn that the essential but bare object for Christian faith is not incarnation or Trinity but what Hebrews lists: "In every age and for all human beings it has been necessary to believe these two truths that God is and that he rewards, but still that is not sufficient for every age and every person" (II-II, 2, 8, 1). Moreover, God's great goodness (III, 1, 1)— the source and goal of the plan and economy of grace—can be grasped without knowing the Trinity, even if ultimately "the missions of the divine persons bring us to beatitude" (II-II, 2, 8, 3). Included in the rich idea of God who would reward us are the source, the medium (Christ) and the goal of grace (II-II, 1, 7). The dynamic human personality, as it directs itself toward the

---

[25]"The time of grace *revelatae*" (II-II, 11, 7) has in the next article (11, 8) become "the time of grace *divulgatae*" ("spread among people" or "made known widely").

provident God of creation, touches de facto the loving God of grace. So the central topic of implicit faith appears here too and suggests subtle modes of grace in diverse stages of human history apart from an individual's clear knowledge of Christian revelation.[26]

Stages of faith correspond to stages of history. "In all places the new law is proposed, but, however, not in all times, although in every time there were people who belonged to the New Law (as was mentioned above)" (I-II, 106, 1, 3). Since the work of Max Seckler, scholars have observed in Aquinas' theology a modest entry of history in the exposition of revelation and faith. For instance, Thomas asked why the New Law was revealed in time and not at the beginning of the world, and his response gave two reasons: the human race maturing in time, and the sobering education of humanity by the spread of sin. Both human knowledge of God and sin became in time more diverse and widespread. In the realm of faith too there are different stages: Eve and Adam before the fall, the elders and the ordinary people in the Hebrew covenant, nations obeying natural law, pagan peoples with implicit revelations or with private revelations. Each historical stage has a reference to Christ, its telos. "And nevertheless it was by faith in the passion of Christ that the ancients were justified, just as we are. The sacraments of the old law were certain protestations of that faith in that they were signifying the passion of Christ and its effect" (III, 62, 6). Of Cornelius before Peter's preaching to him, Aquinas wrote: "He was not an *infidelis*; otherwise his actions would not have been accepted by God whom no one can please without faith. He had, however, implicit faith

---

[26]The commentary on Hebrews is, according to Weisheipl, possibly written by Bernard Gui but more or less accurately conveys Aquinas' thought: "No one can please God unless he approaches him. . ., but no one approaches God except by faith, because faith is a light of the intellect. . .No one would come to this (God) if one does not hope for some remuneration from him. . . . It must be said that after the sin of the primal parent no one could be saved from the guilt of original sin except by faith in a mediator. But that faith is diversified according to the mode of the one believing within a diversity of times and conditions." Aquinas goes on to show how historically different groups, e. g., Jews, Christians, educated Christians, are required to believe more. "But for the gentiles who were saved it was sufficient to believe God to be a rewarder, for that reward exists only through Christ. So they believed implicity in a mediator." *Super Epistolas S. Pauli Lectura, Ad Hebraeos*, (11:2 - 4) (Turin, 1953) 462f. On the texts from Hebrews in Aquinas, see L. Caperan, 1, 193ff.

in the truth of the Gospel not yet manifested" (II-II, 10, 4, 3). The example of Cornelius shows that a less than explicitly Christian faith can justify after the event of Christ.

Once Christ made the Gospel explicit, can anyone ignorant of it be saved? "Through Christ and then through the Apostles it (faith in the Trinity) was made manifest to the whole world" (II-II, 2, 8, 2). Here and in the mention of public proclamation (II-II, 2, 7) Aquinas presupposed that the Christian Gospel is widely known. How widely known is an issue medieval theologians (and their patristic sources) touched upon, although not as extensively as one would like. When is the Gospel actually proclaimed to all peoples, and when did the hearing of the Gospel in this time or place become normally or universally linked with peoples' reception of grace? In commenting on the Sentences, Aquinas affirmed three ages in the human race's faith in the redeemer but then concluded that after Christ the mystery of redemption was visibly fulfilled corporeally, and was preached. Thus all are expected to believe explicitly ("And if anyone does not have an instructor God would reveal to that one so that fault would be removed.")[27] A few years later commenting on Matthew in the late 1250s, Aquinas combined Chrysostom's view that everyone had heard something of the Christian Gospel, "fama," with Augustine's observation that not all had been reached by the Gospel *cum effectu*.[28] This unresolved ambiguity entered the ST:

---

[27]In *3 Sent.*, d. 25, q. 2, a. 2, ad 2.

[28]*Super Evangelium S. Matthaei Lectura*, (24:14) (Turin, 1951) 299. In the commentary on Romans, Aquinas was reluctant to assert that some nations were not reached by preaching (the view of Augustine) but held John Chrysostom to be saying that, if the preaching has reached all nations, still the church was not established everywhere. Curiously Aquinas does not clearly leave the issue of world-wide evangelization at the time of the fathers and address his own time before he turns to the exception of the abandoned child. "But the explanation by Chrysostom is in better agreement with the present meaning of the Apostle than that of Augustine. For the mere fact that they were going to hear sometime in the future would be no basis for depriving unbelievers of an excuse. And yet one does not maintain because of this that news of the apostles' preaching reached every individual, even though it did reach all nations" (*Ad Romanos* [10:18], p. 158). Origen had already presented a grand but unrealistic view: "All in Britain, all in Mauretania, all under the sun . . . the message of the Lord and Savior has reached." *Homilien zum Lukasevangelium* 1, H. J. Sieben, ed. (Freiburg, 1991) 105. Sabra, 163ff. and others think that the rise of Joachimitism (the end would come since the Gospel had been universally preached) made Aquinas cautious; W. Schacten pursues this topic in *Ordo Salutis.*

> The preaching of the Gospel can be understood in two ways: in one way with regards to the divulgation of the idea of Christ, and in this way the Gospel was preached in the entire world even in the times of the Apostles. . . . In another way the preaching of the Gospel in the entire world can be understood in terms of its full effect, so that in each people the church has been founded . . . and in this sense the Gospel has not been preached in the entire world(I-II, 106, 4, 4).

So the extent of evangelization past and present is left open: the world still holds peoples who might have not been evangelized, even if the texts indicate that this was a new, unsettling idea for Aquinas.

The question on faith's opposite, *infidelitas*, is very important. Most of the articles in this question are about the culpable rejection of belief, but there is no damnation of the non-believer simply because of a lack of faith. The first article concerns those who do have non-belief but who have "an infidelity which is purely negative" (II-II, 10, 1), and Aquinas argued here against the damnation of those lacking faith through an absence of evangelization through no fault of their own. Only those who freely and consciously place an obstacle to grace are culpable.[29] There is, however, mention that the loss of the non-believer might come through other sins "which cannot be remitted without faith" (II-II, 10, 1).

Earlier Aquinas had presented a theology of the new law. Only metaphorically a law, it consists in terms of its "dynamic principle" in the presence of the Holy Spirit, while "secondarily" it is the words and writings of the Gospel (I-II, 106, 1). Faith has a structure similar to the Spirit's "law": both lead from material objects to formal dynamic, from diversity to transcendental unity. The formal object of both is God, while the material objects are articulated teachings and sacraments (II-II, 1, 1). Periodically Aquinas liked to call his readers away from verbal analyses and

---

Das Gesetz als Weise der Heilsvermittlung. Zur Kritik des Hl. Thomas von Aquin an Joachim von Fiore (Münster, 1980).

[29]*Summa contra gentiles* III, 159.

lead them back to the divine presence which sustained objects and activities. "First truth is the object of faith" (II-II, 1, 1). God grounds and pervades the explication and multiplication of religious truths. Faith is important not because it gives one information others do not have, but because it introduces the individual to the order of grace. Faith has a teleological, an eschatological dynamic as it anticipates the future disclosure of its believed realities.[30] Because God decided to have on earth an historical race and a revelation in history, not all men and women will have in their belief the same explicit content. Degrees of implicit faith can justify, certainly in the past and presumably in the present.

Regardless, the ST has set aside any reference to miraculous messengers to explain how the human personality attains grace through faith when evangelization is absent. In theory an individual, apart from explicit Christian revelation, can reach some general belief in the providential mediation of God.[31] Human knowing and willing are dynamic; they pass through finite forms and seek their object's cause or ground. Faith, and this can be all the more true of implicit faith, because of the dynamics of grace and the human personality, can pass beyond mental forms toward horizons and objects. Every faith ends not in propositions but in realities.[32] The *res* of faith is God, but God as helping humanity toward the eschaton (II-II, 1, 1; see I, 1, 1). In short, incomplete forms of faith are not the same as defective modes of living in grace; degrees of orientation toward love are prior to its explanation in explicit faith.[33]

C. Faith's Sacrament: Baptism

Aquinas began his questions on the sacrament of baptism by saying that Christ is the head of a race redeemed, and that normally "incorporation" into Christ as a "member" occurs by the sacraments, particularly by baptism (III, 68, 1). To be "in Christ" is a metaphor for having a new life-principle, the *habitus* grace: "By

---

[30]"Proemium," *Expositio super Librum Boethii de Trinitate*, q. 2, a. 2, ad 7.
[31]See T. C. O'Brien, "Faith", *Summa theologiae* 31 (New York, 1974) 93.
[32]II-II, 1, 2, 2; *De Veritate*, q. 14, a. 8, ad 11.
[33]"Das Haupt aller Menschen," 117ff.

the sacraments God effects grace in the soul" (III, 62, 1). The first article, asking whether people are held to be baptized, affirms that without baptism "there is no salvation for human beings" (III, 68, 1). Still, the first objection raises the issue of those who lived before Christ. Aquinas began his answer by relating baptism to faith—baptism is the sacrament of faith. There were degrees of faith, and so there are kinds of baptism. "Although the very sacrament of baptism was not always necessary for baptism still faith, whose sacrament baptism is, was always necessary" (III, 68, 1). Inner faith is more basic than its sacramental celebration, baptism. People were incorporated into Christ through a faith in future events. The second article poses the same issue by asking whether one can be saved without baptism.

> The sacrament of baptism can be absent from someone in two ways. One way—both in re and in voto—happens in those who neither are baptized nor wish to be. Here there is a kind of contempt of the sacrament by those who have free will. . . . In another way, the sacrament of baptism can be absent in re but not in voto. Someone desires to be baptized but for some reason death intervenes. This person can attain salvation without actual baptism because of the desire of baptism (III, 68, 2).

Aquinas' words suggest that he is thinking here of catechumens and martyrs in whom explicit desire seeks the sacrament. The article ends, however, broadly with the laconic observation: "To this extent the sacrament of baptism is said to be necessary for salvation: there cannot be saving life in a person unless it is, at least, present in the will, which 'with God is viewed as the deed'" (III, 68, 2, 3).[34] What is primary and indispensable is not the ritual or creed but the psychological dynamics of the will intent on God; elsewhere he writes: "Someone can attain the effect of baptism through the power of the Holy Spirit without baptism of water or

---

[34]The quotation is from Augustine, *Enarratio in Psalmos*, 57:3 (Migne, PL, 36, 675ff.). Aquinas saw faith as an actualization, albeit under grace, of a free person, and so for no external religious reasons (*nullo modo* II-II, 10, 8) did he permit forced confessions of Christian faith or receptions of baptism. As with many terms Aquinas viewed "necessity" analogously; Thomas can speak of three sacraments being necessary, but this is a necessity for ordinary Christian life in the church (III, 65, 4).

blood: for someone's heart can be moved by the Holy Spirit to believe, to love God and to have sorrow for sins" (III, 66, 11).

Aquinas does not broaden the range of in voto baptism, although in the ST degrees of sacraments and beliefs lead to Christ. There were also, prior to Christ, anticipated signs of the sacraments. Aquinas studied Jewish rituals closely and evaluated them positively (I-II, 98–106). The sacramental rituals of the Hebrew people are ultimately salvific because they reflect and lead to faith, and this faith anticipates prophetically Christ. "Some of the things pertaining to the Old Testament were signifying the holiness of Christ as holy in himself, and others like the paschal lamb signified his holiness by which we are sanctified" (III, 60, 2, 2).[35] Since all men and women are primally predestined and subsequently redeemed, they have a certain access to grace. However, the conversion of the nations proceeds from the mercy of God "but the salvation of the Jews from justice" (I, 21, 4, 2). In Thomas' theology the covenant with the Jews establishes a distinct era between the law of nature and the era of grace. It brings through prophets and teachers a public, supernatural revelation beyond the natural law, and so this period holds a mixture of the metaphysical knowledge of God and knowledge from the time of

---

[35]There were also, prior to Christ, anticipated signs of the sacraments. The Jews had and have Messianic beliefs and sacramental rites which anticipate Jesus (I- II, 101, 4; 102, 5; 111, 62, 6), and the *majores* had an intimation of Trinity and Incarnation (II - II, 2, 7). "The old law was over time subjected to grace: not because it was bad but because it was lacked the power and suitability to lead to fulfillment" (I-II, 98, 2, 2). Aquinas interpreted the Jewish liturgy as still valuable in his own time because it prefigured the Christian faith (II-II, 10, 11). "The passion of Christ had the effect of salvation among the Jews, and then through the preaching of the Jews the effect of the passion of Christ passed to the nations." (III, 47, 4) On Aquinas and the Dominican Order opposing the forced baptism or conversion of Jews see Ulrich Horst, B. Faes de Mottoni, "Die Zwangstaufe jüdischer Kinder im Urteil scholastischer Theologen," *Münchener Theologische Zeitschrift* 40 (1989) 173ff. The Dominican theologian asked too if all human beings were bound to observe the Jewish law. He replied (in a framework of development) that the law of nature led through the Jewish law to the appearance of Christ. The nations were obliged to observe the law to the extent that it contained natural law; the remainder of the law made the Jews holier and more worthy in the eyes of God (I-II, q. 98, 5), although their election was a matter not of human merit but of divine love. Aquinas thought that "many gentiles" had foreseen the Messiah (*De Veritate*, q. 14, a. 11, ad 6). "The old law was over time subjected to grace: not because it was bad but because it lacked the power and suitability to lead to fulfillment" (I-II, 98, 2, 2).

grace (II-II, 174, 6). Moreover, the ST's theology of faith discussed the right attitude toward religious rituals which were neither Christian nor Jewish but did not necessarily lack all "utility and truth" (II-II, 10, 11).[36] To medieval knights or peasants their falsehood or singularity might seem to be an insult to the deity. Aquinas saw this differently: "Although non-believers in their rites may sin, these rites can be tolerated because of some good coming from them" (II-II, 10, 11).

Sacraments for Aquinas are not obligatory sacred rituals but suitable ways for men and women to make visible in symbol and action that life which is Christ's grace. As knowing and symbol-making animals, human beings live sacramentally in the realm of grace. We surmise that Aquinas would have been reluctant to draw a visible sacrament, baptism, into less tangible modalities of grace present more or less implicitly. Nevertheless, in the *Sentences* he spoke of sacraments existing variously in different states of religion.[37] His theology of faith and of moral choice suggests how the activities of the created personality vis-à-vis grace are broader than signs and miracles, sacred symbols and words. God's contact with the human personality is not limited to religious objects: "God has not bound his power to the sacraments in such a way that he cannot confer the effects of the sacrament without the sacrament" (III, 64, 7).[38] What may escape notice in Aquinas' treatment of different states of religion with their own sacramental forms is a presupposition that there is a single history of religion, one not begun by Christ but flowing from and leading to him.

---

[36]Aquinas asked too if all human beings were bound to observe the Jewish law. He replied (in a framework of development) that the law of nature led through the Jewish law to the appearance of Christ. The nations were obliged to observe the law to the extent it contained natural law; the remainder of the law made the Jews holier and more worthy in the eyes of God (I-II, q. 98, 5).

[37]In 4 *Sent*. d. 1, q. 1, a, 2.

[38]We should note that in the early example the evangelist comes to the isolated person not to baptize but to teach. Interestingly, an *infidelis* can administer a sacrament. "Although one might believe that from what is externally done no interior effect follows, still that one is not ignorant of what the Catholic church intends and through the external actions offers the sacrament. And so infidelity is not an obstacle if what the church intends is intended, although (the infidel) might consider it to be nothing" (III, 64, 9, ad 1).

D. The Capital Grace of Christ

The sacraments continue the incarnation of Jesus Christ who is the visible epitome of grace, its icon and sacrament. The Word gives Jesus not only the grace of the hypostatic union but grace as man and as leader of the human race (III, 8, 5), the savior "of all" (III, Prologue). The God-man has a human life of grace like ours; created grace is not rendered unnecessary by the subsistent Logos. Jesus is not only the way and cause of grace but its icon and sacrament. The mission of the Logos in Jesus grounds Trinitarian missions to all men and women, for Jesus' life and ours are included in one predestination (III, 24, 4). If Christ is the center and ground of grace, nevertheless supernatural salvation has a history, an economy of stages. Pondering the created grace of the man Jesus, Aquinas explained how Jesus was the new head of the predestined and redeemed human race. There are, however, levels of affiliation with that human being who is Logos incarnate and a religious prophet, the exemplar and cause of graced humanity. Questions seven and eight of the Third Part unfold the grace of leadership in Jesus of Nazareth, a theology where the Johannine motif of special fullness is combined with the Pauline name, "Head of the Church." Question eight deals with the grace of Christ as head of the church. Its third article has a theological direction not found among Aquinas' Dominican and Franciscan contemporaries: it inquires whether Jesus is "the head of all human beings." There are different historical ways in which men and women meet salvation through degrees not of faith but of grace. The *caput* of the realm of grace, Jesus Christ, gives the "salvation of the entire human race" (III, 8, 3, 1).

Max Seckler discerns some history in an originality and individuality which pervade these opening questions of the Third Part.[39] Jesus Christ is head of all people and all peoples, and not through some sublime position in the cosmos but through his homogeneity with the human race. He is head not ceremonially but (as Seckler puts it) as the mediator of "grace really offered to all,

---

[39]M. Seckler, "Das Haupt aller Menschen," 108.

even to those who do not know grace or do not want it."[40] The proper
source of this headship is not only the power of the Logos but Jesus'
oneness with us in humanity and created grace. Human nature is the
foundation for membership in the collective body, and the race of
which Christ is the head is one of grace.

> What is essential in the redeemer's lordship is not external
> domination but the 'influence' of grace. The structure of the
> entire event of grace unfolds itself presentationally in the
> image of the head. Being lord in the realm of grace is
> totally different from being lord in the offices of civil
> authority. . . . Here Thomas concentrated on a very clear
> under-standing of the function of Christ as the mediator of
> grace and of life in "the return of the rational creature to
> God."[41]

Grace on earth produces not a miraculous theater but what is
ordinary life in the eyes of God. Since all the human race is called
and altered by grace, Christ's headship unifies all members of
humanity not in a unity of eternal essence but in one of human
freedom in history. Seckler concludes: "This *conformitas* of us to
Christ lies not in a static, unmoving natural phenomenon or
essential structure, nor in an exodus from alienation and loss of self.
Just the opposite. It lies in a movement of freedom in which the
image of God and self-discovery emerge at the same time."[42]

To present ways of belonging to the church, the earlier
Sentences had employed analogies drawn from natural science like
one nature or the spread of vital powers to describe the human race
and the mystical body joined in faith, grace, and love through the
Holy Spirit. Several analogies explain the unity of the human race
which is one of nature and one also of grace in Christ: the first
analogy comes from the oneness of our species; the second refers to
the connection of all in one faith; the third unity is of grace and
love, while the fourth adds the indwelling of the Spirit. Non-
believers are *in potentia* to all levels of the church except the first,
while sinners have the first two potentialities. "So non-believers

---

[40]"Das Haupt aller Menschen," 113.
[41]"Das Haupt aller Menschen," 111.
[42]"Das Haupt aller Menschen," 114.

do not belong to the union of the body of the church . . . and in respect to Christ the head they are only in potency."[43] Here it is a question of belonging to the visible church, but in terms of people before the Incarnation, "in the time of the ancients of the Old Testament," there was an ordination toward the incarnation, a faith, and so a kind of belonging.[44]

Later Aquinas replaced a model from nature with one from history. If the Sentences spoke of the stages of the world resembling "the ages of an individual person,"[45] the ST notes that physical and mystical bodies differ precisely through the factor of history. The members of a physical body exist together *simul*, but "the body of the church is made up of people who lived from the beginning of the world to its end" (III, 8, 3). Grace has its temporal modes: "among those who are living in one age some lack the grace which later they will have along with others who already have it" (III, 8, 3). The members of the mystical body can be considered in act and in potency. Actualization comes in three ways listed in their order of importance: through enjoyment in heaven, through charity in this life, through faith. Potency may or may not reach actualization (in Aristotelianism potentiality is a form of reality, even a most faint actuality). There are "those who are united to Christ only by potency which, though not yet reduced to act, is according to divine predestination to be reduced to act" and "those in potency who will never be reduced to act"; the first group are those who will accept grace, but the second group, pertinacious in evil, ultimately will not. The latter live in this world and out of their powerful freedom resist grace; they are not *praedestinati* (III, 8, 3). Yves Congar saw here a fundamental ecclesiology springing from a Platonic process:

> For St. Thomas the church is the whole economy of the return toward God. . . . Thus in the world of grace a kind of

---

[43]In 3 *Sent.*, d. 13, q. 2, a. 2, ad 2. Seckler compares Aquinas' different historical schemata in *Das Heil in der Geschichte* (Munich, 1964), 199f. and argues that Aquinas tended to see a law of diversity and unfolding, a *motus ad perfectionem* for humanity existing in space and time (120ff.).

[44]In 3 *Sent.*, d. 13, q. 2, a. 2, ad 4 and 5. Aquinas cited Augustine that faith does not change but the times change, although the influence of grace before the incarnation was not as great as now.

[45]In 4 *Sent.*, d. 4, q. 3, a. 1.

Platonism is valid, for Christ contains in himself the fullness of the species grace. . . . Christ bears the economy of the new life, the entirety of humanity reborn moving back to God; the church, the same reality, is a kind of overflow of a fountain or an unfolding and development of what was from the beginning realized in Christ.[46]

"Thus by understanding this in a general way according to the entire time of the world Christ is the head of the human race but in different degrees" (III, 8, 3). Time does not begin and end with Christ, but people exist in different potentialities even after his redemptive life.

The mature Aquinas gave only intimations of a theology of history. "Thomas did not compose a theology of history," Pesch writes,

any more than he composed a theology of the church. But he made decisions about the history of theology in order to compose his *Summa theologiae*. . . .To exist historically means to go out from God and to return to God through the world on the path which is called Christ. . . . This theology of history . . . is indirect and more presupposed than thematized; it is true not only for times and epochs but for every historical act, for each moment of history.[47]

Congar noticed that Aquinas did not accept an apocalyptic view of a Christ about to end time violently (a view nourished by various twelfth century movements) but pursued the theme of the education of the human race through the pedagogy of law. A work by Aquinas on canon law observed that revelation came "through the most orderly disposition of the ages (which excludes the error of the gentiles who mocked the Christian faith because it seemed that after many ages and rather unexpectedly it occurred to the mind of

---

[46]"The Idea of the Church in Thomas Aquinas," *The Mystery of the Church* (London, 1960) 98, 103ff.

[47]Pesch, *Thomas von Aquin*, 309, 314. Congar observes that Aquinas has temporal phases in his theologies of law and in the life of Christ, but that he seeks their connection more with divine wisdom and theological logic than with historical development. "Le Sens de l'économie' salutaire dans la 'théologie' de S. Thomas d'Aquin (Somme théologique)," *Glaube und Geschichte* (Baden-Baden, 1957), pp. 109ff.

God to give the law of the Gospel to people). This was not done suddenly but was arranged through a suitable plan that first there would be a pre-announcement of Christ through the law and the prophets."[48] Among the few facets of this theology of history, some are worthy of note. Christ is clearly the causal center, but the economy of salvation appeared in the course of time in different degrees. Second, he is not the sole proper cause of every event in the supernatural order. Third, a theology of salvation in the Hebrew covenant past and present along with a few observations about other religions observing the natural law suggest a positive view of other religions' faiths and sacraments. "The ancient fathers belonged to the church to which we belong" (III, 8, 3, 3). In the time before Christ and even before Jewish law, "in the state of the law of nature, when there was no code of law given externally, people were moved solely by an interior instinct to worship God and also they were determined by interior instinct to use material things for the worship of God" (III, 60, 5). The human desire for worship need not be suppressed but can be directed by natural law to anticipate Christ: "different sacraments are suitable for different times" (III, 60, 5).

If Christ is the head even of those who will only remain in potency, still the group designated as non-predestined remain in their mode of potential belonging, not because of their location in history and geography vis-à-vis the announcement of the Gospel but because of their free, evil activity. They reach a basic, psychological orientation which is sinful not because they have not heard the Gospel or because they lack explicit faith, nor even because of original sin. Rather, their free choices fashioning a personal orientation have encouraged the contagion of sin to flower into resolute sinfulness (II-II, 10, 1). The individual response to grace is not a state but occurs in acts at points in time. Thus, again, the efficacy of Christ's mysterious headship is not monoform but dynamic and diverse. In this regard Seckler writes:

> The metaphor "head" implies poetically the grounding of the way opened for all, and in the manner of a creative and communicable primal form in Jesus Christ. He is not such a

---

[48]*Super Primam Decretalem*, 3; see "Le Sens de l'économie' salutaire. . .," 112ff.

head in the style of a natural association or an external
lordship. As a second constitutive facet of the relationship
of head to member Aquinas introduced freedom in being a
disciple. Where this acceptance of Christ's being-the-head
is absent, he is still the real but not realized head. . . . The
difference lies on the side of humans and their freedom. He
is the head, i.e., a real offer of redeemed humanity, even
for those who do not know this or will it. [49]

There is one human race before and after the fall; there is one
initial predestination to grace which influences all human beings
while leaving individual freedom so much a cause that it can
affirm or deny grace; there is one head redeeming the human race
for the original plan of life above nature. "There was no period,"
Aquinas wrote in the Sentences, "in which human nature was
excluded from the way of salvation, so there is no time of life in
which an individual human being is excluded from the way of
salvation."[50] In the ST Aquinas asked about the line from Scripture,
"God wills all to be saved" (1 Tim. 2:4). His solution used John
Damascene's distinction between antecedent and consequent will, a
distinction in God's loving will from our temporal perspective. The
divine will, after "taking into account all particular circumstances"
(I, 19, 6), one of which is individual free-dom at work, permits
some freely and actively to fall away from the offer of grace. All,
however, are initially, "antecedently," willed salvific grace. This
willing, even though a *velleitas*, is not a hope or a wish but a
conditioned act of the divine will. Religious and moral lives exist
within the one supernatural order and move toward or away from
that supernatural end which includes other natural and religious
teleologies.[51] In these texts on Christ's headship, Aquinas set aside
an unqualified closure upon negative non-believers. An objection

---

[49]"Das Haupt aller Menschen," 112f. There is no question on the church in the
ST: Yves Congar believes this was intentional, and he with J. Geiselmann and
Seckler find ecclesial theology in the capital grace of Christ (J. Geiselmann,
"Christus und die Kirche nach Thomas von Aquin," *Theologische Quartalschrift* 107
[1926] 198ff.; 108 [1927] 233ff.). By the nineteenth century, the topic of the extent of
grace is treated in ecclesiology and no longer in the areas of faith, baptism, and
grace where it was to be found during the baroque period.

[50]In *4 Sent.*, d. 4, q. 3, a. 1.

[51]ST I-II, 106, 3; 95, 2; 107, 1–3.

asserted aggressively: "Infidels, however, are in no way members of the church," but to this he responded by affirming their real i f potential relationship. For Aquinas viewed headship in Christ in two ways: *principaliter* as the power of Christ which is sufficient for the salvation of the entire human race; *secundario* in terms of humanity's free will (III, 8, 3, 1). This solution looks not on the fallen self lost in a religion void of grace but toward the next area: a theology of freedom and self. But here Aquinas said no more and left the ages to ponder the extent and interplay of freedom, original sin, and grace in religious history.

E.   Grace's Entry in the Human Personality

The final encounter with our issue is given in Aquinas' psychological theology of the maturing human being. While that analysis of initial moral actions gave no direct reference to our topic, its teaching, though brief, is significant.

We know that for Christianity there is no neutral world. Humans do not live out the days of their lives apart from moral choice, away from depravity or sanctity. An individual lives amid the competing milieus of the fallen human condition and the offer of grace. For Aquinas the first truly moral act of the human person (with its real freedom and limited sovereignty) involves grace. "When, however, a person has begun to have the use of reason . . . . now at that point in life the first thing that occurs to the individual is to deliberate about himself, and if he orders himself to his rightful end, by grace he attains the remission of original sin" (I-II, 89, 6).[52] Any conversion-movement away from fallenness to a personal and salvific God implies contact with grace. Moral choice has cognitive and voluntary facets: they ground its specificity, but they also bring a deeper orientation to goals. The movement of choice when adult free will chooses what is good is enabled by God's help, grace. "God moves all things, but according to their own ways . . . so that the motion from God toward justification does not happen without the motion of free will toward receiving the gift of grace in those who are capable of that

---

[52]The same problematic appears three times in the commentary on the Sentences (e.g., In 2 Sent., d. 28, q. 1, a. 3, ad 5), twice in the *De Veritate* (e.g., 24, 12, ad 2), and in the *De Malo*, q. 5, a. 2, ad 8.

motion" (I-II, 113, 3). What is important is that an initial active
orientation of the self is not primarily and basically graced because
something religious has been chosen or because baptism has been
received, but because its freedom is enabled by grace. Maturity
brings the inevitable choice of a fundamental orientation of life.
That decision will involve a movement of the will, and in that
movement there is an acceptance or a rejection, implicit or explicit,
of the grace of God (I, 89, 6). This is a pattern for all adults. It
would seem that all human beings receive grace, but in the
interplay of grace and freedom not all receive grace with the same
intensity, and some do freely will to abandon grace (I, 23, 5; 23, 3,
2). Grace meets and bears these choices because a person is seeking a
good orientation, however unreflexively, toward self, neighbor,
and God. (Of course, how the precedence of grace relates to freedom
is the subject of centuries of discussion.) In the *Summa contra
gentiles* Thomas seemed to presume not a flawed or perverted order
of humanity but a theology of generosity and an anthropology of
real contribution:

> Someone cannot be directed to their ultimate destiny
> without the help of divine grace, because without this no
> one can have those things which are necessary for that
> movement to destiny like faith, hope, love and
> perseverance. . . . Now, although one cannot merit or
> summon forth divine grace through the movement of free
> will, one can hinder oneself from receiving it. So it lies in
> the power of free will to impede or not to impede the
> reception of divine grace. . . . God, as he is in himself, is
> ready to give grace to all and 'wills all to be saved and to
> come to the knowledge of the truth' (as is said in *1
> Timothy*). But those alone are deprived of grace who in
> themselves present an impediment to grace, like someone
> who closes his eyes to the sun illuminating the world. . . .[53]

What are the theological motifs behind this positive
anthropology, this moment where human psychology and divine
grace meet? First, creation is good, and the natures of creation are

---

[53]*Summa contra gentiles* 3, 159; see In *4 Sent.*, d. 1, q. 1, a. 2; *ST* III, 68, 2, ad 3; In
2 Sent., d. 28, q. 1, a. 4.

good not just in their being but in their actions. Second, God provides means for all beings to achieve actions and goals (III, 61, 1). Third, the human creature is an image of God, a dignity coming not first from grace but from intelligence and freedom (I, 93, 6 and 7). The Creator is glorified by the success of active natures. Unless grace and life have an opportunity to meet in those creatures called to a higher life, the Source of nature and supernature appears as a failure, in plan and in execution.

> It is not suitable that God provide more for creatures being led by divine love to a natural good than for those creatures to whom that love offers a supernatural good. For natural creatures God provides generously . . . kinds of forms and powers which are principle of acts so that they are inclined to activity through their own beings. . . . Even more for those moved to reach an eternal supernatural good he infuses certain forms or qualities of the supernatural order according to which easily and enthusiastically they are moved by God to attain that good which is eternal. And so the gift of grace is a kind of quality (I-II, 110, 2).

A bleak original sin blocking every divine favor for human beings is missing from this theology. For Aquinas original sin is an injurious, misleading influence; human nature is not fully healthy and has a "sickness," a "fever" (I-II, 109, 2). But original sin, while weakening or misdirecting human personality in terms of grace, does not remove or pervert the drives of human life. Moreover, we need not imagine that this fundamental moral choice happens at an unusually early age, or that it occurs only once. Aquinas' psychological theology can be applied to the first deliberation about life's direction or to deliberations about vocation or conversion. In the *De Veritate* this universal psychology of personality and grace went beyond the older example of peoples meeting angels—"Someone growing up among animals or alone in the woods . . . would follow the leadership of natural reason desiring good and fleeing evil."—and a passage cited from the commentary on Romans mentioned this principle: "He Paul spoke of gentiles converted to faith who have begun to keep the moral precepts of the law through the help of grace. . . . The light of natural reason includes in us that which is the image of God. And yet, this does not exclude grace being necessary to move human affectivity."[54]

In the ST this theology of the first moral act did not refer to those living in extraordinary isolation but to all men and women orienting themselves to or away from the holy or moral. This subtle enablement of serious moral choice by grace is a kind of counterpart to implicit faith. Implicit faith describes a trajectory of consciousness to something believed; through and beyond that object (however minimal) faith touches a richer reality. In a basic moral choice grace sustains an action which can have implications and effects greater than those immediately perceptible in the object chosen. Seckler observes: "It seems that Aquinas with his teaching on the instinct of faith and the dialectic of the first moral act reaches the limits of theological statements, for then human discourse must be silent before the imponderable depths of the ways of God."[55] Without grace fallen humanity sins. Grace as an "interior instinct" for the religious and moral good (III, 60, 5) must reach each human being because, Aquinas explained, "it is not possible that an adult, without grace, would be only in original sin, because as soon as he has attained the use of free choice, if he has prepared himself for grace, he will have grace; otherwise his very negligence will lead to mortal sin."[56] This recalls not only the theology of faith but that of the Spirit as the interior new law.

Some Christian theologians have solved the problem of the damnation of distant peoples by a sovereign act of negative predestination. For Thomas Aquinas, however, God is not a capricious deity or a malevolent judge but the loving source of being; the goodness of beings reflects supreme intelligence. Providence for life

---

[54]*De Veritate*, 14, 11, ad 1; *Ad Romanos* (2:14) 39f. A further area of some consequence can be introduced here, the primary role of reason and conscience in determining right or wrong for the will. "To believe in Christ is good in itself and necessary for salvation; all the same this does not win the will unless it be recommended by reason. If the reason presents it as bad, then the will reaches to it in that light, not that it really is bad in itself, but because it appears so because of a condition that happens to be attached by the reason apprehending it." (I-II, 19, 5) This would have considerable consequence for the evaluation of other religions' rites and teachings.

[55]M. Seckler, "Das Heil der Nichtevangelisierten in thomistischer Sicht," *Theologische Quartalschrift* 140 (1960) 40ff.

[56]*De Veritate*, 24, 12, ad 2.

and predestination to grace come before the fall of the human race. In a brief theological exposition Aquinas observed: "It belongs to divine providence not to destroy the order of things but to serve it. The wisdom of God appears in an extraordinary fashion by the preservation of the orders of justice and of nature. And further, from mercy it provided a remedy of human salvation through the incarnation and death of his son."[57] Predestination is the suitable and admirable decision of providence that there be a supernatural order for human beings (I, 23, 1). Predestination established an order and milieu of grace in which human life unfolds. Predestination is not a haughty selection of a remnant people, nor is it a choice of damnation for a large part of humanity but a plan or *ratio* inevitably establishing the dialectic between human freedom and divine grace. Pesch summarizes: "The sole ground for predestination is the goodness of God; the choice of grace for an individual is an act of the love of God, and those predestined are the beloved of God for whom the model and ground of their predestination is the predestination of Christ."[58] What we call graces are realizations of the basic dynamics of God's loving predestination. The planned offer to humanity of grace from divine goodness (I, 23, 5) leaves human wills free to reject this order's life principle of grace (I, 23, 3) but for Aquinas there was no predestination to the opposite of grace, although there was a further nuanced modality of providence which "permits someone to fall into fault" (I, 23, 3). The divine permission for creatures to choose freely this or that sin is "not a will."[59] God's active relationship to free will in the realm of grace was treated by Thomas with sparseness and depth. All human beings receive grace, but in the interplay of grace and freedom not all receive grace with the same intensity (I, 23, 5, 3), and some will to abandon grace: "fault comes from the free will of the one who has deserted grace" (I, 23, 3, 2). As we saw, the divine will existing in an eternal now but including in its view secondary causes wills "antecedently" that every man and woman be saved and this includes "individuals from every kind of peoples" (I, 19, 6, 1).

---

[57]*De Rationibus Fidei*, c. 7.
[58]Pesch, *Thomas von Aquin*, 157.
[59]Pesch, *Thomas von Aquin*, 153.

If the dynamic ground for the supernatural order (for the incarnation and for grace) is the goodness and love of God (I, 23, 5; I-II, 110, 1), and if grace is the greatest good for humans, grace will be given widely and generously, since God "is most generous to the highest degree."[60] Aquinas' theology of grace in history preserves both essential and contingent perspectives; a divine plan and power eventually realizes this plan amid all that is contingent, historical and sinful.[61] "With regards to the directing of human actions prophetic revelation is diverse, not only according to the procession of time but according to the conditions of activities . . . and so in every age people are divinely instructed about how to live—which [teaching] was expedient for the salvation of the elect" (II-II, 174, 6).

IV

The thirteenth century, in architecture and jurisprudence as well as in theology, was drawn to the epochal structure of summa, and Thomas assembled in the several thousand articles of the ST an extraordinary number and variety of sources. But what Chenu noted fifty years ago is still true: we do not know a great deal about the formal theological structures of that great work, and the threads of Christian themes or of patristic sources running from part to part remain to be studied.[62] Aquinas' attention to order and to cross references as well as his introductions to clusters of questions encourage us to study his theology in its patterns and relationships. Despite the lack of a formal treatment and the infrequency of pertinent articles important themes have given us a limited theology of grace beyond explicit Christianity.

---

[60]". . .maxime liberalis." In 2 Sent., d. 3, q. 4, a. 1, ad 3.

[61]A. Patfoort, "L'unité de la Ia pars et le mouvement interne de la Somme théologique de S. Thomas d'Aquin," Revue des sciences philosophiques et théologiques 47 (1963) 13ff. Predestination displays the themes not only of grace but of Christology. In the ST, however, the dynamics and telos of grace appear as the most basic structure, and yet Christ is central to the order of grace. Christ is the model and image in social and ecclesial history for the human order of participation in the divine. Our predestination and Christ's predestination have a dual relationship; in one approach Christ is unique, but in another Christ is included with us in the one predestined supernatural order (III, 24, 3 and 4).

[62]Toward Understanding . . . ., 310, 308.

(1) The opening article of the ST states that there is no human destiny or life planned for the human race outside the real order of grace. The preceding essay has explored a mystery-laden facet of God's special revealed life on earth. Grace is centered in Jesus Christ but is given by the Trinity to human lives in various modes. Grace either contacts in some way those separated by space and time from any possible evangelization, or God by an a priori decision has withheld the salvific missions of the divine persons to earth because of human temporal and cultural conditions. The Dominican theologian mentioned no national or religious groups explicitly and permanently isolated from the supernatural order. Love is not elitist or hostile, and God is not the failed supervisor of a world where many or most are damned by historical circumstance. The ordinary but historical entry of a human being into salvation through explicit faith and love are not contradicted by Aquinas' brief treatments of implicit faith or grace and natural law.

Looking back at the few texts treating our issue, one can see a pattern. (a) A traditional, often biblical access to grace was presented; but then it was challenged by an objection which would limit grace, one excluding abstract groups of the human race from salvation through no fault of their own. This pattern is found in faith (II-II, 2, 3), faith in Christ (2, 7), faith in the Trinity (2, 8), a sacrament (III, 61, 1), the sacrament of baptism (III, 68, 2), the sacrament of the Eucharist (III, 73, 3), incorporation into Christ (III, 8, 3), and grace (I-II, 109, 5). (b) Each traditional, explicit access to Christian grace was affirmed, but (c) Aquinas showed each time how that particular access had broader, exceptional modes. (d) Aquinas did not treat, much less condemn, groups (*gentes*, *infideles*) living before Christ, but rather he introduced them and then preserved them from a factor which would exclude their salvation. (e) He went on to offer a wider interpretation of a factor, e.g., faith, which had been introduced as potentially exclusionary.

Aquinas was reluctant to close God's plan and action or to limit God's presence. Nevertheless, his generous perspective lacks precision and concretization in geography and time. The texts indicate that somehow when Aquinas was treating grace outside explicit faith or baptism he had in mind the ages before Christ. He seems nowhere to refer explicitly to the problem in his own time but occasionally treated it from the period before Moses or Christ, or from the age of the ministry of the Apostles. Other texts, however, refer to a universal and timeless situation (a timeless example is given in the present tense). It can be argued that in Aquinas' mind the theology of earlier times (like the example of Cornelius) do apply to centuries after Christ. Sometimes he applies principles drawn from the time of primal and Mosaic law to an imprecisely delineated but clearly different situation: the pattern of God moving early peoples within their perception of natural law followed by the graced convenant with Israel would be applicable to peoples living in later centuries "in the state of natural law" (III, 60, 5).

The articles which treat our topic offer openings which modify a strict tying of grace to church, doctrine or baptism, because the ST pays more attention to human psychology and to the development of faith and grace in terms of degrees and ages. "The grace of God is the sufficient cause of human salvation, but God gives grace to people according to modes convenient to them" (III, 61, 1, 2).

(2) Aquinas' theology of the extent of grace was developed from areas like grace, faith, and baptism but not from the issues of theodicy or through comparisons of doctrines from different religions. The expressions of religion, its conceptualities and propositions held only a secondary role for him; a new mode of life, not only believed but enacted, came first. Questions on God's existence and being are propaedeutic to the presence of God called "grace," but the deepest orientation of the individual, life in touch with personal salvation, responsibility before the natural moral law, or levels of meaning in rituals are the themes of the *Summa*.

God loves into existence (and then respects) natures and their individuals. Creatures are adorned with "the gift of being a cause" (I, 22, 3); free and intelligent causes ("secondary causes") unfold a world both stable and moving. Neither God nor the theologian should ask more from a nature—including a graced nature—than it can give. Grace, described as a form and a "habitus," that is, as a life principle,[63] enables the Christian to live as a citizen of God's

---

[63]". . .something by which human nature itself should be raised to a dignity which would make such an end suitable,. . . a spiritual existence." *De Veritate*, q. 27, a. 2.

Kingdom. Human nature cannot on its own enter the world of grace even if that realm is ultimately the one "ordo" for human beings. The exclusion of blocks of loving creatures from God's love apart from their activity does not fit with Aquinas' theology of Creator or Redeemer. God would aim in the world of grace, as in the world of beings, at maximum life. "God could have, by his infinite power, saved the human race in ways other than the incarnation . . . but i t was the most suitable way by which people could achieve most easily their salvation" (III, 1, 2). There is, however, a tension between internal revelations and movements of grace in isolated individuals and the social history of salvation. This theological topic is an example of the difficulty of combining a physics of divine presence with a historical economy of grace, and a psychology of graced freedom. But Aquinas' theology encourages wider, analogous contacts by God to peoples.[64]

(3) Aquinas sought in the areas of faith, baptism, grace and Christ what is fundamental as he pondered in a few articles how grace comes in degrees of history, degrees of faith, and degrees of personal receptivity. The distinction between ground and realization appears inevitably whenever the human mind describes divine action. Religion with its doctrines and rituals serves something higher and deeper: the "new law" which is the presence of the Holy Spirit. Aquinas spoke of degrees of the presence of the New Law of the Spirit just as he spoke of degrees of implicit and explicit faith. Grace which is the life of the Holy Spirit has an unchanging divine source, and it is a "law" of fulfillment; nonetheless, "the state of the New Law is subject to change with regard to various places, times and persons" (I-II, 106, 4). "The New Law's foundation consists in that grace which is given to believers interiorly . . . . Secondarily it consists in certain facts, moral teaching and sacraments" (I-II, 107, 1, 3). The dialectic

---

[64]"Thomas sees the *ordo salutis* in a radical way as salvation-history: salvation is realized in an event, and too, every event between heaven and earth is either salvation-history or its opposite." M. Seckler, *Das Heil in der Geschichte,* 121; see Y. Congar, "Le moment 'économique' et le moment 'ontologique' dans la sacra doctrina," *Mélanges offerts à M. D. Chenu* (Paris, 1967), 135ff. U. Horst, "über die Frage einer heilsökonomischen Theologie bei Thomas von Aquin," in K. Bernath, *Thomas von Aquin* (Darmstadt, 1978) 1, 373ff.

of ground and realization is true also of faith. "In the divine *esse* are included all those things we.believe exist in God eternally and in which our happiness consists. In faith in providence, however, are included all those things which are offered by God in time for human salvation, which fashion a road to happiness" (II-II, 1, 7). Aquinas asked whether the faith of the "moderns" and the "ancients" is one (but not "the same"). "If we take the object of faith, the reality believed, as it is outside of our soul, then faith is one as it refers to us and to the ancients, and so faith receives its unity from the unity of the reality. If we consider it as it is in our receptivity faith is made plural through diverse propositions, but from this diversification faith is not diversified."[65] Aquinas was always a realist: faith moves through propositions in particular languages to reach beyond to the reality expressed in belief, while baptism sacramentalizes the reality of grace which a personality accepts. The distinctions between ground and realization, e.g., implicit and explicit, Spirit and form, are open to further analyses, and they will stimulate no small number of Thomist theologies on this topic.[66]

(4) Pesch thinks that Aquinas' later views stimulated by the discovery of a wider world beyond lonely forest-folk led to an Augustinian pessimism: many would be lost. "With the help of grace we do have this power [to believe]."[67] As Augustine says, "to whomever this help is given by God it is given in mercy; to whomever it is denied, it is denied in justice, namely because of previous sin, even if only original sin" (II-II 2, 5, 1).[68] On the other hand, the few passages on how original sin in an individual leads to vice are nowhere expanded into global damnation. Except for this oblique reference to turning from grace through other sins (but not through a lack of explicit faith II-II, 10, 1), the dynamic of Aquinas' theology is positive: universal predestination to grace,

---

[65]*De Veritate*, 14, 12.

[66]S. Harent surveys how the topic of wider grace is from 1520 to 1920 treated in theories on implicit faith; see "*Infidèles* (Salut des)," *Dictionnaire de théologie catholique* (Paris, 1923) 7:2, 1726–1930.

[67]Pesch, *Thomas von Aquin*, 56 and 712. Pesch observes that the Augustinianism of the later Aquinas does not overbalance the other dynamic lines leading to grace being more powerful than original sin. "Besinnung. . .," 282.

[68]The quotation is incorrectly attributed to Augustine.

God's loving attention to the orders established, a presumption that beings reach their goals, the offer of grace at key moments of moral choice. The devastating contagion of primal sin comes to each individual by nature, but grace, whether before or after Calvary, comes by a personal encounter with God (III, 8, 1). Within human freedom the Trinitarian life-principle can be rejected by sin (II-II, 10, 1) or contempt (III, 68, 2), but not by conditions of birth or an inculpable ignorance of religious truths.

Aquinas did not hesitate to raise the question of those outside the *fama* of Christ, or to assert that grace contacts people obeying the natural law or having implicit faith. Every human being seems to have a chance to accept or to reject grace; people are not born into a frozen isolation from grace where they remain enchained and condemned. Aquinas thought that grace is normatively present in the Christian Gospel and sacraments (I-II, 106, 4), but nonetheless God gives grace to people not only according to a certain diversity (their individuality and their place in a particular society) but also "in ways suited to them" (III, 61, 13).

* * *

If Aquinas was aware of his Dominican brothers' trips to the court of the Mongols or their publication of studies on the Koran, why does he not have a formal treatment of faith and grace outside of European Christendom? Is it because Europe contacted Islam through bloody wars or learned of the Mongols through their dangerous invasions? Is it because Aquinas, despite his positive anthropology of grace in theory, saw too much of the violence of life among Christians to make salvation impersonal or automatic? Caperan concluded in the 1930s:

> Thomas Aquinas consistently taught that the non-believers themselves in whatever milieu the chance of birth has placed them have the means to be saved. . . . Without denying any essential element of Augustinian teaching, he takes us far from St. Augustine in whose perspective the darkness of ignorance covering the nations seems to resist any penetration of a ray of divine grace."[69]

---

[69]Caperan 1, 199.

We have seen that Aquinas' ideas here have a challenging depth but also a lack of resolution. Seckler thinks that the scholastics first confused and then never fully untangled two issues— individuals hidden from society and peoples never evangelized— and that the lines of his theology were left unresolved: "Thomas Aquinas offers to our topic no clear answer. Opposite a series of optimistic statements stands the silence of his later writings on decisive points. . . . One might think that Thomas did not write down all his thoughts, or that he did not see the problem of salvation of non-Christians in its true sharpness."[70]

Learning of peoples to the East and in Africa may have suggested to Thomas Aquinas a new broader horizon for the reach of grace. Ahead in the future was the discovery of not just clusters of peoples and religions but of entire continents not yet touched by evangelization. Within fifteen years after Spain's first contacts with the Americas, the Dominican theologians at Salamanca and their students in Hispaniola, themselves students of a neo-Thomist revival, were drawing upon texts in the *Summa theologiae* to defend the natural rights of non-Christians, to reject the idea that lack of faith damns, and to argue that grace can exist outside baptism. In subsequent centuries forms of neo-Thomism rooted in a theology of personality and grace, implicit faith, and baptism in voto addressed the issues of the extent of grace. Implicit and explicit faith was a dominant topic around 1900, while a decade or so later Reginald Garrigou-Lagrange and Jacques Maritain were moved by the reports of mysticism in Islam and Hinduism to appreciate wider circles of grace in religions.[71] The famous recent theoretician in this area has been Karl Rahner, and these pages show that the problematic and the principles of his theology are

---

[70]M. Seckler, "Das Heil. . .," 45, 39; Pesch (*Thomas von Aquin*, 54) and Sabra, 156f. agree.

[71]See T. O'Meara, "Exploring the Depths. A Theological Tradition in Viewing the World Religions," In *Verantwortung für den Glauben* (Freiburg, 1992) 375. For a survey of various Thomisms on this topic see Sullivan, *Salvation outside the Church? Tracing the History of the Catholic Response*; a bibliographical summary of Thomist theology concerning the Indies can be found in T. O'Meara, "The Dominican School of Salamanca and the Spanish Conquest of America," *The Thomist* 56 (1992) 555ff.

not shockingly new. Knowledgeable in Aquinas and the history of Thomism and aware of the anthropological dimension in the New Testament as well as in modern theology, Rahner's approach too was an exploration of degrees of faith and grace. Long before Rahner, however, working from a Thomist tradition, Domingo Bañez had distinguished between the reality of responding to grace and the designation of "Christian." He wrote: "One might respond that it is sufficient that they be Christians in reality, for they have implicit faith, although this would not suffice for them to be called Christians."[72] And Domingo de Soto had a similar observation: "Although nothing is expressed in the gospel concerning baptism of desire, it is manifest that where the reality itself is not possible . . . the intention [for it] has an effect with respect to justifying grace."[73] So the areas of Aquinas' theology which we explored have influenced the theological mystery and understanding of grace given through the event of Christ but lived outside of Christian faith for four centuries. Indeed up to the present moment Catholic theologians have not gone far beyond him.

---

[72]D. Bañez, *Commentaria in 2am 2ae. . . .* (Venice, 1586) 419.
[73]D. de Soto, *De Natura et Gratia* 1, 12 (Paris, 1549) 130.

TROPICS OF DESIRE:

Mystical Interpretation of the Song of Songs

Bernard McGinn

Divinity School, University of Chicago

The modern French thinker and mystic Simone Weil once said: "To reproach mystics with loving God by means of the faculty of sexual love is as though one were to reproach a painter with making pictures by means of colors composed of material substances. We haven't anything else with which to love."[1] Weil's remark reminds us that no more personal and more potent way of portraying God's love for humanity, both for his people and for the individual, can be imagined than the language of human erotic love. But is it also an appropriate way? Jewish and Christian tradition over the span of many centuries insisted that it was. It is only in the modern era when both the religious-minded and the non-religious have conspired to place a barrier between sex and sacrality that the admittedly complex and delicate task of showing how human sexuality signifies and perhaps even makes present God's eros seems troubling if not even bizarre.

It was for this reason that the classical Jewish and Christian masters of exegesis put the Song of Songs at the center of their partly common book. As Rabbi Akiva said: "The whole world is not worthy of the day the Song of Songs was given to Israel, for all of Scripture is holy, but the Song of Songs is the Holy of Holies."[2] The earliest great Christian exegete, Origen of Alexandria, held the same position:

---

[1] *The Notebooks of Simone Weil*, translated from the French by Arthur Wills, 2 vols. (London and Henley: Routledge & Kegan Paul, 1976) 2: 72.

[2] Tosefta, Sanhedrin XII, 10.

And so this Song is rightly to be preferred to all songs. The other songs that the Law and the Prophets sang were sung to the Bride while she was still a little girl and had not yet entered the threshold of maturity. This Song is sung to her now that she is adult, quite strong, and ready for a husband's power and the perfect mystery.[3]

While accepting this common starting point, however, there were significant differences in the ways in which the Jewish and Christian exegetes demonstrated how the erotic language of the Song inscribed and actualized the message of God's love.[4] Although both religions based their interpretation on God's love for his people, that is on a communal reading, and though both also made use of personal, individual or mystical readings, the latter were more widespread in Christianity and also more ambiguous, precisely because of the Christian debate about the value of sexuality.

The complexity of motivations in Christian attitudes toward sexuality, particularly as the ideal of virginity as a higher way of life came to the fore in the second and third centuries CE, has been much studied in recent years. Fear of sexuality and the body, masochism and mysogyny doubtless all play their part, but they are scarcely the whole of the story. Having rejected Gnosticism (though Gnostic ideas were influential in some Christian circles for several centuries), Christian leaders could not easily deny the basic goodness of sexuality as a part of the Creator's intention. The triumph of the ideal of virginity, a triumph not achieved without a struggle, was primarily a way in which Christian thinkers worked out their own versions of the religious and social control of sexuality which was an integral part of all ancient society. Virginity was more about the freedom and power to be found in the

---

[3]*Origenis Commentarium in Cantica Canticorum*, Prologus, ed. W. A. Baehrens, *Origenes Werke*, vol. 8 (Leipzig: J. C. Hinrichs, 1925) 80: *Unde et omnibus canticis merito praefertur; videntur enim caetera cantica, quae "lex et prophetae" cecinerunt, parvulae adhuc sponsae, et quae nondum vestibula maturae aetatis ingressa sit, decantata, hoc vero canticum adultae iam et valde robustae et quae capax iam sit virilis potentiae perfectique mysterii, decantari.*

[4] I have explored some of these differences in an earlier paper, "The Language of Love in Jewish and Christian Mysticism," *Mysticism and Language*, edited by Steven T. Katz (New York: Oxford University Press, 1992) 202-35.

new religion than it was about masochism and mysogyny.[5] The role that the interpretation of the Song of Songs had in this process was that of providing a lens to focus the debate over the true meaning of eros so that the ideal of the erotic encounter between the human virgin, male or female, and the Divine Lover could appear in all its true splendor. Hence, the "tropics of desire," that is, the tropes or literary strategies and devices that Christian exegetes used to transform the descriptions of human sexual beauty and activity in the Song of Songs into a message about the relation between Christ and the Church and Christ and the believer, are vital for understanding the history of Christian attitudes toward sexuality, as well as for the history of Christian mysticism.

It is a common-place that classic Christian spiritual exegesis of the Song falls into three broad categories: (1) a communal or ecclesiological reading concerning Christ and the Church; (2) the individual or mystical meaning where the lovers are the Word made flesh and the believer; and (3) a Mariological reading in which the Song describes the special relation between Christ and his Mother who is both the paradigm of all believers and a type of the Church.[6] These readings were rarely totally discrete. Origen pioneered the combined ecclesiological-mystical interpretation in the third century, and as early as the late fourth century Ambrose of Milan had introduced elements of a Mariological reading.[7] In

---

[5]For an overview, see Peter Brown, "The Notion of Virginity in the Early Church," in *Christian Spirituality: Origins to the Twelfth Century*, edited by Bernard McGinn and John Meyendorff (New York: Crossroad, 1986) 427-43. For more detail, consult P. Brown, *The Body and Society. Men, Women and Sexual Renunciation in Early Christianity* (New York: Columbia University Press, 1988).

[6] Considerable literature has been devoted to the history of Christian exegesis of the Song of Songs, though most of the detailed studies do not go beyond the twelfth century. The best account remains that of Friedrich Ohly, *Hohelied-Studien. Grundzüge einer Geschichte der Hoheliedauslegung des Abendlandes bis um 1200* (Wiesbaden: Franz Steiner, 1958). In English, see E. Ann Matter, *The Voice of My Beloved. The Song of Songs in Western Medieval Christianity* (Philadelphia: University of Pennsylvania Press, 1990); and Denys Turner, *Eros and Allegory. Medieval Exegesis of the Song of Songs* (Kalamazoo-Spencer: Cistercian Publications, 1995). For a survey of recent literature, see B. McGinn, "With 'the Kisses of the Mouth': Recent Works on the Song of Songs," *The Journal of Religion* 72(1992): 269-75.

[7]For comments on the Song of Songs interpretations of Origen and Ambrose, see Bernard McGinn, *The Foundations of Mysticism. Origins to the Fifth Century* (New York: Crossroad, 1991) 118-27 and 209-15, respectively.

the East, Gregory of Nyssa, a contemporary of Ambrose, concentrated on the mystical reading, whereas most early medieval Western interpretations, like that of Gregory the Great, were primarily ecclesiological. The twelfth-century Cistercians, especially Bernard of Clairvaux and William of Saint Thierry, recreated the ecclesiological-mystical reading in a way that put the dominant emphasis on the second component, at the same time that other authors, like Rupert of Deutz and Alan of Lille, fashioned the first systematically Mariological readings.

The flood of commentary on the Song of Songs did not end at 1200, though late medieval exegesis of the text is largely a *terra incognita*, little studied by scholars. Recent work has also shown that to discern the full impact of the Song of Songs in the later medieval and early modern periods we need to look beyond the explicit commentarial tradition to a broad range of literary and artistic evidence. It is especially interesting to note that although women were *ex officio* barred from taking on the task of becoming professional interpreters of Scripture, the female mystics who from the thirteenth century on contributed so powerfully to the creation of what I call vernacular theology,[8] often used the Song of Songs, both directly and indirectly, in their writings. By the early modern period some of the boldest of these women, such as Teresa of Avila in the sixteenth century and Madame Guyon in the seventeenth, even wrote commentaries on the book.

In what follows I would like to take a brief look at four of the major Christian commentators on the Song of Songs—Origen and Gregory of Nyssa among the Greeks, and Bernard and William among the Latins. My treatment will emphasize the tropes that they employed to create their distinctive mystical readings of the text. I believe that it is possible to concentrate primarily on the mystical interpretation of these authors because Christian exegetes always insisted that the personal meaning of the book rests upon the ecclesiological sense, that is, that the same principles that allow the Bride to be read as God's people are those that are the

---

[8]See "Introduction: Meister Eckhart and the Beguines in the Context of Vernacular Theology," *Meister Eckhart and the Beguine Mystics. Hadewijch of Brabant, Mechthild of Magdeburg and Marguerite Porete*, edited by Bernard McGinn (New York: Continuum, 1994) 1-14.

basis of further applications of the tropics of desire to each believer. Bernard of Clairvaux put it well: "No one among us would dare to claim for himself the title of Bride of Christ for his soul, but because we belong to the Church which rightly glories in this name and its reality, we not unjustly appropriate a share in this glory."[9] It is not enough, however, just to analyze the fundamental principles which enabled these exegetes to effect their transformative readings of the Song. In order to appreciate something of the richness and variety of their mystical interpretations, it will be helpful to provide an illustration of how such readings actually worked by looking at the interpretation of one of the key erotic images of the Song—the wound of love (*vulnus amoris*) that appears in Song 2:5 (at least in the Septuagint and Old Latin versions),[10] as well as in Song 4:9 of the Vulgate translation.[11]

---

[9]*Sermones super Cantica Canticorum* 12.11, in *Sancti Bernardi Opera*, edited by Jean Leclercq et al., 8 vols. (Rome: Editiones Cistercienses, 1957-77) 1:7: *Quod etsi nemo nostrum sibi arrogare praesumat, ut animam suam quis audeat sponsam Domini appellare, quoniam tamen de Ecclesia sumus, quae merito hoc nomine et re nominis gloriatur, non immerito gloriae huius participium usurpamus.*

[10]The theme of the *vulnus amoris*, though rooted in the Song of Songs, has had many other manifestations in the history of Christian mysticism. For a brief introduction, see André Cabassut, "Blessure d'amour," *Dictionnaire de spiritualité, ascétique et mystique*, 16 vols. (Paris: Beauchesne, 1937-94) 1:724-29.

[11]A comparison of the Septuagint-Old Latin text and the Vulgate in relation to the Hebrew of these two passages demonstrates considerable variation. (For the Hebrew I will use the translation of Roland E. Murphy, *The Song of Songs. A Commentary on the Book of Canticles or The Song of Songs* [Minneapolis: Fortress Press, 1990. Hermeneia—A Critical and Historical Commentary on the Bible]).

Song 2:4 (5)

Hebrew	*LXX-Vetus Latina*	*Vulgate*
Strengthen me	Strengthen me	Strengthen me
with raisin cakes,	with perfumes,	with flowers,
refresh me with	surround me with	surround me with
apples,	apples,	apples,
for I am sick	for I am wounded	for I am sick
with love.	with love	with love
	quia vulnerata	*quia amore*
	caritatis ego sum.	*langueo.*

Song 4:9

Hebrew	*LXX-Vetus Latina*	*Vulgate*
You have ravished	You have instructed	You have wounded
	instruxisti	*vulnerasti*

Two Greek Commentators

Origen wrote his commentary on the Song of Songs about 240 during his time at Caesarea where he had considerable access to rabbinic exegesis.[12] Like all his commentaries, that on the Song of Songs was meant for the mature, or "spiritual," Christian. The fundamental principle upon which Origen grounds his reading he expresses as follows: "There isn't any difference between saying that God is to be loved or to be desired. I wouldn't blame anyone who called God 'Love' (*amor/eros*), just as John calls him 'Charity'" (*caritas/agapé*).[13] Thus, he can assert that, "Take whatever Scripture says about charity as if it had been said with reference to love, having no thought of the difference of terms; the same meaning is demonstrated in both cases."[14] Origen was the first Christian author to explicitly equate *amor/eros* and *caritas/ agapé*; he was also the first in the Hellenic tradition, either pagan or Christian, to make passionate love (*eros*) a transcendental divine attribute.[15] Though the Alexandrian could cite two passages in the Septuagint which described human relations to God in terms of eros, there is no question that the main source for his daring claim was the erotic language of the Song of Songs which he

---

my heart, my sister, Bride!	my heart, my sister, Bride!	my heart, my sister, Bride!
You have ravished my heart with one (glance) of your eyes.	You have instructed my heart with one of your eyes.	You have wounded my heart with one of your eyes.

[12]On Origen's relation to Jewish exegesis, see Ephraim E. Urbach, "The Homiletic Interpretation of the Sages and the Expositions of Origen on Canticles, and the Jewish-Christian Disputation," *Scripta Hiersolymitana* 22(1971):47-75; and Nicholas de Lange, *Origen and the Jews* (Cambridge: Cambridge University Press, 1976).

[13]*Comm. in Cant.*, Prol. (ed. Baehrens, 71.22-25): *Non ergo interest, utrum amari dicatur Deus aut diligi, nec puto quod culpari possit, si quis Deum, sicut Iohannes "caritatem," ita ipse amorem nominet.*

[14]*Comm. in Cant.*, Prol. (ed. Baehrens, 70.32-71.1): *Sic ergo quaecumque de caritate scripta sunt, quasi de amore dicta suscipe nihil de omnibus curans; eademque namque in utroque virtus ostenditur.*

[15]For a survey of this development and Origen's place in it, see Bernard McGinn, "God as Eros: Metaphysical Foundations of Christian Mysticism," *New Perspectives on Historical Theology. Essays in Memory of John Meyendorff*, edited by Bradley Nassif (Grand Rapids: Eerdmans, 1996) 189-209.

obviously was reading on the basis of the premiss already shared both Christians and Jews, namely that the book speaks not of human lovers, but of God and his community.

The implications of identifying God with eros tell us much about Origen's doctrine of God, and also about subsequent mystical understandings of God in the Christian tradition. If God really is eros, then we should expect him to exhibit in some way what we humans experience as eros, that is, some kind of passion or yearning. Though Origen's doctrine of unchanging divine perfection taken over from Greek philosophy would seem to rule this out, a few places in his surviving writings hint at a surprising teaching on the "passion of God."[16] More important for us, however, are the implications for the use of erotic language to describe the divine-human encounter. If eros pertains primarily to God conceived of a pure Spirit (let us call this EROS I), then all human expressions of passionate yearning (sexual desire being the primary case) are essentially participations in this reality, however rightly or wrongly directed (let us call these EROS II). Insofar as they are essentially manifestations, their primary purpose (however perverted by the Fall of humanity) is to help humans regain the ultimate EROS I, that is, God. Thus, all human experience of erotic power, and all language about eros, is directed toward a transformative (Origen would say "anagogic") function for the person who understands and uses it in the proper way.

The essence of eros resides in the subject's experience of yearning desire. Its myriad manifestations are in the actual pursuit and attainment of desired objects, as well as in the verbal descriptions of such experiences. In their efforts to transform erotic consciousness in the service of this higher goal the Christian commentators, beginning with Origen, made a sharp distinction between erotic activity and erotic language, at least after the Fall. Unlike the erotic mysticism of the theosophical Kabbalists, for example, who strove to incorporate human sexual activity itself as a part of mystical transformation, Origen and the later Christian commentators on the Song did not conceive of sexual activity, even marital life, as having any place in the itinerary to God.

---

[16]The most important of these passages is found in the sixth of the surviving homilies on Ezechiel (*In Ezech* 6.6; ed. Baehrens, 384-85).

The reasons for this—at least those explicitly given—originate in their understanding of human inability since the Fall to properly relate matter and spirit. Eros as directed to something material may be *derived* from the eros that is God, but it can no longer lead to it. Hence, the erotic transformation of Origen and his successors involves only a mutation in the language of love, especially as found in the Song of Songs. It has no contact with erotic activity.

How is the transformative power of language actually engaged in the mystical life? Origen lays down two fundamental principles, two tropes for transforming desire, which became basic to the whole subsequent Christian tradition. The contrast between matter and spirit grounds the distinction between the outer and the inner person which the Alexandrian took over from Paul (see, e.g., 2 Cor. 4:16) but adapted to his own purposes. Only the inner spiritual person who has directed her yearning away from material things can profit from the Song.

If the outer, material person, and inner one are at such odds, how can the physical descriptions, especially the potent erotic ones of the Song, allow for spiritual transformation? Origen's solution is through an investigation of the spiritual senses, perhaps his most original contribution to the Christian tropics of desire. As he puts it: "We want to show that the Divine Scriptures use homonyms, that is, similar terms, so that you will find the names of the members of the body are used to refer to those of the soul; or rather, these two kinds of things can be compared to each other not only in expression but also in reality."[17] Thus, the inner person possesses spiritual senses of taste, touch, smell, hearing and sight in relation to the realities of the divine world that are not unlike, but far superior to, our physical senses. Every physical description of the Song of Songs, when properly understood, helps the fallen soul activate these dormant powers of spiritual perception. Origen's often pedantic style occasionally quickens to life when he attempts to describe the spiritual senses at work.

---

[17]*Comm. in Cant.*, Prol. (ed. Baehrens, 64.16-65.19): *Ostendere enim ex his volumus quod scripturis divinis per homonymas, id est per similes appellationes, immo per eadem vocabula et exterioris hominis membra et illius interioris partes affectusque nominantur eaque non solum vocabulis, sed et rebus ipsis sibi invicem comparantur.*

For an example, we can glance at the Alexandrian's interpretation of the wound of love in Song 2:5. The Septuagint text
(followed by the Old Latin version) has the Bride address the
Groom with the words: "Strengthen me with perfumes, surround me
with apples, because I am wounded with charity" (*Confirmate me
in unguentis, stipate me in malis, quia vulnerata caritatis ego
sum*).[18] In explaining what it means to be "wounded by charity,"
Origen provides an exemplary illustration of his transformative
exegesis at work. Following the usual progression of five levels of
interpretation he employed throughout his exegetical works,[19] he
first establishes the literal meaning of the text in two stages,
according to the grammar of the words (*pros rhéton*), and according
to the speakers and events described (*pros historian*). In the third
stage he integrates the text into the life of the Church by
analyzing what these images have to tell us about Christ's love for
the Church.

The Alexandrian's investigation of the difficulties of the
literal sense prompt him to take the first two phrases (i.e., those
concerning the perfumes and the apples) as references to various
kinds of trees. The ecclesiological meaning, then, centers on the
Church's request to Christ to nourish the fruitful and fragrant
"trees," that is, those within her body who are being reformed
according to the model of Christ, who is here identified "as an
apple tree among the trees of the wood" (a Christological reading
of the Bridegroom's self-description in Song 2:3). The personal and
mystical application of the verse, found on the fourth and fifth
levels, are often fused in Origen's presentation. Basically, the
fourth level applies the general ecclesiological sense to all
Christians. In the Song of Songs commentary this is often
accomplished through the invocation of the spiritual senses. As he
puts it here: "The Word of God gave to each according to their
desire. . . . He not only offers himself as bread to those who hunger
and wine to those who thirst, but he presents himself as fragrant

---

[18]Origen's interpretation of Song 2:5 can be found in *Comm. in Cant. Cant.* (ed.
Baehrens, 191-95).

[19]On the five levels of Origen's exegesis, see Karen J. Torjesen, *Hermeneutical
Procedure and Theological Method in Origen's Exegesis* (Berlin: De Gruyter, 1986)
especially 54-57.

apples to those who crave delights."[20] (Note the invocation of spiritual taste and smell.) Then, in the fifth stage, Origen turns to personal appropriation, speaking in the "we" voice, and asking his readers to make the inner meaning real in their own lives.

In exegeting Song 2:5, Origen does not really discuss the wound motif until he reaches this fifth stage. His evocation is powerful:

> If there was ever anyone who at some time burned with this faithful love of the Word of God; if there is anyone who, as the prophet says [cf. Is. 49:2], has received the sweet wound of him who is the chosen dart; if there is anyone who has been pierced with the loving spear of his knowledge so that he yearns and longs for him by day and night, can speak of nothing but him, can hear of nothing but him, can think of nothing else, and cannot desire nor long nor hope for anything save him, that soul then truly says: "I have been wounded by charity."[21]

The intensity of his language here, taken in conjunction with his other mentions of the wound of love,[22] brings us closer to Origen's own mystical consciousness than perhaps any other passage in his writings.

It is noteworthy that Origen defends the appropriateness of speaking of the Incarnate Word as a "wounding love" through his appeal to a complex of texts from the Old and the New Testament read as images of how Christ seeks to penetrate our minds and hearts with his saving knowledge, especially Isaiah 49:2 (LXX: "He set me as a chosen arrow...") and Ephesians 6:17 ("Receive the

---

[20]*Comment. in Cant. Cant.* (ed. Baehrens, 193.25-195.3): *Omnia namque haec Verbum Dei unicuique efficitur, prout mensura vel desiderium participantis exposcit;. . . . Praebet ergo semet ipsum non solum esurientibus "panem" et sitientibus "vinum," sed et deliciari volentibus semet ipsum fraglantia exhibet poma.*

[21]*Comm. in Cant.* (ed Baehrens, 194.6-13): *Si quis unquam est, qui fideli hoc amore est Verbi Dei arsit aliquando, si quis est, ut propheta dicit, qui "electi iaculi" eius dulce vulnus accepit, si quis est, qui scientiae amabili confixus est telo, ita ut diurnis eum desideriis nocturnisque suspiret, aliud qui loqui non possit, audire aliud nolit, cogitare aliud nescit, desiderare praeter ipsum aut cupere aliud vel sperare non libeat, ista anima merito dicit: "vulnerata caritatis ego sum". . . .*

[22]The most extended other discussion is to be found in Origen's *Homilia II in Cantica Canticorum* 8 (ed. Baehrens, 53-54). The theme also comes in for brief mentions in the Prologus of the *Comm. in Cant. Cant.* (ed. Baehrens, 67.12-16, and 69.8-12).

Word of God from the Spirit to use as a sword.")[23] Although the Alexandrian's language about the piercing activity of the Divine Word is passionate and personal in reference to these texts, the wound he describes is primarily one of knowledge in keeping with the generally intellectual character of his mystical theology. For Origen all the interior senses are primarily modes of cognition that give the soul different forms of insight into the mysteries of the Logos. The wound of love is a fissure that opens the soul to the depths of saving *gnōsis*.

Between 390 and 394, Gregory of Nyssa delivered fifteen homilies to his congregation commenting on Song of Songs 1:1 to 6:9.[24] Gregory includes both a general defense of spiritual exegesis in the Prologue to his work, as well as a specific explanation of his own tropics of desire in the first half of the first homily. There is no need to dwell on the general defense, but the discussion of the special principles related to the exegesis of the Song is worthy of investigation.

Before entering upon the "mystical contemplation of the Song of Songs," Gregory, like Origen, warns against those who would approach the mysteries of the book with "passionate, fleshly thoughts" which would "drag the pure words of the Bridegroom and the Bride down to earthly, irrational passions."[25] Also like Origen, he holds that the three books of Solomon (who is a type of Christ) form a pedagogy of the ascent to perfection, with Proverbs marking the first stage, that of the instruction of the infant son through the study of the beauty of Wisdom. Solomon-Christ then instructs the person trained to desire virtue by means of the book of

---

[23]On this conjunction of texts and their mystical use, see Henri Crouzel, "Origines patristiques d'un thème mystique: Le trait et la blessure d'amour chez Origène," *Kyriakon: Festschrift Johannes Quasten*, edited by Patrick Granfield and Josef Jungmann, 2 vols. (Münster: Aschendorff, 1970) 1:11-19.

[24]The text has been edited by Hermann Langerbeck, *Gregorii Nysseni In Canticum Canticorum* (Leiden: Brill, 1960. *Gregorii Nysseni Opera*, Vol. VI). There is an English translation (not always accurate) by Casimir McCambley, *Gregory of Nyssa. Commentary on the Song of Songs* (Brookline: Hellenic College Press, 1987). (In what follows I will note where I am using McCambley's version.) In contrast to Origen, little has been written about this important commentary. The most detailed study is Guido-Innocenzo Gargano, *Le teoria di Gregorio di Nissa sul Cantico dei Cantici. Indagine su alcune indicazioni di metodo esegetico* (Rome: Pontificium Institutum Studiorum Orientalium, 1981).

[25]Ed., 15.4-12 (trans. McCambley, 43).

Ecclesiastes. Finally, he lifts up "the desiring motion of our souls to invisible beauty" and "initiates (*mystagōgei*) the understanding into the divine sanctuary through the Song of Songs."[26]

The movement toward joining, communion or mingling, not union,[27] with God that is the goal of this process of training involves a series of three transformations which Gregory spells out with care. First comes the moral transformation through adherence to Christ's teaching, the presupposition of the proper reading of the Song. The act of interpreting the Song itself involves two other transformations: first, a reversal of gender identities in the divine-human love affair; and finally a metamorphosis of passion. The "soul" who is addressed in Proverbs as a "son" must become the female bride of the Song, just as the feminine divine Wisdom (*Sophia*) becomes the male Bridegroom, the Incarnate Logos. This takes place "so that a person may be espoused to God by becoming a pure virgin instead of a human bridegroom, and, clinging to the Lord, might become one spirit [see 1 Cor. 6:17] through joining with what is pure and passionless. . . ."[28] This gender reversal reflects not so much an emphasis on human passivity in the higher stages of mystical experience (as it might with later mystics) as it does the paradoxes of mystical desire for God. While unrestrained desire is evil in human eros, "passion for bodiless things is passionless," so we should love as strongly and madly as we can on this level.[29]

The Holy of Holies to which the Song of Songs introduces the now female soul is characterized by a transformation of passion that human understanding could never grasp on its own. Gregory's account deserves to be quoted in full:

> The most acute physical pleasure (I mean erotic pleasure) is used mysteriously in the exposition of these teachings. It teaches us the need for the soul to reach out to the divine nature's invisible beauty and to love it as much as the body

---

[26]Ed., 21.15-22.17 (trans. McCambley, 46).

[27]Gregory describes this joining as a *syzygia* (ed., 15.15 and 24.20), *anakrasis* (ed., 23.1), *synapheia* (ed., 28.22), or *koinōnia* (ed., 109.1), but never as a *henōsis*, the term for indistinct union with the One that he would have known from his reading of Plotinus.

[28]Ed., 23.3-6.

[29]Ed., 23.6-12. The key phrase translated here is *kai apathes epi tōn asōmatōn to pathos* (23.10).

is inclined to love what is akin and like itself. The soul must transform passion into passionlessnesss so that when every corporeal affection has been quenched, our mind may seeth with passion for the spirit alone and be warmed by the fire which the Lord came to cast on earth [Lk. 12:49].[30]

This appeal to "passionless passion" or "erotic apatheia" is a typical mystical oxymoron. Such reversals of ordinary language are inscripted into the whole Song of Songs, because in teaching mortification of the impulses of the flesh in this book Solomon-Christ does not use the direct language of prohibition, but "he disposes the soul to be attentive to purity through words which seem to indicate the opposite."[31] What is the reason for this odd teaching device? Gregory's answer is that this best conforms with the central meaning of all loving experience of God's presence in Christ by highlighting the fact that such an *aisthésis theou*, or "perception of the divine," is always a paradoxical state in which enjoyment or pleasure is also simultaneously unceasing desire for more. Moses (Gregory's exemplar for the mystical path in his *Life of Moses*), as well as the bride of the Song, continue to seek God at the very same moment as they are enjoying his kiss: "So it is with all others in whom the desire for God is deeply embedded -- they never cease to desire, but every enjoyment of God they turn into the kindling of a still more intense desire."[32] This notion, which Gregory called *epektasis*, that is, the constant movement forward of the soul into an ever-deeper encounter with God, both in this life and in the next, is found in almost all Christian mystics, but nowhere more powerfully than in the bishop of Nyssa.[33]

Gregory adopted Origen's teaching about the spiritual senses, but very much to his own ends. In turning to the actual exegesis of Song of Songs 1:2-4 in the second part of the Homily 1, he begins by

---

[30]Ed., 27.5-15 (trans. McCambley, 49).

[31]Ed., 29.2-10 (trans. McCambley, 50).

[32]Ed., 32.2-5 (trans. McCambley, 51).

[33]For some major appearances in the *Comm. in Cant. Cant.*, see, e.g., Hom. 5 (ed., 119); Hom. 6 (ed., 174-83), Hom. 8 (ed., 245-47); Hom. 12 (ed., 353-57). Gregory often employed Philippians 3:13 as a key prooftext for this teaching. The significance of *epektasis* for Gregory's thought was first stressed by Jean Daniélou in his groundbreaking work, *Platonisme et théologie mystique: Doctrine spirituelle de Saint Grégoire de Nysse* (Paris: Aubier, 1944).

identifying the fountain of spiritual life with the Bridegroom's mouth which humans desire to kiss in order to attain salvation (Sg. 1:2a). This sense image, and the following one of the Groom's breasts "better than wine" (Sg. 1:2b), prompt the comment that the "philosophy of this book" indirectly teaches that perception is twofold—bodily and divine. Gregory illustrates the "analogy between the activities of the soul and the sense organs of the body" by appealing to a variety of spiritual senses found in the opening verses of the Song.[34]

The tasting of the milk from the divine breasts indicates the primacy of Christ's teaching over all human knowledge.[35] The scent of the Bridegroom's ointments (Sg., 1:3a) refers to the eminence of his virtues. The verse "Your name is as ointment poured forth" (Sg. 1:3b) is read as the perfume of divinity whose traces we detect from creation, but which really "transcends every name and thought."[36] Thus the bishop of Nyssa's use of the spiritual senses, like those of many other Christian mystics, involves a synaesthesia, or mingling of the sense images, by which one sense takes on the characteristics of another.

This is well illustrated in the remainder of his commentary in the Homily as Gregory melds the *smell* of the perfume of the divine nature in creation with the *sight* of divine traces in the universe as a springboard for a discussion of the invisible Beauty of the Word which the "young maidens" of Song 1:3b-4a draw to themselves by their desire. This combination of sense images allows an entry for Gregory's favorite theme of *epektasis* and a concluding invocation of the sense of *touch*. The young maidens, "stretch out to what is ahead, forgetting what is behind" (Phil. 3:13), while the more perfect soul of the bride herself, "having stretched forward more earnestly to what is ahead," has already entered into the King's bedchamber and touched him with the lips of her prayer (Sg. 1:4a).[37] The latter portion of this first Homily, then, reveals how Gregory used the exegetical tools created by

---

[34]Ed., 34.1-6 (the translated passage is from McCambley, 52).
[35]Ed., 35.3-15.
[36]Ed., 36.12-38.2.
[37]Ed., 39.9-40.12.

Origen, but gave them his own stamp through his erotic trope of epektetic mystical paradox.

The same transformative process can be found in his exegesis of the "wound of love" in Song 2:5. Following Origen, Gregory collates the Song's "wound of love" with the "chosen arrow" of Isaiah, but he gives the theme a more explicit trinitarian meaning than Origen had. God the Father, who is Love, sends his Arrow, the Only-Begotten Son, whose triple point (faith, hope and charity) has been dipped in the Holy Spirit, into the believer's heart. When both the Divine Arrow and Divine Archer have entered the heart, the Bride breaks out into praise of "the beautiful wound and sweet blow by which Life penetrates within."[38] Gregory delights in playing with the polyvalent symbolism of the Song here. The wounding imagery by which the right and left hands of the Archer send love into the human heart merge with the nuptial imagery of the following verse (Sg. 2:6), "His left hand is under my head, and his right hand shall embrace me." "God is both the Bridegroom and the Archer," Gregory says. When Divine Love has entered the soul, she herself can become an arrow directed back at God by God. Because God is both the source of our flight to him and the goal towards which we fly, "Simultaneously I am carried away by his act of shooting and I am at rest in the hands of the Bowman."[39] The gist of this teaching, then, is pure *epektasis*, that is, the loving soul is always both at rest in God and flying forward toward the ineffable goal that continues to elude her.

Two Latin Commentators

In the second decade of the twelfth century, the young Cistercian abbot, Bernard of Clairvaux, shared time in the monastic infirmary with his friend the somewhat older Benedictine abbot, William of Saint Thierry. During this enforced period of rest and conversation, they created a new erotic interpretation of the Song, which, though deeply endebted to

---

[38]Ed., 128.3 (trans. McCambley, 103).
[39]Ed., 129.14-16 (trans. McCambley, 104).

Origen, marked a significant turning point in the history of Western mysticism.[40]

Bernard certainly knew Origen, as a glance at his first sermon on the Song, in which he discusses the three books of Solomon, indicates.[41] He also used Ambrose and Gregory the Great, but not Gregory of Nyssa whose commentary had not been translated into Latin. Unlike Origen and Gregory, Bernard does not begin his famous commentary, the eighty-six *Sermons on the Song of Songs*, with an explicit explanation of his tropics of desire.[42] Though the Cistercian abbot is among the greatest of the medieval tropological, or moral-mystical, exegetes, he provides few explicit discussions of his hermeneutical principles.[43] In studying the first six sermons of Bernard's commentary (all eighty-six only get as far as Song 3:4), we can, nonetheless, discern the main lines of the Cistercian abbot's principles for the proper exegesis of the song of love.[44] Bernard frames his solution to the problem of the erotic language of the Song within the wider issue of the use of anthropomorphic language in the Bible and what this means for Christian understanding of salvation. How can God who is a pure

---

[40]The story of this discussion is found in William's *Vita Prima Bernardi* 12.59 (PL 185:259BC). This conversation appears to have been the initiation for the work known as the *Brevis commentatio super Cantica Canticorum*, which William compiled from his reminiscences and from written sources of his own and of Bernard. See Thomas X. Davis, "A Further Study of the *Brevis commentatio*," *Bernardus Magister: Papers Presented at the Nonacentenary Celebration of the Birth of Bernard of Clairvaux, Kalamazoo, Michigan*, edited by John R. Sommerfeldt (Kalamazoo: Cistercian Publications, 1992) 187-202.

[41]Bernard, *Super Cantica* 1.1-3 (*Opera omnia* 1:3-4).

[42]I have treated Bernard's exegesis of the Song in greater detail in chapter 5 of my book *The Growth of Mysticism. Gregory the Great through the Twelfth Century* (New York: Crossroad, 1994). There is a large literature on these sermons; here I mention only the excellent study of Michael Casey, *Athirst for God. Spiritual Desire in Bernard of Clairvaux's Sermons on the Song of Songs* (Kalamazoo: Cistercian Publications, 1987).

[43]In *Super Cantica* 23, however, he does interpret the three places of the soul's encounter with the divine Bridegroom (i.e., the garden, the storerooms, and the bed chamber of Sg. 5:1, 1:3 and 3:4) as representing the three levels of access to God found in the biblical text: Hortus est historicus sensus, cellarium moralis intellectus, cubiculum spiritualis vel mysticus (cf. SC 23.1 [*Opera omnia* 1:140]). For a brief summary of Bernard's exegesis, see Dennis Farkasfalvy, "The Role of the Bible in Bernard's Spirituality," *Analecta Sacri Ordinis Cisterciensis* 25(1969): 3-13.

[44]Bernard also has a rich, if diffuse, doctrine of the spiritual senses, which cannot be taken up here. For some remarks, see *The Growth of Mysticism*, 209-10.

Spirit be spoken of in a human way, as the Old Testament does on almost every page? Not only does the Bible speak of the Blessed One as acting in ways that humans do, but also as possessing hands and feet, head and lips—and in the Song of Songs more besides. Bernard's first explanation, given in Sermon 4, is typical of most Jewish and Christian reponses. "God has a mouth by which he teaches humanity knowledge, a hand by which he provides nourishment to all flesh, he has feet whose footstool is the earth. . . . God has all these things, I say, not naturally, but effectively" [that is, by reason of what he does].[45] But the Abbot is not satisfied with this answer, and herein lies his originality. Sermons 5 and 6 develop a new, Christological response to this issue which goes to the heart of Bernard's theology.

Human beings, though a union of matter and spirit, were created to have access to the pure Spirit that is God. Since the Fall, this access is blocked. We are enslaved to materiality and sensual carnality. God's response, effected through the Incarnation, is to offer a new route, the only one now possible, back to him. "He offered his flesh," says Bernard, "to those who knew only flesh so that through it they might come to know spirit too."[46] Therefore, now God in the person of the Incarnate Word has head, feet and hands, not only metaphorically, but also literally. The historical deeds of Jesus, as recorded in the Gospels, are the starting point of the process of salvation. We have to begin on the level of what Bernard called the *amor carnalis Christi*, that is, the carnal love of Jesus the perfect model of human humility, love and self-sacrifice in order to return to God.

In contrast to Origen and Gregory, therefore, Bernard gives carnal or physical love a foundational role in his mystical itinerary. Materiality is not merely to be rejected; rather, a redirected form of carnal love, that which is emotionally attracted to Christ's human life, is the beginning of the mystical ascent to God. The application of this principle to the erotic descriptions of

---

[45]Bernard of Clairvaux, *Super Cantica* 4.4 (*Opera omnia* 1:20): *Sed enim et os habet Deus quo docet hominem scientiam, et manum habet qua dat escam omni carni, et pedes habet quorum terra scabellum est. . . . Haec, inquam, habet Deus omnia per effectum, non per naturam.*

[46]Bernard, *Super Cantica* 6.3 (*Opera omnia* 1:27): *Obtulit carnem sapientibus carnem, per quam discernet sapere et spiritum.*

the Song of Songs allows for new dynamics in the tropics of desire, especially evident in Bernard's willingness to linger over the images of kiss, embrace, wound, and the like, in a way that is highly affective in tone, both in its starting place, that is, as it relates to the believer's devotion to the events of Christ's life, and in its conclusion, namely, in the descriptions of the transformed affectivity of the mystical marriage between God and the soul that is the goal of the Christian life as a foretaste of heaven.

The second major element in Bernard's reading of the Song is his emphasis on the necessity for personal experience in understanding all scripture, but especially the Song of love. "Only anointing [by the Spirit] teaches a Song of this kind; only experience really learns it. Let those who have had the experience realize it; let those who have not burn with desire not so much to learn about it as to have it."[47] He begins his exegesis of Song 1:1 in Sermon 3 with the famous proclamation: *Hodie legimus in libro experientiae* ("Today we read in the book of experience"). Neither Origen nor Gregory had neglected the role of the reader's experience in appropriating the inner meaning of the Song, but Bernard and his followers placed the *liber experientiae* at the center of their reading, elevating it to a correlative position with that of the biblical text itself. In his sermons, the abbot continually strives to locate his reader *between* the book of scripture and the book of experience, inviting her or him to compare one with the other to draw out deeper meanings from both. To give just one example, consider the passage from Sermon 9, where Bernard, in discussing the kiss that the Bride receives while speaking to the Divine Lover (still commenting on Song 1:1), says: "Such is the power of that holy kiss that as soon as she has received it, the Bride conceives, and her breasts overflow copiously, bearing witness with an abundance of milk. Those who try to pray frequently will have experience of what I say."[48] In other words, the experience of

---

[47]Bernard, *Super Cantica* 1.11 (*Opera omnia* 1:7): *Istiusmodi canticum sola unctio docet, sola addiscit experientia. Experti recognoscant, inexperti inardescant desiderio, non tam cognoscendi quam experiendi.*

[48]Bernard, *Super Cantica* 9.7 (*Opera omnia* 1:46): *Tantae nempe efficaciae osculum sanctum est, ut ex ipso mox, cum acceperit illud, sponsa concipiat, tumescentibus nimium uberibus, et lacte quasi pinguentibus in testimonium. Quibus studium est orare frequenter, experti sunt quod dico.*

receiving the kiss in prayer is necessary to unlock the inner meaning of the text of the Song.

These same principles are well illustrated in the abbot's comment on the wound of love of Song of Songs 2:5. Bernard's remarks on this verse are surprising brief. Using the Vulgate text, which reads "because I am sick with love," rather than "because I am wounded by charity" as found in the Old Latin version, he applies the entire verse to the Bride's complaint when she is abandoned by her Divine Lover after the brief experience of the kiss. "When that which is loved is near, love flourishes; when it is absent love is sick. This is only the weariness of impatient desire which necessarily strongly affects the mind of the lover when the one she loves is absent." But Bernard goes on to say more than Origen and Gregory were willing to commit themselves to, at least in direct fashion—"I am telling you of what *I myself* have experienced."[49]

Bernard puts this brief comment in the context of one of the central themes of his mystical teaching, the notion of the "order of charity" (*ordo caritatis*), that is, the proper relation between the affective love of contemplation and the active love of service to others.[50] The abbot prefers the spiritual "fruits and fragrances" he gains through the activity of preaching to others over his own private "pursuit of the delights of contemplation."[51] The Cistercian's comment on Song 2:4, then, brief though it be, provides a helpful insight into key aspects of his mystical thought, especially the necessity for using personal experience in the interpretive process, the recognition that any encounter with the Divine Lover will follow the pattern of an oscillation between brief experiences of presence and more frequent painful absences,[52] and finally, the necessity of balancing affective love and active love in the Christian life.

---

[49]Bernard, *Super Cantica* 51.3 (*Opera omnia* 2:85): *Cum prope est quod amatur, viget amor; languet cum abest. Quod non est aliud, quam taedium quoddam impatientis desiderii, quo necesse est affici mentem vehementer amantis, absente quem amat. . . . Loquor vobis experimentum meum quod expertus sum.*

[50]This is the major theme of *Super Cantica* 50 and 51.1-2 (*Opera omnia* 2:78-85). For a more extended analysis, see *The Growth of Mysticism*, 217-23.

[51]*Super Cantica* 51.3 (*Opera omnia* 2:86).

[52]On this theme in the *Super Cantica*, see Casey, *Athirst for God*, chap. 6.

At the end of this brief treatment in Sermon 51, however, Bernard reminds his audience that he had previously treated this verse differently in his treatise *On Loving God*. When we turn to this text, we find that it emphasizes the other component of Bernard's new form of reading noted above, that is, carnal love for the flesh of Christ. In *On Loving God* the abbot employs the Old Latin version rather than the Vulgate (i.e., "I am wounded by charity") and thus can read the text as a reference to the wound that all good Christians feel when they behold Jesus on the Cross pierced and dying for their salvation.[53] Despite the brevity of these two passages, Bernard's interpretation of the wound of love gives us a good insight into his distinctive form of the tropics of desire.

Bernard's friend William of Saint Thierry finally attained his longtime desire to become a Cistercian in 1135 when he was able to join the abbey of Signy as a simple monk. Here he embarked on his own commentary on the Song, the *Exposition on the Song of Songs*, which he abandoned about 1138 (having reached Song 3:3) when he began his theological dispute with Peter Abelard.[54] Despite its unfinished state, William's commentary is in some ways the most coherent of the four surveyed here, especially because of its Preface which tries to understand the Song as a totality.[55] William begins not from the Origenist distinction between the inner and outer person, but from Augustine's understanding of the difference between use and enjoyment. "For when we love any kind of creature," as he says, "not to use it for you but to enjoy it for itself, love is no longer love but greed or lust or something of the sort, losing the pleasing name of love along with suffering the loss of

---

[53]Bernard, *De diligendo Deo* 7 (*Opera omnia* 3:124).

[54]William had prepared for writing this commentary by compiling two books of excerpts from the commentaries on the Song of Songs by Ambrose and by Gregory the Great (these are available respectively in PL 15:947-2060 and PL 180:41-74). The edition of William's *Expositio* used here is that of J.-M. Déchanet, *Guillaume de Saint-Thierry: Expose sur le Cantique des Cantiques* (Paris: Cerf, 1962. Sources Chrétiennes 82).

[55]In the Preface (*Expositio* 7-9 [ed., 78-82]) William remarks on the genre of the Song of Songs and also divides the text into four songs, each having the same basic fourfold structure (*irritamen amoris-actus purgatorius-epithalamium-accubitus*) (cf. also *Expositio* 28 [ed., 106-08]).

liberty."[56] It is only the action of the Holy Spirit which can set such chained love free and begin to restore our lost likeness to God.

God's speaking in the heart frees love in us, as we are taught in exemplary fashion in the Song of Songs. Like Bernard, William insists that we can only understand the Song if we share the experience of love, and he asks the Holy Spirit to place us within the very conversation between bride and Bridegroom in order to achieve this:

> We beseech You, O Holy Spirit, O Love, that you would fill us with your love, so that we can understand the Song of love, and so that we may be made partakers in some way of the conversation of the bride and the Groom in order to have performed within us what we read about.[57]

This emphasis on the Holy Spirit is characteristic of William's mysticism, which I have elsewhere described as preeminently Spirit-centered.[58] But William is also close to Bernard, not only in his insistence on the reciprocity between the reading of the Song and the believer's personal experience,[59] but also in his recognition of the role of the *amor carnalis Christi*.[60]

Although he makes a few remarks on the literal meaning of the text and occasionally refers to the ecclesiological inter-pretation, William's *Exposition*, even more than Bernard's commentary, concentrates on the *moralis sensus*, that is, how the book tells the story of the soul's continuous movement between experiences of delight in the Divine Lover's presence and periods of absence in which she must be cleansed of vices and adorned with the virtues that make her acceptable for "the mystical drawing

---

[56]*Expositio* n.2 (ed., 72): Cum enim amamus quamcumque creaturam, non ad utendum ad te, sed ad fruendum in se, fit amor jam non amor, sed cupiditas, vel libido, sive aliquod hujusmodi, cum damno libertatis, perdens etiam gratiam nominis...This doctrine of use and enjoyment depends on Augustine, *De doctrina christiana* 1.3-5 and 22-35.

[57]William, *Expositio* 4 (ed., 74):. . . *sancte Spiritus, te invocamus, ut amore tuo repleamur, o amor, ad intelligendum canticum amoris; ut et nos colloquii Sponsi et Sponsae, aliquatenus efficiamur participes; ut agatur in nobis quod legitur a nobis.*

[58]See *The Growth of Mysticism*, chap. 6.

[59]See, for example, *Expositio* 12 (ed., 84), where William begins to discuss how the three states of prayer are revealed in the Song.

[60]See, for example, *Expositio* 16-18 (ed., 88-92).

together of divine and human joining" (*mysticum contractum divinae et humanae conjunctionis*).[61]

William's choice of vocabulary for this goal is interesting. Though he agrees with Origen that all the names for love (*amor-caritas-dilectio*) effectively mean the same thing,[62] he makes an effort to distinguish between normal erotic language and the special erotic vocabulary of the Song of Songs. Thus, the Song uses *accubitus* (literally, "lying toward or near," Sg. 1:11) rather than *concubitus* ("lying with or next to").[63] He also gives special weight to the term *conjunctio* as signifying the kind of union which is suggested by the physical experience of the kiss, but which finds its true reality only on the spiritual level.[64] William seems more concerned than the other commentators with marking out a separate domain for spiritual erotic language.

We may well wonder, then, why God chose to use erotic language at all. Like Origen and the other commentators, William is not willing to give up eros to those who have misunderstood or misused it. Towards the end of the Preface to the *Exposition*, he gives an original defense of scripture's use of erotic language. Since no one can always live on the highest, or spiritual, level in this life, William argues, it is part of the divine economy that prayer will be aided at times by images that help the soul's upward journey. Because we are accustomed to the sight of bodily things, these images bear the spirit of the one who prays onward toward the truth. He concludes:

> Therefore, the Holy Spirit, being about to hand over to humans the Song of spiritual love, clothed a work that is inwardly totally spiritual and divine with images of carnal love on the outside. Since only love itself fully understands divine things, the love of the flesh must be drawn to and changed into the love of the spirit so that it may quickly grasp what is like itself.[65]

---

[61]William, *Expositio* 8 (ed., 80).

[62]William, *Expositio* n. 6 (ed., 78).

[63]William, *Expositio* 7 (ed., 78-80). See also *Expositio* 74-76 and 147 (ed., 184-90 and 312-14).

[64]William, *Expositio* 30 and 95 (ed., 112-14 and 220-22).

[65]William, *Expositio* 24 (ed., 100): *Ideo Spiritus sanctus, canticum amoris spiritualis traditurus hominibus, totum spirituale vel divinum ejus interius*

It seems that William was not so much concerned with the paradox of using carnal terms to describe what is spiritual, as Gregory of Nyssa was, but rather with what we might call their pedagogic necessity.

In practice, William's exegesis of the Song uses most of the tropes that we have already seen, including the invocation of the spiritual senses.[66] Given his practice of organizing the text of the Song into separate pericopes or songs, however, what is perhaps most distinctive about his reading is his tendency to recapitulate the soul's itinerary, especially its oscillation between presence and absence, in each section. A consideration of his treatment of Song 2:5 will bring this out.

This verse, which William reads according to the Vulgate text (*quia amore langueo*), occurs in the *epithalamium* section of what William identifies as the first song.[67] The King, that is, the Bridegroom, brings the soul into the wine cellar (Sg. 2:4a) when he feeds her love and affection. The wine cellar is to be identified with "our little flowery bed" (*lectulus floridus noster*; Sg. 1:15b) understood as the perfect good conscience where everything is converted into wine by the fire of the Holy Spirit.[68] The joy of the Holy Spirit which is the wine of the cellar leads to mystical inebriation. In this state, "at the first experiences of that good, [the soul] cannot bear with either measure or reason, due to the abundance of the wine, and she abandons order in favor of the drunkenness of exceeding fervor and the sickness of that human weakness that faints for God's salvation."[69]

---

negotium, exterius vestivit carnalis amoris imaginibus; ut cum non nisi amor plene capiat quae sunt divina, adducendus et migraturus amor carnis in amorem spiritus, cito apprehenderet sibi similia. . . .

[66]For some remarks on William's use of the spiritual senses, see James Walsh, "Guillaume de Saint-Thierry et les sens spirituels," *Revue d'ascétique et de mystique* 35(1959):7-42.

[67]Following the editor, Fr. Déchanet, we can identify the first song as consisting of the following parts: *praeludium*; *irritamen amoris* (Sg. 1:1-6); *actus purgatorius* (Sg. 1:7-2:3); *epithalamium* (Sg. 2:4-5); *accubitus* (Sg. 2:6); and *finale* (Sg. 2:7-8a). The *epithalamium* of the first song occupies nn. 114-131 (ed., 250-80) of Déchanet's edition.

[68]William, *Expositio* 115-16 (ed., 250-52).

[69]William, *Expositio* 120 (ed., 258): . . . sed ad primas boni illius experientias, modi et rationis impatiens a vini copia exordinatur usque ad ebrietatem nimii fervoris, usque ad languorem infirmitatis humanae deficientis in salutare Dei.

In analyzing the sickness of the soul which has experienced too much of the Spirit's wine, William goes on to distinguish two forms of such malady. The first is the madness of love in which the soul conceives a hatred of its own life, desiring rather to die and to be with Christ, and therefore becomes confused about the proper relation between love of God and love of neighbor. The second form of illness is an imbalance in the relation of the faculties of memory, understanding and willing that takes place when memory is remiss, flitting here and there and impeding the transformation of the understanding into love.[70] The soul who suffers this, whose love is therefore prevented from flying up to its true home, should respond by pouring "herself out wholly upon her neighbor," loving all the goodness seen in other souls, even if they are not as advanced as she is.[71] This movement of active love helps begin to reestablish the *ordo caritatis* which is also the "rightful goal of languishing love," so that William can summarize by saying: "He whose charity is well-ordered loves the Lord his God, and himself in him, and his neighbor as himself—with a love of the same quality and quantity."[72]

Thus, the *epithalamium* section commenting on Song 2:4-5 provides a picture in miniature of the soul's progress, at least in its higher stages. The bride is first brought into the wine cellar, that is, is given the experience of divine love that leads her to a state of inebriation and confusion. One aspect of this confusion is to lead her to a return to active charity in which she no longer has a sense of direct divine presence but in which she practices the virtues that will help her prepare for the next time when the King will intervene to set charity in order in her (Sg. 2:4a) and give her a new experience of union in which: "The one who was drunken becomes sober, the one who was sick becomes whole, the impetuous one is put in order; the drunken one hastens to sleep, the sick one to the flowery bed, the impetuous one to the embrace—and thus there is

---

[70]The interpenetration of understanding and love, expressed in the formulas *amor ipse intellectus est* and *intellectus amoris*, is among the most important themes in William's mystical thought. See *The Growth of Mysticism*, 250-60.

[71]William, *Expositio* 122-23 (ed., 264-70).

[72]William, *Expositio* 127-28 (ed., 272-74; the passage cited is on 274): *Sic qui ordinatae caritatis est, diligit Dominum Deum suum, et in ipso seipsum, et proximum suum sicut seipsum, ipsa qualitate, ipsa quantitate.*

the most delightful joining of bride and Groom."[73] The passionate and yet penetrating character of William's systematic use of the tropics of desire is well set forth in this extended treatment.

This brief comparison of four examples of mystical interpretation of the erotic language of the Song of Songs has attempted to present what the exegetes thought they were doing and what principles they set down to guide their interpretive task. Although these mystics shared a common approach to reading the Song and made use of many of the same tropes, their theological applications reveal significant nuances and differences. It is only by studying a much wider range of their erotic imagery that we might arrive a full sense of the classical Christian "tropics of desire."

I will close with a brief reflection on the possible contemporary meaning of such readings of the Bible's great Song of love. Modern readers who find it hard to imagine how the traditional Christian interpretations of the Song of Songs could so easily pass over the human concrete and physical eroticism of the book in favor of the spiritual reading live in a different textual (and sexual) world than did our ancestors. The differences in the contemporary textual world—given the influence of hermeneutical theories like those of Hans-Georg Gadamer and Paul Riceour—are perhaps not as great as the sexual ones. The fundamental divide here is that the ancient biblical interpreters, both Jews and Christians, were convinced that eros was more than sexuality.

Many moderns find no reason at all for admitting any eros beyond the *EROS II* mentioned above and see any attempt to do so either as a dangerous deception or else possibly as an act of sexual oppression. Even those who may admit that physical libido is not the source and meaning of all eros, still find it hard to agree with the mystical interpreters that transcendental *EROS I* can be best attained by the denial of human erotic love.[74] But is there nothing at all to be discovered in these ancient readings aside from insight into a chapter in the history of Christian exegesis and the story of

---

[73]William, *Expositio* 130 (ed., 276): . . . *ebriusque fit sobrius, languens fit sanus, et vehemens ordinatus, ebrius festinat ad somnum, languens ad lectum floridum, vehemens ad amplexum; sicque Sponsi et sponsae juncundissima conjunctio fit.*

[74] For some reflections on this problematic, see Bernard McGinn, "Mysticism and Sexuality," *Celibacy. The Way Supplement* 77(1993): 46-54.

Christian mysticism? I would submit that there is much, but here I will limit myself to one suggestion. The Christian mystical interpreters were convinced that the transformation of eros implied that gender-identity (as distinct from sex-specification) needed to become more malleable than society usually allowed in order to appreciate dimensions of eros that were not restricted to ordinary sexuality. This also meant, of course, that women could not be excluded from playing an important part in the exploration of the tropics of desire. Although the four figures investigated here were all men, a fuller exploration of the Christian mystical tradition, especially after 1200 when the historical record becomes more extensive, would show that the Song of Songs remained a prism for focussing on the meaning of eros for women as much as for men. The exploration of the true meaning of eros still remains the common task of all those who believe, along with Origen and his successors, that to call God love (*amor/eros*) is not really different from calling God charity (*caritas/agapé*).

HOW TO READ THE BIBLE
According to John of La Rochelle

Girard J. Etzkorn

St. Bonaventure University

In today's world, we seem to be witness to a wide gap between highly-trained and sophisticated biblical scholars[1] and a deeply-rooted fundamentalism. The former include those who can read the languages of biblical times with ease as well as those scholars who can decipher a text found in the Dead Sea Scrolls. The fundamentalists are found in virtually every religious sect and show a decided penchant toward taking everything literally, often coupled in many Christian denominations with a fascination for the Book of Revelation.

Since this article makes no pretense at academic profundity, perhaps I may be indulged a personal anecdote. When my son Kevin was about six years old, the mother of a family whom we had befriended—the mother was a Pentecostal—asked if Kevin might read the Bible with them. I consented with the proviso that there be no proselytizing (not thinking that this might not be understood). After several readings of the Bible with the family, my son came home and announced that only 50,000 people would ever get to heaven. End of that genre of Bible reading sessions!

It may not be too much off the mark to claim that such a gap between highly-sophisticated scholars and fundamentalist literalists was not so wide in the Middle Ages. Or to put it another way, there was certainly a framework of interpretation available whereby the teachers could aid the beginners (and the funda-

---

[1] In my rather tangential and incidental acquaintance with modern biblical scholarship, I find it disappointing and regretable that they seem to know so little about medieval biblical interpretation, an ignorance—in my view—that impoverishes their approach to the Scriptures. It is worthy of note that many scriptural commentaries of medieval authors are still found only in manuscripts and await good critical editions.

mentalists, if they could be so persuaded) to understand the Bible and derive the most from its multi-faceted messages. It was the message of the Good News that preoccupied the theologians of the Middle Ages. To borrow a Gertrude Steinian tactic: the message is the message is the message. This was true, in spite of (or perhaps because of) the fact that few medieval Christian scholars knew Greek or Hebrew and a comparably small number of Jewish scholars knew Latin. Hence, they generally lacked the ability to do etymological analyses and it is commonly conceded that they had little sense of historical context, believing as they did that over the centuries Jews, Greeks, and Latins had a common mental 'language' even though they spoke differently. While this may have been a defect in their hermeneutical skills, it may explain in part their preoccupation with teaching and preaching the message.

A remarkably gifted teacher was the Franciscan theologian and summist John of La Rochelle.[2] Although frequently adumbrated by his colleague, Alexander of Hales, John nevertheless made significant contributions, not only to the famous *Summa Fratris Alexandri*, but also by composing many philosophical and theological treatises of his own making.[3]

John had a genius for organization and clear presentation. Because of his flair for synthesizing and orderly presentation, coupled with an ample array of mnemonic devices,[4] his students were given the keys to biblical treasures. However, we would be remiss if we did not quickly add here that for John of La Rochelle, in the same vein as his illustrious successor Bonaventure, theology

---

[2] For a brief summary of John's life and works, see my article "John of La Rochelle's View of Christ as King, Teacher and Priest," in *Franciscan Christology*, 40-46.

[3] He is credited with *summae* on the soul, on virtues, on vices, on the articles of faith and on the sacraments. While many of La Rochelle's views and writings have been incorporated into the *Summa Fratris Alexandri* (of Hales), many of his treatises must still be edited critically.

[4] Such organizational and mnemonic devices were particularly important in the Middle Ages, since students were required to have extraordinary audial (not optical) memories in order to follow and retain what they heard from their teachers. Manuscripts were rare and expensive. Classroom devices for writing were limited, for the most part, to wax tablets. Needless to say, the atrophying of audial memory in contemporary students and teachers is proportionately disastrous to their ignorance of the need thereof.

and the study of Scripture was not simply an exercise in intellectual acumen, whose sole purpose was to provide insight. Rather knowledge was meant to edify and to lead to wisdom, to effect growth in affectivity which knows how to love both God and humankind with discretion (in the medieval sense of the term, i. e. prudent judgmental discrimination). The Bible, then, —let it be said—was a means for understanding the heritage of faith and putting its tenets into practice. As we have said, it was the meaning of the text for thought and behavior that preoccupied the great theologians of the Middle Ages. Mere etymological archeology was simply pedantry if the message were neglected.

John's approach to the Bible is exemplified in his *Introduction to Theology*.[5] Commenting on the passage from Revelation 10, 10, *So I took the book from the angel's hand and ate it*, he says:

> Here the Evangelist speaks of the office of the teacher of Sacred Scripture, for which office three things are necessary: knowledge, life and doctrine. . . . Knowledge, which is a gift of grace rather than a result of human curiosity. . . [Life,] because the wise man first assimilates sacred knowledge by his good will and good deeds before he tries to influence others by lecturing or preaching. . . Prophecy signifies the office of doctrine.

John of La Rochelle's flair for organization and clear presentation is beautifully exemplified in his treatise on *The Introduction to the Four Gospels*.[6] Having made the claim that the best way to understand the Old Testament was to begin with the study of the Gospels, John introduces his treatise with a passage from Ezekiel[7] describing the vision of the four-faced winged

---

[5]Ioannes de Rupella, *Generalis Introitus ad Sacram Doctrinam*, ed. F. Delorme in *La France Franciscaine*, 16 (1933) : 347.

[6]G. Etzkorn, "John of La Rochelle's View of Christ as King, Teacher and Priest," in *Franciscan Christology*, ed. D. McElrath (St. Bonaventure, New York: 1980) 40-46.

[7]Ezekiel 1, 10: "As far as the appearance of their faces, each had the face of a man, yet each of the four looked like a lion when seen from the right, like an ox when seen from the left, like an eagle when seen from above." Ezech. 1, 6-8: "Each had four faces and two pairs of wings. Either leg was straight-formed, yet ended in a calf's hoof. On each of the four sides, human hands showed beneath the wings."

'creature': the face of a man, a lion, an ox and an eagle. This is almost immediately related, traversing the Bible full circle as it were, to a vision from Revelation.[8] And so, drawing on his Christian tradition and principally on Augustine, John relates each of the creatures to one of the Gospels which variously portray the person and the message of Christ, the central figure of all the Gospels. Hence, the approach is frankly Christocentric. The lion symbolizes Christ as King of creation as emphasized by the Gospel of Matthew. The man is a symbol of Christ's humanity as the theme of Mark's Gospel. The calf or ox is related to the Gospel of Luke which portrays Christ as priest and victim. Thus, the synoptic Gospels concentrate on Christ's humanity. The fourth symbol, the eagle, is obviously reserved to the Gospel of John who focussed on the divinity of Jesus. The insight of the beloved Evangelist is illustrated in delightful fashion by the legend of the father eagle who takes the eaglets aloft in his claws to gaze at the sun, and if they blink, he promptly drops them as illegitimate!

The synoptic Gospels in their preoccupation with the humanity of Christ are compared to the active powers of the soul and symbolized by Jacob's first wife, Lea. The Gospel of John is compared to the contemplative power of the soul and symbolized by Jacob's 'favorite' wife, Rachel.

Having assigned the four faces of the vision to the four Gospels, La Rochelle goes on to remark that, of course, the man might well symbolize the Gospel of Matthew and the lion that of the Gospel of Mark, but he goes on to prefer the first assignation. In all of this, John is quite frankly and obviously dependent on the tradition he inherited from the Fathers of the Church and the glosses on Scripture.

Returning to his preferred assignation, the Franciscan theologian proceeds to relate the three synoptic Gospels to three prerogatives of Christ's activity as man: the lion (Matthew) symbolizing his kingly power, the man (Mark) his wisdom as teacher and the ox (Luke) his role as priest and suffering servant. Naturally, the Gospel of John signifies the divinity of Christ, particularly his contemplative insight as symbolized by the eagle.

---

[8]Rev. 4, 7: "The first figure was that of a lion, the second that of an ox, the third had a man's look, and the fourth was that of an eagle in flight."

Having completed his analysis of how the four Gospels differ, La Rochelle now turns to show how they agree among themselves. He continues to employ a fourfold division and relates it to the vision of Ezekiel in the text with which he began his treatise. Here John begins to teach his students the interpretative framework with which to approach the reading of the Bible. There is no studied attempt at originality; rather John is content to be the conduit of the wisdom of the past in handing down (*traditio*) and organizing his intellectual and spiritual inheritance.

In the vision of Ezekiel, according to La Rochelle, the face refers to the literal meaning of the Scriptures, and since each had four faces, the literal sense comprises four modes of expression, namely historical, prophetic, proverbial and didactic. The historical mode is primordial, the latter three incidental. History is simply the narration of deeds. Prophecy is the divinely-inspired revelation of hidden past, present, and future things. Proverbial expression is the use of figurative speech. Finally, the didactic mode refers to the teaching of faith and morals whether by positive command or negative prohibition, whether by persuasion or dissuasion.

The wings in the winged-effigies of Ezekiel's vision are made to symbolize allegorical passages found in the bible. Here we fly aloft, as it were, on the wings of poetic imagination. Like the literal sense, allegory has four distinct modes of expression, i.e. transference, imagination, comparison, and proverb. Transference is essentially La Rochelle's term for anthropomorphism, namely attributing human characteristics to non-humans. In the search for causes, says John borrowing from Iunilius,[9] the Scriptures attribute movements of the soul, such as anger or remembering, to God. Similarly, the Bible often ascribes bodily members or functions to the divinity. We find, for example, passages refering to the 'right hand of the Lord' or the 'eye of God' or pleas are made in the Psalms that God should 'bend an ear' to the pleas of the one who prays. The imaginary mode of expression is found when a real person or thing is alluded to by way of an imaginary person or thing. The

---

[9]Ioannes de Rupella, *Introitus in Quattuor Evangelia*, ed. G. Etzkorn, *op. cit.*, 54-56: "Translatio est cum animae motus sive humana membra 'ad insinuandas causas transferúntur ad Deum' [Iunilius]."

examples of the steward of the vineyard and the good Samaritan
are adduced as illustrations of this imaginary mode of allegory.
The comparative mode of expression is found in passages which
make relations between things, events or persons. The text of Matt.
13: 31 The kingdom of heaven. . . is like a grain of mustard seed is
adduced as a case in point. Although John does not say so, the
proverbial mode of expression is not easily distinguished from the
comparative mode—perhaps he saw no point in confusing beginning
students of the Scriptures—and he simply refers to the proverb of
the false shepherd who sneaks into the sheepfold to steal and
plunder (John 10, 1).

Each effigy in the vision had four hands and since in the
human context, it is often the hands whereby we do things, it is
appropriate that the hands symbolize the moral sense of the
Scriptures. As with the literal and allegorical senses, the moral
has four modes of expression to which, says John borrowing from
Pseudo-Jerome,[10] four qualities are associated. The precepts have to
do with justice, charity is associated with mandates, good example
is expressive of perfection and testimony is witness to faith. Each
of the four modes of moral expression is exemplified by John with
appropriate Scriptural texts. The four modes are further related to
the divinity: precepts as directive are related to the divine
majesty, mandates to the divine goodness, testimony to divine
truth, and example to the second person of the Trinity who became
man to teach us how to behave.

The final bodily members in the vision of Ezekiel were two
straight legs with cloven hooves. According to John, these are
meant to symbolize the teleological aspect of the Scriptures,
namely, the final goal and purpose of creation. Not unsurprisingly,
this goal is twofold: namely, the struggle to attain the rectitude
(standing upright and straight-legged) of truth through faith and
the acquisition of twofold charitable affection towards God and
one's fellow human beings.

In this way John of La Rochelle has introduced his students to
an understanding which could aid them in discriminating the
various senses whereby the richly varied meanings of the

---

[10]Ps.-Hieronymus, *Prolog. in Marcum* (PL 30, 590B).

Scriptures can be grasped. As a good teacher, his approach is clear, well-organized and abounding in anecdotes and imagery to aid his listeners' audial and visual memories. John's treatment is frankly Christocentric—let that be called his Christian bias, if you will. While his inability to do philological archeology and his apparent ignorance regarding historical criticism may seem naive to modern Scripture scholars, this is more than compensated by his preoccupation with the fundamental meanings to be retrieved from the biblical texts.

Hence, John of La Rochelle's *Introduction to the Four Gospels* contains a rich harvest which can be gleaned by both the fundamentalists and contemporary Scripture scholars: the former because of the need for a more sophisticated approach to the infinite variety of biblical literature, the latter because of the need to recall that even the most highly erudite hermeneutics ought to have as its final goal the message of the Scriptures.

Images of the Crucified Christ

in Clare of Assisi and Angela of Foligno

Ingrid Peterson, OSF

Tau Center, Winona, MN

This essay surveys images of the Crucified Christ in the writings of Clare of Assisi and Angela of Foligno.[1] Their visions of Christ in the context of the Trinity are examined in light of Bonaventure's understanding of the mystery of Christ as the union of the Word of God with human nature in the historical Jesus of Nazareth.[2] Because of the prominence of the figure of the Crucified Christ in the writings of Clare and Angela, their mysticism is most frequently read in the light of its Christological implications. Yet Christ is presented within the heart of the Trinitarian God in the visionary writings of both Clare and Angela. Bonaventure's work, systematizing a theology with Christ as the center of the Trinity, further develops an understanding of the experience of God articulated by Clare and Angela.

The experience of the crucified Christ in Clare (1193-1253), Angela (1248-1309) and Bonaventure (1221-1274) follows the heritage of Francis of Assisi (1182-1226). Francis's desire to act out the gospel, "to set before our bodily eyes in some way" an external portrait of the first Christmas scene, illustrates his emphasis on visualizing the historical events of Jesus' life. The imprint of the marks of the crucified Christ on Francis's body manifests the centrality of Christ and the cross in his inner life. Bonaventure describes how Francis taught the first brothers who gathered

---

[1] I am indebted to Michael Blastic, OFM Conv., Paul Lachance OFM, and Michaela Eschbacher whose friendship and scholarly critique contributed invaluably to this essay. The insights and knowledge of my students in the course on the Franciscan Mystics during the summer sessions at the Franciscan Institute also enriched me as we worked through Angela's *Memorial* and *Instructions*.

[2] Zachary Hayes, OFM, *The Hidden Center: Spirituality and Speculative Christology in St. Bonaventure* (St. Bonaventure, NY: Franciscan Institute, 1981, 1992 rpt.) 56-57.

around Francis at Rivo Torto to pray by visualizing the cross of Christ, especially because they had no books: Christ's cross was their book and they studied it day and night, at the exhortation and after the example of their father who never stopped talking to them about the cross (*LM, IV.3b*).[3]

Francis's method of prayer as graphic meditation was taken up and appears in the writings of the sisters and brothers who began to follow his teachings. The writings of Clare of Assisi, a Poor Lady of the Second Order, and Angela of Foligno, a widowed lay penitent, provide textual evidence of how God was envisioned by Francis's followers, and how a Franciscan mystical tradition in prayer began to evolve. Their experience of God provided Clare and Angela with content to teach others the progress of the soul's journey. The experience of Francis and the writings of Clare and Angela began to shape a distinctive way to God, later systematized in the writings of Saint Bonaventure, especially in his *Soul's Journey into God*. This comparative study of Angela and Clare's experience of the crucified in the light of Bonaventure's Christology reveals the importance of interpreting their Christology in the context of the Trinity.

While Francis's prayers and biographies indicate that his inner journey was a quest in imitation of the human Christ, his writings and his prayers concern themselves more with the mystery of the Trinitarian God than with the Passion of Christ. Upon receiving the stigmata on LaVerna on September 17, 1224, Francis did not write of Christ's Passion, but composed the *Praises of God* found on the parchment given to Brother Leo. Nguyên-Van-Khanh's thorough study of Francis's Christology concludes

> It is not enough to say that the spirituality of Francis is Christocentric; we need to add that its point of departure is the Holy Spirit and that it is directed to the Father. In the light of the Holy Spirit, through the beloved Son, to the

---

[3] "Major Life of St. Francis," by St. Bonaventure in *St. Francis of Assisi, Writings and Early Biographies; English Omnibus of the Sources for the Life of St. Francis*, Marion A. Habig, ed. (Chicago: Franciscan Herald Press, 1993) 655.

heavenly Father. This is the itinerary that Francis of Assisi followed and that he proposes to all people."[4]

The itinerary followed by Clare and Angela shares some of the same Trinitarian elements, but is much more specific in addressing the crucified Christ.[5] It is these followers of Francis and particularly Bonaventure, who began to develop the passion mysticism of the Franciscan tradition.[6]

This essay turns to the specific writings of Clare and Angela that focus on the passion of Christ and illustrates how Bonaventure's theology articulates their experience of God. Their writings and the religious texts of other medieval men and women demonstrate the inner transformations that flowed from the spiritual exercises practiced during the thirteenth century.[7] Enclosed women, such as Clare, recited the seven canonical hours which followed the liturgical cycle. Women and men involved in the penitential movement performed bodily acts of mortification, including fasting and self-flagellation. Members of lay religious

---

[4]Norbert Nguyên-Van-Khanh, *The Teacher of His Heart; Jesus Christ in the Thought and Writings of St. Francis* (St. Bonaventure, NY: Franciscan Institute, 1994) 244.

[5]In juxtaposing the spiritual journeys of these early Franciscan writers in order to glimpse the emergence of a tradition, it is essential to acknowledge that their writings are presented in different literary genres: many of Francis's prayers are poetry; the spirituality found in Clare's Letters to Agnes employs an epistolary genre which is governed by classical rhetorical theory; Angela is a visionary attempting to be faithful to what was given her by God; and Bonaventure writes as a theologian with a poetic heart. While each genre is defined by its own formal characteristics which provide useful descriptive devices for composition and reading, all are part of the broader stylistic developments of the thirteenth and fourteenth centuries which produced affective, meditative works, representing a visual literary imagination.

[6]Paul Lachance pointed out the need to delineate the individual contributions of Francis, Clare, Angela and Bonaventure in the development of the tradition of a passion mysticism. Bonaventure describes Francis at the time of the vision of the stigmata, "Francis was dumbfounded at the sight and his heart was flooded with a mixture of joy and sorrow. He was overjoyed at the way Christ regarded him so graciously under the appearance of a Seraph, but the fact that he was nailed to a cross pierced his soul with a sword of compassionate sorrow." (*Major Life* XIII.3). *St. Francis of Assisi: Writings and Early Biographies*, ed. Marion Habig, OFM. (Chicago: Franciscan Herald Press, 1972) 730.

[7]Elizabeth A. Petroff, *Medieval Women's Visionary Literature* (New York: Oxford, 1986), provides an excellent introduction to the visionary tradition in women's writing and includes a number of primary texts.

groups, such as the beguines, beghards, and tertiaries performed works of mercy in an effort to respond to society's sick and poor. The illiterate memorized vocal prayers while women and laity unable to read Latin visualized the lives of Jesus and Mary in their devotional prayers, which were often modeled upon the pictorial cycles and panels that decorated the churches and instructed the faithful.

Clare of Assisi's writings are rooted in scripture and the readings used in celebrating the liturgical calendar. Angela of Foligno's writings trace the movement of her spiritual growth from devotional exercises to visionary experiences. As Angela's prayer moved beyond the discursive level, her visionary writings become more detailed, sensuous, and centered on the human and divine body of Christ crucified. So, too, as Clare advanced in imitation of Christ's human experience, she described her participation as mirroring the drama of his passion, death and triumph in God. Both Clare and Angela describe their participation in the life of Christ through imitation of the virtues of poverty, humility, and contempt.[8] Their identity with the suffering of the crucified Christ led them to understand the suffering of their lives and to discover meaning in "feeling what his friends feel (3LAg 14)." In their union with God, Christ's transfixed body becomes their body, so that his triumph over pain and suffering prefigures the transformation of their souls.

In their writings, Clare and Angela both describe their experience of God as a vision of the crucified Christ hidden within the Trinity. For both of these Franciscan mystics, imitation of the humanity of the crucified Christ drew them into the experience of God in which Christ, the Word of God, in Bonaventure's theology is the hidden center. Clare's "glorious vision" of the "heavenly Jerusalem" is the "mirror without blemish" in which she sees the incarnate and crucified Christ. In her *Memorial* and *Instructions*, Angela describes the suffering of the crucified Christ as she

---

[8]Angela repeatedly refers to poverty, humility, and contempt as the "company of Christ," whereas Clare names poverty, humility, and charity as the human virtues necessary to imitate Christ. However, Clare makes frequent reference to the contempt suffered by Christ. In her second letter, Clare directs Agnes of Prague to "Look upon Him Who became contemptible for you, and follow Him, making yourself contemptible in this world and for Him" (2LAg 19).

envisions herself on the "bed of the cross," from which she is drawn into a vision of God as Trinity.

The writings of Clare and Angela reveal an understanding of the divine and human Christ dwelling within the heart of the Triune God. Clare's experience of God in contemplation provides the basis for her spiritual instruction to Agnes of Prague. Clare's Fourth Letter to Agnes of Prague (4LAg), in which she reveals her Christocentric understanding of God, was written in 1253 in her late fifties or at the age of sixty after living forty years in the enclosure of San Damiano. Angela, a lay tertiary, dictated her visionary experiences to Brother A. between 1292 and 1296 in her late fifties. Angela's teachings, preserved as her *Instructions*, were given in Foligno to a group of followers with specific references to the friars. Many of Angela's *Instructions* expand upon the detailed visions of the *Memorial* and are recorded by various redactors between 1296 and the time of her death in 1309.

The Writings of Clare of Assisi:
  Letters, Testament, and Form of Life

In the Fourth Letter to Agnes of Prague, Clare leads Agnes through the following of Christ toward union with God, symbolized through nuptial imagery.[9] Clare introduces four themes to present the mystical journey: singing a new song on Mount Zion, participating in the sacred banquet, becoming a mirror of God who in turn reflects God's goodness to others, and experiencing the embrace and kiss of God.[10] At this stage of the spiritual journey, the inward focus of the soul moves from the self to God, and as the soul passes over into God, the action of the soul is passive. St. Bonaventure describes the transformative journey of the soul to God in his classical mystical treatise, the *Soul's Journey into God*.[11] In

---

[9]See Jean Leclerc, "St Clare and Nuptial Spirituality," trans. Edward Hagman, OFM Cap. *Greyfriars Review* 10.2 (1996): 171-78.

[10]These four themes are named by Sister Pacelli Millane, "The Search for God in the Tradition of St. Clare," unpublished dissertation, Franciscan Institute, St. Bonaventure University, St. Bonaventure, NY, 1994: 50-55.

[11]Two popular English translations of this work appear with different translations of the Latin *mentis*. Philotheus Boehner and M. Francis Laughlin's edition, *Works of Saint Bonaventure*, vol 2 (St. Bonaventure, NY: Franciscan

the Preface, Bonaventure announces that "There is no other path but through the burning love of the crucified." Bonaventure's mystical theology, starting from the crucified seraph and Francis's stigmata, depicts a journey of return to God in the mystery of the Trinity.

The images of God used in Clare's writings are varied and indicate a relationship with each of the persons of the Trinity.[12] In her *Testament*, Clare makes frequent references to God as Father, such as the "Father of Mercies" and glorious Father of Jesus Christ. Sister Agnes, daughter of Messer Oportula de Bernardo of Assisi, mayor of Assisi, said that when she said the Prayer of the Five Wounds of the Lord at Clare's deathbed that Clare "kept the Passion of the Lord on her lips and so the name of the Lord Jesus Christ" (*Proc X. 10*). Both in her Letters to Agnes and in her *Form of Life*, Clare names God as author of salvation, giver of grace, and father of perfection. Clare's early companion, Sister Benvenuta of Lady Diambra of Assisi, said that Clare on her deathbed described her heavenly vision and named seeing the Holy Spirit, the Blessed Virgin and a multitude of virgins (*Proc 11.3-4*).[13]

Clare narrates an experience of the vision of God in her Fourth Letter to Agnes. Because she has "abandoned the vanities of the world," Clare describes the vision awaiting Agnes before the throne of God, the "sacred banquet" of eternity, in which persons who are united to God participate.

Institute, 1956, 1990 rpt.), 105, argue that *mens* refers to the soul with its three powers of memory, intelligence, and will which make it an image of God.

Ewert Cousins's translation in The Classics of Western Spirituality series, *Bonaventure* (New York: Paulist Press, 1978) 21 describes his preference for "soul" because the Latin *mens* is eytomologically linked to our English "mind" but does not connote the fullness of the soul as an image of God. Cousins also argues that in the last phrase of the title Bonaventure does not use the expected phrase *ad Deum*, but rather *in Deum* to indicate that the movement of the soul is not toward God but into God, emphasizing the mystical nature of the entire journey.

[12]10 Jesús Maria Bezunartea, "Clare and the Discernment of Spirits, *Greyfriars Review 8*, Supplement (*1994*): 3-110 and Optatus Van Assoldonk, O.F.M., Cap., "The Spirit of the Lord and Its Holy Activity in the Writings of Francis, *Greyfriars Review* 5 (1991): 103-58, respectively treat the activity of the Spirit in Clare and Francis.

[13]Armstrong, 172-73.

Happy, indeed is she
> to whom it is given to share in this sacred banquet
> so that she might cling with all her heart to Him

Whose beauty all the blessed hosts of heaven
> unceasingly admire
>> Whose affection excites,
>> Whose contemplation refreshes,
>> Whose kindness fulfills,
>> Whose delight replenishes,
>> Whose remembrance delightfully shines,
>> By whose fragrance the dead are revived,
>> Whose glorious vision will bless
>> all the citizens of the heavenly Jerusalem:
>> which, since it is the splendor of eternal glory, is
>> the brilliance of eternal light
>> and the mirror without blemish (4LAg 9-14).

Clare's experience of the Trinitarian God as a "sacred banquet" presents a portrait of "all the blessed hosts of heaven unceasingly" praising God. This is the "glorious vision" that reigns in continual blessing over "all the citizens of the heavenly Jerusalem." Clare perceives a vision of God who "is the splendor of eternal glory," "the brilliance of eternal light," and "the mirror without blemish."

Clare directs Agnes of Prague to the image of Christ incarnate and crucified that is the core of her vision of God and at the same time an image of Agnes's human face. Clare directs Agnes to study her face deep within this glorious vision of God, recognizing there the human virtues of Christ's poverty, humility, and charity. These are the virtues Clare suggests as the object of Agnes's contemplation and imitation. Then Clare instructs Agnes in a method of prayer, beginning by gazing "upon that mirror each day," that will lead her to the crucified Christ, and through him enable her to return to the "ineffable delights" of heaven.

Clare instructs Agnes to begin by looking upon the image of Christ as the visible sign of the invisible God to see "the poverty of Him who was placed in a manger and wrapped in swaddling clothes." As Francis was in awe before the mystery of the incarnation, so Clare utters words of incomprehension that "the Lord of heaven and earth is laid in a manger:"

> O marvelous humility!
> O astonishing poverty (4LAg 20)!

In gazing upon the image of the humanity of Christ, Clare directs Agnes to "consider the holy humility, the blessed poverty, the untold labors and burdens that he endured for the redemption of the whole human race" (4LAg 22). Beyond the mystery of the incarnation by which Christ's divinity took on human flesh, Clare directs Agnes to meditate on the mental and physical sufferings of his lifetime. To gaze on the figure of Jesus is an activity engaging the external senses in meditation on the events and meaning of his suffering and death. As Clare engages Agnes to enter into Christ's passion and death, she invites her to "contemplate the ineffable charity that led Him to suffer on the wood of the Cross and to die there the most shameful kind of death" (4LAg23). Because union with God means participation in the life of God, Clare repeats her dialogue with the image of the crucified Christ:

> Therefore,
> that Mirror,
>> suspended on the wood of the Cross,
>> urged those who passed by to consider, saying:
>>> 'All you who pass by the way,
>>> look and see if there is any suffering
>>> like my suffering!'
>
> Let us respond
>> with one voice,
>> with one spirit,
>> to Him crying and grieving Who said:
>> 'Remembering this over and over
>> leaves my soul downcast within me' (4LAg 24-26).

Clare experiences the crucified Christ at the heart of the vision of the Trinitarian God.[14] Dialogue with the humanity and suffering of Christ becomes the entry point of her total identification with God. Clare sees her own face as she studies the face of the crucified and in her illness anticipates the imminence of her own death. Clare, like the crucified Christ, had endured untold labors and burdens, a lifetime of hardship, suffering, and rejection. In this passage, Clare indicates that she understands, loves, and is united for all eternity to a God who is one like her in all things, a God who suffered, cried, grieved, and walked at times with a downcast soul. Such is the image of the crucified to which Clare directed Agnes to respond "with one voice, and with one spirit."

In the early extant correspondence to Agnes of Prague, Clare identified her as "the spouse and the mother and sister of my Lord Jesus Christ," urging Agnes to remain in union with the crucified Christ. Clare counsels:

> But as a poor virgin,
> embrace the poor Christ.
> Look upon Him Who became contemptible for you,
> and follow Him,
> making yourself contemptible in this world for him.

> Your Spouse, though more beautiful than the children of [all], became, for your salvation, the lowest of [all], was despised, struck, scourged untold times throughout his entire body, and then died amid the suffering of the Cross (2LAg18-20).

At the end of her Fourth Letter, Clare draws from the popular nuptial imagery of medieval writers by encouraging Agnes to pass beyond the crucified spouse to be transformed in God. She extends her formula for prayer, from "gaze," "consider," and "contemplate," to "further contemplate" union with God's "ineffable delights" immersed in the brilliance and fragrance of eternity. It is a movement of the heart that extends beyond the human exercise of

---

[14]Boehner 106, n8, comments that the stigmata is Bonaventure's inspiration as well as the model of mystical union in the *Soul's Journey into God*. He portrays mystical union as falling asleep with Christ on the cross.

contemplation. Clare, like Angela of Foligno, refers to Christ under different aspects of both his humanity and divinity: incarnate, crucified and glorious, the sacrificial Lamb, Truth and Spouse. In the fullness of the mystery of the incarnation and redemption represented in their writings, Clare's experience and that of Francis provide the root of Bonaventure's theology that focuses on the birth, passion, and death of the incarnate Christ seen in connection with the power of the resurrection.[15]

The Writings of Angela of Foligno: Memorial and Instructions

Angela's writings are a part of the mystical tradition initiated by Clare. Angela gives a more detailed record than Clare of the steps in her spiritual journey which reveal her union with incarnate and crucified Christ. Angela's conversion began approximately in 1285 when she became conscious of her sinfulness, articulated as the first steps of her journey. She recalled that the process was a gradual one, for it is the fall of 1291 when she made her pilgrimage to the Basilica of Saint Francis in Assisi and experienced the wooing of the Trinity at the crossroads. During the next four years, she dictated her account of the events leading to this experience and her ongoing revelations to Brother A. Angela's later and more intense experiences of God are recorded as the seven supplementary steps of her *Memorial*.

Thus, the first nineteen steps of Angela's *Memorial* narrate her experience as she set out to imitate the suffering Christ. After she passed though the beginning steps which were centered on her perception of herself as a sinner, Angela recalled, "In the seventh step I was given the grace of beginning to look at the cross on which I saw Christ who had died for us" (*Mem I*).[16] For Angela as for Clare, union with God through prayer began by gazing on God.

Angela related that she was "given an even greater perception of the way the Son of God had died for our sins" as she passed

---

[15]For an elucidation of the focus on the crucified Christ in Franciscan mysticism see Ewert H. Cousins, "Francis of Assisi: Christian Mysticism at the Crossroads," in *Mysticism and Religious Traditions*, Ed. Steven T. Katz (New York: Oxford, 19839 163-190.

[16]*Angela of Foligno: Complete Works*, Paul Lachance, trans. (Mahwah, NJ: Paulist Press, 1993) 125. This translation will be used for all quotations from Angela's work.

through the purgative steps of her journey (*Mem I*).[17] Because of her awareness of her sins, Angela said, "I felt that I myself had crucified Christ . . . this perception of the meaning of the cross set me so afire that, standing near the cross, I stripped myself of all my clothing and offered my whole self to him" (*Mem I*).[18] From this point, Angela referred to the fire that burned within her; "it was given to me to seek the way of the cross that I too might stand at the foot of the cross where all sinners find refuge." This ninth step demanded two things of Angela: to strip herself of her possessions and to forgive all who had offended her.

As her soul's journey advanced, Christ crucified on the cross appeared many times to Angela, both while she was asleep and awake. He showed her how he had endured all his wounds for her and how he had endured suffering from each of the wounds. She said, "He spoke to me just as he had when I was sleeping, showing me his afflictions from head to toe. He even showed me how his beard, eyebrows and hair had been plucked out and enumerated each and every one of the blows of the whip he had received. And he said: 'I have endured all these things for you'" (*Mem I*).[19] This revelation heightens Angela's awareness that her sins renew Christ's wounds, drawing her to even greater sorrow and penance.

In her twelfth step in the *Memorial*, Angela described how she resolved to "do the kind of penance I felt called to do and come to the cross as God had inspired me" (*Mem I*).[20] Accordingly, she entered into the sorrow over the passion suffered by the mother of Christ and Saint John. Angela prayed that they would give her a sign by which she could keep the passion of Christ continually in her memory, and so the heart of Christ was shown to her in her sleep. Later, Angela had a clear vision of the cross of Christ, who "called me to place my mouth to the wound in his side. It seemed to me that I saw and drank the blood, which was freely flowing from his side" (*Mem I*).[21] This is the blood, Angela understood, that cleansed her.

---

[17]Lachance, 125-26.
[18]Lachance, 126.
[19]Lachance, 127.
[20]Lachance, 127.
[21]Lachance, 128.

Up to this point in her spiritual journey, Angela continued to feel bitter sorrow for her sins, but she did not experience consolation in prayer. Her transformation into the love of the crucified began as she felt a great consolation and began to taste the sweetness of God. Angela fixed her attention on Saint John and the mother of God in the fifteenth step, "meditating on their sorrow and praying to them to obtain for me the grace of always feeling something of the sorrow of Christ's passion or at least some of their own sorrow"(*Mem I*).[22] In the seventeenth step, once more Angela grieved over the passion of Christ and his mother, and desiring to perform greater penance, announced, "I enclosed myself within the passion of Christ. . ."(*Mem I*).[23] Angela's eighteenth step portrays her so overcome by the fire of the love of God in her heart that whenever she saw a depiction of the passion of Christ she would come down with fever and fall sick.

Angela's Experience of the Trinity and the crucified Christ

The intimate revelation of the Holy Spirit to Angela on the crossroad between Spoleto and Assisi is a key event in her mystical journey, one she often recalls. The twentieth step reports how she received the promise that the Trinity would come to her, and how she swooned and shrieked in the upper basilica before the stained glass window of Christ embracing Francis. On her return from Assisi, Angela continued to reflect upon the vision of the Trinity, and reported to Brother A. that she remained aware of the presence of God speaking to her: " 'You will experience the cross and the love of God within you. This sign will be with you for eternity.' And immediately I felt that cross and that love in the depths of my soul, and even the bodily repercussions of the presence of the cross; and feeling all this, my soul melted in the love of God" (*Mem III*).[24] Angela's union with the crucified Christ began as her soul melted into the love of God.

Brother A., recording her words, questioned Angela how it could be possible that she had been told in her revelation, "I am the Holy Spirit," and a little later, "I am the one who was

---

[22]Lachance, 128.
[23]Lachance, 130.
[24]Lachance, 142.

crucified for you" (*Mem III*).[25] Angela returned to her home, and beginning to doubt her experiences, received the further revelation that "the Trinity has already come into you." This later revelation clarified for Angela that the Father, Son, and Holy Spirit had entered into her and spoke to her, and "that the Trinity was at once one, and a union of many" (*Mem III*).[26] Her experience of the presence of the entire Trinity assured her that she had not been deceived in identifying within both the voice of the Spirit and Christ crucified.

In one of Angela's earliest visions recorded in the *Memorial*, she sees both God's humanity and divinity in the Crucified:

> Once when I was meditating on the great suffering which Christ endured on the cross, I was considering the nails, which, I had heard it said, had driven a little bit of the flesh of his hands and feet into the wood. And I desired to see at least that small amount of Christ's flesh which the nails had driven into the wood. And then such was my sorrow over the pain that Christ had endured that I could no longer stand on my feet. I bent over and sat down; I stretched out my arms on the ground and inclined my head on them. Then Christ showed me his throat and arms. . . . Through this beauty it seemed to me that I was seeing Christ's divinity, and that I was standing in the presence of God; but of that moment that is all I remember seeing. I do not know how to compare the clarity and brightness of that vision with anything or any color in the world except, perhaps, the clarity and brightness of Christ's body, which I sometimes see at the elevation of the host (*Mem III*).[27]

At Brother A.'s prompting, Angela related another vision in which she saw the body of the Christ child while the priest held the host up during the elevation.

---

[25]Lachance, 144.

[26]Lachance, 145. Bonaventure's *Soul's Journey into God* 6.4 (V, 311) Cousins, 108, describes the relation of Christ to the Trinity as a coincidence of opposites of unity and plurality. The Trinity is embodied in the mystery of Christ as both the image of the invisible God and the exemplar of humanity. To turn to the divine image means to turn toward Christ as the center.

[27]Lachance, 145-46.

Although the purification of her soul was no longer a primary spiritual goal, Angela's bodily sufferings continued. She urged all those who love God to "go to the cross to fix their attention and regard upon it, and therein discover what love is" (*Mem IV*).[28] Her second supplementary step tells how God responded to her request for a sign of Love: "The sign which he left me with and which I feel continually is that the right way to salvation consists in loving [Christ] and to want to suffer torments for the sake of his love" (*Mem IV*).[29] These experiences prompt Angela's teaching that God is love as proven by his coming into the world and by his passion on the cross. Detailed images of the crucifixion appeared in Angela's visions, for she explains that God sent her "an explicit demonstration of his passion, the cross, and everything previously mentioned. I saw, finally, and my soul understood with the utmost certainty, that he was nothing but love" (*Mem IV*).[30] This vision is followed by an original parable, presented in the *Instructions*, in which the image of the cross is Christ's final bed (*Mem V*).[31]

Amid Angela's continual doubts of the truth of her spiritual experience, she was consoled by a blessing from God given as a vision of the hand of the crucified Christ. Angela's experience of the crucified recalled to her the wooing of the Holy Spirit at the crossroads on the way to Assisi when the Trinity revealed itself. As Angela was consoled by the hand of the crucified Christ, she immediately perceived the eternal blessing of the Trinity. Angela related in the fourth Supplementary step how she prayed for absolution through the merits of the passion. She heard the voice of God say to her: "Your sins are taken away. I bestow upon all of you a blessing with the flesh of the hand that was crucified on the cross. . . . The blessing of the Father, the Son, and the Holy Spirit will be yours for eternity" (*Mem VI*).[32]

Angela reported an experience of illumination knowing that "Christ was within me, embracing my soul with the very arm with which he was crucified" (*Mem VI*).[33] This vision gave her new

---

[28]Lachance, 160.
[29]Lachance, 151.
[30]Lachance, 154.
[31]Lachance, 243.
[32]Lachance, 172.
[33]Lachance, 175.

understanding that "through him our flesh is made one with God." Later during a presentation of the passion on the Piazza Santa Maria, Angela envisioned her soul entering Christ's side. During the Lenten and liturgical celebration of the Pascal mysteries in 1294, she had a series of visions in which she experienced the poverty and bodily and spiritual sufferings of the passion. Brother A. reported Angela's Holy Saturday vision of intimate union with Christ in the sepulcher:

> She said that she had first of all kissed Christ's breast— and saw that he lay dead, with his eyes closed—then she kissed his mouth, from which, she added, a delightful fragrance emanated, one impossible to describe. This moment lasted only a short while. Afterward, she placed her cheek on Christ's own and he, in turn, placed his hand on her other cheek, pressing her closely to him. At that moment, Christ's faithful one heard him telling her: 'Before I was laid in the sepulcher, I held you this tightly' (*Mem VII*).[34]

Angela's identification with the suffering and passion of Christ is presented as her Sixth Supplemental Step. She experiences Christ's abandonment on the cross and endures bodily torment and the affliction of demons. Angela compares the anguish of her experience of Christ's abandonment to "that of a man hanged by the neck who, with his hands tied behind him and his eyes blindfolded, remains dangling on the gallows and yet lives, with no help, no support, no remedy, swinging in the empty air" (*Mem VII*).[35] Brother A. reports Angela's account of how demons tormented and suspended the activities of her soul and sapped her virtue, leaving her soul without supports:

> The virtues of my soul are undermined, while my soul sees it and knows it and watches what is happening. And when it perceives all its virtues being subverted and departing, and it can do nothing to prevent this process, the pain and the anger that it feels pushes it to such a point of despair that at times it cannot weep and at other times it weeps incon-

---

[34]Lachance, 182.
[35]Lachance, 197.

solably. There are even times when I am so overwhelmed
with rage that I can hardly refrain from tearing myself
apart, while at other moments I cannot refrain from
horribly beating myself and I raise welts on my head and
various parts of my body. When my soul sees all its virtues
fall and leave, then it is overcome with fear and grief. It
wails and cries out to God repeatedly and unceasingly: 'My
son, my son, do not abandon me, my son.'[36]

Angela also felt as if her body had also been handed over to
demons, who reawakened vices within her, especially those
contrary to chastity, assailing her with suffering "beyond
description."

Angela's Visions of the Glorious Christ, Blessed Virgin, and Trinity

A vision of Christ and Mary together in glory which lasted
three days corresponded with Angela's liturgical celebration of the
Easter Triduum in 1294, for Angela saw the Blessed Virgin and the
humanity of Christ in glory. While seeing the Blessed Virgin's
concern for the human race although enthroned in heaven, Angela
said, "Suddenly Christ in his glorified humanity appeared seated
next to her. I perceived then how he had been crucified in his flesh,
tormented and covered with opprobrium. And while I had an
extraordinary perception of all the torments, injuries, humilia-
tions, and defamations which he suffered, nonetheless, for my part
I was in no way grieved over these; rather, they were a source of
such delight that I cannot speak about it" (*Mem VII*).[37]

Angela's glorious vision of heaven is followed by a vision of
the Trinity, which Angela names as the All Good, a concept central
to Francis's expressions of God, and articulated in Bonaventure's *On
Retracing the Arts to Theology*.[38] After receiving communion, she

---

[36]Lachance, 197-98. Lachance notes that "Angela is making her own Christ's
cry of abandonment on the cross," referring to the gospel accounts, *Mt* 27:46 and *Mk*
15:34. 381, n111.

[37]Lachance, 185.

[38]Trans., José de Vinck, *in St. Bonaventure: Opuscula Second Series*, V
(Patterson, NJ: St. Anthony Guild Press, 1966) 324. Bonaventure asserts that because

was told: "Beloved, the All Good is within you, and you come to receive the All Good" (*Mem VII*).[39] Brother Arnaldo asked her if she perceived any form in God, and Angela said she had not. Rather she said, "I saw a plenitude, a beauty wherein I saw the All Good." She saw God's beauty and plentitude within herself and within the Eucharist. Before receiving communion, Angela was told, "The Son of God is on the altar according to his humanity and his divinity, and he is accompanied by a multitude of angels" (*Mem VII*).[40] Angela's revelations confirm her teaching that the mystery of suffering and the sacrament of the Eucharist bring transformation into God.

> This aspect of Christ's love for us was such that even though he saw his death as imminent and experienced such unspeakably acute, deadly, and totally inconceivable sufferings—for every type of suffering converged on his body and soul—still, as if not thinking of himself, he never renounced his intentions, so great was his love for us. Indeed, such is the plan of divine love that its purpose is always to draw back to itself that which it loves; it draws everyone out of themselves and out of all created reality, and totally into the uncreated. Then the soul is made capable of understanding that the whole Trinity was involved in planning this very holy sacrifice (*Mem VII*).[41]

Angela's spirituality indicates an understanding, like that expressed as Bonaventure's theology, that all created reality, including God's Son, are gifts of God's self-effusive goodness giving life and drawing life back into the heart of the Trinity.

In the final supplementary steps of Angela's journey into God, darkness and light occur simultaneously as two dimensions of God. How Angela suffered Christ's abandonment on the cross is described as the sixth step of her *Memorial*, whereas, in the seventh step, Angela's soul is in possession of the All Good. Here she tells of her vision of God as indescribable, but a "secret good, one most certain

---

Christ is the center of the soul, he is the source of divine illumination as eternal sun and the image of the Father and the splendor of God's glory.

[39]Lachance, 186.
[40]Lachance, 186.
[41]Lachance, 292.

and hidden" (*Mem IX*),[42] yet always accompanied by darkness. The paradox of God's light and darkness corresponds to her experience of being both repelled and drawn to God. "For it is in this state, i t seems to me that I am standing or lying in the midst of the Trinity, and that is what I see with such darkness"(*Mem IX*).[43]

Inside Angela's experience of the Trinity, at its hidden center, she finds herself totally immersed in the love of God and of the crucified Christ. Angela's union with God is expressed as a mystical marriage, in which she rests on the bed of the cross:

> What I have spoken of withdraws and stays with me, I see the God-man. He draws my soul with great gentleness and he sometimes says to me, 'You are I and I am you.' I see, then, those eyes and that face so gracious and attractive as he leans to embrace me. In short, what proceeds from those eyes and face is what I said I saw in the previous darkness which comes from within, and which delights me so that I can say nothing about it.' When I am in the God-man my soul is alive. And I am in the God-man much more than in the other vision of seeing God with darkness. . . . It began in this continual fashion on a certain occasion when I was given the assurance that there was no intermediary between God and myself. Since that time there has not been a day or night in which I did not continually experience this joy of the humanity of Christ.
>
> At this moment, my desire is to sing and praise:
>
> > *I praise you God my beloved;*
> > *I have made your cross my bed.*
> > *For a pillow or cushion,*
> > *I have found poverty,*
> > *and for the other parts of the bed,*
> > *suffering and contempt to rest on (Mem IX).*[44]

Angela's vision of the crucified Christ on the bed of the cross extends itself to the Eucharistic Body of Christ. She said that her

---

[42]Lachance, 203.
[43]Lachance, 204.
[44]Lachance, 205.

soul "experienced itself to be within the Trinity and to be within the ciborium wherein the body of Christ is deposited. The soul understood that Christ was at once in the ciborium and yet present everywhere, filling everything" (*Mem IX*).[45] At another time at the elevation of the body of Christ, Angela heard God tell her, "'Behold the man who was crucified'" (*Mem IX*).[46]

Angela's soul is transformed through the humanity of Christ into his divinity in the Trinity—the All Good. Her vision of Christ coming in the sacrament of the Eucharist, demonstrates this understanding.

> It was shown to me how Christ comes accompanied by a mighty throng, or host. Usually I find delight only in Christ, and so I was amazed that this time I found delight both in him and his host, and this was a source of great wonder for me. My perception of him alone was one thing, that of his host another, and I found delight in both of them. And I was told that his host were the Thrones, but I did not understand what this word meant. This host formed an array so imposing, a militia of such great number, that if I did not know that God does all things according to measure, I would believe that the number of this host was without measure, indeed countless (*Mem IX*).[47]

Angela's explanation of the vision describes the ineffable nature of God in the heavens, that "could not be measured either by its length or its breadth."

Imitation of the suffering Christ is the nub of Angela's *Book of Life*, a summation of her teaching that occurs within the *Instructions*. She presents a consistent doctrine of imitation and transformation into God through the crucified Christ whose humanity and divinity are the core of the All-Good Trinity. Angela explains in her *Instructions* that transformation to God occurs through imitation of the poverty of Jesus in his humanity and through contemplation of his divinity:

---

[45]Lachance, 209.

[46]These words during the elevation of the body of Christ inspire another vision which Brother A. describes as a "wonderful transformation," in which Angela's "soul found itself enwrapped within Christ's divinity." Lachance 209.

[47]Lachance, 211.

As I said of love that the more the soul sees, the more i t
loves, I say the same of suffering, that is, the more the soul
sees of the unspeakable suffering of Jesus Christ, God and
man, the more the soul suffers and is transformed into his
suffering. . . . Thus, the transformation of the soul into Jesus
Christ, God and man, through love, is directly in proportion
to its transformation into his suffering (*Inst III.III*).[48]

In a vision that took place during the celebration of Mass on the
Sunday before the feast of the Portiuncula, perhaps on Aug 2, 1300,
according to the redactor of the *Instructions*, "Angela's soul was
absorbed and transported into the uncreated light by the majestic
power of the sovereign and uncreated God" (*Inst IV*).[49] He reported
that "After her absorption into the fathomless depths of God and
while she was still under the impact of this continuous vision, the
image of the blessed crucified God and man appeared to her,
looking as if he had just then been taken down from the cross."
After Angela's detailed vision of Jesus' wounds, distorted joints,
distended sinews and dislocated limbs, she experienced such
compassion that "all her own joints seemed to cry out with fresh
laments, and her whole body and soul felt pierced anew from the
painful impact of this divine vision" (*Inst IV*).[50]

Angela's experience of the divine essence was confirmed in a
revelation of the Trinity: "On one occasion, while I was in that
state, God told me: 'Daughter of divine wisdom, temple of the
beloved, beloved of the beloved, daughter of peace, in you rests the
entire Trinity; indeed, the complete truth rests in you, so that you
hold me and I hold you' " (*Mem. Supp.VII*).[51] This is the condition
in which Angela continually remained during the end of the
period, approximately from 1294 to 1296, during which she

---

[48]Lachance, 242.

[49]Lachance, 245.

[50]Lachance, 246. At the same time Angela sees the cruel death pains of Jesus'
crucifixion, she experiences the restorative splendor of heaven. The redactor of the
Instructions reports that "While she was thus both totally absorbed in the
experience of the sweetness of God and also crucified as a result of the vision of
Christ crucified, while she was filled with joy and sorrow, sated with myrrh and
honey, quasi-deified and crucified," Angela envisions her followers drawn into the
embrace of Christ.

[51]Lachance, 215.

dictated the *Memorial*. She confided in Brother A. that she had experienced this manifestation of God more than one hundred times. Brother A. quoted Angela as saying "that this unspeakable good is the same good enjoyed by the saints in eternal life, but there the experience of it is different. In eternal life the least saint has more of it than can be given to any soul in this life before the death of the body. Christ's faithful one said that she understood this" (*Mem* IX).[52]

Bonaventure's Christological Vision, Clare and Angela's Images of the crucified Christ

The spirituality of Clare and Angela, starting with their interior conversion guided by the Spirit, demonstrate Bonaventure's Christocentric theology. The Word of God that "becomes the visible center of the cosmos and its history in the form of the incarnate Word" is the Christ who, suffering and crucified in human history, became the spiritual core in the writings of Clare and Angela.[53] Zachary Hayes refers to Bonaventure's contention at the beginning of the *Collations on the Six Days of Creation* where he presents Christ as the center of all reality. Bonaventure uses a spatial metaphor to argue that "the Word is the divine person that dwells at the very center of the Godhead."[54] Bonaventure's text in the *Collations* expresses the Christocentric nature of Franciscan theology and spirituality:

> As regards the second point, note that a beginning should be made from the center (*medium*), that is, from Christ. For He Himself is the *Mediator* between God and men, holding the central position in all things, as shall be seen. Hence it is necessary to start from Him if a man wants to reach Christian wisdom (*Col* I.10).[55]

---

[52]Lachance, 217.

[53]Hayes, "Christ, Word of God and Exemplar of Humanity," *The Cord* 46.1 (1996): 9.

[54]Hayes, "Christ, Word of God and Exemplar of Humanity," 9.

[55]*The Works of St. Bonaventure,* V, trans. José de Vinck, (Paterson, N.J.: St. Anthony Guild Pres, 1970): 5-6.

Hayes points to the radical identity between the eternal Word and the incarnate Word.[56] He contends that spirituality is the process of becoming God-like, specifically by becoming like the Son. The style of spirituality graphically expressed by Angela and echoing Clare reveals this Franciscan tradition with its focus on Christ who, in turn "is cast against the background of a distinctive style of Trinitarian theology."[57] In view of Bonaventure's writings, Hayes describes the persons of the Trinity in terms of their origin:

> There is one who is origin alone; there is one who comes forth but is in no way origin of another; and there is one who comes from another and is principle of another. Thus, we might say that in the trinity there is one person who is totally active and communicative; there is another who is totally passive and receptive. In the center is a person who is first receptive and then actively communicative. In these three lies the order of divine life; and in this is grounded the fact that all which flows from God in the form of creation has a beginning, a middle, and an end.[58]

In his study, Zachary Hayes begins the section on the identity of the second person of the Trinity by announcing that "[t]he Christological mystery, as Bonaventure sees it, is grounded deeply in the Trinitarian mystery of God; for it is in the latter that we discover the ultimate condition for both the creation of the world and for the incarnation."[59] He explains that while the meaning of creation and the incarnation lies hidden in God, "in a more specific sense it resides in the person of the Son in whom God 'has disposed all things.'" The mystery and identity of Christ include aspects of Son, Image, and Word. The title Son describes Christ in relation to the Father, "from whom he is," but also in relation to the Spirit "Who is from him." Therefore, Christ is designated as the center of the Trinitarian God, for he holds a middle place between God as father and the world.[60]

---

[56]Hayes, *The Hidden Center*, 61.
[57]Hayes, "Christ, Word of God and Exemplar of Humanity," 4.
[58]Hayes, *The Hidden Center*, 62.
[59]Hayes, *The Hidden Center*, 57.
[60]Hayes, *The Hidden Center*, 58-59.

Zachary Hayes traces how Francis's vision of Christ is directed to the humanity of Christ as evidenced in scenes of Francis before the cross in the little church of San Damiano, his reconstruction of the crib at Greccio, and his stigmata on Mount LaVerna. Francis's incarnational spirituality appears in the writings of Clare and Angela and later is systematized by the great theologians and mystics of the Franciscan movement. While focused on the humanity of Christ, and especially on the crucified Christ, both Angela and Clare seemed to sense that Jesus is about more than helping to overcome sin, but becomes the way to participate fully in the life and love of God.

Christ brings the revelation of what God initiated in creation. The meaning of the Word of God in the structure and meaning of the universe that is articulated in the gospel narratives and Pauline letters plays a significant role in the mysticism and theology articulated by Bonaventure.[61] In *The Triple Way,* Bonaventure states that the embrace of the cross is essential for contemplation, "The cross itself is the key, the door, the way, and the splendor of truth. He who is willing to take up the cross and follow its way, as Christ explained, does not walk in the darkness, but will have the light of life."[62]

The mystery of the crucified Christ as the highest expression of God's goodness is the mystery that Bonaventure perceives at the center of the soul. For Bonaventure, to go to Christ means to go to Christ as the uncreated Word, the dwelling place of God which is the heavenly Jerusalem. The soul does not ascend to God in a purely intellectual manner, but rather contemplation takes place in imitation of Christ. Contemplation is the journey through the uncreated Word which is Christ. In the *Soul's Journey into God,* Bonaventure describes a hierarchization in which the soul enters the heavenly Jerusalem where God is seen as all in all (1Cor 15:28).[63] In the *Collations on the Six Days of Creation,* Bonaventure

---

[61]Hayes, "Christ, Word of God and Exemplar of Humanity," 7-8.

[62]Bonaventure, "The Triple Way, or Love Enkindled," trans., José de Vinck, *The Works of St. Bonaventure, I,* (Paterson, NJ: St. Anthony Guild Press, 1966) 86.

[63] Cousins, trans. 4,4 (V, 307).

portrays the soul standing, coming down, and ascending to the heavenly Jerusalem.[64]

On her deathbed in 1309, Angela experienced a series of visions of heaven including a vision of her soul wed to the Word of God hidden in the Godhead. Angela revealed that her soul heard a voice comfort her with the assurance that she would be eternally united to God in heaven. A multitude of angels appeared, directing her, "Prepare yourself to receive the one who has espoused you with the ring of his love. This union with him has already been realized. Now, he wishes to renew it" (*Inst* XXXVI).[65] Then God showed her the robe of light which he had won for her through the Passion and with which he longed to adorn her. One of Angela's final visions assures her that God's eternal Word and incarnate Word are one:

> Then God showed me the Word, so that now I would understand what is meant by the Word and what it is to speak the Word. And he said to me: 'This is the Word who wished to incarnate himself for you.' At that very moment the Word came to me and went all through me, touched all of me, and embraced me (*Inst XXXVI*).[66]

As Angela's death approached, this vision of God revealed that in her lifetime as she had participated in the mystery of the incarnate Word through her pain and suffering, so in eternity she would continue to participate in the mystery of God by understanding what it means for God to speak the eternal Word. As Angela's death approached, the unspoken Word—the hidden center—of God came to her, penetrated her, touched her and embraced her in a way corresponding to the way she had come to the spoken Incarnate Word, penetrated, touched, embraced and received the embrace of Jesus Christ on her earthly journey.

In presenting the triple transformation of the soul in the *Instructions*—transformation into God, with God, and within God and God within the soul—Angela distinguishes the work of the

---

[64] "Collations on the Six Days, trans. José de Vinck, *The Works of Bonaventure*, V (Paterson, NJ: St. Anthony Guild Press, 1970) 307.

[65]Lachance, 312.

[66]Lachance, 315.

soul on this earth from the action of soul when it is "in possession of the full vision of God" (*Inst 11*).[67] In this life, all the soul can do, in imitation of Jesus' suffering, is follow the only way he knew which is the way of the cross:

> His life began on the cross, continued on the cross, and ended on the cross. He was always on the cross of poverty, continual pain, contempt, true obedience, and other harsh deeds of penance. Since the heritage of the father should be handed down to his sons, God the Father handed the heritage of the cross and penance to his only Son. As a consequence, it is fitting that all the sons of God, the more they reach perfection, assume this heritage and adhere to its implications all their life. For the entire life of the suffering God-man was filled with the most bitter cross and penance. How long does penance last, and how much of it is there? As long as one lives. As much as one can bear? This is the meaning of being transformed into the will of God. But when the soul is truly transformed into God or within God and is in that state of perfect union and enjoys the full vision of him, it seeks nothing more (*Inst II*).[68]

The crucified Christ is, however, more than a starting point for contemplation. Imitation and conformity to the crucified Christ prepare the soul for eternal life where the humanity of Christ, crucified and glorious, continues as center. Bonaventure's *Tree of Life* presents the eternity of his reign, "as in a mirror containing the beauty of all forms and lights and as in a book in which all things are written according to the deep secrets of God."[69] Jesus, crucified and glorious, is the desired end of union with God. The Christo-centric character of Franciscan mysticism and theology stems from Francis's deep faith and love for the crucified and glorious person of Christ. This spirit of Francis, centered on the human figure of Christ, pervades the writings of the early Franciscan mystics and doctors of the church.[70]

---

[67]Lachance, 224.

[68]Lachance, 224.

[69]Bonaventure, *The Tree of Life*, trans., Cousins 170.

[70]Eric Doyle, OFM., and Damien McElrath, "St. Francis of Assisi and the Christocentric Character of Franciscan Life and Doctrine," *Franciscan Christology* (St. Bonaventure, NY: Franciscan Institute Publications, 1994) 3, n3, point out that

Hayes concludes that Bonaventure and the Franciscan theological tradition present a way of "finding the world in its truest reality in its deepest relation to God, the ultimate origin and end of all that is."[71] For Clare and Angela, the historical life and mystery of Jesus are at the center of what Hayes describes as "the core of our spiritual journey in and with the world into the mystery of God." The images of the crucified Christ that are prominent in the writings of Clare and Angela anticipate their own death, resurrection, and transformation into the Trinitarian God. What God initiated in their creation had eternal significance for them and is completed in the mystery of the eternal God. The final outcome of the human history of Clare and Angela, as recorded in their writings, is that of Christ's history: transformation from a human image into an invisible presence of the living God.

---

often the same person is both doctor and mystic, citing St. Anthony of Padua, Bonaventure, Peter Olivi and John Duns Scotus.

[71]Hayes, "Christ, Word of God, and Exemplar of Humanity," 12.

A Theological View of Philosophy: Revelation and Reason

University of Chicago

I. Introduction: Revelation and Philosophy — Ideal Types

In the history of Christian theology, philosophy has played many roles. The crucial factor, from the theological side, is some notion of revelation as well as the divinely-engifted reception of that revelation called faith—a knowledge born of revelation. A theological position is this: if there is divine self-revelation and if there is a form of human knowledge constituted by that revelation, then theology can neither ignore nor be sublated by philosophy. Many modern philosophies focus on the category 'religion' and any claims to divine self-revelation will be philosophically interpreted under a philosophical construal of religion. Indeed, that peculiarly modern discipline, philosophy of religion, is a discipline invented by modern thinkers. Its most characteristic moves are twofold: first, to religionize the traditional question of God and revelation and thereby any understanding of divine self-revelation: second to render philosophically intelligible the cultural and empirical category of religion. Philosophy of religion is the discipline most clearly allied to theology in modernity. And yet the two disciplines are constituted entirely differently. Philosophy of religion must clarify the category 'religion' and, through that strictly philosophical clarification, any further philosophical notion of 'revelation' or even "God". Theology must clarify the strictly theological category 'revelation' and, through that clarification , any theological claim to a form of knowledge ('faith') constituted by a divine self-disclosure. Only after a self-clarification of their distinct subject-matters (and therefore

---

[1] It is my sincere hope that this brief paper expresses some of my admiration for Zachary Hayes, a scholar and thinker who has helped me, and so many others, to begin to understand Bonaventure and thereby ourselves in theology and philosophy.

methods) can a philosophy of religion and a theology of revelation clarify their further relationships to each other. Such, at least, is my basic hypothesis. Since I have elsewhere written on the 'origins' of modern philosophy of religion and how the category 'religion' (not God or revelation) began to play the major philosophical role in Hume, Kant and Hegel, I will here turn to the second discipline in conversation, Christian theology. My hope is to clarify one way in which a theology grounded not in religion but in revelation may nonetheless relate in significant ways to philosophy—indeed must relate to philosophy insofar as a revelation-constituted understanding of faith as knowledge is a meaningful cognitive claim.

First, however, it is important to eliminate two often employed models as not useful for understanding, much less assessing, the relationship of philosophy and theology. These models are fideism and rationalism. These models are almost never used by a thinker for a self-description but are often used by other thinkers in describing what is judged to be an inadequate alternative. But since such ideal-types are used so widely in both philosophical and theological forms, it is well to eliminate, at the very beginning, at least the 'vulgar' (both as intellectually unsophisticated and, alas, also as popular-especially in the textbooks) understanding of these two much used and much abused terms: fideism and rationalism.

I admit that just as Leslek Kolakowski claims that what is often called vulgar Marxism is, in fact, Marxism (however unhappy that thought may be to revisionary Marxists), so too what I am here naming 'vulgar fideism' and 'vulgar rationalism' may actually prove in some rare individual cases to be fideism and rationalism. Even if that proves to be one case, it would not remove the need to develop some further distinction for the large majority of theological options between something like the vulgar and revisionary forms of each option. Indeed, when one observes the fuller complexity of a position like Karl Barth's, on the one hand, or Schubert Ogden's on the other, the labels 'fideism' (Barth) and 'rationalism' (Ogden) begin to seem entirely inappropriate.[2]

---

[2]On Barth, for some recent assessments, see H. Martin Rumscheidt, ed., *Karl Barth in Re-View* (Pittsburgh: Pickwick Press, 1981); for Ogden, see Schubert M. Ogden, *On Theology* (San Francisco: Harper & Row, 1986). For a helpful study of

Strictly speaking, a fideist position insists that faith is the only relevant form of knowledge on matters of revelation. Philosophy, therefore, may be useful on other topics like science (or even religion!) but is irrelevant for understanding faith (except in relatively trivial ways). It is difficult to find a pure form of fideism (hence its ideal type status) since even fundamentalists usually admit that every believing theologian uses some philosophical categories at least for the expression of one's understanding of faith. Therefore, at the very least, philosophy as clarificatory conceptual analysis of some categories inevitably used by theologians (e.g. causality) is necessary even for a fideist perspective. But this 'conceptual analysis' position, on strictly fideist grounds, cannot play the more ambitious (if still philosophically modest) role that several analytical 'Christian philosophers' accord their philosophy of understanding Christian faith as knowledge. For these Christian philosophies after all, include both defensive moves against philosophical critiques of faith and constructive (or better, reconstructive) moves to clarify and sometimes even to develop the understanding and thus intelligibility of Christian beliefs as forms of knowledge. The better position (like its theological counterpart Karl Barth) is far more complex than the usual meaning of 'fideism' allows.

The same kind of intellectual difficulty holds for the category 'rationalism'. Strictly speaking, a rationalist position holds that only reason is relevant for understanding and judging any cognitive claims implicit in Christian faith. Just as there are some strict fideists, so too there are some strict rationalists. However, the very turn to religion as the central category needing analysis in modern philosophies of religion has occasioned a hesitation in assuming that religion can be adequately interpreted and thereby assessed or judged by reason—this move to the acknowledgment of the complexity of the religious phenomenon as non-reducible to other phenomena, ever as understood by Kant in 'Religion Within the Limits of Reason', is, in various forms, a now familiar position in modern philosophies of religion. No more than Kant can be considered a strict rationalist in relationship to religion (as

these issues, see Ingolf V. Dalforth, *Theology and Philosophy* (Oxford: Basil Blackwell, 1988).

D'Holbach or Brand Blanshard can be) so too most philosophers of religion and most liberal or revisionary theologians employing some philosophical analysis of 'religion' (beginning with Schleiermacher) cannot be construed as rationalist. Something more complex is at stake in positions often named fideism by opponents or rationalism by adversaries. This complexity can be viewed by observing it in two familiar theological candidates for these labels: Karl Barth (often named a fideist) and Schubert Ogden (often called a rationalist). Karl Barth's position is well known: Christian theology must be based in God's self-revelation and should not search, via philosophy or any other discipline, for any point of contact between human experience and knowledge and that revelation. At the same time Barth insists that reason and all human culture should be reconstructed from the viewpoint of the new knowledge gained through the gift of faith. In short, faith as knowledge clarified through the discipline theology precisely as *theological* knowledge, can reconstruct philosophical knowledge in such a manner that philosophy too can acknowledge the reasonableness although not the truth (that is constituted by faith alone) of the knowledge constituted as faith by revelation.

At the other end of the spectrum, Schubert Ogden insists from his work on Bultmann to the present constructive work in the Hartshornian tradition that theology is accountable to the 'right i.e. correct philosophy' in order to develop criteria of credibility or intelligibility for assessing the cognitive claims of Christian faith. However, the strictly existential character of Christian faith, in Ogden's view, does not allow faith to be existentially reducible to philosophy. Philosophy, on this view, provides a metaphysics for understanding and assessing all relevant cognitive claims. God, existentially, however—the God of Christian faith—is the God experienced through Jesus Christ as revelatory and salvific *pro me*. To understand and assess this existential relationship to God, therefore, demands explicitly theological criteria, including criteria of appropriateness to scripture including a Christology as well as criteria of existential meaningfulness. The latter criteria need include but are not existentially exhausted by an understanding of 'religion' as a category for human wholeness.

There can be little doubt that Karl Barth inclines to fideism but opens up to' a reconstruction of philosophy by theology in such manner that 'Christian philosophers' can employ his work for their own strictly philosophical purposes. At the same time, Schubert Ogden's theology, however dependent upon and indeed philosophically creative in his use of and development of philosophy, may incline to classical Enlightenment rationalism but is distinct from such rationalism by his strictly christological (and thereby strictly theological) interpretation of his position on the full use of philosophy in theology. Strict Enlightenment rationalisms, when interpreting and assessing Christian faith, needed something like a theory of religion (or 'natural religion') but surely no christology!

My point in recalling so briefly the main outlines of the complex positions of Barth and Ogden is not to suggest that there do not exist fideists or rationalists on the issue of the relationship of philosophy and theology. Clearly there are. But the more interesting and influential theological positions—that is, complex positions like Barth and Ogde —are, I believe, too complex and too nuanced to lend themselves to so wooden a designation as fideism or rationalism.

This is even more the case for the mediating positions on the theological spectrum, especially but not solely the Roman Catholic and Anglican positions. There are real differences, for example, between Karl Rahner and Hans Urs von Balthasar, on the relationship of theology and philosophy.[3] But those real differences are not clarified, despite the claims of some of their followers, by such terms as fideist or rationalist. Indeed von Balthasar is even more open to the reconstructive task of philosophy's use in theology than Barth is. This is partly dependent on von Balthasar's use of the Catholic model of grace and nature as distinct from Barth's understanding of grace as power and his Reformation model of grace-sin and gospel-law. There should be little surprise that von Balthasar remains analogical in language and in his construal of basic continuities involved in the relationship of philosophy and theology while Barth, even after

---

[3]For a good study, see Rowan Williams, "Balthasar and Rahner," in ed. John Riches, *The Analogy of Beauty* (Edinburgh: T & T Clark, 1986).

Romans, remains dialectical in his analysis of that relationship, even after developing his 'analogy' of faith positions. Those classical nature-grace (Catholic) grace-sin (Reformed) differences remain real and deeply influential upon the use of philosophy by a particular theology.

Moreover, Karl Rahner's transcendental reformulation of both philosophy and theology does insist that philosophy can show that the condition of possibility of human being is that we are none other than contingent, temporal, and historical hearers of a possible word of revelation. But that Word comes to us as pure gift, sheer grace, categorical revelation which correlates to but is not equivalent to transcendental revelation. This transcendental position frees Rahner to a greater intrinsic use of philosophy in his theology than von Balthasar. But both work within the same grace-nature Catholic model, so that the differences, although real, are not mutually exclusive.

II. Revelation and the Knowledge of Faith

The first need, from the viewpoint of theology, is to clarify the category revelation, not religion. Theologically construed, revelation is an event of divine self-manifestation in the event and person of Jesus the Christ.[3] Each of these categories demands clarification:

1) event— 'Event' language in contemporary theology is indicative of the gratuitous or gracious character of divine revelation. The very fact that God reveals Godself *is* grace, event, happening. Theologically, revelation is never a human achievement, work, or necessity; revelation must be understood as event, happening, gratuity, grace. Hermeneutically, the category event (*Ereignis*) is applicable even to word as Word-event (*Sprach-Ereignis*) as a happening of language itself and as therefore not under the control of the modern subject.

---

[4]For an expanded version of my hermeneutical analysis here, see my essay to the former conference on 'Word, Language and Religion' in the volume edited by Marco Olivetti entitled *Religione, Parola, Scrittura* (1992) Archivio de Filosofia—Rome.

2) 'The event of divine self-manifestation' —The language of divine self-manifestation indicates, theologically, that revelation is not construed primarily (as in the older manual scholastic traditions) as propositional truths that would otherwise be unknown (that is, 'supernatural or revealed' truths). Rather in modern theologies revelation is primarily construed on an interpersonal or encounter model as an event of divine self-manifestation to humanity. This interpersonal model of revelation further assumes that some person-like characteristics (namely, intelligence and love) must be employed to understand the reality of God as God manifests God's self as Wisdom and Love even if they also employ impersonal models for the Divine Mystery. The dangers of anthropomorphism here are real but finally unavoidable (as Buber insisted in his critique of Spinoza and his insistence on the biblical God as Thou). Indeed, despite some strong qualifications on the use of personal language for God (e.g., Schleiermacher), all modern theologians who employ the category of revelation as divine self-manifestation must, if they wish to be hermeneutically faithful to scripture, at some point also employ (biblical) personal language and thereby interpersonal models for God as Wisdom and Love.

Hermeneutically, this use of the category 'manifestation' is also, as we shall see below, suggestive of the hermeneutical notion of truth as primordially an event of manifestation (or disclosure-concealment). The subjective correlate to the objectivity of manifestation is 're-cognition'. In an analogous manner, the theological counterpart to the event-gift-grace of revelation as divine self-manifestation is the gift, grace, happening (never 'work' or personal achievement) of faith as re-orientation of trust in and loyalty to the God disclosing Godself in the Word, Jesus Christ.

3) "Event of divine self-manifestation in the Word, Jesus Christ"—the decisive event of God's self-manifestation is, as Karl Barth insisted, not merely an event but a person, that is, the person of Jesus of Nazareth proclaimed and

manifested as the Christ and thereby as the decisive
Word-event of divine self-manifestation. In and through
this Jesus Christ the Christian learns the identity of the
God disclosing Godself in Jesus Christ. Here one cannot find
a strict hermeneutical correlate but rather the possibility
of hermeneutically clarifying the nature of Word as Divine
Self-Expression. In Christian theism, the ultimate
understanding of the Word is as the Second Person of the
Trinity. Any full Christian theological understanding of
God would need that further Trinitarian clarification in
order to understand both the intrinsically relational
character of the doctrine or symbol of revelation and to the
intrinsically relational (that is, explicitly Trinitarian)
reality of the Christian understanding of God.

For present purposes these further important questions on the
Trinitarian nature of God as clarified by the Christian understanding of revelation in the Word Jesus Christ need not be pursued
further here. Rather there is a prior need to clarify how Word
enters the Christian understanding of revelation as an entirely
dialectical reality that determines the Christian understanding of
Word.

The dialectic of the Word in Christian theological self-
understanding begins with the hermeneutical insight that Word
may take the form of either Logos or Kerygma. Hermeneutically
word is, therefore, both disclosure-manifestation (Word in the
Form of Logos) and proclamation-disruption (Word in the Form of
Kerygma). In history of religion terms, Logos becomes 'religion as
manifestation,' especially the manifestation of primordial
correspondences obtaining throughout all reality. The archaic,
meditative, and mystical traditions analyzed by Mircea Eliade
and others are the clearest illustrations of these 'Logos' traditions,
just as sacrament, nature, creation, cosmos, and analogical correspondences are the clearest Christian analogies of Word in the
form of Logos manifesting all reality (God-cosmos-history-the self)
as a vast system of disclosive and participating, analogical
correspondences. The reality of participating symbol (sacrament) is
crucial for the Word as Logos.

In history of religion terms, Word in the form of kerygma or proclamation also becomes word as interruption, disruption; i.e., word as a distancing from a sense of manifestory participation. Where Word as Logos discloses a vast system of participatory and analogical correspondences, Word as proclamation both discloses and conceals Word as proclamatory interruption of all senses of continuity, participation, and rootedness (all now labelled 'paganism'). When Johann Baptist Metz (here, following Walter Benjamin) describes religion with the one word 'interruption', he well describes this classical trajectory of the prophetic, apocalyptic proclamatory Word in Judaism and Christianity.

In Christian theology the dialectic of Word in the form of Logos and Word in the form of Interruptive Kerygma can be found in all the classic dichotomies become dialectical antinomies of Christian theological self-understanding. Consider the contrast between Logos Christologies beginning with the disclosive manifestory Gospel of John and apocalyptic christologies like Mark's or proclamatory and disruptive Christologies of the Cross like Paul's Christology of Christ crucified. Or consider the contrast in Christian theologies between the Comprehensible-Incomprehensible *Logos* traditions' understanding of God in Aquinas and Rahner and the Hidden-Revealed proclamatory God of Luther and Calvin. Recall Tillich's formulation of the dialectic of Protestant principle (word as disruptive, critical, suspicious proclamation) and Catholic substance (word as participatory logos). Or recall, in conceptual terms, the differences between the analogical languages of classical Orthodox, Anglican, and Roman Catholic theologies and the negative dialectical theologies of classical Protestant theologies.

Even in terms of the symbols of incarnation-cross-resurrection, Word as Logos instinctively appeals to the symbol of incarnation whereas Word as kerygma instinctively appeals to cross. Both find the need for one another in their distinct appeals to the symbol of resurrection to complete the dialectic of Christian symbols. Only the fuller symbol system of incarnation-cross-resurrection clarifies the dialectic of Jesus the Christ as the Word, that is, as both Logos and Kerygma, both John's Word of Glory and Paul's Crucified

Christ, both Mark's word of the cross and Luke's word of resurrection-ascension.

It would be possible to clarify further the Christian understanding of Word through a further exposition of one or another of the classical dialectics noted above (incarnation-cross; sacrament-word; cosmos-history; symbol-allegory; icon-idol; analogy-dialectic; Comprehensible-Incomprehensible God or Hidden-Revealed God; creation-redemption; nature-grace or grace-sin; love-justice; participation-distance; continuity-discontinuity; continuity-interruption). Pervading all these dialectics is the originating Christian dialectic of revelation as Word: Jesus the Christ as Word—Word in the form of Logos and Word in the form of Proclamation. It would also be possible to see this same dialectic continued in the two distinct readings of the tradition: either the prophetic-apocalyptic reading of the Word-as-proclamation tradition beginning with Mark and Paul or the meditative tradition which yields wisdom, mystical, and archaic (cosmic) readings of Word as disclosive Logos beginning with John.

As anyone familiar with the history of Christian theological reflection can readily see, all these formulations of the Christian dialectic of Word have been tried and reformulated over and over again in the history of Christian reflection in both philosophy and theology. Each of them has yielded genuine fruit. However, too many of those theological formulations of the dialectic of the Christian revelation as Word have ignored the fact that Jesus Christ as Word *is* both disclosive/Logos and disruptive/Proclamation of God and humanity, of cosmos and history. Word therefore manifests both nearness and distance, both participation and interruption.

To ignore this dual function of Jesus as the Christ is to ignore the fact that the Word, Jesus Christ, is testified to and indeed rendered in written words and written forms like narratives in scripture. This singular fact of revelation as written and there in-formed by forms —in scripture cannot be hermeneutically and theologically irrelevant. The fuller Christian description of revelation, in the event of divine self-manifestation in the Word, Jesus the Christ, is testified to and witnessed to in the written words of the scriptures. Christianity must affirm its self-understanding in its scriptural-biblical base and its Jewish, not Greek, roots. Christian theology, moreover, must leave behind both naive and Gnostic notions of the Letter and the Spirit in order to understand the place of written scripture in Christian self-understanding. Only by a focus on scripture as written word, may any adequate hermeneutics of the Christian understanding of revelation through Word in writing occur.

For Christianity, the New Testament and the Christian Old Testament is scripture: the written original witness to the revelation. The decisive revelation for the Christian occurs in the event and person of Jesus Christ as true Word of God. The Word, Jesus Christ, is affirmed as present to the community and the individual Christian in two principal forms: word (proclamation) and sacrament (those disclosive signs which render present what they signify). Even the common confession of the principal Christian churches— "We believe *in* Jesus Christ *with* the apostles" —is dependent on this notion of the Word's presence to the community. The rule for the *lex credendi* is the *lex orandi*. The present worshipping community renders present the same Jesus Christ in word and sacrament to all Christian believers. The scripture remains the authoritative *normans non normata*. The written texts called Scripture assures that the Christ of the present Christian community is the same Christ witnessed to and testified to by the apostolic witnesses as the decisive self-manifestation of God and humanity. Neither "Scripture Alone" nor "Scripture and tradition" clarify this important hermeneutical role of scripture for the Christian. Rather one may speak of Scripture-in-tradition, i.e., the rendering present in word and sacrament of the Word witnessed to in the scriptures as decisively present in Jesus Christ.

The recent recovery of the import of the genre 'gospel' as a proclamatory narrative has clarified this peculiar, indeed unique, role of form as indispensable in the written narrative and confessional scriptural texts for Christian self-understanding. If gospel is both proclamation and narrative, gospel is both a proclamatory confession of faith and a disclosive narration of the identity of this Jesus and as the Christ and of Jesus Christ and thereby ultimately of God. *Lex credendi* is based on the presence of the Word as Logos and Kerygma to the worshipping community (*lex orandi*). Both are held together, by what may be named the peculiar role of narrative writing as rendering present what is absent, the identity of the God manifesting Godself in Jesus Christ.

III. Faith as Knowledge:
   Event, Manifestation, Possibility, Exercise

In Christian self-understanding faith is a gift. Faith is the gift-grace for the reception of revelation. Faith is constituted by God's own self-manifestation. In and through the Spirit, Jesus is recognized in faith as the very Christ of God. Jesus Christ is acknowledged as God's own self-manifestation. Who God is — Love (I John 4:16) —is known to faith in and through knowing God's identity as that identity is manifested primarily in the form of the passion narrative of Jesus Christ. Who Christians may become those commanded and empowered to love—is known by Christians in and through their faith in Jesus Christ. Bernard Lonergan's understanding of faith as 'a knowledge born of love' is surely a correct, if somewhat cryptic, description of the kind of knowledge which Christian faith is.[5] For faith is a knowledge born of revelation and what revelation in Jesus Christ manifests to those engifted by the Spirit to that faith is Love: God is love and human beings are loved and therefore, commanded and empowered to love in their turn. Indeed all Being is now known as gracious. Here, as Lonergan suggests, is the one great exception to the dictum: *non amatum nisi cognitum.*

What of knowledge is this knowledge of faith? Here the traditional analogy of love seems entirely appropriate. What love fundamentally gives is a new understanding of possibility. What kind once seemed 'reality', more exactly 'actuality', now seems in the light of love's new understanding, relatively narrow in scope and small in spirit. The new knowledge born of all human love is the knowledge, above all, of new possibility. The knowledge born of Christian revelation—the knowledge of God as Loving Father and Mother, a knowledge obtained through Jesus Christ in the Spirit, is a knowledge in and through the manifold forms of

---

[5]For Bernard Lonergan, see *Method in Theology* (Philadelphia: Westminster, 1982).

revelation, beginning with and grounded in the form of the passion narrative—that narrative which identifies who this Jesus is and thereby who Christ is. In identifying Jesus as the Christ the narrative also identifies the God manifesting Godself in Jesus Christ as none other than Pure Unbounded Love.

The knowledge born of that revelation of God as Love is the new knowledge of faith—the gift/power/grace of faith. Such faithful knowledge disrupts (knowledge as disruptive procla- mation) our sinful, self-deluding grasp of what we consider 'reality' and 'realistic' knowledge. The new knowledge of faith also gives the gift of Love now understood to be pervasive of all reality within which we, as thus engifted to love, now understand the possibility to love beyond even our best actualities. The further development of such knowledge—the knowledge born of revelation now become the new knowledge of new possibility (faith, hope and love)—also demands, as the ancient philosophers knew, the discernment and development of what Pierre Hadot nicely named 'spiritual exercises' (of which more below).

It is little wonder that so many ancient Christian thinkers found Platonism in its many forms so natural a philosophical ally to the new knowledge of the revelation of Jesus Christ. For Platonism, in its many forms, does live in and by a sense of sheer wonder at the engifted, gracious possibilities within which we live and move and have our being. From Plato's own vision of Beauty occurring 'suddenly' (as event, happening) in the *Symposium* to his 'Good beyond Being' (and beyond the achievements even of dialectic) in the *Republic* to his final mythic—philosophical vision of all reality in the *Timaeus*, one cannot but sense in Plato, as in his Platonist successors, a sense of the sheer wonder of existence as a feeling of genuine participation in the possibilities opened by Beauty, by the Good, by the One, by Intelligence and by all the Forms.

The Christian Platonists, moreover, sensed this wondrous, participatory reality in Plato and the Platonists. The Christian thinkers did not hesitate to transform the forms of Platonism, when necessary, to cohere with *the* form of God, the Form where God is manifested in and through Form, Jesus the Christ. This incarnational christology freed Dante to understand the necessity

for the particularity of Beatrice, that is, the necessary particular
form in and through which essence manifests itself and without
which the manifestation could not occur. Thus can a new ethic of
the Good be worked out through manifold forms in the theology of
Augustine. Thus could a new understanding of truth itself as
manifestation in and through christological form occur for
Christian thinkers from Bonaventure to von Balthasar. Plato and
Platonism, once reconstructed or transformed through the possibilities disclosed by a new form of forms, Jesus Christ as
proclamatory and manifesting Word, was far more religiously
available to Christians than were either Aristotle or Stoicism.

And so today, in the twilight of Platonism, other philosophies
may seem more appropriate to the Christian insight into faith as
knowledge of possibility born of that love empowered by the
revelation of Christ in the Spirit. Among contemporary philosophies, I continue to believe that hermeneutical philosophy
provides the kind of contemporary philosophy needed by a
revelational theology.[6] Although I have argued the case elsewhere, for the present purposes, the following summary statement
of why hermeneutics aids theology in its understanding of
revelation can be stated as follows:

1) Hermeneutics, philosophically, accords a priority to
   'possibility' over 'actuality' analogous to revelation's
   disclosure of new divine possibility over present actuality.

2) Hermeneutics (unlike Platonism) takes history and
   historicity with full philosophical seriousness. For
   Judaism and Christianity with their revelation in and
   through historical events, this need is crucial.

3) As Paul Ricoeur argues, truth is primordially, on the
   hermeneutical vision, an event of manifestation (Ricoeur)
   or disclosure (Gadamer) or disclosure-concealment
   (Heidegger). This defense of how manifestation (not correspondence or coherence) is the primary, indeed primordial,

---

[6]Inter alia see Hans-Georg Gadamer, *Wahrheit und Methode* (Tübingen: J.C.B.
Mohr, 1965); Martin Heidegger, *Zur Sache des Denkens* (Tübingen: Max Niemeyer
Verlag, 1969); Paul Ricoeur, *Hermeneutics and the Human Sciences* (Cambridge:
Cambridge University Press, 1981).

notion of truth in hermeneutics is clearly fruitful for a philosophical clarification of the meaning of revelation as the self-manifestation of God in and through form as event.

4) Hermeneutics, by its concentration on text (or even action as text), provides philosophical clarification of how essential form is for rendering manifestation. Form is not dispensable but crucial for understanding the manifested essence. Moreover, precisely the interest in the in-form-ing of text by such strategies of form as composition, genre, and style (Ricoeur) opens to exactly what a theology of revelation needs: an understanding of the text disclosing in and through form (Dar-stelling) a *possible* mode of being in the world. Philosophically, the hermeneutical world of possibility[7] is an appeal to the productive imagination. Theologically, it is persuasive not argumentatively coercive as a Christian revelation's appeal to new possibility—the self-manifestation of this hermeneutical understanding of imagination is analogous to God in and through the indispensable and unsubstitutable Form of Jesus Christ as witnessed to in all the scriptural forms, especially the passion narratives which render that self into three identities: Jesus, Christ, and God.

5) Hermeneutics, through its dialogical model for under-standing, encourages the philosopher, in my judgment, to develop an ethics of the Good as the Good transforms reality by theologically understanding all Being as gracious.

All these moves suggest that philosophy (here hermeneutical philosophy) has two central roles in a theology grounded in revelation: first, to reconstruct the hermeneutical categories (possibility, event, historicity, manifestation, form, dialogue) in accordance with the Form of Christian revelation in and through Jesus Christ. This theological reconstruction, moreover, will itself be informed by hermeneutical philosophy by finding categories

---

[7]For the spectrum of reception of this possibility, see Hans Robert Jauss, *Toward an Aesthetics of Reception* (Minneapolis: University of Minnesota, 1982).

(via hermeneutics) which genuinely clarify and develop the meaning of revelation itself. Second, hermeneutical philosophy— especially through its development of the notion of the productive imagination in and through forms—provides a new way to clarify and, when necessary, challenge and correct theology's own self-understanding of revelation as manifestation of *reasonable* even i f formerly unimagined possibility. Whether such correlation occurs in an *ad hoc* or more general (inevitably transcendental) way is a further question that demands both further philosophical and further theological analysis. For the moment, it is enough to see that a correlation can and does occur between revelational theology and hermeneutical philosophy even without prior decisions on the general or *ad hoc* question.

Like Platonism before it, contemporary hermeneutical philosophy keeps alive the sense of wonder and participation crucial to revelation and philosophy alike. Unlike Platonism, moreover, hermeneutical philosophy can open philosophy itself to its ancient heritage by uniting theory to the praxis of spiritual exercises.

As theology struggles to undo the nearly fatal separation (not distinction) between theology and spirituality, perhaps theology may also suggest new ways for philosophy itself (including hermeneutical philosophy) to abandon all modern separations of theory and practice and retrieve the ancient philosophers' understanding of the role of spiritual exercises in and for theory itself. As Pierre Hadot's work has shown,[8] the ancients, whether in the schools of Stoics, Epicureans, Aristotelians, or Platonists, or in the non-institutionalized movements of skepticism and cynicism, all insisted on philosophy as a way of life. As a way of life, philosophy united theory to praxis (and vice versa) partly by means of the regular, systematic use of spiritual exercises (e.g. exercises of a tensive attentiveness to the *Logos* for the Stoic, exercises for letting-go in the Epicureans). The loss of such exercises —even the classical use of mathematics for understanding pure intelligibility in Pythagoras and Plato, much less the exercise of ancient dialectic and the Hellenistic spiritual exercises of the Platonists—is peculiar to modern Western philosophy and

---

[8]See Pierre Hadot, *Exercises spirituels et philosophie antique* (Paris: Etudes Augustiniennes, 1987).

theology. As our Western philosophy and theology learns to acknowledge the cognitive point of such exercises in, for example, Buddhist philosophies, perhaps at least 'Christian philosophers' might join their theological colleagues in new, if tentative, attempts to recover what was once held together in both our disciplines—spiritual practice and theory, theory and a way of life. The new global cross-cultural understanding of both disciplines can encourage all responsible thinkers to that new intellectual journey back to the future of both theology and philosophy as thoughtful ways of life.

Bonaventure's Christology
A Resource for the Third Millennium

Ewert Cousins

Fordham University

On the eve of the third millennium, we are being drawn—at an ever accelerating rate—towards a future that is challenging, threatening, and pregnant with hope. Some are bewildered by the crosscurrents of history. Others are inspired by the excitement that the future holds. However we respond, many perceive that the human race as a whole is undergoing the most radical, far-reaching transformation in history. Forces that have been building up for centuries have in our day reached an intensity that is drawing the human race into a global network and the religions of the world into a global spiritual community.[1]

This move toward a global spiritual community is generating a new spirituality of matter. Awakened only recently to our global ecological crisis, the human community must address this challenge not only pragmatically but also spiritually. This new spirituality of matter must go beyond ecology and alert all peoples of the earth to our "run away" economy that is destroying natural resources. At the same time we must become aware of the plight of the oppressed around the world: the poor, women, racial groups, and other minorities. We cannot continue to ignore poverty and injustice in the third world. Our problems are no longer regional, but global, calling for global solutions.

Fullness of the Mystery of Christ

At this decisive moment in history Christians must draw upon the fullness of their tradition. Unfortunately, we have been

---

[1] For an analysis of the present global transformation in its larger historical context, see my treatment in *Christ of the 21st Century* (Rockport, MA: Element, 1992 especially, 1- 14); see also Karl Jaspers, *The Origin and Goal of History,* trans. Michael Bullock (New Haven: Yale University Press, 1953).

conditioned to move in the opposite direction. For more than four hundred years Christian theologians have felt pressured to adjust their vision to fit into the limits of scientific and secular culture. Our present challenge is the exact reverse, for our transformation into a global community is bringing to light even new depths of our tradition and of our individual and collective spirit. Moreover, scientific and secular culture itself has been undergoing a transformation. Now our task is to retrieve the fullness of our religious heritage, just as Hindus and Buddhists must retrieve theirs, so that we may enter creatively and collaboratively into the on-going transformation that will unfold in the third millennium.

At this critical moment of transformation, Bonaventure can be a major resource both because of his strategic point in our history and because of the richness and relevance of his thought. Bonaventure appeared at an early stage in the second millennium, summing up in a remarkable synthesis the Christology of the first millennium and, at the same time, ushering in the creative transformation brought about by Francis of Assisi's devotion to the humanity of Christ, which has permeated the second millennium, leading us to the threshold of the third millennium.

Bonaventure offers us the fullness of the mystery of Christ as this had been manifested in the first millennium. He recaptured for the West the Eastern patristic tradition of the cosmic Christ, seeing the Logos as the divine expression of the fecundity of the Father and immanent in all creatures and the entire cosmos. To this he added Augustine's spirituality of Christ as interior teacher of wisdom in the innermost depth of the soul, and Bernard of Clairvaux's love of Christ as the bridegroom of the soul. In continuity with the Eastern and Western patristic view, he made central the transformation brought about by the incarnation, death, and resurrection of Christ. Into this he integrated Anselm's theory of redemption from the burden of sin, as expressed in *Cur Deus Homo*. He enlarged this rich heritage by channeling into it the revolution of spirituality effected by Francis of Assisi in focusing on the humanity and suffering of Christ. It was Bonaventure who wrote the classic volume of meditations on the scenes of the life of Christ, which Ignatius of Loyola later made the centerpiece of his

Spiritual Exercises. This focus on the humanity of Christ has transformed the religious sensibility and visual art of Western culture even to today. In the Middle Ages this led to the Franciscan claim of the primacy of Christ in creation, that if Adam had not sinned, Christ would have come. Bonaventure also developed one of the richest theologies of history in Christianity. Although influenced by Joachim of Fiore and highlighting the role of the Holy Spirit, Bonaventure's theology of history focused emphatically on Christ the center.

It is this rich heritage that Bonaventure offers to the third millennium. He not only presents a comprehensive view of the fulness of the mystery of Christ, but provides a holistic metaphysical structure which undergirds his theology and spirituality. It is precisely this holistic structure that is coming to light now in many areas, for example, in ecology, interreligious dialogue, and in the emerging global community.

In the light of this, I will examine three aspects of Bonaventure's thought: (1) His metaphysics of exemplarism as providing a holistic structure of reality. This structure is emerging more and more in consciousness as the human race is being drawn towards a holistic global spiritual community. (2) I will examine its significance for an ecological spirituality based on the vision of Francis of Assisi. (3) I will explore how this structure has been manifested in interreligious dialogue. In each area I will show how Bonaventure's Christology throws light on the central issues of the third millennium.

It is especially gratifying for me to make a contribution to this volume in honor of Zachary Hayes. For over twenty years he and I have shared our explorations of Bonaventure. I have been profoundly enriched by our friendship and am indebted, in countless ways that I cannot fully articulate, for the precision and wisdom of his knowledge and the richness that he has opened up for me in Bonaventure's thought.

Holistic Metaphysical Structure

In the first of the *Collationes in Hexaemeron*, Bonaventure summarizes the metaphysical structure that permeates his entire thought: "This is our whole metaphysics: emanation, exemplarity, consummation—to be illumined by spiritual rays and to be led back to the highest Reality."[2] This text presents us with a twofold perspective: in one direction it refers to the process of creation in which all things flow out from God, manifest God, and return to God. From this perspective the text focuses on the cosmic Christ as eternal Logos, the locus of the eternal ideas of all that God can create. In this context Bonaventure refers to Christ as the "metaphysical center" (*medium metaphysicum*), and comments that when you contemplate creatures and Christ in this way "you will thus be a true metaphysician (*sic eris verus metaphysicus*)."[3] But the text offers another perspective: it points to the inner life of the Trinity since in the same context Bonaventure speaks of the Son as the metaphysical center in his eternal generation from the Father. Here emanation suggests the Father as eternal, fecund source of the Trinitarian processions. The Son is generated by the Father, as Image of the Father, reflecting the fulness of the Father's fecundity, thus encompassing in the Son the eternal ideas of all that can be created. Finally, the Holy Spirit is the fulness of love between the Father and the Son, bringing the circle of intra-Trinitarian love to a perfect completion in the loving union of the Father and Son. This intra-Trinitarian dynamic structure provides the ground and archetype for the holistic metaphysical structure of all of creation. Foundational in this structure is fecundity. Bonaventure calls the Father in the Trinity "fountain-fulness (*fontalis plenitudo*)."[4] It is out of the fountain-fulness of the Father's fecundity that the Son, along with the eternal ideas of all creatures, is begotten, and it is out of this same fecundity that the Holy Spirit is breathed forth as the fulness of the fecund love of the Father and the Son.

In a book written some twenty years ago, I called this metaphysical structure a coincidence of opposites, not a coincidence of dialectical opposition, rather one of mutually affirming comple-

---

[2] *Collationes in Hexaemeron*, I, 17; English translations of Bonaventure are my own.

[3] See below for a discussion of the meanings that Bonaventure attaches to the Latin term *medium*.

[4] Bonaventure, *I Sent*, d.27, p.1, a.un., q.2, ad 3.

mentarity.[5] The relatedness of these opposites is not based on negative energy repelling each other, or even on distancing each from the other, but by way of creative interpenetration, like the I-Thou relation in the interpersonal sphere. The more 'other' they become in mutually relating, the more they are affirmed in themselves.

In the last three chapters of Bonaventure's *Itinerarium*, these mutually affirming relations abound. For example, speaking of the Trinity, which is the supreme archetype of creation taken as a whole and in all its parts, Bonaventure says: From supreme goodness it is necessary that there be "supreme mutual intimacy, by which one is necessarily in the other by supreme interpenetration and one acts with the other in absolute lack of division of the substance, power, and operation of the most Blessed Trinity itself."[6] By the coincidence of opposites, then, I mean an organic, interrelated structure of the entire created universe, reflecting the divine archetype of this structure within the inner life of the Trinity.

Five Classes of the Coincidence of Opposites

In Bonaventure there is not one uniform type of the coincidence of opposites that permeates his thought. Quite the contrary! Each area of his thought contains a specific type of the coincidence of opposites based on the specific metaphysical status of that area. For example, within the Godhead, there is a coincidence of the non-manifesting and the manifesting aspects of the divinity. Within the manifesting aspect of the divinity, there is the coincidence of the dynamic opposites of the Trinity: in the Father's self-expression in the Son and the return through the Son in the unity of the Spirit. The dynamic emanation within the Trinity provides the basis for the coincidence of unity and plurality, for the persons of the Trinity coexist in the unity of the divine nature. These opposites within the Godhead are eternal and necessary, since they are part of the very being of God. This means that

---

[5] *Bonaventure and the Coincidence of Opposites* (Chicago: Franciscan Herald Press, 1978), see especially 18-22.

[6] *Itinerarium*, VI, 2.

within the divinity, there is the coincidence of silence and speech, of darkness and light, of simplicity and fecundity, of the ground and of emanation, of self-sufficiency and self-communication, of unity and plurality. This differentiation and polarity within the divinity is not based on creatures: on either a necessary emanation of creatures from the divine nature or on God's free-will decision to create. Even if there were no creatures, this polarity would exist, for it is bound up with the divine mystery itself. It follows, then, that it is of paramount importance to be conscious of the coincidence of opposites within the divinity, for the Christian mystery of the Trinity implies that there is a coincidence of opposites in God, independent of creatures. Because of what has been revealed to the Christian community, God cannot be seen merely as the timeless Absolute, the undivided One, or Pure Act. Of course, God is all of these—but also more! For he is the self-diffusive Good, the dynamic Trinity: the one divine nature in three divine persons.

The next class of the coincidence of opposites involves God and creation. Here we find the coincidence of the creator and the creature, the infinite and the finite, the eternal and the temporal, the beginning and the end. This necessarily involves another generic class because the elements here constitute a different meta-physical configuration from those of the first class, mentioned immediately above. In the first class, we focused exclusively on the divinity and found there, independently of creation, several specific types of the coincidence of opposites. In this second class, we add to the divinity the realm of creation, which stands on a different metaphysical level; and in so doing, we constitute a different generic class of the coincidence of opposites.

In Bonaventure the same *medium* (or center) that links the divinity and creation also links the two classes of the coincidence of opposites: namely, Christ as *medium metaphysicum* (meta-physical center) and the *persona media* (central person) of the Trinity. For Bonaventure the Latin term *medium* means the midpoint between extremes, the center, and the means by which some result is effected.

Bonaventure develops this meaning of *medium* as center in the first of the *Collationes in Hexaemeron*, which he entitles "Christ the Center of All the Sciences."[7] In a systematic fashion he explores Christ as the center of the seven sciences: metaphysics, physics, mathematics, logic, ethics, politics, and theology. As center, Christ mediates the coincidence of opposites in each of these spheres. For Bonaventure, Christ is the *medium metaphysicum* (metaphysical center) in his eternal generation. When the Father generates the Son, he produces in the Son the *rationes aeternae* (eternal forms) of all that he can make; thus all creatures have an eternal existence in the Son as the Art of the Father. The two metaphysical spheres—the divinity and creation, the infinite and the finite, the eternal and the temporal—are united in and through Christ the *medium metaphysicum* (metaphysical center) in his eternal generation as the Son and Word of the Father. Not only does Christ link the two metaphysical spheres, but he also links the specific types of the coincidence of opposites within each class. Christ is the *persona media* (central person) of the Trinity. Yet precisely because he is the *persona media* (central person) in the divine sphere, he is the *medium metaphysicum* (metaphysical center) linking the divine sphere with the sphere of creation. Through Christ as *medium metaphysicum* (metaphysical center) this second class is constituted as the class of exemplarism, in which creatures reflect their divine Exemplar in various types of the coincidence of opposites graded in a hierarchical pattern: as shadow, vestige, image, and similitude. Based on exemplarism, Bonaventure's epistemology of illumination involves a coincidence of opposites in all certain knowledge through the "contuition" of the changeable, concrete finite particular and the unchangeable *rationes aeternae*. At the same time that we experience object in the sense world, we "contuit", or intuit along with the sense object the divinity as Truth, Goodness, and Beauty.[8]

The third class of the coincidence of opposites is constituted by Christ as the *medium physicum* (physical center) in his incarnation. As in the second class, we see here the coincidence of the creator and the creature, the infinite and the finite, the eternal and the temporal, the beginning and the end. But what constitutes

---

[7] *Collationes in Hexaemeron*, I.

[8] On Bonaventure's understanding of "contuition", see his *Quaestiones Disputatae de Scientia Christi*, q.4, concl.

the difference is the Incarnation. Whereas in exemplarism all creation is united to the divinity through the Word, in the Incarnation the Word is hypostatically united to human nature in such a way as to constitute a single person. This establishes a much more intimate and complex union of the divinity and creation than was realized in universal exemplarism. It also introduces a new cluster of the coincidence of opposites which can be called the specifically Christological or Incarnational opposites to distinguish them from the coincidence of opposites in exemplarism.

The Christological opposites are based on the hypostatic union and involve three types of the coincidence of opposites which I have termed cosmological since they deal with dimensions and aspects of the cosmos. This first is the *maximum-minimum* (greatest-least) because in Christ the highest is joined to the lowest, the divinity with creation, even with matter. The second is the microcosm-macrocosm; for the Incarnation takes place in human nature which is the microcosm reflecting the macrocosm of all creation, since human nature combines both matter and spirit, thus reflecting all the grades of material creation and the angels as well. The combination of the *maximum-minimum* and microcosm-macrocosm constitutes the third type of cosmological coincidence of opposites: namely, Alpha-Omega. The union of the *maximum* (divine nature) in the microcosm (human nature) establishes in Christ the greatest intensity of perfection in the universe, recapitulating in himself all creation and at the same time bringing it into a new and more intimate union with the divinity. Thus Christ is the pinnacle of creation, the Alpha and Omega of the entire cosmos, the firstborn of all creatures and the goal towards which all are striving. Together these three types of the coincidence of opposites form the complex notion of Christ the center, which is the culmination of all Bonaventure's forms of the coincidence of opposites. As *maximum-minimum*, microcosm-macrocosm, and Alpha-Omega, Christ stands at the center of the universe, uniting the opposites of matter and divinity through human nature the microcosm. Thus Christ is established as the center to which all the universe is related and through which it will realize its goal. In this way Christ becomes the center of the Christian mandala, the great archetypal symbol of total integration, which is at the same time a cosmogram, a psychogram, and an itinerary of the return of all things to the Father.[9]

The fourth class of the coincidence of opposites is based on the metaphysical difference between good and evil and is concerned with sin and redemption. In my book on Bonaventure and the coincidence of opposites, I called these soteriological opposites and explored them from the standpoint of Bonaventure's notion of Christ the *medium mathematicum* (mathematical center) and *medium logicum* (logical center). Sin introduces into the world an entirely new type of the coincidence of opposites: with its own power, structure, and logic. Instead of being related in a harmonious balance of complementarity, like the cosmological opposites, good and evil are contraries, constantly at war one with the other. Evil is the negation of good; it distorts good, deludes, seduces, and deceives. It promises life and brings death; it offers fulfillment and ends in destruction. In fact, it inverts and upturns all the creative power and inner logic of the good. Evil turns the creativity of the good into destruction, the truth of the good into deception. When Adam sinned, he upset the order of the good with its creative power and harmony and turned these to their opposite: creativity to destruction, truth to deception, reward to punishment, the positive logic of the good to the negative logic of evil.

Into this sinful world, with its distortion of the good, the God-man came to redeem human beings from the destructive opposites of evil. Within Bonaventure's Christology, the cosmological opposites in the God-man bring about the soteriological opposites. The positive opposites of the God-man confront the negative opposites of evil and transform them into their opposites: namely, the good. As *medium mathematicum* (mathematical center) Christ enters into the depths of the universe and as *medium logicum* (logical center) he transforms the logic of evil into its opposite; out of death he brings life, deceiving the deceiver to re-establish truth. Bonaventure incorporates Anselm's satisfaction theory into his soteriology and throws new light on its meaning through his logic of the coincidence of opposites. Anselm's entire theory of the redemption can be seen as an application of the logic of opposites:

---

[9] For a treatment of mandala symbolism in Bonaventure, see my *Bonaventure and the Coincidence of Opposites*, 161-197.

sin involves an infinite offense effected by finite human beings. This infinite offense establishes a debt which humanity cannot remove; it is necessary for a new coincidence of opposites to enter the universe—the God-man who by accepting the punishment for sin can unite the shattered poles and restore harmony in the universe. This is done, according to Bonaventure, by Christ's accepting the logic of evil. Christ enters into a dispute with Satan, taking upon himself the destructive logic of evil. Because he is the God-man, containing within himself all the opposites of the incarnational class—*maximum-minimum*, microcosm-macrocosm, Alpha-Omega, and universal center—he is able to win a victory over Satan and his destructive logic. By following the logic of evil through suffering and death, he is able to transform death into life through his resurrection. Thus he is the *medium logicum* (logical center) in his resurrection, transforming the entire sphere of evil, along with its logic of destruction, into its opposite.

The Fifth class of the coincidence of opposites concerns the return of all things to the Father and deals with Bonaventure's spirituality, mystical theology and his theology of history. Bonaventure treats this return through the notion of Christ the *medium ethicum, politicum,* and *theologicum,* (ethical, political, and theological center), and through Christ the spouse of the soul and the greatest coincidence of opposites who leads to the passage of the soul into mystical ecstasy. The return of the soul is based on the fact that the soul is the image of God: a coincidence of the finite and the infinite. Through sin the soul is turned away from its Archetype, but is restored by the incarnate Word and his work of redemption. As *medium mathematicum* (mathematical center), Christ restores the lost center of the soul through two perpendicular lines intersecting in the form of a cross.[10] Once the soteriological opposites of evil have been transformed by the cosmological opposites of the Word incarnate, the soul with Christ as its center can grow as image of God in the moral and theological virtues and through contemplation to mystical ecstasy and rapture. Even in these states and in the beatific vision, the soul is not absorbed into an undifferentiated unity with the divinity. The coincidence of opposites remains to the end of time and through

---

[10] See *Collationes in Hexaemeron,* I, 24.

eternity; for the more intimate the union of the soul with God, the more its uniqueness is intensified.

Not only does the soul return to its Archetype, but all of creation and history are on a journey back to their divine source. As *medium metaphysicum* (metaphysical center), the eternal Word is both the Alpha and Omega of the *exitus* (going out) and *reditus* (return) of creatures. All things emanate through him in the act of creation, and all things refer back to him through exemplarism. In him all creatures find the coincidence of their beginning and their end.

Christ the 'Medium' Links the Five Classes

These five classes of the coincidence of opposites, which are differentiated by the different metaphysical elements in each class, have a single unifying factor in the notion of Christ the *medium* (center). As we have pointed out, the notion of Christ the *medium* functions differently in each class according to the metaphysical differences involved. For example, in the Trinity he is the *persona media* (middle person), at the center of the dynamic Trinitarian life. As incarnate Word he is the *medium physicum*, summing up in himself the opposite poles of reality. Thus the notion of Christ the center unifies the classes of opposites while maintaining their differences. Although the coincidence of opposites is the universal logic of Bonaventure's system, each major area of his thought has its own specific form of the coincidence of opposites based on the metaphysical structure of that area. The notion of Christ the center, then, accounts for the common logic at the same time that it sustains the specific difference of each class. The notion of Christ the *medium* (center) not only provides a unifying thread running through the five classes of opposites; it also designates the specific form of the coincidence of opposites that operates in all of the classes. Bonaventure's notion of Christ the *medium* (center) implies that Christ is the center in which opposites converge and are maintained. For example, in the Trinity he is the *persona media* (middle person), eternally the center of the Father and the Spirit. In the Incarnation, the divine and the human natures are united in the person of the Word in such a way that the identity of each is maintained. The divinity does not swallow up the humanity, nor does the humanity contract the divinity to the point of losing itself in finitude. Yet both are genuinely united, not merely juxtaposed. In each of the above cases there is a coincidence of mutually affirming complementarity. In neither case does Bonaventure's coincidence of opposites slide into an all-consuming unity nor polarize itself into a radical separation. Thus through his notion of Christ the *medium* (center), each class of Bonaventure's system is clearly situated within the architectonic model of complementarity and avoids being drawn into the other two architectonic models: either the model of non-differentiated unity in which opposites coincide to the point of losing their opposition, or the model of polarized differentiation in which no genuine coincidence occurs. Thus in each of the five classes unity and difference are maintained in mutually affirming complementarity through the notion of Christ the *medium* (center), applied consistently to each class according to the metaphysical differences of that class.

Challenge of Ecology

Against the background of Bonaventure's metaphysical model of the coincidence of opposites as described above, we can now see how it throws light on two issues which have already emerged and will increasingly characterize the beginning of the third millennium: our ecological crisis and interreligious dialogue. As we enter the third millennium, one of the most challenging issues we face is the preservation of the environment. Fortunately, since the publication of the Meadows report entitled, *The Limits to Growth* in 1972, the general public has become increasingly aware of the magnitude of our ecological crisis.[11] There has steadily grown an awareness that this is not merely a pragmatic problem, but an issue of our own attitude of mind, and ultimately a spiritual problem. After millennia of ignoring and destroying the environment, we humans must rapidly develop a spirituality that will help us protect and preserve the environment. Fortunately in Francis of Assisi and Bonaventure we have rich resources for such a

---

[11]Donella H. Meadows, et al., *The Limits to Growth: A Report for the Club of Rome's Project on the Predicament of Mankind* (New York: Universe Books, 1972).

spirituality. Each of them can lead us to a vision which is holistic, for they see an interpenetrating relationship between God, the human person, and physical nature. In addition to Francis' *Canticle of Brother Sun*, we can turn to one of the most beautiful passages in Bonaventure's biography of Francis:

> [Francis] *rejoiced* in all *the works of the Lord's* Hands[12]
> and from these joy-producing manifestations
> he rose to their life-giving
> principle and cause.
> In beautiful things
> he saw Beauty itself
> and through his *vestiges* imprinted on creation
> *he followed his Beloved* everywhere,[13]
> making from all things a ladder
> by which he could climb up
> and embrace him *who is utterly desirable*[14]
> With a feeling of unprecedented devotion
> he savored
> in each and every creature—
> as in so many rivulets—
> that Goodness
> which is their fountain-source.
> And he perceived a heavenly harmony
> in the consonance
> of powers and activities
> God has given them,
> and like the prophet David
> sweetly exhorted them to praise the Lord.[15]

This is an eloquent example of the second class of the coincidence of opposites described above, which links the divinity and creation through the medium of Christ the metaphysical

---

[12] Ps. 91, 5.

[13] Job 23, 11; Cant. 5, 17.

[14] Cant. 5, 16.

[15] *Legenda Maior*, IX, 1; the translation is my own from the Bonaventure volume of The Classics of Western Spirituality, *Bonaventure: The Soul's Journey into God, The Tree of Life, The Life of St. Francis* (New York: Paulist Press, 1978) 262-263. I have retained here the sense lines as these appear in that version.

center, the perfect Image and Word of the Father. In his boundless
fecundity, the Father generates the Son and in the Son the eternal
ideas of all that he can make. When creation occurs in time, it
flows ultimately from the Father's fecundity and the eternal ideas
in the Son. In the light of this, Bonaventure can say of Francis that
"in beautiful things he saw Beauty itself" and that he climbed the
ladder of creatures to embrace his Beloved and that in "unprecedented devotion" he "savored" in creatures the fountain-source of
Goodness. These poetic phrases express Bonaventure's metaphysics
of exemplarism, according to which all creatures are expressions of
the Word in the Trinity, as the exemplar of creation. The final line
is a reference to Francis' *Canticle of Brother Son,* and in the above
context suggests an exemplaristic interpretation of the *Canticle.*[16]

In the first two chapters of the *Itinerarium,* Bonaventure
follows the metaphysics of exemplarism as he leads the reader in
a meditation on the sacrality of matter by seeing God's reflection
throughout the sense world. Inspired by Francis, he adds a new
dimension to the classical Neoplatonic tradition. More than any
previous pagan Greek or Christian Neoplatonic writer, he focuses
on the reflection of God in the material world, thus highlighting
how the divine fecundity of the fountain-fulness of the Father
flows out from the Trinity and, through the self-diffusiveness of
the Good, penetrates to the depth of matter, permeating the
panorama of the sense world in a holistic fashion, drawing all
things back to their source:

> . . .all the creatures of the sense world
> lead the mind
> of the contemplative and wise man
> to the eternal God.
> For these creatures are shadows, echoes and pictures
> of that first, most powerful, most wise and most perfect
> Principle,
> of that eternal Source, Light and Fulness,
> of that efficient, exemplary and ordering Art.

---

[16]The exemplaristic interpretation of the *Canticle* is adopted in the translation
by Regis Armstrong and Ignatius Brady in *Francis and Clare: The Complete Works*
(New York: Paulist Press, 1982) 38-39. See also Ilia Delio "The *Canticle of Brother
Sun*: A Song of Christ Mysticism," *Franciscan Studies,* 52 (1992) 1-22.

They are
vestiges, representations, spectacles
proposed to us
and signs divinely given
so that we can see God.
These creatures, I say, are
exemplars
or rather exemplifications
presented to souls still untrained
and immersed in sensible things
so that through sensible things
which they see
they will be carried over to intelligible things
which they do not see
as through signs to what is signified.[17]

For years I interpreted Francis' nature mysticism from the standpoint of Bonaventure's metaphysics of exemplarism and the epistemology of "contuition," whereby, along with our experience of material objects, we intuit the divine Beauty, the Cosmic Christ, the Son as the Art of the Father. I found that this provided a rich resource for a spirituality of ecology; for if the material universe reflects God, then it must be respected in its own right as sacred and a divine manifestation. It ceases to be merely a tool or a plaything to be used by us only for our own pragmatic purposes. More recently, however, I have come to see another dimension of Francis' nature mysticism. While I still hold that he is an exemplaristic mystic, seeing God reflected in all material things, I believe that he is at the same time a mystic of the family of creatures. Although exemplarism and contuition play a major role in the *Canticle of Brother Sun,* they do not fully account for Francis' calling the sun his brother and the moon his sister. This latter response expresses the intimate family relation he experienced with creatures. Bonaventure acknowledges this in his biography of Francis: "When he considered the primordial source of all things, he was filled with even more abundant piety, calling creatures, no matter how

---

[17]*Itinerium,* II, 11.

small, by the name of brother or sister, because he knew they had
the same source as himself."[18]

Bonaventure, it is true, directs attention to what can be called
Francis' mysticism of the family of creatures; but he does not extend
his holistic metaphysics explicitly into that realm. Yet the
resources for his doing so were available in the very Christian
Neoplatonism that provided him with the exemplarism which
permeated his thought. I am referring to the doctrine of the World
Soul, which was articulated in the *Timaeus* of Plato and later
flowed into Neoplatonism, where it was given an eloquent
articulation by Plotinus, as is evidenced from the following quote
from the *Enneads*:

> Now to understand how life is imparted to the universe and
> to each individual, the soul must rise to the contemplation
> of The Soul, the soul of the world. The individual soul,
> though different from The Soul, is itself no slight thing.
> Yet it must become worthy of this contemplation: freed of
> the errors and seductions to which other souls are subject, it
> must be quiet. Let us assume that quiet too is the body that
> wraps it round—quiet the earth, quiet the air and the sea,
> quiet the high heavens. Then picture The Soul flowing into
> this tranquil mass from all sides, streaming into it,
> spreading through it until it is luminous. As the rays of the
> sun lighten and gild the blackest cloud, so The Soul by
> entering the body of the universe gives it life and immor-
> tality; the abject it lifts up. The universe, moved eternally
> by an intelligent Soul, becomes blessed and alive. The
> Soul's presence gives value to a universe that before was no
> more than an inert corpse, water and earth. . . ."[19]

This text shows the holistic nature of the Neoplatonic
universe. Flowing from the One through Intelligence, the World
Soul brings the eternal forms into the material world and imparts
to it the organic interrelatedness of a living thing, not unlike the
perception of the earth in our contemporary Gaia hypothesis. Why
do we not find such a theme in Bonaventure? The answer lies in the

---

[18] *Legenda Maior*, VIII, 6.

[19] Plotinus, *Enneads*, V, 1,2; translation by Elmer O'Brien, *The Essential Plotinus*
(Indianapolis: Hackett Publishing Company, 1986) 92-93.

intellectual history of the 12th and 13th centuries. The doctrine of the World Soul was central to the 12th century School of Chartres, which had at its disposal the text of Plato's *Timaeus*, where the World Soul is treated extensively. As a result of many intellectual cross–currents the doctrine of the World Soul did not find its way into the 13th century and into the early Franciscan school as did other 12th century doctrines of Christian Neoplatonism.[20] However, spurred by our need for a comprehensive theology and spirituality of ecology in the third millennium, we can fulfill Bonaventure's metaphysics of exemplarism with the doctrine of the World Soul, as developed by the 12th century School of Chartres, and thus complete the holistic metaphysics that is implicit in Francis' *Canticle of Brother Sun*.

Interreligious Dialogue: Hindu-Christian

Bonaventure's holistic metaphysical model, then, can be a major resource for developing a positive spirituality of the environment as we enter the third millennium. In a similar way this same model can serve as a resource for interreligious dialogue. Since the first World's Parliament of Religions in Chicago in 1893, interreligious dialogue has developed at an ever-increasing pace, to the extent that at the time of the second Parliament of the World's Religions in 1993, interreligious dialogue had become a worldwide phenomenon. In fact, one can view the process of interreligious dialogue itself as an example of the holistic paradigm of the coincidence of opposites.

Since I began working in interreligious dialogue over thirty years ago, I have found Bonaventure a rich resource in many ways, but most significantly through his holistic metaphysics of the coincidence of opposites. Although it is possible to see disparate positions in Christianity and other religions related as a coincidence of opposites, the most striking phenomenon to observe is the fact that there is a widespread presence of the metaphysics of the coincidence of opposites within each of the major world religions,

---

[20] On the history of the concept of the World Soul, see Tullio Gregory, *Anima Mundi* (Florence: Sansoni, 1955).

in Hinduism, Buddhism, Taoism, Confucianism, Judaism, Christianity, and Islam, as well as in primal religions.

This can best be seen in Hinduism and Christianity—not in all strands of Hinduism, but in the *bhakti* (love or devotion) tradition as this was articulated by Ramanuja in the late 12th century. In rejecting the non-dualist metaphysics of his predecessor Sankara, Ramanuja developed a metaphysics of qualified non-dualism. Whereas Sankara declared that between God and the world there was no difference, Ramanuja claimed a difference and non-difference, which is generically like Bonaventure's metaphysical model of the coincidence of opposites. It is of utmost importance to make this known in the West. For the non-dualist position of Sankara, since the last century both by European scholars and Hindu teachers in the West, has been presented as the dominant Hindu tradition. On the contrary, the *bhakti* (love or devotion) tradition, supported by the metaphysics of Ramanuja, has been dominant in Hinduism since the medieval period.

Because of the common spiritual path of love and because of the similar metaphysics of the coincidence of opposites, Bonaventure and Ramanuja are ideal dialogue partners.[21] In addition, they fall within the same time period—the 12th to the 13th centuries—and the spiritual path of love which they helped to orchestrate unfolded through similar stages of development in Hinduism and Christianity. In both traditions love poets appeared first: the *alvar* and *nayanmar* mystics, who explored many forms of loving human relationships to awaken their love of God.

In France the troubador poets sang the praise of the love between a man and a woman, awakening in Western culture what was later to be called "courtly love." As the 12th century progressed, a new form of intense love mysticism was evoked by Bernard of Clairvaux in his *Sermons on the Song of Songs*, which paralleled some of the strands of courtly love. In Hinduism and Christianity major metaphysical systems were developed by Ramanuja and Bonaventure which had love as their origin, process, and goal. In each culture, the metaphysical system was followed

---

[21]For a study of Ramanuja and Bonaventure see John C. Plott, *A Philosophy of Devotion: A Study of Bhakti and Prapatti in Visistadvaita and St. Bonaventura and Gabriel Marcel* (Delhi, Varanasi, Patna: Motilal Banarsidass, 1974).

by a major narrative poem whose central theme was the spiritual path of love, awakened by the human love of a man and a woman, leading to the soul's union of love with God: the *Divine Comedy* of Dante and the *Gita Govinda* of Jayadeva.

In the light of this historical background, while I was teaching as a visiting professor at St. Bonaventure University in the fall of 1987, I had a number of interreligious dialogue conversations with K. R. Sundararajan, a Hindu of the *bhakti* tradition and chairman of the Theology Department. Together we organized a dialogue, which took place in the spring semester of 1988, between the *bhakti* tradition of Hinduism and the Franciscan tradition. Speaking on the Franciscan side were Fr. Conrad Harkins, O.F.M., and Fr. Joseph Doino O.F.M. On the Hindu side were K.R. Sundararajan and Krishna Sivaraman, of McMaster University, with myself as chairman. We entitled this dialogue "The Spiritual Path of Love in Hinduism and Christianity." The dialogue was far more successful than I had hoped. The fundamental reason was that it began from common ground: the human experience of love. Implied in this experience was the shared metaphysical model of the coincidence of opposites. It was this model that provided the metaphysical possibility for love, which consists of a union of two persons in an I-Thou relation or analogously a union of two elements in a center to center relation.

So many points of similarity surfaced, along with some illuminating differences, that we decided to hold the dialogue again each year, on specific topics that had emerged that first night, such as divine incarnation, creation, asceticism, world affirmation and world negation, violence and non-violence. A total of ten of these dialogues have taken place and there are plans to continue them on a yearly basis. Throughout, the Christian presenters have drawn from Francis of Assisi and Bonaventure. It has been striking how central a role Bonaventure's metaphysics of the coincidence of opposites has played in the dialogue. A manuscript has grown out of these dialogues, co-authored by K.R. Sundararajan and Fr. Francis Berna, O.F.M., who has joined the dialogue along the way. There are plans for publication of this as a book when the manuscript is completed.

Among the many issues that emerged, the most fruitful were those related to Incarnation. Like Christianity, the *bhakti* tradition holds that God has become incarnate in human form, but the Hindus hold that God has been incarnate in five human forms and in other forms as well. For the Hindus the two most significant incarnations of the divinity in human form have been in Rama and Krishna. The theological reasons for incarnation in Hinduism are very similar to those of Christian theologians. For example, in a line of reasoning like that of Anselm, Hindus believe that God becomes incarnate when accumulated evil requires rectification beyond human capacity. Another line of reasoning follows that of love. God wishes to be close to his devotees by taking on human form like theirs. Another similarity emerged in methods of meditation. In order to cultivate love for the child Krishna, Hindus imagine Krishna's mother expressing her love for her son. By taking on the role of his mother in their imagination, the devotees hope to increase their love for the incarnate divinity. This has striking similarities to the meditations on the life of Christ which began to emerge in the 12th century and reached a high point in the 13th century Franciscan milieu, with Bonaventure writing the first classic in this genre in his *Tree of Life*.

In spite of these similarities, it was precisely in the area of the incarnation that some of the greatest differences appeared. Professor Sivaraman pointed out that the Hindu incarnations in Rama and Krishna were more docetist than real, giving the impression that the divinity did not take on human nature as profoundly as the Christians believe is the case with Christ. He highlighted this by claiming that the Hindu tradition does not have an incarnate *suffering* God. At this moment we realized that we had reached a truly deep level of dialogue where the differences in the midst of many similarities caused both sides to look more profoundly into their own tradition in order to fathom, at least to some extent, the spiritual significance of this difference. At this point of the dialogue we could draw upon the rich resources that Francis and Bonaventure offered for exploring the mystery of the suffering of Christ. We reached the same point again in a later dialogue when K.R. Sundararajan observed that the Hindu tradition sees no salvific value in human suffering. Again we

Christians came to a greater awareness and appreciation of our own beliefs.

The significance of Bonaventurian metaphysics of the coincidence of opposites was constantly highlighted in these Hindu-Christian dialogues. But it is by no means limited to these cases, since it is widespread throughout the history of religions. This was brought to light by my longtime friend and collaborator, Richard Payne, who conceived and developed the series *The Classics of Western Spirituality and World Spirituality: an Encyclopedic History of the Religious Quest.* Richard Payne's most striking discovery was that in all the major religions there was an unprecedented flowering of the spirituality of love in the 12th and 13th centuries, in many cases without the influence of one religion on another. In each case it involved the spiritual path of love— interpersonal love, love of ecstatic union or the love of compassion —and consciously or implicitly the metaphysics of the coincidence of opposites. In order to test this out, we organized a conference that was held in Nantes in France in 1986. About twenty-five scholars from India, Nepal, Japan, Europe, and North America attended and universally concluded that such a global phenomenon had occurred in the 12th and 13th centuries.[22] Later Richard Payne and I had the occasion to spend a retreat weekend in dialogue with the eminent Confucian scholar Tu Wei-ming of Harvard University and came to the same conclusion about New-Confucianism and Bonaventure.

Buddhist-Christian Dialogue

The same focus on the suffering of Christ that had emerged in our Hindu-Christian dialogue surfaced again, this time in the Buddhist-Christian monastic interreligious encounter held at the Abbey of Gethsemani, near Louisville, Kentucky, July 22-27, 1996, which I had the privilege of attending.[23] The seeds for this

---

[22] See the description of the world-wide development of the spirituality of love in the 12th and 13th centuries in my preface to *Bernard of Clairvaux: Selected Works*, trans. G.R. Evans (New York: Paulist Press, 1987) 5-11. In this preface I make reference to the paper delivered by Richard Payne at the conference in Nantes, June 1-4, 1986: "A Mystical Body of Love."

[23] The proceedings of this encounter will be published shortly by Continuum.

dialogue were sown in 1968, when Thomas Merton, who was a monk of this abbey, traveled in Asia and met the Dalai Lama. In their several conversations, the Dalai Lama was awakened to the spiritual significance of Christian monasticism. Through the years this impression grew, leading to an intermonastic exchange which began in 1981. In this program Christian monks and nuns visited and lived for a period in Tibetan Buddhist monasteries and Tibetan Buddhist monks and nuns did the same in Christian monasteries. The similarities between Buddhist and Christian monasticism are striking—for example, in the external structure of their life, prayer, meditation, and chanting.

After a number of years of getting to know one another, the two groups met for an extended interreligious dialogue, at which the Dalai Lama was present, at the Second Parliament of the World's Religions, held in Chicago in 1993. The Intermonastic Encounter a t Gethsemani in 1996 was the next monastic interreligious dialogue after the Parliament. It included Christian monks and nuns from Benedictine, Cistercian, and Camoldolese monasteries and representatives of major strands of Buddhism: Theravada monks from Sri Lanka, Burma, Thailand, and Cambodia; and Mahayana monks from the Tibetan tradition along with Zen monks from Taiwan, Korea, and Japan. There was one Zen nun from Taiwan. The Dalai Lama was present and gave four major presentations on Tibetan Buddhist spirituality. Present also were some Christian non-monastic members of the advisory board and some American Buddhist teachers as well as a number of auditors who were from a variety of Christian monasteries.

I can say unqualifiedly that this event was the most profound and illuminating interreligious dialogue I have ever attended. This was the case because of the common monastic lifestyle which the Buddhists and Christians shared, because of the more than fifteen years of visiting and participating in each other's mona- steries, and most of all because of the spiritual maturity, knowledge, wisdom, and profundity that both sides brought to the dialogue. Since the dialogue focused on monasticism, it dealt with the essential aspects of that life. Papers were presented by Buddhists and Christians on the following topics: the practice of prayer and meditation, the stages in the progress of spiritual development, the role of the spiritual teacher and of the monastic community, and the spiritual goals of personal and social trans-formation. Although these themes dominated the presentations and discussions, the deeper issue of the suffering of Christ broke through. An American Zen Buddhist teacher called attention to a crucifix in the chapter room where the dialogue was taking place and asked how Christians felt in seeing the suffering body of Christ on the cross. A number of Christians came forward to the microphone to state briefly their feelings and their understanding of Christ's suffering. It was clear that we had touched a deep vein in the dialogue, for the Zen teacher had pointed out how alien it is, in the light of the Buddhist ideal of non-violence, for Buddhists to see such a violent act of execution as the central image of Christianity. "How can suffering," another Buddhist asked, "be salvific?" Although we did not pursue the issue further at that time, another Buddhist at seeing the number of Christians who spontaneously came forth to speak, commented, "See how much the Christians love Christ."

Later the issue surfaced again in the context of the discussion of the paper of Fr. Armand Veilleux, O.C.S.O., who described the kidnapping and execution of seven Cistercian monks in Algeria by Muslim fundamentalists. Their execution had occurred shortly before the Gethsemani dialogue. Several months earlier when the political situation in Algeria had become dangerous, the seven monks had gathered to discuss whether they should stay or leave. When they took a vote, only two chose to stay. However, they agreed that they should act in unison, but decided to pray over the matter for twenty-four hours and then vote again. On the second ballot, their decision was unanimous to stay. They were kidnapped and eventually beheaded. After their death, as the official representative of the Cistercian Order, Fr. Veilleux flew to Algeria to identify their bodies. All that he saw were their heads. Before his execution, one of the monks gave eloquent testimony to the love and compassion he felt for his executioners:

> This is what I shall be able to do, if God wills, immerse my gaze in that of the Father to contemplate with him His children of Islam as he sees them, all shining with the glory of Christ, fruit of His Passion, filled with the Gift of

the spirit whose secret joy will always be to establish communion and to refashion the likeness, playing with the differences.[24]

As moving and noble as this statement was, it did not satisfy a Buddhist discussant, who asked whether it would have been more compassionate for the monks to leave Algeria to save their executioners from the bad karma resulting from their deed. I felt that this question opened a deep chasm between Buddhism and Christianity—not an obstacle between us, but a mystery to be explored together. Although both religions focus intently on liberation or redemption from the negativities of the human situation, their perspectives on the solution diverge. Perceiving existence as suffering, Buddhists seek enlightenment to rectify the distorted consciousness which causes suffering. They use mind to overcome the distortions of mind. Christians also use mind in this way, but on another level, they identify with Christ who liberates from the suffering of existence not merely by transforming mind but by plunging into the very depths of suffering and as the cosmic redeemer transforms suffering into joy, death into life. In dialogue with Buddhists, Christians must find the depth of their own mystery. What Gethsemani made clear to the Christians—and I believe to the Buddhists—is that we have not plumbed the depths of our own traditions, and we cannot do that except in dialogue with each other. It is here, I believe, that we can begin to glimpse, however faintly, what it means to enter into a global spiritual community.

On the eve of the third millennium, as we explore the mystery of Christ, we can, I believe, find no better guides than Francis of Assisi and Bonaventure. For at an early stage of the second millennium they explored in new ways the mystery of the suffering Christ, who enters into death to transform it into life. As we move ever further into the transformation towards a global community, we run the risk of encountering unprecedented suffering in ecological

---

[24]Dom Christian de Cherge, quoted in the paper of Fr. Armand Veilleux, O.C.S.O., entitled "The Importance of the Monastic Community and the Church in the Contemplative Life," delivered at the Gethsemani interreligious dialogue, July 25, 1996, to appear in the proceedings.

crises and economic hardships. It is here that the mystery of the suffering cosmic Christ can lead us to successful transformation. It is here, in a special way, that Francis and Bonaventure, having perceived this mystery so deeply, can guide us on our journey into the third millennium.

Reformist Apocalypticism
and
the Friars Minor

E. Randolph Daniel

The University of Kentucky

In my *The Franciscan Concept of Mission in the High Middle Ages* I differentiated between Franciscan eschatology and Joachite apocalypticism. I described Joachim's thinking as evolutionary and progressive. The procession of *status* was a divinely-ordained march toward a coming:

> *ecclesia* of the *uiri spirituales* by whom all mankind—except those reserved to antichrist—would attain a new level of spirituality and live together in universal peace during an indefinitely delimited period of history.[1]

Thus, I then believed, Joachim's three *status* were successive steps, each one qualitatively superior to its predecessor. In contrast I asserted that Pope Gregory VII and the twelfth-century "papal reformers made evangelical renewal a burning issue."[2] The Gregorians, however, "looked back to the apostolic church as the original state of purity"[3] to which they sought to return.

> Franciscan eschatology combined this [papal] idea of reform with an Augustinian understanding of history: the Order had been sent by God in the last age of the world to prepare humankind for the final apocalyptic events that would end history. By renewing the life of the crucified Christ and the apostles, St. Francis and his brothers would

---

[1] E. R. Daniel, *The Franciscan Concept of Mission in the High Middle Ages*. (Lexington, Ky.: University Press of Kentucky, 1975); reprinted (St. Bonaventure, N.Y.: The Franciscan Institute, 1993) 27 [hereafter *Franciscan Concept*].

[2] Daniel.

[3] Daniel.

show men and women how to prepare themselves to face Christ at the last judgment.[4]

Thomas of Celano and St. Bonaventure within the Friars Minor and Jacques de Vitry outside it reflected this "Franciscan eschatology."[5] Joachitism was confined to the Spirituals. Hence while "Franciscan eschatology" characterized the mainstream, Joachitism was sectarian.

After all most "mainline Christians" and most "establishment" scholars insisted that apocalypticism and apocalyptics were sectarian. Robert Alter described the copyists of the Dead Sea Scrolls by saying:

> Perched on the rim of history, looking out toward the End, the Qumran sectarians were scarcely equipped to engage moral life or the political realm with any nuance or complexity. Apocalyptic thunder drums through many of their texts.[6]

The non-biblical Hebrew psalms from the Scrolls were according to Altman:

> Pastiches of biblical poetry, repeatedly taking the urgency of the supplication psalms—Lord save me, my enemies encompass me—and coloring it with the crude emotional hues of apocalyptic *ressentiment*.[7]

Altman discerned a "disquieting note" among these texts. Their writers:

> were not, after all, building a new edifice on the foundation of the Bible like their adversaries the Pharisees, but rather sustaining through literary pastiche and apocalyptic fulmination the illusion that they were still living at the heart of the biblical destiny in all its Davidic and Aaronite glory. . .[8]

---

[4]Daniel, 28.

[5]Daniel, 28-36.

[6]Robert Alter, "How Important are the Dead Sea Scrolls?" *Commentary* 93[Feb., 1992] 34-41. The quotation is from page 39. (Hereafter *How Important*).

[7]Alter.

[8]Alter.

Crude, emotional, full of fulmination, disquieting. Altman marshals a series of adjectives that have repeatedly been used to distinguish between "sectarians" and "mainline" texts. Apocalyptics and apocalypticism *could never be* mainline. Hence Qumran must have been a "monastery," the headquarters of an "Essene" group that had separated itself from the proto-rabbinic leaders in Jerusalem in order to propagate their unrealistic, fanciful dreams.

Norman Golb has made a strong case that Qumran was a Hasmonean military fortress or a country villa, not a monastery. The scrolls probably came from Jerusalem along with the treasures described in the Copper Scroll that were hidden in the desert as the Roman armies neared Jerusalem c. 68 C.E. Hence the Dead Sea Scrolls represent a cross-section of the currents of thought among Palestinian Jews on the eve of the First Jewish War [66-70 C.E.]. Although the Manual of Discipline came from a party or *hairesis*, nothing connects this "Unity" group with Qumran. Apocalypticism pervades the Scrolls as a whole and thus would seem to have pervaded Palestinian Judaism on the eve of the war. Apocalypticism was most probably the key cause of the revolt. Apocalypticism prior to 66 was characteristic of the mainstream, rather than sectarian.[9]

Altman accuses Golb of "special pleading" when Golb cites the diversity and even contradictions between various of the texts and when Golb argues that neither "rabbinic Judaism [nor] Christianity [existed] as movements" prior to 70 C.E.[10] Altman, however, is the scholar who has to ignore or dismiss the growing mound of evidence against his and the "Qumranologists" position.

Reading about the controversy over Qumran and the Scrolls, I cannot escape the conviction that apocalypticism is at the core of the argument. Were Altman and the other defenders of the "sectarian" hypothesis to admit that the scrolls came from

---

[9]Norman Golb, *Who Wrote the Dead Sea Scrolls: The Search for the Secret of Qumran*, (New York: Simon and Schuster, 1995). See especially chapter twelve, 327-360 where Golb convincingly analyses and refutes Altman's article. Although *hairesis* is the Greek term from which our word heresy derives, the original meaning was party or sect or school and it is used in this sense in Acts 5:17 and 15:5. See William F. Arndt and F. Wilbur Gingrich, *A Greek-English Lexicon of the New Testament*, 4th rev. and augmented ed., (Chicago: The University of Chicago Press, 1957) 23.

[10]Altman, *How Important*, 38.

Jerusalem, they would have to acknowledge that they represent
the mainstream and, therefore, they would be compelled to confess
that pre-revolt Judaism and Christianity were most likely deeply
affected by apocalypticism.

Norman Cohn continues to insist that millenialism—which is
his characterization of apocalypticism—has always been
sectarian from Zoroaster [c. 1500 B.C.E.] to the sixteenth-century
C.E. rebels at Münster.[11] Marjorie Reeves, on the contrary, argued
that Joachimism became "mainstream" in Western Europe after
1200.[12]

How do the dispute about the Dead Sea Scrolls and the
different theories of Cohn and Reeves pertain to the Franciscans?
Historians, concerned with Franciscan history and theology, still
continue to see Joachite apocalypticism as sectarian. Many
Spirituals were apocalyptics but they were not mainstream
friars.[13]

My thesis in this article is that Joachim belonged to the group
of reformist apocalyptics who appeared in the second half of the
twelfth century and who represented a *mainstream view of clerical
reform*. From the standpoint of reformist apocalypticism,
"Franciscan eschatology" and "Joachite Apocalypticism" were
substantially the same. Therefore, although all Franciscan
apocalypticism was not necessarily derived from Joachim, apocalypticism, including Joachimism, belonged to the Franciscan
mainstream, not just to a revolutionary minority.

Reformist apocalypticism is comprehended by beginning with
the exodus of the Hebrews from Egypt, because for this type of

---

[11]Norman Cohn, *Cosmos, Chaos and the World To Come: The Ancient Roots of
Apocalyptic Faith*, (New Haven and London: Yale University Press, 1993) p. 96;
Idem, *The Pursuit of the Millenium*, rev. and expanded ed. (New York: Oxford
University Press, 1970) 261-280. [Hereafter, *Pursuit*].

[12] Marjorie Reeves, *The Influence of Prophecy in the Later Middle Ages: A
Study in Joachimism*   (Oxford: At the Clarendon Press, 1969; new ed. South Bend
and London: University of Notre Dame Press, 1993).

[13]For Example, Duncan Nimmo, *Reform and Division in the Franciscan Order
(1226-1358])*(Rome: Capuchin Historical institute, 1987) 158-190. On page 189,
Nimmo characterizes Olivi's Joachitism as "a self-contained, watertight, divinely
guaranteed doctrine of total opposition to the existing dispensation and total
confidence in future triumph. It [was] surely one of the most perfect revolutionary
ideologies ever fashioned." [Hereafter *Reform and Division*].

apocalypticism the exodus was the underlying paradigm.[14] Michael Walzer pointed out that the Hebrew exodus included three separate phases: the liberation from oppression as slaves in Egypt; the journey through the wilderness to the promised land; and finally the conquest of the promised land. The first of these has usually been the most readily accomplished. The Hebrews escaped Egypt successfully with God's help. Cyrus liberated the Judean exiles when he gave them permission to return to Judea. Jesus liberated us from the power of sin and death by his crucifixion and resurrection. The French revolutionaries overthrew the monarchy and established a republic.[15]

The most difficult part of the exodus was the journey through the wilderness. Paradigmatically, this represents the effort to become sufficiently pure and holy to merit the promised land. Any reader familiar with Exodus, Numbers, and Deuteronomy knows that the Hebrews continually sinned and that none of the first generation, not even Moses, was allowed to enter the promised land. Only a fraction of the Judean exiles chose to go back to Jerusalem and there they encountered not the "promised land" but Persian Rule, the Macedonian Conquest and the consequent Hellenization that helped lead to the Maccabean war. The early christians began to form factions within the lifetime of Paul.

The promised land itself has never been completely satisfactory. The Palestinian Hebrews were repeatedly subjugated by their neighbors. In the eighth to sixth centuries B.C.E. the powerful empires of the Assyrians and the Babylonians overran both Israel and Judah because they lay beside the route to Egypt. Only the brief era of David and Solomon [1000-922] had real promise. When first Israel and then Judea were overrun and the peoples deported, Second Isaiah promised a new exodus [Isa. 40:1-5]. First the Persians and then the Greeks controlled Palestine, however, and finally the Romans incorporated it into their empire.

---

[14]Reformist apocalypticism was coined by Kathryn Kerby-Fulton in her *Reformist Apocalypticism and 'Piers Plowman'* (Cambridge: Cambridge University Press, 1990). "'Reformist' apocalypticism is my own term to denote the medieval 'school' of alternative apocalypticism which is concerned primarily with clerical reform. This is usually to be accomplished by imminent chastisement, and followed by spiritual renewal." [p. 3] (Hereafter *Reformist Apocalypticism*).

[15]Michael Walzer, *Exodus and Revolution* (New York: Basic Books, 1984).

The two Jewish revolts [66-70 and 132-135 C.E.] were apocalyptically motivated and both failed.

Thus history has repeatedly seen peoples "liberated" only to
find themselves struggling endlessly through the "wilderness" and
if they arrive at all, coming to a "promised land" that turns out to
be more a slum than a "holy city." Afro· Americans were liberated
from slavery during and after the Civil War, but their journey
became renewed oppression under "Jim Crow." The Civil Rights
movement seemed to liberate them once again but for many of them
the journey has been extremely slow and harsh from the ghettos of
our cities to any kind of genuine equality and freedom.
Nevertheless the dream persists not only among Zionists and Afro-
Americans but many others.

Hence the exodus represents the beginning of an apocalyptic
crisis. The journey stands for the struggle to realize holiness among
the chosen people and to become worthy to enter the holy city. The
promised land is the new aeon that will come after the struggle
within history. For reformist apocalyptics the liberation coincided
with Pope Leo IX and the ensuing struggle to actualize the *libertas
ecclesie*, to emancipate the papacy itself, the episcopate, and
eventually all of the clergy from lay control. The journey was much
more difficult; to subordinate the episcopate and the clergy under
the control of the reforming popes and to reform them both.
Clerical reform sought to eliminate simony in both its narrowest
and broadest sense and to redirect bishops and clerics from seeking
worldly wealth and privilege to seeking spiritual benefits. The
reformers bogged down precisely on this journey. The promised land
was a clergy whose manifest holiness would convert both the laity
and non-christians.

Reformist apocalyptics focused on clerical reform as an
unprecedented crisis of truly apocalyptic significance with God's
forces massed against those of Satan. Satan countered by sending
"antichrists" to oppose the reformers. The Reformists saw their
opponents as multiple emissaries of the devil, not as the final
Antichrist. The outcome of reform would be a renewed church that
would be genuinely evangelical or Christlike, marked by poverty
of worldly goods, and a superabundance of spiritual ones. This
reformed church would not be perfect but only holier than the

church had been at least since the very earliest days and it would still live in this world.

For the Reformists, as has been noted above, the liberation began in 1049 with the selection of Pope Leo IX. Gregory VII was among the first to view the investiture conflicts as apocalyptic battles against anti-christian forces. Gregory sought to liberate the clergy from lay control in order to achieve clerical reform and, thus, a purified, holy church. St. Bernard of Clairvaux was the key champion of reformist apocalypticism. In his *Liber de consideratione* addressed to Pope Eugenius III, he reminded the pope that he, Bernard, bore Eugenius in his womb. Now like a mother Bernard expected Eugenius to accomplish fully the reform of the clergy of which the abbot of Clairvaux had dreamed when Eugenius was elected to the papal throne. Instead Bernard saw Eugenius becoming more and more absorbed in hearing legal suits and listening more attentively to the lawyers than to reformers like Bernard.[16]

After Eugenius died, Gerhoch of Reichersberg [1092/1093-1169] in his *Liber de nouitatibus huius temporis* [late 1155 or early 1156] urged Hadrian IV to accomplish the reforms that Eugenius had left undone.[17] Gerhoch urged that Hadrian read Bernard's *Liber de consideratione*.[18] Gerhoch compared Hadrian to Joshua and urged him to lead the church into the promised land.[19] Hadrian instead allied with the Sicilian Normans and became more hostile toward the emperor, Frederick Barbarossa. When Hadrian died in 1159, Pope Alexander III had the support of the pro-Sicilian group and Victor IV of those who favored a continued alliance with Frederick. Gerhoch regarded Alexander as the legitimate pope but grave charges amounting to simony had been made against Alexander and Alexander refused to clear himself. Gerhoch

---

[16]Bernard of Clairvaux. *Five Books on Consideration: Advice to a Pope*, Trans. by John D. Anderson and Elizabeth T. Kennan, Cistercian Fathers Series (Kalamazoo, Michigan: Cistercian Publications, 1976). This and the following treatment is drawn from a nearly completed book manuscript. Obviously I cannot lay out the evidence here at any length.

[17]Gerhoch of Reichersberg, *Letter to Pope Hadrian about the Novelties of the Day* [*Liber de nouitatibus huius temporis*], ed. by Nikolaus Haring, S.A.C., Studies and Text 24 (Toronto: Pontifical Institute of mediaeval Studies, 1974).

[18]Gerhoch, ch.43, s. 9, 105-106.

[19]Gerhoch, prol. s. 4, 23.

regretfully concluded that Alexander must be guilty and, as a simoniac on the *cathedra* of Peter, Alexander was hence an antichrist, despite being the *legitimate* pope.[20] Gerhoch could no longer hope for Alexander to realize clerical reform. Hence in his last work, the *De quarta uigilia noctis*, Gerhoch clung to the hope that Christ would somehow reform the clergy in the near future just as Jesus had come to the disciples in the storm-tossed boat on the sea of Galilee during the fourth watch of the night. Gerhoch no longer could see how that reform would be accomplished but he kept his dream and his faith that Christ would not let his church sink in the simoniac ocean. Gerhoch compared the coming of Christ to renew and reform the church to the dawn that both precedes and heralds the sunrise. By his coming Christ will destroy the antichrist, i.e. avarice. Thus the church will be genuinely reformed before the coming of the final Antichrist and the end of history.[21]

Hildegard of Bingen [1098-1179] like most prophets refused to reveal the content of her visions until she was assured by Pope Eugenius III that they were from God.[22] *Sciuias* is Hildegard's unique form of *summa*. She introduces five beasts, a fiery dog, a tawny lion, a pale horse, a dark pig, and finally a gray wolf that symbolize periods of history but these are only briefly sketched as eras of human corruption before the arrival of the final Antichrist whom Hildegard describes in Adsonian terms, although with Hildegard's own unique elements. Afterward there will be a brief era when the purified church will shine brightly preceding the actual end of history.[23]

---

[20]Gerhoch, *De inuestigatione antichristi liber I*, ed. by E. Sackur, MGH, Libelli de Lite (Hannover: impensis Bibliopolii Hahniani, 1897) III:304-395.

[21]Gerhoch of Reichersberg, *De quarta uigilia noctis*, ed. by E. Sackur, MGH, Libelli de Lite (Hannover: impensis Bibliopolii Hahniani, 1897) III:503-525. On the reform see chps. 13, 19, 514, 523.

[22]For a succinct life see Barbara Newman's introduction to *Hildegard of Bingen: Scivias*, trans. by Mother Columba Hart and Jane Bishop, Classics of Western Spirituality [New York and Mahwah: Paulist Press, 1990] 9-22. [Hereafter *Scivias*]; *Vita sanctae Hildegardis*, edited by Moniace Klaes, CCCM vol. 126 (Turnhout: Brepols, 1993) is partly autobiographical; Hildegard, *Epistolarium: Pars Prima I-XC*, edited by L. Van Acker, CCCM, vol. 91 [Turnhout: Brepols, 1991] contains Hildegard's letters to Bernard and to Eugenius III.

[23]*Scivias*, bk. 3, vision 11, 493-511. The most detailed study of Hildegard's apocalypticism is Charles Czarski, The Prophecies of St. Hildegard of Bingen, unpublished dissertation (Lexington, Ky.: The University of Kentucky, 1983). My

The *Sciuias* appeared in 1151. Twelve years later Hildegard began her *Liber diuinorum operum*. This later work comments on the same vision that Hildegard had interpreted in her earlier work, but the tone and thrust are strikingly different. From the time of Jesus until the late eleventh century the church had enjoyed a period of virile strength, but then a "regal judge," probably Henry IV began a new time of feminine weakness [*muliebris debilitas*]. This era of weakness will lead to the period of the fiery dog during which lay princes will strip the clergy of their temporal wealth and purge all of society. Under the lion an era of peace, earthly prosperity, and holiness will ensue as if at the end of a new wilderness journey the pilgrims had come at last to the true Jerusalem.[24]

Prosperity and peace will gradually soften and corrupt the christians who will then be attacked by ferocious pagans during the period of the pale horse. Michael will fight for the christians, however, and the pagans will eventually be defeated and convert to christianity. Both an emperor and the pope will lose their universal authority. Princes and kings will rule the laity and archbishops and bishops the dioceses. Another era of peace and prosperity will result from this.[25]

During the era of the pig, prophets will appear but so will heresies. Sin and evil will flourish alarmingly and will usher in the era of the wolf, the final Antichrist.[26]

Hildegard had become a reformist apocalyptic when she wrote the *Liber diuinorum operum*. She had lost all hope that the popes would reform the clergy, a reform that she had expected from Eugenius. Like Gerhoch she had not given up on reform but had turned to the lay princes and the episcopate instead.

Joachim of Fiore [middle 1130's-1202] was at least two generations younger than Gerhoch and Hildegard. By the time he

---

work on Hildegard draws heavily on his as does that of Kathryn Kerby-Fulton, *Reformist Apocalypticism* 26-51. Czarski first pointed out the differences between the apocalypticism of the *Scivias* and that of the *Liber diuinorum operum* and also attributed the shift to Hildegard's reaction to the popes after Eugenius and the Alexandrian schism.

[24]*Liber diuinorum operum*, PL. 197, 3:10:16-20:1018-1023. The notion of the new wilderness journey comes from Isaiah 4:2 and of peace from Isa. 2:4.

[25]*Liber diuinorum operum*, 3:10:21-25: 1023-1027.

[26]*Liber diuinorum operum*, 3:10:26-38; 1027-1038.

began to write his major works the Alexandrian schism was over. When Joachim wrote his Testamentary Letter, Innocent III [1198-1216] was pope. Joachim was, however, very much a disciple of St. Bernard. The *De consideratione* is virtually the only book written in the twelfth century that Joachim quotes.[27] Joachim saw Bernard as the Moses of the third *status*.

In Book Two of the *Liber de concordia* Joachim explained the concords of generations from which he drew his patterns of history. The *prima diffinitio* consists of three *status*, each of forty-two generations which are preceded by an introductory phase of twenty-one generations. The *status* correspond to the processional relationships between the persons of the trinity and between the three orders, the laity, the clergy, and the monks. The second *status* of the Son proceeds from the first and the third *status* of the Holy Spirit both from the Father and from Son, i.e. from both the two preceding *status* and, therefore, the third *status* overlaps the second. The clergy and the monks both come from the laity and the monks additionally from the clergy. The *secunda diffinitio* comprises two tempora that also have initial phases and that consist of forty-two generations each. These two *tempora* parallel the two peoples, the Jewish and the Christian, as well as the two Testaments. From the two peoples proceed the *uiri spirituali* and from the two testaments the spiritual understanding of the scriptures.[28]

In Book Four, Part One of the *Liber de concordia*, Joachim, explaining the two *tempora*, discusses the spiritual meaning of the two series of generations [i.e. those from Abraham to Jesus and those from Jesus to the end of the second *tempus*] side by side, demonstrating how events in the Old Testament parallel those since the incarnation. Joachim's aim was to demonstrate that the events that occurred in Judah from the reign of Josiah [640-609 B.C.E.] to the return of the exiles under Joshua and Zerrubbel

---

[27]Joachim of Fiore, *Liber de concordia noui ac ueteris testamenti: Books 1-4*, edited by E. Randolph Daniel, Transactions of the American Philosophical Society vol. 73, pt. 8 (Philadelphia: The American Philosophical Society, 1983), bk. 4, pt. 2, chp. chp. 2, 417-419 [hereafter *Liber de concordia* 4:2:2:417-419].

[28]For the relationship between these two *diffinitiones* see E. R. Daniel, "The Double Procession of the Holy Spirit in Joachim of Fiore's Understanding of History," *Speculum* 55(1980): 469-483.

parallel the history of the popes from Leo IX to the forty-third generation of the second *tempus*. The struggle for papal reform was a second Babylonian Exile in the eyes of Joachim who was living in the fortieth generation [1170-1200 C.E.] and writing between c. 1184 and 1195. The situation of the church resembled the Babylonian exile because the church was so infected with avarice that it was Babylonian in a spiritual, not a literal sense. Just as Holophernes and Haman, according to Judith and Esther, had persecuted the exiled Jews, so the church would suffer from two antichrists. This would occur during the forty-first generation. During the forty-second a "universal pontiff of the new Jerusalem, i.e. from mother church, will ascend from Babylon like a new leader [*dux*]." This will be the angel of the sixth seal [Apoc. 7:2]. He will go up from Babylon because "to him will be given complete liberty to innovate the christian religion and to preach the word of God."[29] What needs to be reformed?

> The church of Peter or rather [the church] of Christ that had been constituted empress [*domina*] of the entire world in the days of Constantine Augustus. . . [that] at some time was full but is now empty, because even if it appears to be full of people even now, they are not its own people but an alien [population]. [They are not] sons of the heavenly Jerusalem but sons of Babylon.[30]

The sons of Babylon fill Peter's church because bishops seek their own good rather than that of their sheep. The priesthood ought to be golden because of its wisdom but instead is like black lead. Clerical reform was for Joachim the central issue.[31]

---

[29]Joachim, *Liber de concordia*, 4:1:28-45: 373-403. On the carnal church as Babylon see especially Joachim of Fiore, *Expositio in Apocalypsim* (Venice, 1527; reprinted Frankfurt am Main: Minerva G.M.B.H., 1964) pt. 6, distinctio 1, fols. 191va-202vb. [Hereafter *Expositio in Apocalypsim*]. On Joachim's understanding of *carnalis* and *spiritualis* see *Liber de concordia* 2:2:1:51-61, where carnal refers to all those who believe that God has promised material fulfillment as he did to Abraham according to the literal sense of Genesis, while spiritual refers to those who see in the literal merely a pointer toward spiritual reward, especially the *spiritualis intelligentia scripture*.

[30]Joachim, *Liber de concordia* 4:1:39:390.

[31]Joachim,*Liber de conccordia*, 4:1:39:390-394. Joachim put his condemnation of the clergy of his time in the form of a commentary on Lamentations.

Exegeting Apocalypse 11:2, Joachim argued that the two witnesses ought to be identified with Moses and Elijah rather than Enoch and Elijah as tradition has done, because the duties of the witnesses go better with Moses than with Enoch. Joachim then cited Jerome saying "that entire book [i.e. the Apocalypse] ought to be understood spiritually, because if we understand it carnally we ought to acquiesce in Jewish fables, rebuild Jerusalem and the temple and reinstitute the sacrifices. . . ."[32] According to the spiritual sense the two witnesses are two coming orders, one of clerics and one of monks.[33]

Moreover, the third *status* of the *prima diffinitio* has already begun like a new exodus. St. Bernard stood for Moses. Cîteaux and its first four daughter houses equated in the new *status* to those five tribes that received their inheritance first and to the five patriarchates, Rome, Alexandria, Antioch, Jerusalem, and Constantinople.[34] Joachim left unstated who would be the concord to the seven tribes and the seven churches, but Stephen Wessley has suggested that the abbot had originally intended the Florensians to fill that role.[35]

The new "exodus from Babylon" has already begun under the leadership of Bernard. Joachim expected the full crisis to come shortly after 1200 and to end with a truly reformed church here under earth sometime thereafter. Only after this would the final Antichrist come and the world end.[36]

In 1204 or 1205 an anonymous author, whom Beatrice Hirsch-Reich thought was a monk at the Michelsberg in Bamberg, wrote the *De seminibus scripturarum*.[37] The premise of the work is that

---

[32] Jerome, *Epistula LIX ad Marcellam de quinque noui testamenti quaestionibus*, edited Isidorus Hilberg, CSEL, vol. 54 (Vienna: F. Tempsky, 1910) section 3, 543-544.

[33] Joachim of Fiore, *Expositio in Apocalypsim*, Pt. 3, fols 146ra-149vb.

[34] Joachim, *Liber de concordia* 4:2:2:408-422.

[35] Stephen E. Wessley, *Joachim of Fiore and Monastic Reform* (New York: Peter Lang, 1990). [Hereafter *Joachim of Fiore*].

[36] Joachim, *Liber de concordia* 4:1:46:404.

[37] On the authorship see Beatrice Hirsch-Reich, "Alexander von Roes Stellung zu den Prophetien," *Mitteilungen des Instituts für österreichische Geschichtsforschung* 38[1959] 306-316, at 305-308. The encomium to the spiritual marriage of the emperor Henry II and his empress, Cunegund, under the letter "s" strongly suggests Bamberg, a city much favored by Henry and his spouse. The *De seminibus scripturarum* has never been published. I have used transcriptions of Vat. Lat. 3819, fols. 1r-18v and of Cambridge, Corpus Christi College 404, fols. 44r-63v. In

the key clues to the history of the church may be found in the twenty-one letters of the Latin alphabet [a, b, c, d, e, f, g, h, i, k, l, m, n, o, p, q, r, s, t, u, x] to which were added y and z from Greek and the connective "et." The twenty-three letters stood for the same number of centuries beginning from the founding of Rome in 752 B.C.E.[38] Jesus was born in the century of "h" [52 B.C.E.-48 C.E.] and died in 33 B.C.E.[39] The key centuries were those of "i" [49-148 C.E.], "m" [349-448 C.E.] and "x" [1249-1348]. Under "i" Peter and Paul brought Christianity to Rome. Under "m" the fathers defended the equality of the trinity—symbolized by the three equal minims in Gothic bookhand—against the Arrians. In "x" Jesus will reform the clergy which has been contaminated by simony. This section concludes with quotations from Bernard's *Sermones* number 23 and number 33 on the Song of Songs, in which Bernard excoriated the clergy, who "are all ministers of Christ and, nevertheless serve antichrist."[40] Under "y" [1349-1448] the fullness of the Gentiles will have been realized by the reform of the church—the three arms of the "y" represent Asia, Africa and Europe—and the Jews will be converted to Christianity [Rom. 11:25-26].[41] Finally under "z" [1449-1548] the final Antichrist will appear. "Et" stands for the final period of "less than a century" before the end of history and the second coming of Christ.[42]

Corpus Christi 404 the explicit occurs on fol. 64v but fols. 63v-64v is a comment by the owner of the manuscript, Henry of Kirkestede. Vat. Lat. 3819 probably dates from the late 13th or early 14th century. Henry dates his text to 1370 [fol. 65r]. Hereafter Vat. Lat. 3819 is designated as A and Corpus Christi 404 as B. An abbreviated version is found in Vat. Lat. 5732, fols. 64r-70v.

[38] *De seminibus*, under "i", A, fol. 3va: "Siquidem a condicione urbis anno septingentesimo .lii⁰., mediante .h. litera, natus est christus, anno autem urbis condite septingentesimo .lxxxu⁰. redempcionis nostre cursum in celos ascendendo consummauit." B, fol. 47r, places this section under "h" and says: "Siquidem a condicione urbis anno septingentesimo huius mediante .h. litera natus est christus. Anno autem a condicione septingentesimo octogesimo quinto redemptionis nostre cursum in celos ascendendo consummauit."

[39] *De seminibus*, A, fol. 3va and B, fol. 47r: "Et quindecim anni .h. litere restabant ex quibus .xii. apostoli in Iudeam .xii. annis predicauerunt."

[40] Bernard of Clairvaux, *Sermones super cantica canticorum*, *Sermo 23*, paragraphs 12-13 and *Sermo 33*, paragraphs 15-16, in *Sancti Bernardi opera*, edited by J. Leclercq, C. H. Talbot, H. M. Rochais, 8 vols. (Romae: Editiones Cistercienses, 1957-1977) I:146-147, 244-245. The quotation is from *Sermo 33* par. 15, 244, l. 9.

[41] *De seminibus* under "y," A fols. 16va-17rb; B, 61v-62v.

[42] *De seminibus* A, fol. 17rb-va; B, fol. 62v.

Reformist apocalypticism represented an important part of the mainstream of twelth-century thought, notably the "monastic theologians" as Jean Leclercq called them.[43] All of them held intensely to the dream of clerical reform, but after the death of Eugenius III none of them trusted the papacy to carry it out. The means, not the goal was in question.

Another powerful current competed with the Reformists. This combined the Last World Emperor with the final Antichrist and often with the brief period after the annihilation of Antichrist that Robert Lerner called the "Refreshment of the Saints."[44] The *Tiburtine Sibyl* and Pseudo-Methodius' *Reuelationes* both made a messianic Roman Emperor the immediate predecessor of the final Antichrist. Adso suggested that the messianic ruler would be a Frankish king instead of a Roman emperor.[45] The critical edition of Adso indicates how widely his text circulated and how many revised versions appeared often under the name of other authors.[46] M. Laureys and D. Verhelst have recently published a list of the manuscripts of the Pseudo-Methodius that indicate that it also was popular in the eleventh, twelfth, and thirteenth centuries.[47] Benzo of Alba in his polemic against the Gregorians, depicted

---

[43]Jean Leclercq, osb, *The Love of Learning and the Desire for God: A Study of Monastic Culture*, trans. by Catharine Misrahi (New York: Fordham University Press, 1982) 153-251. Horst Dieter Rauh, *Das Bild des Antichrist im Mittelalter: von Tyconius zum deutschen Symbolismus*, Beiträge zur Geschichte der Philosophie und Theologie des Mittelalters. Texte und Untersuchungen, n.f. bd. 9 (Münster: Verlag Aschendorff, 1973) described Gerhoch and Hildegard as "German symbolists" but in fact the term equally applies to Bernard, Joachim and the *De seminibus*.

[44]Robert E. Lerner, "The Refreshment of the Saints," *Traditio* 32(1976): 97-144. Lerner has interpreted Joachim's third *status* as a development of this last post-Antichrist period, but, as should be obvious from what has been said above, I cannot accept his hypothesis.

[45]Bernard McGinn, *Visions of the End: Apocalyptic Traditions in the Middle Ages* (New York: Columbia University Press, 1979), 43-50, 70-76, 82-87. Idem, *Apocalyptic Spirituality* (New York: Paulist Press, 1979), 81-96 has a complete translation of Adso's Letter. For the Frankish ruler see 92-93. The period after the death of Antichrist is on p. 96.

[46]Adso of Montier-en-Der, *De ortu et tempore antichristi*, edited by D. Verhelst, CCCM 45 (Turnhout: Brepols, 1976).

[47] Marc Laureys and Daniel Verhelst, "Pseudo-Methodius, *Revelationes*: Textgeschichte und kritsche Edition. Ein Leuven-Groninger Forschungsprojekt," *The Use and Abuse of Eschatology in the Middle Ages*, Medievalia Lovaniensia, ser. 1, Studia 15 (Leuven: Leuven University Press, 1988) 112-136.

Henry IV as a Last World Emperor.[48] Count Emich of Leisingen conceived himself as such a messiah.[49] Messianic enthusiasm for Frederick I Barbarossa is reflected in the *Play of Antichrist*.[50] The Last World Emperor was traditionally one who would defeat all of christianity's enemies and bring peace. Hence in a sense such a ruler was a reformer and even more the period after Antichrist would be an era for repentance and holiness.

Both of these apocalyptic currents were main currents, not mere eddies. Apocalypticism was mainstream in 1200, not confined to sectarians. What then of the Franciscans? Francis certainly had a strong sense that the Lord had called him to bring all persons, cleric and lay, members of the church, heretic, or non-christian to the evangelical life of *imitatio Christi* by example and by word. Clare shared this same mission. Both sought to renew the church in this manner. Beyond this I do not think that it is possible to go. I can imagine Francis and Clare as reformist apocalyptics but I can equally believe that neither was aware of this type of thinking. On the other hand when Thomas of Celano and Jacques de Vitry described the friars as being sent *in nouissimis diebus*, or in the "twilight of the world," reformist apocalypticism seems to be in their thinking. De Vitry saw the friars "as a reproach to the prelates who resemble 'mute watchdogs unable to bark.'" Thomas at the least implied that the clergy were failing to fulfill their function.[51]

Reformist apocalypticism ought to make us rethink the issue of "clericalization." If reform of the clergy were a priority, then using the friars to perform clerical functions and even promoting them to the episcopate could well have been a necessary step toward reform. In fact it is hard to imagine the Franciscans effectively reforming the clergy without becoming "clericalized" to some extent, if only by the enlistment of clerics "converted" to the evangelical life.[52]

---

[48]Benzo, Bishop of Alba, *Ad Heinricum IV imperatorem libri uii.* edited by K. Pertz, MGH. SS. vol. 11 (Hannover, 1854) 591-681.

[49]Cohn, *Pursuit* .73.

[50]*The Play of Antichrist*, trans. by John Wright (Toronto: The Pontifical Institute of Mediaeval Studies, 1967).

[51]Daniel, *Franciscan Concept* 28.

[52]Nimmo, *Reform and Division*,.52-55.

Hugh of Digne and John of Parma remain enigmas because we do
not know what they thought. Gerard of Borgo San Donnino is still
known only from what his enemies said. Moreover, the Pseudo-
Joachim *Expositio super Hieremiam* clearly was influential on
Gerard and most likely on the other two. Robert Moynihan argues
that the *Expositio* was produced in three separate stages of which
the first might go back to Joachim himself, but without an edition
of it scholarship still cannot really tell how it altered and thus
affected the perception of Joachim's thought.[53] Alexander Minorita
cited the prophecies of two coming orders from the *Super
Hieremiam* and applied them to the Dominicans and the
Franciscans.[54] Roger Bacon, who cited the *De seminibus
scripturarum*, was a reformist apocalyptic who pled with Clement
IV and Gregory X to realize reform.[55]

In an article discussing Bonaventure and Joachim I wrote that

> [in his works up to the *Legenda maior*] Bonaventure
> developed a Franciscan eschatology. He identified St.
> Francis, who bore the stigmata, with the angel of the sixth
> seal who bears the sign of the living God [Apoc. 7:2].
> Francis is the exemplar of evangelical perfection, the
> model for those who would conform themselves to Christ by
> humility, poverty and obedience. Francis has made the
> *transitus*, the passover from the speculative level of the
> cherubim to the affective unity of the seraphim. As the
> initiator of evangelical renewal, Francis is John the
> Baptist or Elijah, the herald of the coming of Christ in
> glory. The role of the Franciscans who have embraced
> poverty is to mark the foreheads of the servants of God
> with the *tau*, the sign of the living God. In other words the

---

[53]Robert Moynihan, "The Development of the `Pseudo-Joachim' Commentary
Super Hieremiam: New Manuscript Evidence," *Mélanges de l'École Française de
Rome, Moyen âge-Temps modernes* 98(1986) 109-142. Stephen Wessley, *Joachim of
Fiore*, pp. 101-124, discusses the authorship, attributing it either to a Cistercian
sympathetic to Joachim—such as Luke of Cosenza—or what is more likely to a
Florensian.

[54]Alexander Minorita, *Expositio in Apocalypsim*, edited by Alois Wachtel,
MGH, Quellen zur Geistesgeschichte des Mittelalter bd. 1 (Weimar: Hermann
Böhlaus Nachfolger, 1955) 436-440.

[55]E. R. Daniel, "Roger Bacon and the *De seminibus scripturarum*," *Mediaeval
Studies* 34(1972): 462-467.

friars are sent by Christ to renew the apostolic life in this last hour of the world as a preparation for the end.[56]

Subsequently in that same article I argued that Bonventure adopted Joachim's *secunda diffinitio* and that this pattern underlay the minister general's *Collationes in Hexaemeron*. Thus it seemed to me that Bonaventure had significantly changed his thinking after 1261.[57] Reformist apocalypticism leads me to conclude that "Franciscan Eschatology" and Bonaventure's "Joachimism" were essentially the same thing. In his lectures in the 1270's, Bonaventure was only clarifying what had at least been implicit from much earlier, not converting to some sectarian ideology.[58]

Bonaventure now seems to me to have been quite consistent and to have been representing a Franciscan mainstream from his earliest efforts to his final, unfinished lectures.

---

[56] E. R. Daniel, "St. Bonaventure's Debt to Joachim," *Medievalia et humanistica* n.s. 11(1982) 61-75. The quotation is from 62.

[57] E. R. Daniel, "St. Bonaventure's Debt to Joachim," 64-69.

[58] In an interesting paper that was read at the Kalamazoo Conference in 1993 or 1994, Ilia Delio, osf, argued that the apocalypticism of the *Collationes* was already implicit in the *Itinerarium mentis in deum*. She of course did not imply that such was sectarian.

"Non propheta, sed prophanus apostata":

The Eschatology of Elias of Cortona
and His Deposition as
Minister General in 1239

Michael F. Cusato, O.F.M.[*]

St. John's University (Collegeville)

On 15 May 1239, a general chapter of the Order of Friars Minor opened in Rome, having been called into session not by its Minister General, Brother Elias (as would have been customary), but by Pope Gregory IX. In the course of this historic chapter, Gregory, after hearing the complaints of the friars, proceeded to depose Elias

[*]A first draft of this article was read at the Twenty-Ninth International Congress on Medieval Studies in Kalamazoo, Michigan (May 5-8, 1994) in a session devoted to Frederick II and the Church. I should like to express my thanks to Dr. John P. Lomax, organizer and co-presenter of the session, for the invitation to be a part of the panel and to Fr. Augustine Thompson, O.P. whose comments on the original version were both insightful and helpful. The present text is a substantially expanded version of the original, refocussing more sharply on the eschatology of Elias of Cortona. This revised version is offered in honor of Zachary Hayes, O.F.M., whose translation of Joseph Ratzinger's *The Theology of History in Bonaventure* (Chicago, 1971) first introduced me to the issues of eschatology and apocalypticism.

**Abbreviations used:

AF = Analecta Francescana sive chronica aliaque varia documenta ad historiam Fratrum Minorum

BF = Bullarium Franciscanum

BR = Bullarium Romanum

HB = Historia diplomatica Friderici secundi sive Constitutiones, privilegia, mandata, instrumenta quae supersunt istius imperatoris et filiorum eius, 6 vols., ed. J.-L.-A. Huillard-Bréholles (Paris, 1852-61)

MGH EP = Monumenta Germaniae Historica. Epistolae saeculi XIII et regestis pontificum Romanorum selectae, 3 vols., ed. Carl Rodenberg (Berlin, 1883-94)

MGH LEGUM = Monumenta Germaniae Historica. Legum sectio IV. Constitutiones et acta publica imperatorum et regum, 4 vols., ed. Louis Weiland (Hanover, 1883-1911)

from office and then closely scrutinized and approved the election
of his successor, Albert of Pisa, the first friar-priest to lead the
community.[1] As a result, the Chapter of 1239 has been considered a
major turning point in the history of the Franciscan Order as it
embarked upon a more decidedly clerical direction.[2]

Yet the events leading up to Elias' inglorious fall from grace
are important not only to historians of the Franciscan Order; they
also unexpectedly shed light on what was at stake in the great
conflict which erupted in 1239 between the Papacy and Emperor
Frederick II. Indeed, it is by viewing this well-known conflict
through the lens of Franciscan history that one begins to realize
that the apocalyptic language used between the two adversaries in
the polemical exchanges of 1239 needs to be taken seriously: that is
to say, not merely as over-heated and inflated propaganda, but as
the language of two worldviews which were in direct conflict with
each other—and which Gregory perceived as threatening the very
survival of the Papacy in its present form. The stakes were thus
very high; and the general chapter of 1239 illuminates just how
high, as Gregory removed as head of the Franciscan Order his
friend and confidant: Brother Elias.[3]

---

[1]The two sources which provide the key details about the events at the
Chapter of 1239 are: Thomas of Eccleston, *De adventu Fratrum Minorum in Angliam*,
ed. A. G. Little (Manchester, 1951), c. 13, 67-69 [hereafter cited as Eccleston]; and
Salimbene, *Cronica fratris Salimbene de Adam Ordinis Minorum*, ed. O. Holder-
Egger, *MGH SS*, 32 (Hannover, 1905-1913): 96-108 and 157-63, *passim* [hereafter
cited as Salimbene]. The chronicle of Jordan of Giano, crucial for other information
on Elias, simply notes the fact of Elias' deposition: *Chronica fratris Jordani*, ed.
Heinrich Boehmer, *Collection d'Études et de Documents*, 6 (Paris, 1908): 58
[Hereafter cited as Jordan].

[2]Such is the historiographical approach adopted by, for example, Lawrence
Landini, *The Causes of the Clericalization of the Order of Friars Minor 1209-1260 in
the Light of Early Franciscan Sources* (Chicago, 1968); and Raoul Manselli, "La
clericalizzazione dei Minori e san Bonaventura," in *S. Bonaventura francescano*,
Convegni del Centro di Studi sulla Spiritualità Medievale, 14 (Todi, 1974): 181-208.

[3]The most judicious treatments of the controversial figure of Elias are Rosalind
Brooke, *Early Franciscan Government. Elias to Bonaventure* (Cambridge, 1959) 83-
122 and 137-77; Lorenzo di Fonzo, "Élie d'Assise," DHGE, 15 (Paris, 1963), cols. 167-
83; Giulia Barone, "Frate Elia," *Bulletino di Istituto Storico Italiano per il Medio
Evo e Archivio Muratoriani* 85 (1974): 89-144 [hereafter cited as Barone, "Frate
Elia"], to be complemented by her more recent contribution: eadem, "Frate Elia:
suggestioni da una rilettura," in *I compagni di Francesco e la prima generazione
minoritica* (Spoleto, 1992) 59-80 [hereafter cited as Barone, "Rilettura"]; and

THE RELATIONSHIP OF GREGORY IX
AND BROTHER ELIAS.

The question is: what happened to change Gregory's opinion of the ill-fated brother? Until his deposition in 1239, Elias had been one of the most respected Friars Minor of his day. Not only had he enjoyed the esteem of people like Francis, Clare and Robert Grosseteste (to name only the most well-known),[4] he was also, to use Salimbene's phrase, a *"specialis amicus"* of Gregory IX.[5] Indeed, the two had, over the years, collaborated closely on a number of important projects, the most ambitious of which being the planning and construction—against strong opposition within the Order itself—of the basilica of Saint Francis outside Assisi, completed and dedicated in 1235.[6] Moreover, even as late as February 1238, Gregory was sending Elias to the court of Frederick II as his personal envoy (*unus et idem*) to spearhead sensitive negotiations with the Emperor at a critical juncture.[7] It is thus not surprising that, when a group of friar-clerics arrived at the Curia later in 1238 to present their grievances against Elias, Gregory showed himself at first very reluctant to move against his friend.

But if the Pope was reticent to support the movement against Elias in 1238, by May 1239 all such hesitation had vanished. What caused this change in attitude? Surely the dissatisfaction of certain clerics with Elias' heavy-handed governance of the Order was putting pressure on the Pope to act; but this is only part of the

---

Dieter Berg, "Elias von Cortona. Studien zu Leben und Werk des zweiten Generalministers im Franziskanerorden," *Wissenschaft und Weisheit* 41 (1978): 102-26 [hereafter cited as Berg, "Elias Von Cortona"]. Valuable for their insights, but to be used with caution, are: Primo Dallari, *Frate Elia architetto della Basilica d'Assisi e di Cortona* (Milan, 1970); and idem, *Il dramma di Frate Elia. Primo organizzatore del movimento francescano e ispiratore del Rinascimento* (Milan, 1974).

[4]Giulia Barone discusses the various personnages drawn to Elias in her magisterial article, "Frate Elia," 110-19.

[5]Salimbene, 96 (see below, n. 7).

[6]On the issue of Elias, Gregory and the Basilica, see chapter 2 of my forthcoming book, currently in preparation and tentatively titled: *The Renunciation of Power: The Search for Franciscan Identity in the World (1206-1250).*

[7]Salimbene, 96: *Ibat (Elias) enim Cremonam ad imperatorem missus a domino papa Gregorio nono, cum esset specialis amicus utriusque.*

story and, to my mind, not the most decisive factor.[8] An answer to our question can better be found in the relationship of Elias with Emperor Frederick II. But first we need to briefly examine the context in which this drama was unfolding.

THE CONFLICT BETWEEN GREGORY IX AND FREDERICK II.

The deposition of Elias occurred at a time when relations between Papacy and Empire were extremely tense. Even though the events of this period have been frequently rehearsed elsewhere,[9] a brief outline of the evolution of their relationship prior to the explosion of hostilities in 1239 will help illuminate the context out of which the conflict arose.

After Gregory's excommunication of Frederick in 1227[10] and the papal invasion of the Kingdom of Sicily in 1229, the Treaty of San Germano, signed in July 1230, inaugurated a period of relative calm between the two men, allowing each to concern himself for a time with affairs in his own domain. The Emperor, however, had never

---

[8] The limited scope of this presentation does not allow me to demonstrate the evidence for this assertion. Suffice it to say here that the mission of the clerics to the papal court (reported by Jordan, cc. 63-64, 56-57) and the testimony presented against Elias at the chapter itself (reported by Eccleston, c. 13, 67-68), make for fascinating, if frustrating, reading, since the reasons adduced for wanting Elias deposed in 1238 are not the same as those presented in 1239. Quite possibly the reasons forwarded in 1238 were judged to be insufficient grounds for deposition so that by 1239 the clerical opposition was reduced to advancing *ad hominem* attacks against the general. In this way they hoped to show that the friars had lost confidence in the ability of the minister general to lead the Order: legitimate grounds for deposition, according to the Rule. Hence, the clerical disenchantment with Elias, though significant, was neither persuasive nor ultimately decisive in Gregory's decision to move against Elias. The most solid reconstructions of this question are Berg, "Elias von Cortona," 102-26, and Barone, "Frate Elia," 116-27, but see my own review of the matter as well (cf. above, n. 6, chapter 3).

[9] The bibliography for the conflict is extensive. Good surveys of the major events can be found in Thomas Van Cleve, *The Emperor Frederick II of Hohenstaufen* (Oxford, 1972) 344-85 [hereafter as Van Cleve]; and Ernst Kantorowicz, *Kaiser Friederich der Zweite*, 2 vols. (Düsseldorf, 1963 ; Berlin, 1931²), I: 402-70 [hereafter as Kantorowicz].

[10] Kantorowicz, I: 158. The ostensible reason was his failure to embark on his long-promised Crusade to the Holy Land: a task which he eventually fulfilled in 1228. The following year, however, the Emperor's peace treaty with Malek al-Kamil, the sultan of Egypt, not only horrified the Pontiff but scandalized those ecclesiastics intent upon the destruction of Islam: a theme which will recur in the polemical exchanges of 1239.

renounced his claim to the full restitution of his imperial rights over territories in Italy which Gregory's predecessors, in league with the communal movement, had removed from Hohenstaufen control. Nor had he renounced the ambition of his grandfather, Frederick Barbarossa, to establish a *renovatio imperii* within the Hohenstaufen domains, with Rome as its center.[11]

Accordingly, in the autumn of 1236 Frederick began to make good on his intentions by moving against Brescia and Milan: two key centers of resistence to imperial rule. With his decisive victory at Cortenuovo in 1237, the Emperor was at the summit of his power. But the advantage quickly vanished. First, his seige of Brescia failed; then negotiations with Milan broke down; and finally, in 1238, the Papacy decided to rouse itself and challenge the Emperor's claims of hegemony over the peninsula.

On 1 March 1239 Frederick issued a call to his allies to take up arms against Milan and all other centers of resistance: the battle for the *renovatio imperii* had been engaged—but not without opposition.[12] On Palm Sunday, 20 March, Gregory IX announced from the pulpit his second sentence of excommunication against Frederick II.[13] The ostensible reason for the sentence: grave and persistent obstruction of the liberty of the Church, particularly in the Kingdom of Sicily which the Emperor refused to cede to papal sovereignty. A few days later, another bull of excommunication *latae sententiae* was issued against anyone who would swear obedience to him.[14]

Frederick did not delay long in responding. On 20 April, the imperial chancery, led by Piero della Vigna, issued an *Encyclica accusatoria* against Gregory IX, sending it to the kings and princes

---

[11]Kantorowicz, I: 402-16; but especially the more trenchant article of Hans Martin Schaller, "Die Kaiseridee Friedrichs II.," in *Probleme um Friedrich II.*, ed. Josef Fleckenstein, *Vorträge und Forschungen*, 16 (Sigmaringen, 1974): 109-34 (rpt. most recently in idem, *Stauferzeit. Ausgewählte Aufsätze*, MGH *Schriften*, 38 (Hanover, 1993): 53-83. [Hereafter cited as Schaller, *Stauferzeit*].

[12]One can follow the unfolding events of the conflict in Friedrich Graefe, *Die Publizistik in der letzten Epoche Kaiser Friedrichs II. Ein Beitrag zur Geschichte der Jahren 1239-50* (Heidelberg, 1909).

[13]MGH EP, 1: 637-39.

[14]MGH EP, 1: 640-41 (7 April 1239). The following month, on 22 May 1239 - that is, a few days after the General Chapter of Rome - the same bull was addressed to, among others, the Order of Friars Minor: MGH EP, 1: 643-44.

(both temporal and spiritual) of Europe.[15] Beginning with the evocative citation from Isaiah *"Levate in circuitu oculos vestros"*, Frederick presented a spirited defense of his conduct during the pontificate of Gregory IX and an account of the persecution which he himself had been enduring at the hands of this Pontiff. He then proceeded to advance a radical interpretation of the doctrine of apostolic succession and authority: namely, that the true descendants of St. Peter are not the Popes but rather the College of Cardinals, of which the Pope is only its chief representative.[16] In asserting that ecclesiastical authority was, in fact, a shared authority, Frederick was outlining a conception of the papal office radically different from the one under which the 13th century Papacy was certainly operating.

Gregory's response to the April salvo had to wait, however, until the summer, detained as he was, among other things, by the Franciscan general chapter in Rome. But respond he did: the claims of the bull of 20 June are not only astonishing but the language used to depict the conflict has now become explicitly apocalyptic.[17] Taking as his point of departure images drawn from Rev. 13 and 17, Gregory begins his letter with the dire words: "Ascendit de mari bestia blasphemie, plena nominibus". In other words, comparing Frederick to the Beast rising from the sea in the Last Days, Gregory was depicting the Emperor not as the precursor of Antichrist—the *preambulum Antichristi* which, according to the Pope, Frederick liked to style himself—but as Antichrist himself![18] He then goes on to list a number of accusations bolstering his charge.

---

[15]MGH LEGUM, 4/2: 290-98.

[16]Van Cleve, 429-31.

[17]MGH EP, 1: 645-54. On the apocalyptic current in the controversy, see Hans Martin Schaller, "Endzeit-Ewartung und Antichrist-Vorstellungen in der Politik des 13. Jahrhunderts," in *Festschrift für Hermann Heimpel zum 70. Geburtstag* (Göttingen, 1972), II: 924-47, esp. 935-38 (rpt. in idem, *Stauferzeit*, 25-52); and, more recently, Peter Segl, "Die Feinbilder in der politischen Propaganda Friedrichs II. und seiner Gegner," in *Feindbilder. Die Darstellung des Gegners in der politischen Publizistik des Mittelalters und der Neuzeit*, ed. Franz Bosbach, *Bayreuther Historische Kolloquien*, 6 (Cologne, 1992) 41-71.

[18]MGH EP, 1: 653: *"gaudet se nominari preambulum antichristi."*

Frederick responded immediately in a letter sent directly to the Cardinals, rejecting the charges of the Pope.[19] Drawing on Rev. 6.4, he accuses Gregory of being the one who sits upon the red horse, sowing discord on the earth. Frederick thus does not identify Gregory, tit-for-tat, as the Antichrist, but rather as an agent of Antichrist who, in seizing power not his own—a reference to the claims of papal supremacy over all imperial rights—has sown destruction and disorder into an order established by God himself.

It is this background which is essential for understanding the actions of Gregory IX against Elias one month earlier in May 1239.

THE RELATIONSHIP OF FREDERICK II AND BROTHER ELIAS.

Some historians have assumed, correctly, that Elias' dismissal from office must have been in some way connected to his relationship with the excommunicated Emperor. The problem with this supposition is that, with the exception of the mission of Elias to the imperial court on behalf of Gregory IX in 1238, there is no solid evidence of any political involvement with the Frederick prior to this date.[20] Indeed, documentary evidence of any overt political sympathies for the Emperor on the part of Elias is to be found only in events which unfolded **after** his deposition at the General Chapter of May 1239.

After his fall from grace, Elias and several companions, we are told, went to do penance in a hermitage outside of Cortona.[21] In December of that year, according to the *Chronica XXIV Generalium*, it was Frederick who invited Elias—and not *vice versa*—to come to the imperial court in Pisa.[22] Frederick had been keenly aware of Gregory's actions against Elias at the Chapter of Rome; indeed, in a letter of July of that same year, Frederick had

---

[19]*Acta imperii inedita saeculi XIII et XIV*, 2 vols, ed. E. Winklemann (Aalen, 1964; Innsbruck, 1880), I: 314 [Hereafter cited as Winklemann]; HB, 5/1: 348.

[20]There is, nonetheless, some general evidence of a personal rapport between the two men. For example, see Salimbene, 157: *"Raro enim ibat quoquam, nisi dumtaxat ad papam Gregorium nonum et ad imperatorem Fridericum secundum, quorum intimus erat..."*; as well as the casual asides made on pp. 96 and 99.

[21]Eccleston, c. 13, 69.

[22]AF, 3: 249. It is Richard of San Germano (*Chronica*, ed. G. H. Pertz, MGH SS, 19 (Hanover, 1866) 379) who tells us that Elias appeared in the imperial camp around the time of Christmas.

even written to the Pope protesting the deposition of the Franciscan general and accusing Gregory of trying to trap and arrest him.[23] In the imperial camp, the Emperor could at least offer him protection.

By accepting the invitation, however, Elias automatically incurred the indirect sentence of excommunication issued by the Pope the previous March.[24] Then, after a failed attempt to make contact with Gregory to explain his actions resulted in his direct excommunication,[25] Elias was seen, according to Salimbene, at the side of Frederick II during the sieges of Faenza and Ravenna (between August 1240 and April 1241), having becoming the counselor and intimate of the Emperor.[26] Commenting upon this development, Gregory IX informs us that both Elias and a certain Henry had wheedled their way into the good graces of the Emperor, but that they were, he says disparagingly, contrary to their claims, *"non prophetae sed prophani apostatae"*: a highly significant remark, as we shall see.[27]

After the death of Gregory IX on 21 August 1241, Frederick sent Elias on mission to the East (from the winter of 1241 until 1243), entrusting him with leading the difficult negotiations between Baldwin IV, Emperor of the Latin Kingdom of Constantinople, and John III Vatazes, exiled Greek Emperor of Nicaea with whom

---

[23]HB, 5/1: 346-48.

[24]The documentary evidence on the issue of the excommunications is confused. Eccleston (c. 13, 69) correctly mentions, shortly after Elias' removal to Cortona, two different sentences of excommunication levied against him by Gregory IX. However, he incorrectly attributes the first sentence - by his own admission, he is guessing - to Elias' violation of the prohibition to visit the Poor Ladies without authorization. He then places the initiative for crossing into the territory of the Emperor with Elias himself, whereas, it appears, the opposite was true: it was Frederick who called Elias to his side.

[25]Angelo Clareno, (*Historia septem tribulationum ordinis Minorum*, ed. Alberto Ghinato (Rome, 1959) 79 [hereafter cited as Angelo Clareno, *Historia*]) relates how Elias, fearful of being trapped and arrested by the Pope in an arranged meeting, drafted a letter explaining his actions and entrusted it to the new general, Albert of Pisa, to deliver to Gregory. En route, however, the courier took ill, died and, according to Clareno, the letter vanished. Unaware of the details arranged between Albert and Elias, Gregory excommunicated Elias outright. On the date of the death of Albert, see Jordan, c. 70, 59-60.

[26]Salimbene, 160: *"et ipse miser semper in imperatoris exercitu morabatur dando imperatori concilium et favorem."*

[27]HB, 5/1: 777.

Frederick enjoyed good relations.[28] The mission appears to have as its aim some form of reconciliation between the two kingdoms and the creation of a solid Christian front on Europe's southeastern border with Islam. Overly ambitious, the negotiations proved ultimately fruitless. By the time of his return to Europe,[29] a new pontiff, Innocent IV, had been installed on the throne of St. Peter. Nevertheless, in spite of the change of the Chair's occupant, several attempts of the friars to reconcile Elias to the Order over the next years all ended in failure.[30] Elias' adhesion to the Emperor, in other words, transcended any personal antagonism or antipathy towards Gregory himself. The issue was not Gregory; it was Frederick. Salimbene states it baldly: Elias did not want to break with the Emperor.[31] Indeed, it is only in the years following Frederick's unexpected death in December 1250 that Elias appeared more amenable to any talk of reconciliation: whether he did so before his death in 1253 still remains a matter of conjecture.[32]

We need, therefore, to ask: what would have led Elias to knowingly incur excommunication from Gregory IX, persistently

---

[28]HB, 6/1: 147-48.

[29]It is after this mission that we should date Elias' quasi-permanent establishment at La Cella outside Cortona with his group of companions (Salimbene, 157-58). For, by 1245, he had undertaken the construction of the church of San Francesco within the city of Cortona.

[30]Eccleston (c. 9, 42) relates that at the General Chapter of Genoa (1252), the English friar, John of Kethene, persuaded the assembled friars to attempt to reconcile Elias by sending word that he should consider returning to the obedience of the Church and Order. Quite possibly linked to this new impulse was the unsuccessful mission undertaken by Gerard of Modena with the direct encouragement of the minister general, John of Parma (Salimbene, 162).

[31]Salimbene, 162.

[32]Giulia Barone ("Frate Elia," 132-33) believes that Elias was reconciled a few months before his death on 22 April 1253. For this judgement, she relies upon a document, cited by Édouard Lempp (*Frère Élie de Cortone. Étude biographique* (Paris, 1901) 79-187, here at 184) which purports to be both an admission of guilt by Elias and a request for absolution. The key words supposedly dictated by Elias are cited by Barone ("Frate Elia," 133): *"quia adhaesi Federico contra mandatum Ecclesiae et quia non portavi ordinem meum sicut debui."* Salimbene (162-63) seems uncertain as to the actual outcome of the matter. Moreover, he reports that some time later, an indignant and irate custos of Cortona, scandalized at the burial of an excommunicant in the friars' cemetery, exhumed Elias' remains and tossed them on a dung heap! Angelo Clareno (*Historia*, 79), for whom, it must be remembered, Elias was one of the major villains in his review of Franciscan history, states categorically that Elias was never reconciled.

remain in excommunication long after Gregory's death, and waver, perhaps, only after the death of the Emperor? Moralizers prefer to believe it was his arrogance and pride; historians would do better to look to the issue of eschatology.[33]

THE ESCHATOLOGICAL UNDERPINNINGS
OF THE CONTROVERSY.

Even though the activities of Elias prior to 1239 revealed no strong political sympathies with regard to Frederick, we have seen that his activities between December 1239 and December 1250 did indeed manifest a new and definite posture toward the Emperor. Is it possible to determine what might have prompted this newly-found attitude toward Frederick? Indeed: on the basis of the documentary record, we can demonstrate a clear connection between the values and projects to which Elias had been dedicating his energies since joining the Friars Minor and that which he would find attractive and compelling about the person of the German Emperor.

One such area of concern was the situation in the Holy Land. The first historical reference we have of Elias as a friar reports him being sent to the Holy Land in 1217 as the first provincial of Syria.[34] A second, more general concern was his active promotion of the missionary effort of the Order. His first generalate (1222-28) but even more so the second (1233-1239) testify to an extraordinary interest in sending the friars on mission beyond the confines of Christian Europe. By way of illustration, the year 1233 represents perhaps the best example of these efforts, with papal letters of

---

[33]It is of paramount importance to recall that the man whom Salimbene calls *Bonusbaro* (96), upon entry into the Franciscan Order, changed his name to that of *Elias*: the one who, along with Enoch, were to be, according to medieval apocalypticism, the two prophet-witnesses of the End Time (see Rev. 11.3). On this theme, consult Ernesto Buonaiuti, "Gioacchino da Fiore ed Elia da Cortona," *Ricerche religiose* 7 (1931): 53-59.

[34]Jordan, c. 9, 7-8. According to John Moorman (*A History of the Franciscan Order From Its Origins to the Year 1517* (Oxford, 1968) 46, n. 3), Elias probably sailed in 1218. It is not without interest that the first three minister generals of the Order—Francis, Peter Catani and Elias—all went to and lived for a time in the Holy Land. Preoccupation with the Holy Land—or, more particularly, the conversion of the Muslim world - held a prime place in the values of the early Franciscan community.

introduction being sent to three different groups of people: (1) leaders of the Muslim world (the sultan of Damascus,[35] the caliph of Bagdad[36] and the miramolin of Morocco);[37] (2) the Greek patriarch of Nicaea;[38] and (3) the king of Georgia in the Caucasus Mountains.[39]

It is important to note, however, that all of the missionary activities promoted by Elias were being carried out under the authority of Pope Gregory IX. We thus witness here a conjunction of interests between the two men in four specific areas of mission: (1) the conversion of the Muslims in the Near East and North Africa; (2) conversion of pagans on the un-christianized peripheries of Europe;[40] (3) the reunion of the Latin and Greek Churches; and (4) the confrontation of the new menace of the Mongols, rumored since the 1220s to be stirring in the area of Alexander's Gate, just south of the Caucasus Mountains.[41]

Now, that which underpins the activities undertaken by Elias and supported by Gregory IX—all before the deposition of 1239—is not only a shared interest in mission but, more profoundly, a common **eschatological vision of the world**. In other words, beyond any issue of personal rapport, the relationship of Elias and Gregory was also grounded in a shared understanding of events which had to occur to inaugurate the Last Days.

---

[35]BF, 1: 93-96 (Coelestis altitudo, 15 February 1233).

[36]BF, 1: 105-106 (Coelestis altitudo, 26 May 1233).

[37]BF, 1: 106 (In aliis litteris, 27 May 1233).

[38]BF, 1: 103-105 (Cum iuxta testimonium, 18 May 1233).

[39]BF, 1: 101-102 (Cum sit omnis, 11 april 1233). This mission was spearheaded by James of Russano and his companions (cf. Girolamo Golubovich, *Biblioteca bio-bibliografica della Terra Santa e dell'Oriente francescano* (Quaracchi, 1906), I: 162).

[40]A perusal of the *Bullarium Franciscanum* between the years 1233-1238 yields a number of papal letters of introduction for the Friars Minors in the areas of northeastern Europe: an effort largely spearheaded by John of Piancarpine, minister provincial of Saxony (1233-1239). See Williel R. Thomsom, *Friars in the Cathedral* (Toronto, 1975) 45.

[41]On this theme, see A. R. Anderson, *Alexander's Gate, Gog and Magog, and the Enclosed Nations, Monographs Mediaeval Academy of America,* 5 of the (Cambridge, Mass., 1932) and Raoul Manselli, "I popoli immaginari: Gog and Magog," in *Popoli e paesi nelle cultura altomedievale,* Settimane di Studio del Centro Italiano di Studi sull'Alto Medioevo, 29 (Spoleto, 1983), II: 487-517. See also below, n. 69.

In what did this common eschatological framework consist? First, both men believed, as did many of their day, that they were living *in undecima hora*: that history was hastening towards its consummation and that the events of their day, read in the light of Scripture, could yield some understanding of their meaning. Second, on the evidence of the just-cited papal bulls, both men concerned themselves with gathering the known world under the one sign of Christianity through the conversion of Muslims and pagans, the reconciliation of the Greek and Latin Churches and through a unified defense against the new threat of the Mongols. A third element, not part of the traditional eschatological framework but one shared by both men, was the key role to be played in the events of the Last Days by the Order of Friars Minor.[42]

It is at this point, however, that the eschatological agreement between the two men ceased and the troubles for Elias began. For as the activities of the Franciscan after 1239 reveal, Elias had come to believe that Frederick II was none other than the anticipated eschatological figure of the Last World Emperor.[43]

According to that particular current of medieval apocalyptic, which had as its touchstone the Latin transcriptions of the Pseudo-Methodius[44] and which had entered into the imperial propaganda of the Hohenstaufens in the mid-12th century,[45] the Last World

---

[42]See chapter 2 of my forthcoming book (cited above, n. 6).

[43]This theme has been overlooked in two otherwise outstanding articles on early Franciscan involvement in apocalypticism: Dieter Berg, "Staufische Herrschaftsideologie und Mendikantenspiritualität. Studien zum Verhältnis Kaiser Friedrichs II. zu den Bettelorden," *Wissenschaft und Weisheit* 51 (1988): 26-51 and 52 (1988): 185-209; and Robert E. Lerner, "Frederick II, Alive, Aloft and Allayed in Franciscan Joachite Eschatology," in *The Use and Abuse of Eschatology in the Middle Ages*, eds. W. Verbecke, D. Verhelst and A. Welkenhysen, *Mediaevalia Lovaniensia. Series I/Studia*, 15 (Louvain, 1988) 359-84 [hereafter cited as *Use and Abuse*].

[44]The standard latin version of the Pseudo-Methodius is found in *Sibyllinische Texte und Forschungen*, ed. Ernst Sackur (Halle, 1898) 59-96; but we await a new critical edition announced by Daniel Verhelst, "Pseudo-Methodius, *Revelationes*: Textgeschichte und kritische Edition," in *Use and Abuse*, 112-36. Germane to the theme of the Last World Emperor, also in the same volume, is G. J. Reinink, "Pseudo-Methodius und die Legende vom römischen Endkaiser," 82-111. An English translation of the Syriac text can be found in Paul J. Alexander, *The Byzantine Apocalyptic Tradition* (Berkeley, 1985) 36-51.

[45]Particularly in the anonymous *Ludus de Antichristo*. The text is found in: *Geistliche Spiele. Lateinische Dramen des Mittelalters mit deutschen Versen*, ed.

Emperor had a positive and constructive role to play in the events of the Last Days. As anointed head of the Holy Roman Empire, he —and not the Pope—had been given the dual role of drawing the whole of Christendom into unity and, once achieved, of gathering the rest of the world under the obedience of Christ. To accomplish this second task, this "king of the Greeks and Romans"[46] would go to Jerusalem, convert (or defeat) the infidel and then destroy the unclean forces of Gog and Magog, now released from behind Alexander's Gate. His work of unification completed, he would hand over his crown—and his soul—to God. Such would be the signal for the Antichrist to appear upon the scene, concomitantly prompting the return of Christ who, after dispatching Antichrist and his minions, would bring human history to its glorious close.[47]

Elias saw in Frederick II the one who would establish peace in Christianity by reuniting the Latin and Greek Churches, effect the conversion of the Muslims, and confront the Mongol menace. When and what might have prompted such a dramatic attribution of these eschatological roles with the German Emperor? Such an identification occurred, I suggest, some time after his mission to the imperial court in February 1238 and in direct correlation with the news filtering in from the East that the Mongols were once again on the move.[48] Indeed, we know that the report of the Mongol ultimatum sent to King Bela IV of Hungary in late 1237 by the Mongol leader, Batu Khan, had been transmitted to the patriarch of Aquileia (in northeastern Italy) by the following spring 1238.[49]

Karl Langosch (Darmstadt, 1957) 179-239. For an excellent overview, see Franco Cardini, "Il *'Ludus de Antichristo'* e la teologia imperiale di Federico I," in idem, *Dal Medioevo alla Medievistica* (Genoa: 1989) 151-63.

[46]As he was called in the Latin transcriptions of the Pseudo-Methodius.

[47]A competent, if somewhat disjointed, summary of the unfolding drama of the Ludus de Antichristo can be found in Richard Emmerson, *Antichrist in the Middle Ages. A Study of Medieval Apocalypticism, Art and Literature* (Seattle, 1984) 48-49, 58-59, 84-85 and 87-89.

[48]Accessible surveys of the Mongol advance towards Europe can be found in John J. Saunders, *The History of the Mongol Conquests* (London, 1971) 73-89; Davide Bigalli, *I tartari e l'Apocalisse* (Florence, 1971) 7-49; and Jean Richard, *La papauté et les missions d'Orient au Moyen Age (XIIIe-XVe siècles)* (Rome, 1977) 26-30.

[49]This ultimatum, threatening the conquest of Hungary and to advance "to Rome and beyond", was delivered to the king by the Dominican missionary, Brother Julian, at the beginning of 1238. A succinct account of these events is found in Robert

Salimbene informs us, moreover, that in that same year, Elias had received two delegations at the convent of Fano in northeastern Italy: one from the friars of the province of Hungary and another, shortly thereafter, sent from the king of Hungary himself.[50] It is thus news of the Mongol ultimatum that seems to have convinced Elias that the time of testing had come and that Frederick was indeed the man of the hour whose special task would be to save the Church from the onslaught of Gog and Magog.[51] Recall, too, that Gregory himself had told us that Frederick liked to style himself the *preambulum Antichristo*: the one who must come **before** the appearance of Antichrist—in short, the Last World Emperor.[52]

Gregory IX, however, did not share this positive assessment of Frederick and his role within the Church. For him Frederick's treaty with the sultan in 1229; his claims to hegemony over the territories of northern and central Italy; his insistence on the existence of imperial authority in its own right independent of the Papacy; and, most recently, his advancing of specious notions of apostolic succession: all represented a negative and dangerous threat to the Church. Frederick, in other words, was a destroyer and perverter, indeed the monstrous persecutor *par excellence*, of the Church and its institutions, whom Joachim of Fiore had identified as the seventh head of the Beast arising out of the sea in Rev. 13: that first and most terrible Antichrist who, as secular leader in the West, would ally himself with Islam **against** the Church![53] To combat this assault on the very existence of the

---

E. Lerner, *The Powers of Prophecy* (Berkeley, 1983) 10-11 (relying on Heinrich Dorrie, *Drei Texte zur Geshcichte der Ungarn und Mongolen* Göttingen, 1956).

[50]Salimbene, 107. The chronicler notes that this occurred while he was a novice (that is, in 1238: idem, 96).

[51]An interesting detail, whose meaning at present remains elusive, is the report by Salimbene that Elias was fond of wearing a type of "Armenian cap" (*capellam Armenicam in capite suo*, p. 96) and that his lay brother companions *semper barbam longam portabant, sicut faciunt Armeni et Greci, qui barbas nutriunt et conservant* (p. 102). Armenia is, of course, the area just to the south of the Caucasus Mountains, not far from the region of Alexander's Gate.

[52]See above, n. 18. Independent of my own research on Elias, Giulia Barone has also begun to appreciate the importance of the eschatological thematic in the life of the Franciscan general ("Rilettura," 75-76).

[53]*Il libro delle figure dell'abate Gioacchino da Fiore*, eds. Leone Tondelli, Marjorie Reeves and Beatrice Hirsch-Reich, 2 ed. (Turin, 1953), plate XIV; Marjorie Reeves and Beatrice Hirsch-Reich, *The "Figurae" of Joachim of Fiore* (Oxford,

Church and the papacy, Gregory would need the loyal support of his Churchmen; and in the first line of defense were to be the new mendicant Orders, whom he had already been grooming for such a task *in undecima hora*.[54]

The role which Elias envisioned for Frederick in the Last Days was thus diametrically opposed to how Gregory perceived him, thereby placing the Friar Minor in the camp of the enemy. The content of his eschatological hopes and the fact that Elias stood at the head of a community on whose loyalty the Pope needed to rely in the struggle which was reaching its culmination in the spring of 1239: these are the factors which led to his ruin at the General Chapter of May 1239. The fact that opposition to Elias' governance of the Order had been gathering among certain clerics merely sealed his fate.

EVIDENCE OF ELIAS' ESCHATOLOGICAL HOPES (1239-1241).

Thus far, we have attempted to present the broader context in which the Franciscan General Chapter of 1239 took place, showing how the deposition of Brother Elias by Gregory IX could conceivably have been connected to the erupting controversy between himself and Frederick II. In other words, what we have presented up to this point is a strong case based on solid circumstantial evidence. But do we have any direct evidence in the sources which might provide more convincing proof that Gregory had indeed moved against Elias primarily because of eschatological beliefs which had placed him at variance with the pope at a critical juncture in the controversy? We have, I believe, three pieces of evidence which, if read correctly, do in fact point us in this direction.

1972) 146-52; and the lucid article of Robert E. Lerner, "Antichrists and Antichrist in Joachim of Fiore," *Speculum* 60 (1985): 553-70, esp. 562-66.

[54]For Gregory's use of the Mendicant Orders against Frederick II, see Giulia Barone, "Federico II Svevia e gli Ordini mendicanti," *Mélanges de l'École française de Rome* 90 (1978): 607-26; and, most recently, eadem, "Forme e temi della propaganda anti imperiale nell'Italia federiciana: l'azione degli Ordini Mendicanti," in *Federico II e le città italiane*, eds. Pierre Toubert and Agostino Paravicini Bagliani (Turin, 1994) 278-89.

1. Elias' request to the friars prior to the Chapter.

It is Salimbene who, in his wide-ranging screed against Elias, tells us that during the run-up to the General Chapter, the minister general had made a special request to the friars:

> While Brother Elias was still Minister General but when he had already become aware that the General Chapter of the Order was on the verge of condemning him, he sent a message to the various convents of the brothers ordering the reading, after the *Pretiosa*, of that particular psalm which begins "You who reign in Israel, listen". . .[55]

Salimbene reports an event: Elias' request that the friars include in their recitation of the office the praying of Psalm 79 during the month prior to the Chapter which, Salimbene comments, "I have never seen done before or since". He then goes on to offer us both the reason why Elias had made this request—"He did this because that Psalm appeared to speak about the Order through the metaphor of the vine"—as well as an interpretation of the imagery of the psalm. However, both the reason imputed to Elias as well as his explanation of the psalm bristle with contradictions, casting doubt, not on the veracity of the event itself but on Salimbene's reading of the event.

The Franciscan chronicler wants us to believe that Elias chose this particular psalm for two reasons. First, Salimbene says that Elias believed the psalm referred to the Order which has "stretched forth its branches unto the sea and its boughs unto the river" (v. 12). And second, aware that a movement was afoot to depose him, Elias wanted to have the friars pray for him personally, seeing himself mirrored in the words of the psalm: "Let thy hand be upon the man of thy right hand and upon the son of man whom thou has confirmed for thyself" (v. 18). Salimbene found the request highly unusual since, he says, the psalm was sometimes indeed prayed prior to a Chapter, but only after a minister general had died, leaving his office vacant and thus the Order at risk.[56]

---

[55]Salimbene, 158.
[56]idem, 158-59.

Salimbene then goes on to give us his own interpretation of the psalm's imagery. First, he says that the psalm does indeed contain a reference to Elias ("that evil Minister General of the Order of Friars Minor"). However, it is not the phrase which he claims Elias believed referred to himself, but rather this one: "The boar out of the wood has laid it [the vine = the Order] waste; and a singular wild beast has devoured it" (v. 13). Then, he says that the verse which serves as the culmination of the psalm—"Let your hand be upon the man of your right hand; and upon the son of man whom you have confirmed for yourself" (v. 18)—actually refers, not to Elias but to "the **good** Minister General, that is to say, all the Ministers General **except** Elias".[57]

There are at least three problems with Salimbene's interpretation of Elias's use of this psalm.

First, if Salimbene's reading of the psalm imagery is correct, it seems odd indeed that Elias would have deliberately chosen a text which referred so damningly to himself. It is, therefore, obvious that Elias read the psalm differently than Salimbene and probably not at all as referring to himself.

Second, it must be asserted that prior to 1239, no minister general of Order had as of yet died in office.[58] Hence, Salimbene's reference to the practice of the friars reciting this psalm upon the death of the general and on behalf of the Order—as opposed to for an individual, Elias—could not possibly have occurred. Thus, Elias' request of the friars, though admittedly unusual, would not have had the aberrant significance attributed to it by Salimbene.

Third, Salimbene's assertion that the psalm, with its image of the vine/vineyard, refers to the Order of Friars Minor is, of

---

[57]idem, 159 (emphasis added).

[58]I exclude Francis himself from this assertion since he had already given up the charge of minister general five years prior to his death. Even if one would assume that Francis, as virtual leader of the Order, had died in office, it is interesting to note that in Elias' famous Encyclical Letter, amid the numerous biblical references lamenting the fate of the Order after the death of Francis, there is not a single reference to Psalm 79.

course, highly debateable in itself. That Elias agreed with Salimbene that such was the interpretation is also highly unlikely.

If Salimbene's reading of Elias' request and of the psalm itself was thus skewed by his own need to heap invectives upon his disgraced brother, we still need to explain why Elias would have ordered the friars to pray Psalm 79 in preparation for Chapter. An answer lies in the more customary interpretation of the psalm.

The traditional interpretation of the image of the vine is that it refers to Israel and, in an explicitly Christian context, to the new Israel: the Church. Given the charged context in which the upcoming chapter was unfolding—the threat of a Mongol incursion from the East and the resurgence of the conflict between papacy and empire—Elias would have been asking the friars to pray, not for the fate of the Order, but for the fate of the Church. As a selection from the text of the psalm makes rather clear:

> Give ear, you who rule Israel; you who lead Joseph like a sheep . . . Stir up your might and come to save us.

> Convert us, O God, and show us your face and we shall be saved.

> O Lord God of hosts, how long will you be angry against the prayer of your servant? How long will your feed us with the bread of tears. . . You have made us to be a contradiction to our neighbors and our enemies have scoffed at us.

> O God of hosts, convert us. . .

> You have brought a vineyard out of Egypt; you have cast out the Gentiles and planted it. . . you planted the roots thereof and it filled the land. . . It stretched forth its branches unto the sea and its boughs unto the river.

> Then why have you broken down the hedge thereof so that all who pass by the way do pluck it? The boar out of the wood has laid it waste and a singular wild beast has devoured it.

> Turn again, O God of hosts; look down from heaven and see, and visit this vineyard; and perfect the same which your

right hand has planted and upon the son of man whom you have established for yourself. . . Let your hand be upon the man of your right hand and upon the son of man whom you have confirmed for yourself.

O Lord God of hosts, convert us. . .[59]

If we are correct in assuming that Elias' eschatological hopes took on a new coloration with the incursion of the Mongols from the East in 1237-1238, then psalm 79—with its references to "the boar out of the wood", "the singular wild beast" and "the broken down hedge" —could all be read as referring to the inrush of Gog and Magog through Alexander's Gate, the reputed area of Mongol settlement since the 1220s. Moreover, if the Church was now threatened from the outside as well as from the inside by internal dissension— "you have made us a contradiction to our neighbors": a reference to the conflict between pope and emperor contradicting the Christian law of love?—who then was able to save it from total destruction? Elias appears to have interpreted the phrase in the psalm of "the son of man whom you have established for yourself" to refer not to himself but to the figure of the Last World Emperor and its historical manifestation: Frederick II. Elias, in short, was asking the Order to pray for the Church and for that forthcoming battle on behalf of the Church which was to be led by the German Emperor.

It is of interest that Elias' reading of events and of this psalm finds an echo in a letter written on behalf of Frederick II to the princes of the world by Piero della Vigna, chief legal advisor of the emperor.[60] This letter[61] is to be dated some time between the

---

[59]I use the English translation of the Douay-Reims version of the Vulgate with some minor stylistic alterations.

[60]On this important figure at the court of Frederick II, see, for example, Hans Martin Schaller, "della Vigna, Pietro," in *Dizionario biografico degli italiani*, Vol. 37 (Rome, 1989) 776-84; and Antonio Casertano, *Un oscuro dramma politico del secolo XIII. Pietro della Vigna* (Rome, 1928).

[61]Petrus de Vinea, *Friderici II. Imperatoris epistulae*, novum editionem curavit Johannes Rudolphus Iselius (Hildesheim, 1991), I: 73-80 [hereafter cited as Petrus de Vinea]. See also Hans Martin Schaller, "Die Antwort Gregors IX. auf Petrus de Vinea I, 1 'Collegerunt pontifices'," *Deutsches Archiv*, 11 (1954): 140-65 (rpt. in idem, *Stauferzeit*, 197-223) [hereafter cited as Schaller, "Antwort"].

issuance of Frederick II's *encyclica accusatoria* of 20 April and
Gregory's scathing reply *"Ascendit de mari bestia"* of 20 June. In
short, it was written during the polemical struggle between Gregory
and Frederick and was contemporaneous to the Franciscan General
Chapter.

The letter is important for our discussion since it uses as one of
its primary biblical touchstones the same-cited Psalm 79. Indeed,
one of its leading images is the same image of the Church as the
vineyard, introduced right at the opening of the letter:

> The chief priests and Pharisees have taken counsel
> together against the leader and Emperor of the Romans.
> They say: ". . . if we let this man go, he will subdue all of
> Lombardy and, coming like Caesar, he will not hesitate to
> take our place away from us and destroy our kind. He will
> then hire out the vineyard of the Lord of hosts to other
> laborers, he will judge with a judgement separate from us
> and he will shamefully destroy us. . ."[62]

In addition to his use of the central image of the Church as a
vineyard and the repetition of the metaphors of sheep and
planting, there are two other textual resonances with Psalm 79
which are worthy of note. First, Piero della Vigna's use of the
phrase *"Dominus Sabaoth"* is virtually identical with the
"Domine Deus virtutum" —or its alternate *"Deus virtutum"* —
employed as a refrain four times in the Vulgate translation of the
psalm.[63] Second, the very opening plea of the psalm is likewise
quoted by the imperial advisor within the text of his letter: *"At
qui regis Israel, intende"*.

Yet even beyond the issue of direct textual borrowings, the
whole intent of the letter is to lament the sad state into which the
Church has fallen. Indeed, since Gregory has failed to act in the
manner of a true descendent of Peter, unjustly persecuting the
Emperor, the Church finds itself riven with heresy and unable to
meet the present threat to its integrity. Moreover, echoing Elias'
use of the *"filius hominis"* imagery applied to Frederick, Piero
implores the pontiff:

---

[62]Petrus de Vinea, I/1: 73.

[63]Both phrases are translated as "God of hosts".

". . .do not oppose yourself to the Emperor, defender of Mother Church. . . Receive back then your noble son. . . otherwise our strong lion . . . will roar and bring fat bulls from the ends of the earth and, by planting justice, he will reform the Church, plucking out the horns of the proud."[64]

Thus, Piero della Vigna and Elias of Cortona appear to be drawing from a similar—though certainly not identical—pool of ideas about the German Emperor and his role in the Church in the Last Days. That these ideas surfaced at precisely the same time only lends credence to our assertion of that the eschatology of Elias was a prime issue at the Chapter in May 1239.

2. The sermon of Gregory IX at the Franciscan General Chapter.

A second, even more striking source confirming that the eschatological views of Elias led to his deposition comes from the Chapter itself. It is Thomas of Eccleston who reports that, immediately after calling the Chapter into session, Gregory preached a sermon to the friars, using as his theme words drawn from the second chapter of the Book of Daniel: *"Tu, rex, cogitare coepisti, quid esset"*. The full citation of this verse 29 reads: "You, O King, did begin to think in your bed on what should come to pass hereafter".[65] Gregory's sermon, in other words, was based on the famous dream of King Nebuchadnezzar of the statue of various metals wherein a stone "not made by human hands" detaches itself from a mountain and smashes the feet of the statue, bringing the entire edifice to a crashing end.[66]

The dream of the statue is, of course, one of the most widely used images in apocalyptic literature, interpreted often as the four empires which were to succeed each other until the end of time.[67]

---

[64]Petrus de Vinea, I/1: 79-80: ". . . nec opponas te Principi matris Ecclesiae defensori [...] recipias filium singularem . . . alioquin leo noster fortissimus . . . rugitu solo terribili trahet omnes à terrae finibus tauros pingues, et plantando justitiam, Ecclesiam diriget, evellens prorsus ac destruens cornua superborum."

[65]Eccleston, c. 13, 67.

[66]Dan 2.25-45.

[67]Indeed, the twelfth century saw a renewed interest in the image and its application to the political realities of the German Empire. See Alois Dempf, *Sacrum Imperium. Geschichts- und Staatsphilosophie des Mittelalters und der politischen Renaissance* (Munich, 1962) 229-68; of only limited use is Giorgio Piaia,

The emphasis in the text, of course, is upon the fate of the fourth and final kingdom: the Roman Empire and its medieval successors. It is destined, however, to be crushed by a stone not of human but divine origin: the Church, whose action against the last earthly kingdom will inaugurate the kingdom that will have no end. Hence, this pessimistic view of the Empire is in sharp contrast to its more positive role in the eschatological scenarios of the Last World Emperor.

Now the question is: given the strong political overtones associated with the dream of Nebuchadnezzar in Daniel 2, why would Gregory use this particular text in addressing the Friars Minor at their Chapter?

Eccleston gives us a reason; and yet, not unlike Salimbene, his account poses several critical problems to the reader. At first glance, his account appears fairly straightforward. Gregory preached a sermon based on the text of Daniel which dealt with, we are told, "the golden statue";[68] faced with accusations of his violations against poverty, Elias attempted to defend himself before the assembly; Haymo of Faversham, an English friar, insisted that his offenses were more grievous than Elias allowed; charges and counter-charges ensued; Elias refused to resign whereupon Gregory removed him from office.[69]

The problem with this account is that it is not entirely coherent. That a furious debate took place about the personal excesses of Elias and the shortcomings of his governance is not in doubt. However, Eccleston **assumes** that there was a necessary connection between the sermon preached by the pope and the ensuing debate about Elias' lifestyle; and, furthermore, that the connecting thread between them was the thematic of gold:[70] the gold of the statue as foreshadowing the moral failings of Elias (which are cast in the language of gold = excesses against poverty as well as charges of alchemy). I would suggest, however, that

---

"Interpretazione allegorica ed uso ideologico della prima profezia di Daniele agli inizi del Trecento," in *Soziale Ordnungen im Selbstverständnis des Mittelalters*, ed. A. Zimmermann, Miscellanea Mediaevalia, 12 (Berlin, 1979), II: 351-68, esp. 351-54.

[68]Eccleston, c. 13, 67: ". . .*quae erat de statua aurea."*

[69]idem, 67-68.

[70]It is Eccleston who calls it a *statua aurea*, not the Vulgate.

Eccleston **assumes** this to be the connection because this *ad hominem* attack on the excesses of Elias was in fact the very argument forwarded most vigorously by his English confrères. In other words, the report which Eccleston received about the chapter proceedings from his confrères—and upon which he was basing his chronicle narrative nearly two decades later—emphasized quite naturally the triumph of the English position in achieving their goal—getting Elias deposed—but to the exclusion of other issues.

Yet, the connection made by Eccleston between the sermon and the debate is somewhat tendentious for at least two reasons. First, the statue in the king's dream is not a golden statue; it is composed not of one but of four different metals, only one of which—the head—is gold. Moreover, the focus of the narrative is not on the head of the statue but rather on the fourth part, the feet composed of iron and clay. In fact, it is precisely the declining value of the four metals, from head to toe, which allows the dream to be interpreted in Christian history as an allegory of decline, particularly the decline of four great historical kingdoms. Indeed, it is the fourth kingdom, the Holy Roman Empire of the Hohenstaufens which will find itself destroyed by a stone "not made by human hands", the Church led by its pope, Gregory IX, thereby ushering in the Last Days.[71]

Second, if the intention of Gregory in his opening sermon was to lay the groundwork for a debate over the moral failings and violations of poverty of Brother Elias, then it seems bizarre in the extreme that he would have chosen as his text a passage so heavily freighted with eschatological significance as the dream

---

[71]A thorough study of the use of the text of Dan 2 in the 13th century has yet to be done. It must be observed, however, that, beginning in the late 12th century with the *Bible moralisée*, the interpretation of the dream of the statue of various metals starts to take on more moralistic overtones but almost always remaining an allegory of decline, that is, of declining virtue; see, Peter Kern, "Die Auslegung von Nebuchodonosors Traumgesicht (Dan 2, 31-35) auf die Lebensalter des Menschen," in *Les ages de la vie au Moyen Age*, eds. Henri Dubois and Michel Zink, *Cultures et Civilisations Médiévales*, 7 (Paris: 1992) 37-55. Nevertheless, it must also be said that the traditional, that is to say, historical reading of this text as representing the four kingdoms continued to be prevalent in the universities and clerical circles, as evidenced, for example, by a sermon of Eudes de Châteauroux in the 1260s about the downfall of Manfred Hohenstaufen. I wish to thank André Charansonnet for his private communication to me of this valuable information.

of Nebuchadnezzar. Indeed, there would have been no shortage of other scriptural texts, especially in the Gospels themselves, which would have made the criticism of Elias' lavish living far more pointed and obvious. To accept Eccleston's assumption of a necessary connection between sermon and debate on the basis of a golden thread is to accept that Gregory had either opted to use a deliberately oblique reference to the extravagances of Elias or that he misconstrued the thrust of the passage he was citing. It is far easier to believe that Gregory simply had another idea in mind when he lifted up the passage of Daniel 2 for the friars' reflection.

Indeed, placed within the politically-charged context which frames this Chapter, the sermon must be viewed as a dire warning to the friars at large and a direct challenge to the leadership of Elias, whose conception of the apocalyptic role of Frederick II was presenting a grave obstacle to the pope in his struggle against the Emperor.[72] Gregory had to be able to count on the Order to help him in a conflict which was gathering apocalyptic significance. In opening the Chapter on an apocalyptic note, Gregory was thus attempting to orient the friars towards a more proper interpretation of their role on behalf of the Papacy in its struggle with the Emperor and also to signal to the friars that he had called the Chapter to deal with what had become one of his main obstacles in this struggle: the generalate of Elias.

3. Elias and his companions in the imperial camp, 1241.

One final confirmation of the eschatological underpinnings of the deposition comes from a few salient details embedded in two sources: Salimbene's report of Elias' activities in the years following his fall from grace and a letter of Gregory IX written in February 1240.

We have already seen how, upon the request of Frederick II, Elias and several of his companions had joined the imperial camp in Pisa in December 1239. Salimbene then goes on to note:

---

[72]Moreover, the fact that the citation from Daniel used by Gregory in his sermon is pointedly addressed *Tu, rex*, would seem to indicate that he was thinking specifically of Frederick II, thus lending far greater weight to an eschatological (rather than a moralistic) use of this text in 1239.

And while living at the Imperial court, Brother Elias accompanied the Emperor on horseback, although he continued to wear the habit of the Order (as did all the other members of his retinue) . . . All this in spite of the fact that the Emperor was excommunicate. And even during the seige of Faenza and Ravenna, this wretch remained with the Imperial army, giving the Emperor advice and support.[73]

Although the seige of Ravenna was accomplished swiftly in August 1240, that of Faenza proved to be far more difficult, lasting from September 1240 to 14 April 1241.[74] Now according to Matthew Paris, immediately after the fall of Faenza, Frederick II, spurred on by news of the fall of Liegnitz to the Mongols in Silesia on the 10th, sent a letter, aided by his philosopher-astrologer Theodore of Antioch, to all the monarchs of Europe, warning them of the imminent danger of invasion.[75] To face the threat, he was thereby announcing the launching of a new crusade against the Mongols to be led by his son, Conrad.[76]

Given that a critical turning point in Elias' eschatological views appears to have occured in 1238 with the news of the Mongol threat, it is tempting to see a connection between the initiation of

---

[73]Salimbene, 160.

[74]Kantorowicz, I: 492-495, 499-500.

[75]Matthew Paris, *Chronica maiora*, ed. Henry R. Luard, *Rolls Series* (London 1877), 4: 112-119. Charles Burnett asserts that an *Epistola prudenti vero*, addressed to "Theodore, philosopher of the most invincible Emperor" and drawing upon the eschatological scenario of Pseudo-Methodius, must have been written at about the same time since it urges immediate action against the Mongols who are explicitly identified as the unclean peoples of Gog and Magog, previously shut up behind Alexander's Gate (cf. C.S.F. Burnett, "An Apocryphal Letter from the Arabic Philosopher al-Kindi to Theodore, Frederick II's Astrologer concerning Gog and Magog, the Enclosed Nations and the Scourge of the Mongols," *Viator* 15 (1984): 151-167). In a more recent article ("Attitudes towards the Mongols in Medieval Literature: the XXII Kings of Gog and Magog from the Court of Frederick II to Jean de Mandeville", *Viator* 22 (1991) 153-67), Burnett and Patrick Gautier Dalché state unequivocally (at p. 159): "By 1236 the Mongols had conquered Georgia - they had literally broken through the Caspian Gates". And in the accompanying note: "These were commonly identified as either the pass of Dariel in the central Caucasus or the pass of Derbend on the Caspian Sea in present-day Dagestan." The location is consistent with the region know as Alexander's Gate.

[76]The crusade was launched by Conrad at a Diet in Esslingen in May 1241. For a brief overview of these events, see Kantorowicz, I: 502-506.

this new crusade by Frederick and the "advice and support" offered by Elias and companions in the imperial camp. For such a battle to save not only the Empire but all Christendom from the unclean forces of Gog and Magog would have been perfectly in line with the eschatological role reserved to the Last World Emperor. Indeed, Gregory himself appears to have been aware that these were the eschatological hopes of Elias and a companion, Henry; for, in a letter in early 1240, he derides them for having ingratiated themselves to the Emperor in the imperial camp, whereas they were, in fact, contrary to their self-promotion, *"non prophetae, sed prophani apostatae"*.[77] In other words, in Gregory's view, they may wish to appear like prophets of the End Time, announcing the coming of Gog and Magog and placing their hopes in Frederick II,[78] but they are no more than renegades from their Order and the Church.

Hence, the eschatology of Elias and his circle—which surfaced in the sources in 1238 in connection with news of a Mongol threat of invasion and which prompted the wearing of Armenian hats and long beards in the style of Greeks and Armenians—surfaces once again in the sources in 1241: and again in connection with the threat of a Mongol incursion. The common thread tying the two events together is the positive eschatological role assigned to the German Emperor to meet this threat on behalf of the Christian Church.

THE ESCHATOLOGICAL VIEWS OF GREGORY IX.

Before we conclude our examination of the eschatological issues which shaped the deposition of Elias at the Chapter of 1239, it

---

[77]HB, 5/1: 777: "*Verum idem non sub pastoris virga humiliatus est verbere, quin potius super omne quod dicitur Deus aut colitur elevatus, Helia et Henrico quibusdam non prophetis, sed prophanis apostatis, testibus sue perversitatis assumptis, in lucis angelum in monte superbie transformatus, Christi claves et Petri privilegium vilipendens, irreverenter divinis interesse presumit, ministros ecclesie sub pena capitis et perpetui edicto exilii ad sue dampnationis cumulum divina prophanare compellens, pro summe sedis orantes antistite ac orare pro ipso publice contemptnentes simili puniturus edicto.*"

[78]One wonders whether they might not also have perceived themselves in the role of the two witnesses of Revelation 11—often identified with Enoch and Elijah—dressed in sackcloth, whose role in the Pseudo-Methodius apocalyptic scenario was to confront the Antichrist in Jerusalem with their preaching (cf. Buonaiuti, 56).

might be helpful to add one final element to the total picture: the contrasting eschatology of his primary opponent at the Chapter, Gregory IX. Unfortunately, to date, no systematic or comprehensive treatment of his eschatological views has yet been attempted. Hence, we can only hope to give a cursory treatment of the sources of Gregory's ideas and their ramification on the actions he took against Elias.

Several elements of Gregory's eschatology noted above might lead one to believe that he had been strongly influenced by the Calabrian abbot, Joachim of Fiore: namely, his efforts on behalf of the reunion of the Greek and Latin Churches; the central role which the Church must play in the inauguration of the End Time; the importance of evangelical preaching in the reform of the Church; his explicit assertion, in the liturgical sequence *Caput draconis*, that history was in its and final seventh age;[79] and, perhaps most telling, the complete absence of any role for a Last World Emperor.[80] Indeed, in Joachim, it is the intervention of a *novus dux*—a Pope, not a secular Emperor—who was to lead the Church through the time of persecution into the Third Age of the Spirit.[81] Thus, this is the primary reason why, contrary to Gregory

---

[79]The sequence, traditionally attributed to Gregory IX, was written most probably at the very end of the 1230s or early 1240s; see Hans Martin Schaller, "Antwort," 152-53 (rpt. in idem, *Stauferzeit*, 209-210). The text of the sequence is found in AF, 10: 401. It is the opening verses which indicate the eschatological time framework:

> Caput draconis ultimum,
> Ultorem ferens gladium,
> Adversus Dei populum
> Excitat bellum septimum.

Joachim believed that he was living at the end of the fifth and at the start of the sixth *aetas* (c. 1200). Since, according to his calculation of time, the seventh *aetas* was to begin in 1230, Gregory's designation of his own time as that of the *bellum septimum* is in perfect accord with the joachite framework.

[80]On this theme, see Marjorie Reeves, "Joachimist Influences on the Idea of a Last World Emperor," *Traditio* 17 (1961): 323-70, *passim*, and especially, Paul J. Alexander, "The Diffusion of Byzantine Apocalypses in the Medieval West and the Beginnings of Joachimism," *in Prophecy and Millenarianism. Essays in Honour of Marjorie Reeves*, ed. Ann Williams (Essex, 1980) 53-106.

[81]See, for example, Bernard McGinn, *The Calabrian Abbot. Joachim of Fiore in the History of Western Thought* (New York, 1985) 67, 112 and 121, n. 73.

IX, one must assert that the eschatology of Elias could not have been directly shaped by the ideas of the Calabrian abbot.

Moreover, the connection between the two men, Gregory and Joachim, can be strengthened by noting the positive esteem in which the pontiff held the Order of Fiore: the reformed Cistercian community founded by Joachim in southern Italy. In *Fons sapientiae*, the bull issued for the canonization of St. Dominic in 1234, Gregory, using Zechariah's apocalyptic vision of the four chariots, identifies the third chariot, drawn by white horses, as the Order of Cîteaux and the Order of Fiore, who by their charism, had been fortifying the Church in anticipation of the eleventh hour.[82]

Nevertheless, there are several problems with positing too close a dependence of Gregory upon Joachim. First, nowhere in the pontiff's writings does one find any signficant use of the major motifs which dominated Joachim's eschatological system: the trinitarian structure of history and the exegetical principle of concordance. Second, Nebuchadnezzar's dream of the statue of various metals plays virtually no role whatsoever in the writings of the Calabrese. And third, Joachim never explicitly identified the First Antichrist with the German Emperor. Gregory's identification of these two figures in June 1239—and his use of the dream of a prophesied destruction of the Empire at the Franciscan Chapter of Rome the previous May—can only be explained as the direct result of his conflict with Frederick. Indeed, the only other contemporary explicit identification of this first and most terrible Antichrist with Frederick II is found in the *Super Ieremiam*, the important pseudo-Joachim commentary on the Book of the prophet Jeremiah, written most probably by a Florensian monk and datable (at least in the form in which we have it) no earlier than 1243. Hence, Gregory's identification precedes that of the commentary and was quite possibly influential in shaping its negative depiction of the German Emperor.[83]

---

[82]BR, 3: 483-85.

[83]Through the 1230s, Frederick had maintained an amicable relationship with Joachim and the Order of Fiore. However, Salimbene (p. 236) recounts an incident which shows how drastically the Emperor's attitude had changed towards the Florensians by the early 1240s. He reports that the abbot of a Florensian monastery on the road between Pisa and Lucca, fled his abbey with copies of *omnes*

CONCLUSION

Though not a full adherent of the eschatological schemas of Joachim of Fiore, Gregory IX did find in the writings of the Calabrian abbot a certain resonance for his own ideas about the Last Days. Moreover, given the explicit identification of Frederick II with the First Antichrist (first in Gregory and then, a few years later, in the Jeremiah commentary) and given the Pontiff's favorable rapport with the Order of Fiore, one might reasonably conclude that Gregory IX was a kind of "joachite before the letter": an important transitional figure between Joachim and joachimism. As a selective exponent of Joachim's eschatology and a formative influence upon the author of the *Super Ieremiam*, Gregory represents, therefore, a crucial conduit of Joachim's ideas about the imminent persecution of the Church: a persecution which Gregory saw unfolding before his own eyes in the person of Frederick II and his most recent champion—the "prophet turned apostate"—the now-deposed Brother Elias of Cortona.

---

libros suos a Ioachim editos and took refuge among the Friars Minor in Pisa. The reason for his flight: *"timens, ne imperator Fridericus monasterium suum destrueret."* For he believed *quod in Friderico tunc temporis omnia essent complenda misteria, eo quod cum ecclesia discordiam habebat non modicam*. It is thus quite possible that Frederick's aim was to destroy all copies of the *Super Ieremiam* which were impugning his character in the eschatological scenario.

Olivi, Prous,
and
The Separation of
Apocalypse from Eschatology

David Burr

Virginia Polytechnic Institute and State University

As any church historian knows, Christianity developed in such a way as to give the study of eschatology a double focus. It referred to last things, but things were "last" in two different senses. There were the final days of earthly history culminating in Judgment Day, and there was the eternal reward and punishment that existed in heaven and hell, beyond history but also concurrent with it. It is on eschatology in the first sense, the end of history, that I shall concentrate in this essay. When I speak of "eschatology" I shall use the word in that sense.

In planning their route to the final judgment, early medieval Christians tended to follow the road map furnished by St. Augustine. It was a remarkably sketchy one, but it nevertheless laid out the general path to be followed, one that led past the standard apocalyptic figures of Elijah, Antichrist, Gog and Magog, then culminated in final judgment. Little attention has been paid to this positive aspect of Augustine's apocalyptic musings, and for two reasons. First, historians have been more interested in what he denied than what he affirmed, and what he denied was a literal thousand-year millenium. In essence he identified the 1,000 years of Apoc. 20 with the Christian era. In the second place, his essential message was that these final events were something about which Christians did not need to be terribly concerned, because they were not scheduled to occur soon. People had better get used to the ecclesiastical order as they knew it, since they would have it for a very long time to come.

Augustine's denial of a literal millennium kept medieval commentators through the twelfth century from taking Apoc. 20

literally but, as Robert Lerner has shown,[1] the sort of eschatological speculation patristic exegetes like Augustine and Jerome ejected from the front door eventually returned through a window opened by Jerome when he tried to make sense of the 1294 and 1335 days mentioned in Daniel 12. Jerome saw the difference, 45 days, as representing the period between the death of Antichrist and the final judgment. From Bede on, exegetes began to combine this notion with a reading of the Apocalypse which saw it as delineating seven periods of church history. The sixth period was that of Antichrist, and the 45 days stood for the seventh period which began with Antichirst's demise.

One might conclude from that fact that the seventh period would be slightly over six weeks in duration, but if the 1,000 years could be seen as symbolic, so could the 45 days. Bede implied as much, and Haimo of Auxerre went a step farther, suggesting that this number represented a minimum figure with more to be added, although his way of stating the matter suggested that the additional time would be brief.[2]

There is little point in tracing the way twelfth-century scholars produced variations on this basic pattern, since Lerner has covered the subject admirably; yet it is worth noting that several expanded the importance of the seventh period by assigning it more functions. Jerome had been genuinely puzzled as to why God should have thrown it in at all, but in his exegesis of Daniel he suggested that it might be there to try the patience of the saints. In his exegesis of Mtt. 24 he repeated that idea but combined it with a further suggestion that it would provide those marked for damnation with a final opportunity to earn that status by eating, drinking and making merry without attention to their souls. Haimo further developed this basic scenario, evoking the image of the elect using the time to do penance while the damned further damned themselves by indulging in carnal delights and rejoicing that, although Antichrist their leader was dead, they still enjoyed peace and security. Twelfth-century scholars developed it still further by working the conversion of the Jews and/or heathens into it. Gerhoh of Reichersberg extended its purpose even further by

---

[1]Robert Lerner, "Refreshment of the Saints," *Traditio* 32 (1976): 97-144.
[2]Lerner, "On Bede and Haimo," 103-7.

predicting that the church would be "cleansed of filth and simony" by "spiritual men" and the elect would rejoice.[3]

With Gerhoh we are in the second half of the twelfth century and rapidly approaching another seminal figure, Joachim of Fiore.[4] Joachim's contribution to the discussion was twofold. First he was the commentator who finally stood up to Augustine on the matter of Apoc. 20, although his defiance was hardly complete. He agreed with Augustine that the thousand years should not be taken literally and that they could be taken as standing for the entire history of the church. Nevertheless he insisted that identification of the thousand years with the seventh period of church history was a "rational opinion" consistent with the faith. Thus Apoc. 20 could be taken as predicting an earthly sabbath of peace and contemplation to occur in the seventh period.

This brings us to the second part of Joachim's contribution. He combined the sevenfold division of church history with a threefold division of history as a whole into the ages of Father, Son and Holy Spirit. The seventh period of church history corresponded to the final disappearance of the second age of history and complete emergence of the third age, a period of greatly increased spiritual gifts and high contemplation. Thus he identified the period after Antichrist with a radically new sort of Christian life. Perhaps the words "radically new" are misleading. Joachim also identified the third age with monasticism and began it with St. Benedict, so in one sense it had been gestating for some time by the seventh age. Nonetheless, the period after Antichrist marked the moment when, like a space ship shedding its booster rocket, the third age would discard the second and proceed to heights that only it could attain.

Having said so much, we arrive at a third point about Joachim, one that seriously qualifies his importance for the present discussion. Having agreed that the 1,000 years should not be taken literally, in his exegesis of Apoc. 20 he simply suggested that we leave the actual duration of the seventh period up to God; but in

---

[3]Lerner, 106-15.

[4]The literature on Joachim is huge. For a good short introduction to his thought on the topic under consideration see Lerner, "Joachim of Fiore's Breakthrough to Chiliasm," *Cristianesimo nella storia*, 6 (1985) 489-512.

dealing with Apoc. 8:1, the "silence in heaven for about half an hour," he suggested that it meant the final period would only last about six months. Thus whether we are dealing with Haymo's expandable 45 days or Joachim's shrinking millennium, we arrive at much the same figure. Six months is certainly more than six weeks, but neither is so huge as to allow anyone to think of the seventh age as anything more than a brief coda to history. The death of Antichrist remained a quintessentially eschatological event because it ushered in the final days in a very literal sense.

By and large, thirteenth-century exegetes adhered to the same pattern. They saw the Apocalypse as delineating seven periods of church history. The fifth period would witness the precursors of Antichrist, Antichrist himself would arrive in the sixth, and the seventh period would be a time of peace when holy men would be allowed to preach freely, sinners would receive a final chance to repent, and the Jews would be converted. They followed Joachim's predecessors rather than Joachim in basing the seventh period on Dan. 12 rather than Apoc. 20 and mentioning the figure of 45 days (or 40, a variant that had crept in along the way), but they also followed at least some of those predecessors in seeing it as a minimum figure.[5]

So far we have said nothing about one important element, the exegete's sense of where he stands in the process. Here it may be helpful to concentrate on three commentaries, two Franciscan and one Dominican, which share a significant amount of common material. They are interesting, not only because of what they say, but also because of the problems involved in determining their authors. The Dominican commentary, which begins with the words *Vidit Iacob*, has been assigned by Lerner to Hugh of St. Cher, or more precisely to the group that wrote commentaries under Hugh's name.[6] Both Franciscan commentaries are attributed by some manuscripts to Vital du Four, but one suspects that this is due to a

---

[5] On these commentators see my "Mendicant Readings of the Apocalypse," in *The Apocalypse in the Middle Ages* (Ithaca and London, Cornell University Press, 1992) 89-102, and *Olivi's Peaceable Kingdom* [hereafter *OPK*] (Philadelphia, University of Pennsylvania Press, 1993) ch. 2.

[6] "Poverty, Preaching and Eschatology in the Revelation Commentaries of 'Hugh of St. Cher,'" in *The Bible in the Medieval World* (Oxford, Blackwell, 1985) 157-89.

confusion produced by their common material. In only one case does Vital seem a serious contender for authorship, and we will refer to that commentary as by him, though without absolute confidence. In the other case one printed edition claims it is by Alexander of Hales, while another attributes it to Bonaventure. The latter seems highly unlikely and the former has been considered equally so by some modern scholars, yet I myself, while I see no reason why it should be attributed to Alexander, am hesitant to treat that attribution as completely impossible and will refer to the author here as "Alexander," if only to give it a name.[7]

All three commentators identify the fifth, sixth and seventh periods in the way described above. In dealing with Apoc. 9,[8] all three say that the fifth period has arrived. All three seem to demonstrate their point with a remarkable endictment of the contemporary church, in fact contemporary society as a whole. To be sure, in discussing Apoc. 8 Vital and Hugh seem to say they are in the fourth period, and "Alexander" too speaks of that chapter as if the ills it allots to the fourth period were present reality.[9] That might seem contradictory, and from one perspective it certainly is; yet from another it makes sense. One suspects that these authors see themselves as just entering the fifth period. This suggestion is strengthened by the fact that as he turns to the opening of Apoc. 9 and the angel who blows the fifth trumpet, Vital suggests that John has been consoling the church about the past but will now warn it about the future.[10] This seems consistent with the use of tenses throughout all three works. These are often confusing, because the total effect of these commentaries is to depict a world in which, though various periods succeed one another, they bring various combinations and degrees of the same basic evils. Thus whatever period they happen to be describing they can illustrate its ills by

---

[7]For further discussion see my *OPK*, 44f. I had hoped to return to these commentaries and pursue the question of their authorships, but as yet I fear I have not. In the following footnotes when citing Hugh I shall refer to the edition in Thomas Aquinas, *Opera*, Parma, P. Fiaccadori, 1860-62, 23:325-511. When citing Vital I shall refer to MS Assisi 66. When citing "Alexander" I shall refer to the edition in Alexander Halensis, *Commentarii in apocalypsim*, Paris, 1647.

[8]See Hugh, 397; Vital, 77rb; "Alexander," 154.

[9]Hugh, 395; Vital, 75va; "Alexander," 151-53.

[10]Vital, 76ra.

appealing to present corruption.[11] Nevertheless one gets the impression that all three authors see the third period as definitely past and the sixth as definitely future (although not distantly so), while the fourth and fifth are more familiar territory, both looking a great deal like the present landscape.

One might expect that their position at the beginning of the fifth period would insulate them from any eschatological anxiety by placing them three periods from the end, but that is not the case. "Alexander" explicitly describes not only the fifth period but the fourth as "toward the end of the world."[12] All three authors accept the standard notion that Antichist will reign for only three and one half years[13] as well as the idea of a brief seventh period. As for the latter, Vital says little about it[14] while Hugh, who has the unsettling habit of shifting back into the sixth period as he begins to discuss the seventh,[15] at least takes the time to announce that "once the Antichrist's persecution is over, the end of the world is at hand."[16] "Alexander" is another story. He is genuinely looking forward to the seventh period, which he describes as a time when the Jews as well as the rest of the Gentiles will be converted and "we will be like sons of God, for there will be no dominations or powers then, but all things will be subject to God alone, and God alone will reign in heaven, on earth and in hell."[17] He notes that some think it will last only forty days, thus paralleling the time given the Jews for repentance after Christ's death;[18] and acknowledges that according to the Apocalypse this respite will be brief, lasting only around "a half hour"; yet he seems hesitant to acknowledge its brevity. He suggests that it is said to last only a half hour either because judgment will follow swiftly or because "the peace from Antichrist's death to judgment day will seem to last only about a half hour." It is difficult to judge what he is

---

[11]Thus Vital, in a passage that should be dealing with the ills of the sixth period, can announce that *ad litteram ita est hodie.*

[12]"Alexander," 153, 158.

[13]"Alexander," 171, 240; Vital, [87=9:15], [145=17:10]; Hugh, 402.

[14]Vital, 71ra-rb, 89ra, 119va.

[15]Hugh, 416, 459.

[16]Hugh, 459.

[17]"Alexander," 204-6.

[18]"Alexander," 137. As Lerner, "Refreshment" shows, this variant on Jerome's 45 days already existed before "Alexander."

suggesting in that second alternative, but it is tempting to interpret him as saying it may *seem* like a half hour because it will be so enjoyable.

Thus Hugh and Vital are willing to envisage a quick run through the sixth and seventh periods, with the whole thing over in less than four years; and even "Alexander" is ready to acknowledge that most scholars would endorse such a timetable. Thus only the fifth period could be seen as placing them at any distance from the final judgment; yet one suspects Vital and Hugh would probably agree with "Alexander's" repeated statement that even then the remaining time is brief. That is, at least, the impression received from scattered passages. For example Vital, in explaining the "great city"of Apoc. 17:18, remarks that John looks backward to the Roman Empire, but also perhaps forward to a future moment "when heresy and all perfidy will reign." At that time, he says, "kings will be gathered to fight against [the great city] and strike at the sons of Babylon, who call themselves sons of Christ and are not, but are rather the synagogue of Satan." These kings will intend to destroy Christianity but will instead purify it. Their attack will crown the just with martyrdom and visit judgment on the evil. Their blow, Vital says, "has now begun in part." When it has run its course, there will be victory for the Christians and joy for those fearing the true God.[19]

It is hard to give this remark any clear meaning. Will the implied devastation of the corrupt church occur at the end of the fifth period and be followed by a further persecution under Antichrist, or is Vital describing a gradual process which will include the fifth period but climax in the sixth? Will victory over this evil be in history or on the other side of final judgment? Or is it naive to imagine that he has any expectation clearly in mind? He cites Joachim in the middle of these ruminations. It would be nice to know which work he means. Vital's scenario can be inferred from Joachim's Apocalypse commentary, but it would take serious effort. On the other hand, it is clearly stated in the pseudo-Joachim Jeremiah commentary.[20] Whatever Vital intends, his sense of impending historical judgment combines with his harsh attack on

---

[19]Vital, 130ra-rb.
[20]See *OPK*, 5-7.

contemporary ecclesiastical corruption to suggest that he places himself at no great remove from the end.

Vital is hardly unique in citing Joachim. Although our three commentators rely mostly on the interpretive tradition descending from Bede and Haymo, there are Joachite grace notes here and there. Nevertheless—and this is the most important point to be made—whether they are citing Bede, Haymo or Joachim, they find it easy to place themselves before Antichrist yet near the end. There is no sense that the rest of history might go on for a very long time.

What generalizations, then, can we make about these three commentators? First, we can say that they are genuinely apocalyptic. At first glance that might seem idiotically self-evident. What else can a person commenting on the Apocalypse be? What I mean by the statement is that, whatever else these scholars do with the text, they read a coherent pattern of historical development into it and place themselves at a critical point within that development. They make the text illuminate the present and relatively near future.

Second, we can say that their apocalyptic awareness is strongly eschatological. That is, the text confirms their feeling that they are living toward the end of history. It would be misleading to speak of the final days, but they seem ready to believe they are in the final years. What we see here is not the chiliasm rejected by Augustine, but it is not Augustinian either. Our commentators are a great deal more optimistic than Augustine about the possibility of finding a historical pattern in the Apocalypse, and they have a bigger reason to look for one because they expect Antichrist to arrive a great deal sooner than Augustine did.

It is perhaps wise to keep these commentators in mind when reading the polemical battles of the mid-thirteenth century, which featured heavy doses of apocalyptic denunciation. One thinks for example of William of St.-Amour's treatises against the mendicants, or Guelf attacks on Frederick II.[21] In the former case

---

[21]On the former see especially M.-M. Dufeil, *Guilaume de Saint-Amour et a l Polémique Universitaire Parisienne, 1250-1259* (Paris, Editions A. et J. Picard, 1972). On the latter see especially Robert Lerner, "Frederick II, Alive, Aloft and Allayed,

the friars were stigmatized as forerunners of Antichrist, and in the second Frederick was identified with Antichrist himself. It might be tempting to see these works as opportunistic, using an apocalyptic rhetoric without actually taking it seriously. That could be at least partly the case, but it would take a much subtler reading of these documents than anyone has provided so far to make the point convincingly.

Having drawn a few conclusions from the documents under consideration, I might pause to note one that should not be drawn. Whatever might be inferred from what has been said so far, it should lead no one to deduce that Joachim's contribution was minimal, a mere switch from "40 days or whatever" to "six months or whatever." In suggesting, *contra* Augustine, that the 1,000 years of Apoc. 20 could be identified with the seventh period of church history, and in seeing that period as the maturation of a third age different in nature from the first two, Joachim offered the basis for a genuine challenge to the ecclesiastical system as it existed. That challenge was never issued by Joachim himself. When he spoke of the woes to come he concentrated his attention on enemies outside the hierarchy like the Cathars, Muslims and Holy Roman Empire, and he was prevented from exploring the full implications of his third age by his agreement with Augustine that the thousand-year figure was purely symbolic; yet even on these terms his influence could lead others down dangerous paths.

That much is evident from the sad adventure of Gerard of Borgo San Donnino in 1254-55.[22] We know of Gerard's "Eternal Gospel" only what its critics and judges said about it, but even they tell us something. Gerard apparently left the length of the third period open, merely noting that the generations within it would be brief. Here he was completely in line with Joachim. Moreover Gerard— like others in his time[23] —thought prophecies concerning the third age would be fulfilled in the year 1260; and 1260 was not an un-Joachite number, although Joachim did not apply it as woodenly as

---

in Franciscan-Joachite Eschatology," in *The Use and Abuse of Eschatology in the Middle Ages* (Louvain, University Press, 1988) 359-384.

[22]For a brief description see *OPK*, 14-21.

[23]See Salimbene, *Cronica*, Bari, G. Laterza, 1966, 441 for the author's own disillusionment when Frederick II died in 1250, thus disqualifying himself for the role Salimbene and others expected him to play in 1260.

Gerard seems to have done, and in any case Joachim was given an entirely different relation to it by the fact that he was writing over a half-century before that date, while Gerard was separated from it by a mere six years. More important, Gerard apparently broke sharply with Joachim in making Joachim's own works the canonical scripture of the third age, replacing the New and Old Testaments. If Gerard really did say that, it is an indication of the way he appropriated elements of Joachim without really appreciating Joachim's central vision, which anticipated a new spirituality rather than a new set of books.

If the possibilities inherent in Joachim's third age were limited by his refusal to envisage a period long enough to do them justice, the idea of a new age was developing in an entirely different way within the Franciscan order. I refer to the idea of Francis as inaugurator of a new order that would play a key role in whatever events, eschatological or otherwise, lay ahead. We see this notion working itself out in various forms,[24] sometimes giving equal attention to the Dominicans and sometimes not. Here we will concentrate on three striking examples. The first is the Apocalypse commentary of Alexander the Minorite, occasionally (and perhaps unjustifiably) called Alexander of Bremen. Far from positioning himself in the final days, Alexander is reasonably confident that at least seventy years stand between him and Antichrist. Nor is he interested in what will happen after Antichrist's demise, or how long it will take. Nevertheless, his commentary is charged with a sense that something radically new has happened in the early thirteenth century with the creation of the Franciscan and Dominican orders, and much of his exegesis after Apoc. 20:6 is devoted to praising the mendicants.[25] He sees them predicted in the New Jerusalem of Apoc. 21 and expects them to provide the elect with leadership in preparing for and eventually weathering the confrontation with Antichrist.

---

[24]It is seen, for example, in the Pseudo-Joachim Jeremiah commentary, in Gerard of Borgo San Donnino, and in the joint letter published by John of Parma and Humbert of Romans in 1255. See Luke Wadding, *Annales Minorum* (Rome: Rochus Bernabò, 1732) 3:80-33.

[25]*Expositio in apocalypsim*, Monumenta Germaniae Historica, Quellen, I (Weimar: Hermann Böhlaus Nachfolger, 1955). For a brief description and further references see *OPK*, 30-33.

Another, equally ambitious attempt to read Francis into the Apocalypse is found in Bonaventure's *Collationes in Hexaemeron*.[26] Here Bonaventure places himself squarely within the sixth period of church history, which began with Charlemagne. He sees that period as a complex mixture of positive and negative elements, major spiritual advancement contrasted with overwhelming temptation. The major temptation will, of course, be provided by Antichrist, whom he seems to expect in the relatively near future, although he refuses to speculate on how long the period will last. The seventh period will bring peace and enlightenment. The church militant "will be conformed with the triumphant as far as is possible on the pilgrim way." How long it will go on, however, "God only knows."[27]

The most important element here is the way Bonaventure works Francis into this process. He is an early manifestation of the contemplative order that will bloom in the seventh period, and thus he links the two periods in a single continuous development. The major question is what the Franciscan order has to do with this development. Does it too link the periods? Joseph Ratzinger has argued that it does not, that Bonaventure saw it as a creature of the sixth period which would give way to another, higher order in the seventh. Others, including E. R. Daniel and myself, have argued for an interpretation which would keep Francis in his own order by seeing a strong continuity between the contemplative order of the seventh period and the spiritual destiny to which Bonaventure is calling his brethren in the *Collationes*.[28] If such is the case, we again have a strong sense of the order as ushering in a new era.

It remained for Peter Olivi to bring these elements together in an even bolder formulation of Franciscan apocalyptic during the final decade of the thirteenth century. In his commentary on the Apocalypse he accepted the Joachite notion of a third age palpably different from the first two; read Francis into it as its co-founder (along with Joachim, who remained something of a junior partner); and completed Joachim's half-finished refutation of

---

[26]*Collationes in Hexaemeron*, in *Opera Omnia* (Quarachi, College of Saint Bonaventure, 1882-1902) vol. 5. For description and references see *OPK*, 33-44.

[27]*Collationes in Hexaemeron*, 16:19, 22, 30.

[28]For brief discussion see *OPK*, 41-44.

Augustine by depicting the third age as a real millennium, albeit a
slightly shrunken one of 700-800 years. Having discussed Olivi's
reading of the Apocalypse at some length I hardly need to do so
again here.[29] The important point for this discussion is that in
proceeding as he did Olivi effectively separated apocalypse from
eschatology. He was conscious of living in an apocalyptically
charged period, but there was nothing particularly eschatological
about it. Final judgment seemed about as far away to Olivi as it
had to Augustine. He expected it to arrive somewhere around the
year 2000 and thus showed little interest in it. The important
ending in his own time was that not of the world but the second age.
It had, in fact, been ending for close to a century. The third age of
peace and contemplative bliss would not be fully realized until the
death of Antichrist, which Olivi expected sometime before the
middle of the fourteenth century, but it was already being realized
at least in part, and the Franciscan rule provided a model of sorts
for it, as did Francis' life.

Olivi's picture of the third age nevertheless remained general.
He was still very much aware of living in the second age and
remarkably cautious in suggesting what the next one would be like
once it became, as it were, free-standing. Nor did he ever offer
himself as an example of the new contemplative knowledge to be
enjoyed in the third age. Like John the Baptist in Grünewald's
Isenheim Altarpiece, he simply pointed.

When we turn from Olivi to his self-proclaimed champion, the
beguine Na Prous Boneta, we see what could happen when someone
stopped merely pointing and started to act like a participant. It is
not a sight Olivi would have enjoyed much. On August 6, 1325
Prous, an inhabitant of Montpellier, gave her testimony before the
Inquisitor at Carcassone.[30] She explained that she had made a vow
of virginity in 1305 and nine months later visited Olivi's tomb at
Narbonne on his feast day, March 14. She was later informed by
Christ that she had been conceived in the spirit on the day she
vowed virginity, and on Olivi's feast day had been born spirit-

---

[29]See OPK,
[30]Published by William May, "The Confession of Prous Boneta, Heretic and
Heresiarch, in *Essays in Medieval Life and Thought*, edited by John H. Mundy et
al., (New York: Biblo and Tannen, 1965) 4-30. [Hereafter "Confession"].

ually. All her sins had been forgiven on the day of her spiritual conception, just as Mary's were in her mother's womb.[31]

The next important experience reported by her occurred around 1321 at Montpellier, in the Franciscan church. While she was at mass on Good Friday she was transported in the spirit to the first heaven and saw God's divinity. The experience lasted two days, and by the time it was over Prous had received the entire trinity in a special way. Nevertheless it particularly involved the Holy Spirit, for she had been chosen as donatrix of the Spirit just as the Virgin Mary was donatrix of the Son, and as herald of the Spirit just as John the Baptist was herald of Christ.[32]

Prous is not our only source for the Olivi cult practiced by the Beguines. We also find it described by Bernard Gui in his *Practica Inquisitionis*.[33] Nevertheless, compared with Prous the version in Gui seems tame. Prous insists that Olivi's writings were dictated by the Holy Spirit and must be believed in order to be saved. Unfortunately just the opposite has occurred. Olivi's writings and memory have been assaulted, especially by Thomas Aquinas and Pope John XXII. Aquinas, like Cain, spiritually slew his brother Olivi by attacking his writing.[34] John XXII too played Cain to Olivi's Abel, but he also became Adam, for his sin in condemning Olivi's writing was equal to Adam's. By condemning Olivi's writing he condemned Christ, for Christ has two natures, and just as destroying the gospel means assaulting Christ's human nature, so destroying the wisdom of the Holy Spirit given to Olivi means assaulting Christ's divine nature. In condemning Christ, of course, he also made himself a new Caiaphas. He is a new Herod as well, for just as Herod ordered the slaughter of the innocents, John ordered that the beguines should be burned.[35]

John is also like Lucibel (or, in post-fall nomenclature, Lucifer). Lucibel received the noblest name among angels, and John received the noblest name among men, "apostle" or "pope."[36] After his fall, however, the former received the most terrible name among all the

---

[31]"Confession," 10f.

[32]"Confession," 7f., 26.

[33]*Practica Inquisitionis* (Paris, Alphonse Picard, 1886) 264-87.

[34]"Confession," 24.

[35]"Confession," 12. John is also likened to Simon Magus.

[36]It is worth remembering that the word used here is *papa*.

demons, "Lucifer," and after John's fall he received the most terrible name among men, "Antichrist." John also resembles Lucifer inasmuch as his fall is irreversible. That is his fault, not Christ's, for the latter has told Prous that he would be willing to forgive John if he repented, just as he would have forgiven Cain, Caiaphas, Simon Magus and Herod. None of them did repent, however, and neither will John.

Moreover, John's fall brought the church down with him. Prous reports a conversation with Christ which took place one day when she had intended to take communion. Christ told her not to bother because the sacraments no longer conferred salvation. Here again Prous sees a parallel with Adam. Just as human nature in its entirety died spiritually when Adam sinned, so Christianity as a whole died spiritually through John's sin.

Has the church, like John, fallen irreversably? Yes and no. The old dispensation is quite dead, but Prous feels that is no bad thing, because she discerns the birth of a new one. Buried in Prous' testimony, obscured partly by her and perhaps partly by the state of the document, is an awareness of Joachim's three ages. She speaks of one sort of power that obtained between the fall and the incarnation. Then the trinity invested all of its power in the Son, and that situation lasted until the trinity later placed its power in the Holy Spirit and deposited the Holy Spirit in Olivi. Here it is Olivi who seems to occupy the role played by Mary in the second age, the role Prous assigns herself elsewhere. She avoids the apparent inconsistency by adding herself alongside Olivi, noting that God had once told her of two women mentioned in holy scripture, Mary and herself, who were to receive the Son and Holy Spirit respectively.[37] Thus Prous identifies her own role with Olivi's, and that identification extends to her claim that she and Olivi are both unquestionable authorities. It is necessary for salvation to believe that God gave Olivi the Holy Spirit in its entirety and, since Prous shares that same Spirit with Olivi, those who would be saved must also believe her.

The important point for our purposes is that, as Prous explicitly states, John's loss of power was part of a more general transfer of

---

[37]"Confession," 20.

power with the birth of a new age. That birth has been a painful one for many. Prous tells us that since the sacrament of the altar lost its power the gates of heaven have been closed and no one has entered. The souls of the elect are being temporarily warehoused in Limbo, where they must remain until Christ dies a second time in his person and spirit That is precisely what is happening, however. Just as the Son of God was sent to the Jewish legal experts and, not recognizing him, they crucified him, so the Christian legal experts are failing to recognize and thus crucifying the Holy Spirit in the person of Prous.[38] Thus Prous' trial is a soteriological event parallel with Christ's death on the cross, and modern church leaders are doing just what Jewish leaders did in the first century: They are simultaneously putting an end to their own authority and bringing the new dispensation to birth.

There is, then, both continuity and discontinuity between the old and new ages. The church remains, although its sacraments may disappear and its leadership change. Christ remains as well. He is not replaced by the Holy Spirit. Prous recognizes that these are two aspects of the same trinity. Nevertheless, the two ages are marked by two passions atoning for two different sins. Adam's sin was purged by Christ's passion, and the time of that passion is now over. John XXII's sin, which is as great as Adam's sin, will be purged by the passion now in progress, "the beginning of which is the term and end of the Lord Jesus Christ's passion."[39]

Pushed by her interrogators on the disappearance of the sacraments, Prous shows some hesitation. She is absolutely sure about the Eucharist. "However many chaplains may celebrate masses, saying all the accustomed words at the consecration, it will contribute nothing at all to the salvation of anyone, nor will [those chaplains] confer the body of Christ, because the sacraments have lost their power." She is equally sure that baptism and confesson are neither efficacious nor necessary. All who believe in Olivi's writing and Prous' words, observe the commandments, and feel contrition will be baptized in the Holy Spirit, and the Lord will forgive their sins. Prous is less sure about marriage. She suggests that it should be observed as it was in the cases of Adam and Eve

---

[38]"Confession," 23.
[39]"Confession," 27.

and the marriage at Cana (John 2), but she has no idea what that entails.[40] The important thing is that he who gave the law can rescind it. Christ gave us the sacramental laws and now, because of the pope's sin, he has taken them away.

One might be tempted to observe that Prous is hardly worth the attention given her so far, since her insistence on her own spiritual gifts makes her unique among the beguines of whom we have any knowledge. One might, in fact, be moved to suggest that such insistence makes her interesting more from a clinical than from a theological perspective. It is impossible to read Prous' testimony, though, without seeing something more than emotional illness. A presumably ignorant layperson, she nonetheless constructs a rich, complex theology of history which simultaneously expands and distorts Olivi's.

This is not to suggest that everything in her testimony that goes beyond Olivi should be regarded as her own contribution. One can imagine her listening to someone read a vernacular work like the Catalan text subjected to investigation in 1318 or 1319 by Guido Terreni and Pierre de Palu.[41] The latter apparently included large segments of Olivi's Apocalypse commentary with additions and minor adjustments. Thus whereas in Olivi's commentary the angel of Apoc. 10:1 is Francis, in the Catalan work it is Olivi himself just as Prous claims. Bernard Gui's *Practica inquisitionis* tells us that the beguines encountered by him made the same identification.[42] In fact much else reported by Gui supports the notion that Prous was drawing upon a common set of beliefs. In Gui's description we find the notion that Olivi received his knowledge by divine revelation; that he and and Saint Paul are the only two absolutely infallible authorities; that he "is the light which God sent into the world, and thus those who do not see this light walk in darkness"; that by condemning him the pope became a heretic; that ecclesiastical persecution of the spiritual Franciscans and beguines represents a new passion; and that beyond that passion lies a new age with a

---

[40]"Confession," 27-29.
[41]See Burr, *OPK*, 204, 206-17.
[42]*Practica inquisitionis*, 273, 280.

much different sort of church.[43] We even find reference to the pope as a new Caiaphas, Nero, Herod and Simon Magus.[44]

Obviously some of these assertions claim for Olivi precisely what he denied. He consistently presented himself as a fallible scholar, not an infallible spokesman for God.[45] Nor did he ever attack a specific pope as Prous did John. Nevertheless, it is hard to deny that in condemning John Prous simply accused him of having done what Olivi was sure some pope in the near future would do, and with some reason. John's campaign against the spirituals and beguines looked oddly like the one Olivi expected the carnal church to launch against the new era. The scenario projected by Olivi bore an uncanny resemblance to the one Prous saw unfolding. Thus one can understand why, whereas Olivi simply predicted the new Caiaphas/Nero/Herod/Simon Magus, Prous thought she had seen him at work.

Moreover, their underlying presuppositions were remarkably similar. As she participated in those beguin readings Prous absorbed Olivi's strong sense of history as a dynamic process containing real change, and his Joachite belief in a threefold division of history into the ages of Father, Son and Holy Spirit. She absorbed his conviction that Francis and his movement represented a critical moment in history, the point at which the transfer to the third age began. Something radically new was occurring. She also inherited Olivi's Joachite sense of historical parallelism and his genuine pleasure in elaborating such parallels. Like Prous, Olivi repeatedly underlined the parallel between resistence to change in the first century and resistence to it in the thirteenth. Nevertheless, Prous inherited Olivi's sense that, although Francis played somewhat the same role in inaugurating the third age that Christ had in inaugurating the second, Christ had not been superseded by Francis. Like Olivi, she recognized that

---

[43]*Practica Inquisitionis* , 272f., 281, 287.

[44]*Practica Inquisitionis* , 281.

[45]Nevertheless, the way Olivi combines prophecy, contemplation and biblical exegesis in his discussions of Joachim makes one wonder if he might have granted, however hesitantly, that the sort of interpretation provided in his Apocalypse commentary was a species of *intellectus spiritualis* and thus in some sense the result of a divinely-granted heightened spiritual awareness. See my "Olivi on Prophecy," *Cristianesimo e Storia*, 17 (1996) 367-89.

the second and third ages both lay within the Christian
dispensation. Christ ruled over both; yet he ruled over the third
age in a different way.

Most important for our purposes, Prous learned from Olivi to be
profoundly apocalyptic without being very eschatological. She
was primarily interested in the death of the old age and birth of
the new. In her testimony she never discusses how long the new age
will last now that it is underway, but she acts as if it will be
around for some time to come. Bernard Gui reports that some
beguines expected it to last a century. Perhaps Prous thought so too,
but she never said so. However she might have answered the
question, the significant thing is that it was a question which
simply did not interest her. The end that concerned her was not
that of the world, but that of the old dispensation.

One might ask if Olivi and Prous were part of a more general
change in the nature of apocalyptic awareness. Some scholars
would agree. Stephen Wessley[46] rightly sees the spiritual
Franciscans, beguines, Guglielmites and Dolcinists as connected by
their common reliance on the thirteenth-century themes of *ecclesia
spiritualis*, *imitatio Christi*, and *vita apostolica*. On the precise
question under consideration, however, it is harder to show any
significant parallel. Certainly the Gugliemites, whom the
inquisitors at Milan were attempting to hound out of existence
during Olivi's final years, were similar in their strong sense of
innovation.[47] Guglielma herself, like Olivi, had been subject to
some examination during her lifetime but at her death in 1281 had
died in good enough odor to be venerated as a saint in her own city.
Like Olivi, she was seen by a smaller group as more than a saint,
and credited with major involvement in ushering in a new era. Like
Olivi in Prous' interpretation, she was identified by her admirers
with the Holy Spirit. In Guiglielma's case, this new age of the
Holy Spirit was associated with a widening of the Christian
dispensation in the sense that the priesthood was extended to
women and there would be a major conversion of the Jews and

---

[46]"The Thirteenth-century Guglielmites: Salvation Through Women," in
Medieval Women (Oxford, Basil Blackwell, 1978) 289-303.
[47]Luisa Muraro Vaiani, *Guglielma e Maifreda*, Milan, La Tartaruga, 1985,
offers a brief but competent survey of the process.

Muslims. Like Prous the Guglielmites felt that the pope—in this case Boniface VIII—was without authority. That in itself was not unusual, since a number of more or less orthodox Christians thought the same thing about Boniface. It takes on a new meaning, though, when we discover that Sister Maifreda, one of the two central figures in the group after Guglielma's death, assumed priestly robes, conducted mass, and may have been regarded as pope by her fellow believers. Thus in the Gugliemites' case the denial of Boniface's authority may have been part of a general sense—not unlike Prous's—that the new age had brought a major shift in the locus of authority.

All this is, of course, dependent upon testimony gathered during the inquisitorial process which led to the burning of Maifreda and others in 1300, and inqusitorial records invite suspicion. In fact, they are probably more suspicious in Maifreda's case than in Prous', since it appears that the former consciously attempted to conceal the truth for some time, while Prous' process gives just the opposite impression. At times she seems to take over the interrogation, using it as an opportunity to preach her gospel. Nevertheless, in Maifreda's case the broad outline suggested here is probably accurate.

The Apostles offer another interesting parallel, at least in their later incarnation under Fra Dolcino.[48] Dolcino posited four rather than three ages of world history, but in other ways the pattern is familiar. In his first letter to the faithful, written in 1300, Dolcino saw the final age as having originated under Gerardo Segarelli, founder of the Apostles, and thought Segarelli and himself important enough to be designated by two of the seven angels addressed in the first vision of the Apocalypse, that of the letters to the seven churches of Asia. He looked forward to a cleansing of the church within three years through the violent extermination of existing leaders by Frederick of Sicily, followed by a period of peace and apostolic perfection under Frederick and a holy pope until the arrival of Antichrist, whose death would

---

[48]Raniero Orioli, *Venit Perfidus Heresiarcha* (Rome, Istituto Storico Italiano per il Medio Evo, 1988) offers an excellent extended examination, while Elena Rotelli, *Fra Dolcino e gli Apostolici nella Storia e nella Tradizione* (Torino, Claudiana Editrice, 1979) provides a good outline of Dolcino's letters.

apparently lead to final judgment. In his second letter, written at the end of 1303, the scenario obviously called for some adjustment, which Dolcino provided by postponing the extermination until 1304. Here he spoke of four popes, the first and last good and the middle two evil. The first was Celestine V, the second Boniface VIII, and the third unnamed. Once this third pope was destroyed by Frederick of Sicily,[49] a fourth, holy pope would reign until the end of the world.

Here we have yet another new age of peace strongly associated with the Holy Spirit. Again we see a small group presenting itself as the advanced guard of a major alteration. Beyond that one finds differences. The most important one for our purposes is that according to Dolcino, once the new age was in full bloom, it would only comprise the reign of a single pope before being brought to an end by Antichrist and the final judgment. That made it longer than 45 days or six months but substantially shorter than Olivi's slightly shrunken millenium, shorter even than the hundred years mentioned by Gui in the case of the beguines. Thus Dolcino managed to combine his notion of a new age with a sense of living in the final days. It is hard to find any such feeling in Prous' testimony. It is in precisely this sense that Olivi's influence seems to have been determinative.

Nor was she the last for whom it was determinative. As Robert Lerner has noted,[50] in 1332, seven years after Prous' testimony, a young man studying in Toulouse, Jean of Roquetaillade, discovered Olivi and turned his mind to prophecy. The result was a literal reading of Apoc. 20 that bettered Olivi's 800 years by 200, producing a millenium that extended exactly 1,000 years beyond the death of Antichrist. Jean's wide circulation in following years, combined with the rediscovery of Lactantius' fourth-century argument for a literal millenium, insured that the fissure between apocalyptic and eschatology would remain open throughout the later Middle Ages. That, however, is another, longer story.

---

[49]Frederick also appears in beguin apocalyptic scenarios. See Raoul Manselli, *Spirituali e beghini in Provenza* (Rome, Istituto Storico Italiano per il Medio Evo, 1959) 197-99.

[50]"The Medieval Return to the Thousand-Year Sabbath," in *The Apocalypse in the Middle Ages* (Ithaca and London, Cornell University Press, 1992) 66-68.

Scotus's Eschatology:
Some Reflections

Allan B. Wolter, O.F.M.

Santa Barbara, CA

Pope Paul VI points out in his apostolic letter *Alma parens* that Duns Scotus built his systematic philosophical and theological conception of God upon two passages of Scripture, one from Exodus, namely "I am who am" and the other from the first Johannine epistle, namely: "God is love."[1] As a philosopher Scotus interpreted the first of these to be God's description of himself as 'being' -- the core notion he chose to develop as a philosopher in his *De primo principio*. He gives this prayerful summary of what he believed a skillful metaphysician could prove by natural reason:[2]

> You alone are simply perfect, not just a perfect angel, or a perfect body, but a perfect being, lacking no entity it is possible for anything to have. Nothing can formally possess every perfection, but every entity can exist in something either formally or eminently,[3] as it does in you, O God, who are supreme among beings, the only one of them that is infinite. Communicating the rays of your goodness most liberally, you are boundless good, to whom as the most

---

[1]"Doctor Subtilis . . . suam construit theodiceam principiis et rationibus Deum spectantibus e Sacris Litteris haustis, 'Ego sum qui sum,' et 'Deus caritas est' . . ." *Acta Apostolicae Sedis*, 58 (1966) 612.

[2]A. B. Wolter, *A Treatise on God as First Principle*, 2ed. (Chicago: Franciscan Herald Press, [1983]), p. 144. For the fuller account of the context in which this item occurs see the Introduction to my *Duns Scotus on the Will and Morality* (Washington, D.C.: The Catholic University of America Press, 1986) 8. Hereafter this work is referred to as *Will and Morality*.

[3]God's justice towards creatures is a splendid example of a perfection that does not exist formally, but rather eminently in God as a consequence of that love God has for his own goodness.

lovable thing of all every single being in its own way *comes back to you as its ultimate end.*

Even on purely philosophical grounds, it was clear to Scotus that God himself must somehow be the ultimate end of whatever he creates. What our intellect, unaided by revelation, leaves unexplained is how 'in its own way' (*suo modo*) is to be understood. What divine revelation adds to this picture is what Scotus examined as a theologian. And it was in this role that he explored the implications of the other Scriptural passage, "God is love."

In the monumental *Ordinatio*, Scotus's 'theological legacy to posterity,' as the late Carl Balic liked to call it,[4] Scotus did spell out the various implications of his belief that our triune God is "essentially love."[5] Unfortunately this major work suffers from the fact that, according to university custom of the times it is cast in the form of a so-called 'commentary on the *Sentences.*' As a result John Duns could give us only piecemeal glimpses of the grand theological vision he had of God's supernatural destiny for humankind as he followed the topical divisions of Peter Lombard's four books of *Sentences.* Had he lived as long as Thomas Aquinas, his illustrious Dominican predecessor, he might have extracted in a more systematic way in a work the size of his *De primo principio* or St. Bonaventure's *Breviloquium* a more concise account of his eschatology.[6]

---

[4]This evaluation was Balic's justification for beginning the Vatican critical edition with this particular work. As he argued his case before 1937 meeting of the *Vereinigung deutscher Franziskaner-Lektoren*: "Würde die kritische Edition dieses Werkes, in dem der Doctor Subtilis wie in seinem Testament der Nachwelt seinen letzten Willen hinterlassen hat, in unserer Zeit nicht die besten Früchte bringen können?" C. Balic, "Bemerkungen zur Methode des Studium sowie der Edition der Gesamtwerke des J. Duns Skotus" in *Wissenschaft und Weisheit* 4 (1937): 278. Unfortunately, he underestimated the difficulty of completing such an edition in a reasonable time period.

[5]*Lectura* I, dist. 17, n. 116 (Vat. ed. 17:217): "Deus est dilectio per essentiam."

[6]The overarching plan of Peter Lombard's *Sentences* is based on the principle that everything emanates from God as first principle and returns to its source as its ultimate end. My contention is that Scotus would simply have needed to sum up briefly the basic conclusions he arrived at in key portions of his *Ordinatio* to produce a 'breviloquium' of his own as a companion volume to the *De Primo Principio*.

It seems clear he did plan to compile something of this sort from the words he adds to the quotation from the *De primo principio* above.[7]

> Besides the aforesaid points which philosophers have affirmed of you, Catholics often praise you as omnipotent, immense, omnipresent, just yet merciful, provident of all creatures but looking after intellectual ones in a special way, but these matters are deferred to the next tract. In this first treatise I have tried to show how the metaphysical attributes affirmed of you can be inferred in some way by natural reason. In the tract which follows, those shall be set forth that are the subject of belief, wherein reason is held captive—yet to Catholics, the latter are the more certain since they rest firmly upon your own most solid truth and not upon our intellect which is blind and weak in many things."

Note that the first three attributes of omnipotence, immensity and omnipresence stress the sharp difference between the philosophical and theological conceptions of God in Scotus's day. Unlike the remote transcendent God of the philosophers, dwelling in the third heaven, causally related to the earth and humankind only through a lengthy series of intermediary intelligent beings, for the Catholic he is immanent and active throughout the universe, continually conserving what he created, and indwelling in a personal way in the souls of the just. Omnipotence, also, had a special meaning for the believer.[8] It meant that God could do

---

[7]*A Treatise on God as First Principle*, 146.

[8]Scotus distinguishes the 'omnipotence' of the theologian from that of the philosophers in that the latter extends to all things only through the mediacy of secondary causes, whereas Christians believe God can do immediately whatever he normally does through the cooperation of creatures. For philosophers like Avicenna God only creates immediately *ab aeterno* the first intelligence connected with the movement of the firmament. The first intelligence creates the second, the second the third, etc. The final intelligence, connected with the movement of the moon, creates individual souls and material creation. As Scotus interprets Avicenna's eschatology, the lunar intelligence thus become the beatific object humankind hopes to enjoy fully in the afterlife. See *Ordinatio* I, dist. 1, n. 9 (II, 5): " . . .videtur esse opinio Avicennae quod fruitio ordinata potest esse circa aliud a fine ultimo. Quod probatur ex dictis eius IX *Metaphysicae* cap. 4, ubi vult quod intelligentia superior per actum suum intelligendi causat inferiorem: tunc autem videtur productum esset

immediately whatever could be performed through the secondary
causes. Hence God is the one "in whom we live, move and have our
being" —as Paul explained to the Athenian philosophers (Acts.
17, 28).

'Just yet merciful' stresses the eschatological dimension of
these two attributes of God, for they are treated as inseparably
connected. Justice and mercy are divine attributes, and as such we
might expect them to be presented systematically in the tract on
the triune God as Aquinas does in Bk. I of his *Summa theologica*,
question 21. Lombard, however, defers their treatment to his tract
on eschatology in Bk. IV of his *Sentences* where he deals with hell
and the damned. For it was in their discussion of the punishment of
the damned that the Fathers of the Church considered the justice
of God to be vindicated. In the end-time all wrongs were to be
righted, just as in heaven "all tears—the consequences of all life's
seeming injustices—will be wiped away." Since Scotus was
following Lombard's thematic scenario, it was not until distinction
46 in Bk. IV that he had his first opportunity to deal extensively
with God's justice.[9]

> The inquiry here is about those exceedingly evil, for this
> distinction 46 treats of how God's justice and mercy concur in
> the punishment of evildoers. Therefore four questions are
> raised: First, is there justice in God? Second, is there mercy
> in God? Third, in God is justice distinguished from mercy?
> And fourth, in the punishment of evildoers do justice and
> mercy concur on the part of God?

In the Paris lecture on this distinction where the four questions
are tied together with a single *corpus*, Scotus states the fourth and
most important question first: Do justice and mercy concur in God's

---

perfectum quando attingit suum principium productivum, secundum illam
propositionem Procli 35, quod 'unumquodque natum est converti ad illud a quo
procedit'; in tali autem reditu videtur circulus esse completus et ita perfectio; ergo
intelligentia producta perfecte quietatur in intelligentia producente."

[9]*Ordinatio* IV, dist. 46: "Sed quaeritur hic de valde malis, quia in ista
distinctione 46 agitur de iustitia Dei et misericordia concurrentibus in punitione
malorum; ideo quaeritur quatuor: primo utrum in Deo sit iustitia, secundo utrum in
Deo sit misericordia, tertio an in Deo distinguatur iustitia a misericordia, quarto an
in punitione malorum concurrat ex parte Dei punientis iustitia cum misericordia."
(Codices A [f. 270ra] & M [f. 231rb]; cf. Vivès 20:399)

punishment of evildoers? Only then does he turn to the three subordinate questions that must first be answered to solve it.[10] In revising his work as an *Ordinatio*, he thought it better not to separate the main question so far from its solution, and adopts the more orderly sequence, beginning with the question on justice. He gives this dual description of it:[11]

> Here first as to the definition of justice, Anselm in ch. 12 of *De veritate*, gives the most general notion: "Justice is rectitude of will served for its own sake." This general notion is made specific by the way in which the Philosopher treats justice in Bk. V of the *Ethics*; he adds the further notion that this "has to do with another."
>
> It is clear that God has justice in both senses: the first, because he has rectitude of will—indeed, a will that cannot be gainsaid, because it is the first rule or norm, and is "served for its own sake." Not that "served" here implies any submission or acceptance on the part of the one observing it, but rather it is "served for its own sake" in the sense that it is always spontaneously pre*served*. It is clear he also has justice in the second sense, because he is upright to others, and therefore, in all his actions towards others there is rectitude.

The problem the scholastics tried to solve, as Scotus saw it, was how can God be strictly just to creatures if as Scripture says in

---

[10]*Reportatio* IV, d. 46, qq. 1-4: "Utrum in punitione malorum concurrat misericordia cum iustitia. . . . Respondeo primo ad secundam et tertiam et ad quartam quaestionem, deinde ultimo solvenda est quaestio prima." (Vivès 24:581, 583).

[11]*Ordinatio* IV, dist. 46, q. 1: "Hic primo de definitione iustitiae rationem generalissimam ponit Anselmus, *De veritate* c. 12, quod 'iustitia est rectitudo voluntatis propter se servata.' Haec ratio specificatur per iustitiam secundum quod de ea tractat Philosophus V *Ethicorum*, qui addat ultra istam rationem hoc quod est 'esse ad alterum.' Et utroque modo accipiendo patet quod iustitia competit Deo. Primo modo, habet enim rectitudinem voluntatis, immo voluntatem inobliquabilem, quia prima regula est et servata propter se, non prout "servata" dicit aliquam susceptionem vel passionem respectu alicuius servantis, sed servata propter se, id est, spontanaee semper habita. Secundo etiam modo patet, quia potest habere rectitudinem ad alterum, et ideo in omni actione sua ad alterum est rectitudo. " (Codices A [f. 270ra] & M [f. 236rb]; cf. Vivès n. 2 20:400)

matters of punishment "Mercy triumphs over justice"[12] and in
matters of reward he is overly bountiful. Scotus runs briefly
through some of the classical Aristotelian distinctions in Bk. V of
Nicomachean Ethics that theologians in his day argued were
either applicable or inapplicable to God.[13] He sums up their
conclusions as follows:[14]

> Thus the whole distinction of justice, then, insofar as it is
> applicable to God, could be reduced to two sorts: the first of
> which would be called rectitude of will with respect to
> what is due to divine goodness, the other rectitude of will
> with respect to what the exigencies of the creature demand.
> And we find this distinction in Anselm's Proslogion, ch. 10,
> where he says of God: "When you punish the wicked, it is
> just, because punishment corresponds to their merits," so far
> as the second member goes. And he adds immediately:
> "When you spare the wicked, however, it is just not because
> it corresponds to their merits, but because it befits your
> goodness." This refers to the first member of the division.
> And such is the distinction between these two kinds of
> justice that God cannot operate against or beyond the first
> justice [viz. namely what is due to his goodness], but he can
> go beyond what the second requires, but not in all matters,
> for he cannot damn the just or the blessed.

---

[12]Cf. *Ordinatio* IV, dist. 46, q. 4, n. 17 (Vivès 20:480) where Scotus quotes this
passage from James 2: 13 to prove that if mercy concurs with justice, divine judgment
"is made more perfect that it would be if it proceeded solely from justice."

[13]See for example Thomas Aquinas, *Summa Theologica* I, q. 21, art. 1, ad 3.
"Thus in divine operations debt may be regarded as due either to God or to creatures,
and in either way God pays what is due. . . . Anselm touches on either view where
he says (*Proslogion* 10): 'When you punish the wicked, it is just since it agrees with
their merits; and when you spare the wicked, it is also just because it befits your
goodness.'"

[14]*Ordinatio* IV, dist. 46, q. 1: "Sic ergo in genere tota illa definitio iustitiae eo
modo quod potest ad Deum pertinere, potest reduci ad duo membra, ut primo modo
dicatur iustitia rectitudo voluntatis in ordine ad condecentiam bonitatis divinae;
alio modo rectitudo voluntatis in ordine ad exigentiam eius, quod est in creatura.
Ista distinctio potest haberi ab Anselmo *Proslogion* 10, ubi loquens ad Deum dicit:
'Cum punis malos, iustum est, quia illorum meritis congruit.' —Quantum ad secundum
membrum; subdit statim, 'Cum parcis malis, iustum est, non quia illorum merltis, sed
quia tuae bonitati condecens est.' Et tanta ponitur membrorum istorum distinctio,
quod Deus contra primam iustitiam operari non potest, nec praeter eam, sed praeter
iustitiam secundam potest operari, licet non universaliter, quia non potest damnare
iustum vel beatum." (Codices A [f. 270rb] & M [f. 236va]; cf. Vivès n. 5 20:404-405)

On these matters all theologians in his day seemed to agree. What I find interesting about Scotus's treatment of these 'two sorts of justice' is that, after introducing them like Aquinas did, he cleverly shows they can be reduced to a single aspect, namely, what God owes to himself 'as other.'[15]

> Not by way of disparaging these distinctions, I reply with greater brevity to the question that in God there is but one justice both conceptually and in reality, although by stretching the meaning of "justice" one could say that in addition to the aforesaid, justice [viz. what he owes to himself] there is some justice, or rather something just, about the way he deals with creatures.

The logician in Scotus clearly perceives it is only by "stretching the meaning of the word" that God can be said to be just to his creatures. After all he had no need to create them for there is nothing they can add to his infinitely perfect nature. If he freely does so out of love, —for "God is love" —it is they who are indebted to him, not he to them.[16]

> Nevertheless, one could say that this single justice, which determinately inclines the divine will to its first act, modifies each of these secondary acts, although not in a

---

[15]*Ibid.*: "Non improbando distinctiones, dico brevius ad quaestionem quod in Deo non est nisi unica iustitia re et ratione, tamen praeter illam, extendendo iustitiam, potest poni aliqua iustitia, vel magis aliquid iustum, in creaturis." (Codices A [f. 270rb] & M [f. 236vb]; cf. Vivès n. 7 20:424)

[16]*Ibid.*: "Tamen potest dici quod ista unica iustitia, quae non inclinat determinate nisi ad primum actum, modificat actus secundarios, licet nullum eorum necessario, quin posset modificare oppositum. Nec quasi praevenit voluntatem inclinando eam per modum naturae ad aliquem actum secundarium, sed voluntas primo determinat seipsum ad quodcumque obiectum secundarium. Et ex hoc iste actus est modificatus ab illa prima iustitia, quia consonus voluntati cui adaequatur, quasi pro rectitudine inclinante iustitia prima.

"Secundo modo iustum dicitur in creatura esse ex correspondentia unius creati ad aliquid (sicut iustum est ex parte creaturae ignem esse calidum et aquam frigidam, ignem sursum et aquam deorsum, et huiusmodi), quia ista natura creata hoc exigit tamquam sibi correspondens; sicut possemus dlcere in politiis, quod est quod in solo principe esset iustitia, tamen in rebus ordinatis esset quodammodo iustum, ut scilicet tales res sic disponerentur, et sic tales, quia hoc res ipsae, ut natae cedere in usum civium exigunt." (Codices A [f. 270rb-va] & M [f, 236vb-237ra]; cf. Vivès n. 8-9 20:425-426)

necessary manner, as though it could not also modify the
opposite of each. Neither does this justice precede the will,
as it were, inclining it after the manner of nature to some
secondary act. Rather the will first determines itself in
regard to each secondary act, and by this very fact that act
is modified by that first justice, because that act is in
harmony with the will to which it is conformed as if the
rectitude inclining it this way were the first justice itself.

In this second way God is said to do what is right in a
creature from the way in which he makes one created thing
correspond to another (just as we say it is just on the part of
the creature that fire be hot and water cold, that fire rise
and water descend, and so on), because that created nature
demands this as something suited to it. —Just as we could
say in politics that justice exists as such only in the ruler
himself, nevertheless we could speak of him as being
somehow just in the things he ordains, namely, to the extent
that he arranges things in such and such a way. For this is
something demanded by the things themselves insofar as
they are destined by nature for the use of the citizens.

Like Anselm and Aquinas before him,[17] Scotus admits that God
in creating is in some sense paying a debt, as it were. For when an
objector insists that God is a debtor to no one, Scotus replies:[18]

Speaking simply, I say God is a debtor only to his own
goodness, that he love it; to creatures however he is a
debtor out of his liberality, that he communicate to them
what their nature demands, which exigency in them is set
down as something just, a kind of secondary object of this
justice.

The debt accrues, however, only because God first freely
chooses to create out of charity, and thus puts himself under
obligation as it were by reason of his other attributes like

---

[17]See note 13 above.

[18]*Ordinatio* IV, dist. 46, q. 1: "Dico quod non simpliciter est debitor nisi
bonitati suae, ut diligat eam; creaturis autem est debitor ex liberalitate sua, ut
communicet eis quod natura sua exigit, quae exigentia in eis ponitur quoddam iustum,
quasi secundarium obiectum illius iustitiae." (Codices A [f. 270va] & M [f.437rb]; cf.
Vivès n. 12 20:428)

liberality, mercy and so on. This prompts him to be "provident of all creatures but looking after intellectual ones in a special way." Here the final attribute Scotus ascribes to him as a Catholic comes into play.

Why did Scotus believe a God of love, —being a perfect lover —would be moved to create what he did? And what is the special way in which intellectual creatures come back to God, and in so doing, bring back the whole of the material world as a new heavens and a new earth. Here we touch on the heart of Scotus's eschatology. They have been created to share with the three divine persons the very charitable love they have for the divine nature. That is what he tells us for example in that interesting question in the supplement to Bk. III, distinction 23 of his *Ordinatio*[19] where he explains how God's love extends to all things.

I. How God's love relates to all things

The single question he raises in this distinction is: Does God love everything equally out of charity?[20] Scotus divides his answer to the question into three articles:[21]

---

[19]In distinctions 27-33 of Bk. III of his commentaries on Lombard's *Sentences*, Scotus deals with charity as a perfection of the will's affection for justice. There is some dispute as to whether these are part of his *Ordinatio*, as Codex A seems to consider it, or whether Scotus's final revision of his bachelor lectures did not get beyond distinction 14 as some manuscripts suggest. As the editors of the Vatican edition indicate (I: 297), the supplement to the *Ordinatio*, however, extends at least to distinction 38. The Scotistic Commission has yet to study the relative importance of the manuscripts containing the supplement to Bk. III. If the listing found in the Introductory volume to the Vatican edition, pp. 12* to 126* is indicative of their relative value, however, the two best manuscripts for a reliable text of this section, as far as I can judge, would seem to be Codices A and S.

[20]*Ordinatio* III, suppl. dist. 32: "Circa distinctionem 32 quaero utrum Deus diligit omnia ex caritate aequaliter?" -- The Latin text here and in the following citations is corrected according to the two best codices, viz. Codex A (f. 174ra-va) and Codex S (f. 214va-215ra).

[21]*Ibid.*: "Hic tria sunt videnda: primum quod Deus diligit omnia; secundo, quod iste actus non est proprius alicui personae; tertia, quod est unus actus, et in hoc dicetur quomodo est unus et aequalis, vel quomodo se habet aequaliter vel inaequaliter respectu omnium." (Codices A [f. 174ra] & S [f. 214va]; cf. Vivès n. 2 15:426)

There are three things here to look into: *first* that God
loves all; *second* this act is not proper to any one person;
third, it is a single act, and hence we will explain how it is
both one and equal, or better, how it relates equally or
unequally to all.

In the first article, Scotus proves the fact that God indeed does
love all things, not only everything that actually exists, but also
all that could possibly exist. Just as his omniscient intellect knows
not only the divine nature as its primary object but also all possible
creatures as its secondary object, so the one voluntary act whereby
the three divine persons enjoy the divine nature as the primary
object of their charitable love, must also embrace in some similar
fashion all possible creatures.

Since contrary states and accidental characteristics are
synchronistically possible for any individual substance, however,
one might raise this objection. If God loved all possibles equally
from all eternity, contraries would coexist, which is impossible.
Hence Scotus distinguishes between God's benevolent and his
complacent love. The former love extends only to those creatures he
is pleased from all eternity to create at some future time, whereas
his complacent love extends equally to all possibles,[22] since they
are viewed as consequences, as it were, of his infinitely fertile
intellect.[23]

---

[22]*Ibid.*: "Quaedam etiam diligit voluntate et volitione efficaci, puta illa quae
aliquando producunt in esse; quaedam volitione quadam simplicis complacentiae non
efficaci, quae tunc nunquam producet in esse quae tamen ostenduntur ab intellectu suo
ut possibilia habere tantam bonitatem sicut illa quae diligit volitione efficaci."
(Codices A [f. 174rb] & S [f. 214va]; cf. Vivès 15:426-427)

[23]Though logically speaking possibles are intrinsically or formerly possible of
themselves, that is to say, their constitutive characteristics are not self-
contradictory, their extrinsic possibility depends on whether some efficient or
creative cause exists that can give them existence. According to the common
theological teaching in Scotus's day, however, God's omnipotence is such a cause
since it is limited only by the principle of contradiction. As a metaphysican,
however, Scotus sought to explain what sort of 'being' or entity possibles possess.
Since metaphysically speaking all being is traced back to God, he points out that
possibles have a quasi-exsistence or being as objects of thought (*esse intelligibile*). It
would be derogatory to the perfection of the divine intellect, however, if it were
dependent for its knowledge of possible creatures upon their finite intelligibility.
Like the creative artist who first models his masterpiece mentally before
embodying it some material form, Scotus argues that the infinitely fertile mind of

Though chosen holistically from all eternity, each item that makes up the universe is willed individually. This is a consequence, as I have explained elsewhere, of his doctrine of haecceity.[24]:

> Not only do individuals pertain to the order of God's universe, . . . but in communicating "his goodness as something befitting his beauty, in each species" he delights in producing a multiplicity of individuals. "And in those beings which are the highest and most important, it is the individual that is primarily intended by God." Viewed from this aspect, Scotus's doctrine of haecceity applied to the human person, would seem to invest each with a unique value as one singularly wanted and loved by God, quite apart from any trait that each person shares with another or any contribution he or she might make to society. One could even say 'thisness' is our personal gift from God.

Since what he creates temporally, however, is willed *ab aeterno*, creation though it unfolds in time, is willed holistically as a single object from all eternity. As we read in the book of Jeremiah (31:3): "I have loved thee with an everlasting love, therefore with loving kindness I have drawn thee."

In the second article, Scotus explains that God's charitable love is personal. It is not proper to any one person, however, but is shared equally by Father, Son and Holy Spirit.

God produces each creature as a thought object, thus giving it intelligibility. Hence for Scotus it is correct to say that God does not know creatures because they are intelligible, but they are intelligible because he knows them. *Ordinatio* I, d. 35, nn. 31-32 (VI, 258). See my articles, "Duns Scotus on the Divine Origin of Possibility," in *American Catholic Philosophical Quarterly* 67 (1993), 95-107; and "Ockham and the Textbooks: On the Origin of Possibility" (*Franziskanische Studien* 32, 1950) 70-96 that was reprinted in *Inquiries into Medieval Philosophy*, ed. James F. Ross (Westport, Conn.: Greenwood, 1971), pp. 243-73.

[24]See the preface to *Duns Scotus's Early Oxford Lecture on Individuation* (Santa Barbara: Old Mission Santa Barbara, 1992), xxvii.

It is the third article, however, that is most interesting eschatologically. God's love is one and equal, yet extends unequally to all. Scotus explains the paradox as follows:[25]

> The third or last point becomes clear if we realize this. In God there is but one power to love and one first object [his divine essence] and he has one infinite act equal or proportionate to that power. But it is not necessary that this act regard all things as actualized, as if all were required to be loved [creatively] for the act to be perfect. Rather his actual love of all is a consequence of the perfection of this act, since it tends in a perfect manner to its first object and to all for which this first object is the whole reason for the divine intellect and will acting at all. Now only the divine essence can be the primary reason for God's acting, because if something else were, his power would be denigrated.

Scotus, if I read him aright, seems to be making here two important statements. First, God could not create a purely meaningless universe, though this would seem to be logically possible intrinsically, since his omnipotence extends to whatever does not involve a contradiction. As I pointed out elsewhere,[26] this is a consequence of the divine will's affection for justice.

---

[25]*Ordinatio* III, dist. 32: "Tertium apparet, quia una est potentia et unum obiectum primum, et habet unum actum infinitum adaequatum sibi. Nec oportet istum unum actum esse omnium quia omnia requirantur ad perfectionem huius actus, sed solummodo ex perfectione huius actus consequitur hoc, quia perfecte tendit in primum terminum; tendit etiam in omnia circa quae primus terminus est totalis ratio agendi tam intellectui divino quam voluntati. Sola essentia divina potest esse prima ratio agendi, quia si aliquid aliud posset esse prima ratio, vilesceret ista potentia." (Codices A [f. 174rb] & S [f. 214vb]; cf. Vivès n. 5 15:432)

[26]"Like the scholastics generally, Scotus distinguished between the absolute and orderly will of God, the former being limited only by the principle of non-contradiction. If the *affectio iustitiae* is a pure perfection and a constitutive element of the divine will, then the realistic possibilities of creation represent only a proper subset of the set of all purely logical possibilities, namely, those that do him justice, we might say. . . . Following Anselm again, he sees only one justice in God, that which he owes to his own nature, but this justice, he insists, also affects his dealings with creatures for it 'modifies his creative act,' causing him to 'give to natures such perfections as are due or becoming to them.' Properly, speaking however, so far as creatures are concerned this is not so much justice as liberality." See *Philosophical Theology*, p. 158.

The second is a still stronger statement, namely, that if God does create, creation in some way must be *capax* Dei. It must contain 'co-lovers' of that infinitely perfect and lovable being, that lacks "no entity it is possible for anything to have."[27] In other words, i t must involve rational creatures—creatures endowed with an intellect that has the natural capacity to be perfected, not blinded by the intuitive vision of God, and a free will that spontaneously chooses to love the infinitely lovable essence of God for its own sake.

This still leaves God with many, if not indefinite options, and hence does not compromise the fact that any creation will still be contingent. Furthermore, Scotus makes clear that this seeming limitation of his omnipotence refers only to creation as a whole and not to any individual item it may contain. As he says in the question above on God's justice:[28]

> I say the legislator in matters of state regards one thing as simply just if it is just for the public good, whereas h e regards what is just for a part always in the qualified sense that this is not disproportionate to what is just [for the community at large], and therefore in certain cases he sees it is just not to observe just laws concerning what is only just for a part, namely, when their observation would be detrimental to what is just publicly, namely, to what is in the best interests of the state. In a similar fashion God is determined to do what is just publicly as something just and becoming to his goodness, and to do this not for a group that is only an aggregation of citizens, but rather for *a community whose members are knit together in a far more*

---

[27]Cf. the text associated with note 2 above.

[28]*Ordinatio* IV, dist. 46, q. 1: "Ad tertium dico quod sicut in istis politiis legislator respicit in se simpliciter iustum quod est iustum boni publici, secundum quid respicit alia iusta partialia, semper quidem in proportione ad istud iustum et ideo in quibusdam casibus iustum est non servare leges iustas, respicientes ista iusta partialia, quando scilicet observatio earum vergeret in detrimentum iusti publici, scilicet bene esse reipublicae, ita Deus simpliciter determinatur ad iustum publicum, non communitate aggregationis, sicut est in civitate, sed communitate eminentis continentiae, quod est iustum condecens bonitatem suam. Omne autem aliud iustum est particulare et nunc hoc iustum, nunc illud iustum secundum quod ordinatur vel convenit huic iusto." (Codices A [f. 270rb-va] & M [f. 237ra-rb]; cf. Vivès n. 11 20:427)

excellent way.[29] But whatever is only just for a part, now this is just and now that is just depending on how it is ordered to or in harmony with what is just for all.

He gives this concrete example in answer to the following objection:[30] "If it is just to save Peter, and God justly wills this, then it is unjust to damn Peter, and thus if God can will to do so, he can will something that is unjust."[31]

> I say therefore that God could will that Peter be damned and be right to will such, because this particular instance of what is just, viz. "Peter is saved," is not necessarily required for what is just for the community in the sense that its opposite could not also be ordered to that same end, namely, what is just for the community as befitting divine goodness.[32] For the attainment of this end, indeed, no being represents a definitely necessary requirement."

Viewed holistically, whatever God chooses to create will have a natural goodness about it. In so far as motivating his will to create, however, prior to God's choosing one possible creation rather than another, all possibilities seem to be equally good. He makes this clear in his first article.[33]

> Certain things are loved by an efficacious volition, such as those which are at some time brought into existence; others by a certain volition of simple non-efficacious complacency, which therefore are never brought into existence. Never-

---

[29]Not only is each individual member of this community *capax Dei*, but each is an integral member of mystical body of Christ, whose soul was predestined to become that of the Son of God.

[30]*Ordinatio* IV, dist. 46, q. 1: "Item, si iustum est Petrum salvari, et Deus hoc iuste vult, ergo inustum est Petrum damnari, et ita si Deus potest hoc velle, potest aliquid iniustum velle." (Codices A [f. 270va] & M [f.437ra]; cf. Vivès n. 9 20:426)

[31]*Ibid.*: "Sic ergo quod potest velle Petrum damnari et iuste velle, quia illud particulare iustum 'Petrum salvari' non necessario requiritur ad iustum publicum, quin eius oppositum possit ordinari ad illud idem, scilicet ad condecentiam divinae bonitatis. Est enim illud finis quidem nullum ens ad finem determinate necessario requirens." (Codices A [f. 270va] & M [f.437rb]; cf. Vivès n. 11 20:427)

[32]As nearest to the end, Christ's soul was first predestined, and thus became the relative end for those who would constitute the Christocentric kingdom of God.

[33]See note 22 above.

theless these have as much goodness as those which h e loves by an efficacious love.

But to continue with this third article. Whatever a trinitarian God chooses to create, however, is willed holistically as a single object from all eternity. For this reason Scotus, after asserting creation is a consequence of the perfection of this single act of love "since it tends in a perfect manner to its first object and to all for which this first object is the whole reason for the divine intellect and will acting at all," goes on to say:[34]

> From this, it is clear there is no inequality on the part of God in his love for all things if one compares his act to himself as agent. But if his act be compared to what it connotes, namely to the objects outside himself to which it extends, then inequality does exist, not only because the objects willed are not equal, or because unequal goods are willed to them, but also because of the certain orderly way his act extends to them. For everyone who wills in a reasonable way, first wills the end and secondly that which immediately attains the end, and thirdly other things which are more remotely ordered to the attainment of his end. And so it is that God, who is most reasonable — not of course by different acts, but in one single act which is said to tend in different ways to the different objects ordered in some way to one another—first wills the end,

---

[34]*Ordinatio* III, dist. 32: "Ex hoc patet quod non est inaequalitas Dei in diligendo omnia comparando actum ad agens. Sed comparando actum ad connotata, sive ad ea super quae transit, est inaequalitas, non tantum quia illa volita sunt inaequalia vel inaequalia bona sunt eis volita, sed etiam quia secundum ordinem quemdam transit super ea; nam omnis rationabiliter volens, primo vult finem, et secundo immediate illud quod attingit finem, et tertio alia quae sunt remotius ordinata ad attingendum finem. Sic etiam Deus rationabilissime vult omnia licet non diversis actibus, unico tantum actu, in quantum ille diversimode tendit super obiecta ordinata, primo vult finem, et in hoc est actus suus perfectus, et intellectus suus perfectus, et voluntas eius beata; secundario vult illa quae immediate ordinantur in ipsum praedestinando scilicet electos, qui scilicet immediate attingunt eum, et hoc quasi reflectendo, volendo alios condiligere idem obiectum secum, sicut prius dictum fuit de caritate distinctione 28 huius tertii. Qua re enim se primo amat ordinate et per consequens non inordinate zelando vel invidendo, secundo vult alios habere condiligentes, et hoc est velle alios habere amorem suum in se, et hoc est praedestinare eos, si velit eis habere huiusmodi bonum finaliter et aeternaliter. (Codices A [f. 174rb-va] & "S [f. 214vb]"; cf. Vivès n. 6 15:432-433)

and in this his act is perfect, and his intellect is perfect,
and his will is happy. Secondly, he wills those things
which are immediately ordered to him, predestining
namely the elect who attain him immediately, and this as
it were, by reflecting and willing others to love with him
the very object of his love, as was stated earlier in
distinction 28 of this third book.[35] For it is because he first
loves himself rightly, and consequently not inordinately in
an envious or jealous manner, that he wills secondly to have
other co-lovers, and this is nothing else than willing that
others have his love in themselves. Now this is to
predestine them, if he wishes them to have this good
finally and eternally.[36]

As an earlier countryman, Richard of St. Victor, made clear to
Scotus, the perfect lover is not envious or jealous but wills the
beloved be loved by others.[37] Richard gives this as a necessary
reason why a personal God must be both one and three, for if God's
love is perfect charity, it requires a triad of divine co-lovers to be
fully shared. St. Bonaventure cites this as a plausible explanation
of our belief in the Trinity. Scotus, however, views it rather as a
quasi-motivation why a God of love is creative. In his *Lectura*,
Scotus admitted his shift from a physical to a metaphysical proof
of God was inspired by Richard's argument.[38] Here he suggests
another application of Richard's reasoning. It is through grace or
charity that God continues to dwell in the human soul. Though

---

[35]The reference here is to the fact that Scotus claims the charity whereby we
love God above all is the same as that whereby we love our neighbor as ourselves.
For the perfect love of self or neighbor is to will that we all love God for his own
sake, for in that our human nature finds its most perfect fulfilment. These texts are
found in bilingual form in my *Will and Morality*, pp. 446-455.

[36]God can only wish or will them to possess this good permanently in heaven,
if they have freely co-operated morally with the opportunities he gives them to do
so.

[37]In his *De Trinitate* Richard, the Scot, seeks 'necessary reasons' for his belief
that God must be both one and three. See my selections from this work in J. F.
Wippel and A. B. Wolter, *Medieval Philosophy: From St. Augustine to Nicholas of
Cusa* (New York & London: Free Press/Collier-Macmillan Ltd., 1969), p. 212-225.

[38]*Lectura* I, dist. 2, n. 41 (Vat. ed. 16:126): "Omittendo igitur rationem
physicam, qua probatur primum movens esse, arguitur ex parte entis primum
efficiens esse secundum efficientam entis, et est ratio Richardi I *De Trinitate* cap.
8."

Scripture appropriates this in a special way to the Holy Spirit, Scotus's second article made clear it is not proper to only one or two persons, but to the entire Trinity. When the created will elicits an act of love of God or neighbor, this is nothing other than the Trinity itself loving their beloved deity in and through their own creation.[39] That is why Scotus views God's creativity as "nothing else than willing that others have his love in themselves."

Scotus continues his analysis of this orderly progression as follows:[40]

> Thirdly, however, he wills those things which are necessary to attain his end, namely the gift of grace. Fourthly, he wills for their sake other things that are more remote—for instance, this sensible world —in order that it may serve them, so that what is stated in the second book of [Aristotle's] *Physics*[41] is true: "Man is in

---

[39]In Bk. II of his early Oxford lectures Scotus indicates that the grace Peter Lombard calls an indwelling of the Trinity in the souls of the elect attributed to Holy Spirit (*Sentences* II, dist. 26-27), is formally identical with virtue of charity. "Circa distinctionem vigesimam septimam quaeritur utrum gratia sit virtus. Respondeo quod sic, non tantum per identitatem, sed formaliter; est enim formaliter caritas. Ista enim gratia, de qua Magister loquitur ibi, est caritas, quae virtus est secundum quam Spiritus Sanctus inhabitat, nec sic per fidem atque spem, sicut dictum est in libro I ubi determinata est opinio Magistri" (*Lectura* II, dist. 27, n. 1-2 Vat. ed. 19:271). Scotus's back-reference is to *Lectura* I, dist. 17, n. 32-42 (Vat. ed. 17:194-196) where he explains Peter's view that "mediante gratia et inexistente et inhabitante tota Trinitas, et appropriate Spiritu Sancto, elict voluntas actum meritorium, ita quod Spiritus Sanctus gratificat animam aliquo habitu, inhabitando eam." (n. 41, p. 195).

[40]*Ordinatio* III, dist. 32: "Tertio autem vult illa quae sunt necessaria ad attingendum hunc finem, scilicet bona gratiae. Quarto vult propter ista alia remotiora, puta h unc mundum sensibilem, pro aliis ut serviant eis, ut sic verum sit illud II *Physicorum*: 'Homo quodammodo est finis omnium' −omnium sensibilium; quidem quia propter ipsum volitum a Deo quasi in secundo signo naturae, sunt omnia sensibilia volita quasi in quarto signo. Illud etiam quod est propinquius fini ultimo, consuevit dici finis eorum quae sunt remotiora; sive ergo quia in ordine ad hominem praedestinatum vult Deus mundum sensibilem esse, sive quia quodammodo immediatius vult hominem amare se, quam mundum sensibilem esse, homo erit finis mundi sensibilis." (Codices A [f. 174va] & "S [f. 214vb]"; cf. Vivès n. 6 15:433)

[41]Aristotle, II *Physicorum* II, c. 2 194a 34-35: "Nos sumus quodammodo finis omnium." Confer J. Hamesse, *Les Auctoritates Aristotelis*, (Louvain/Paris, 1974) 145.

some way the end of all sensible things," for all these are willed in the fourth place, because of man's being willed in the second place. Also that which is closer to the ultimate end is customarily said to be the end of those things which are more remote. Hence, man will be the end of the sensible world, whether it be because God wills the sensible world to be ordered to predestined man or whether it be because his more immediate concern is not that the sensible world exists but rather that man love him.

In the light of the above Scotus gives his answer to the original question: Does God love everything equally out of charity?[42]

And so it becomes clear how inequality among things willed is possible so far as these objects are concerned, though not in so far as inequality pertains to the will itself. For it is only because of the external objects, being willed in the order they are, that any inequality is characteristic of his volition. Even this inequality does not actually come about because of some goodness preexisting in any object other than himself, as if that were the reason why such and such objects are willed in this and that order. On the contrary, the reason for God's willing is in the divine will alone. For it is because he accepts other things in such and such a degree, and not vice versa. Or if it be granted to them that objects, as shown to God by his intellect, have a certain measure of essential goodness according to which they deserve to please his will in a reasonable and orderly way, this much at least is certain. That it pleases God to give them actual existence is something that stems exclusively

---

[42]*Ordinatio* III, dist. 32: "Et ita patet inaequalitas volibilium quantum ad ipsa volita, non ut volitio est ipsius voluntatis, sed ut transit super obiecta modo praedicto; nec tamen ista inaequalitas in actu est propter bonitatem praesuppositam in obiectis quibuscumque aliis a se quia sit quasi ratio quare sit sic vel sic volenda, sed ratio est in ipsa voluntate divina solummodo quia enim ipsa accepta alia in tali gradu, et non e converso; vel si detur eis, ut ostensa sunt ab intellectu, sit aliquis gradus bonitatis essentialis, secundum quem rationabiliter debent ordinate complacere voluntati, saltem hoc certum est, quod beneplacita eorum quantum ad actualem existentiam mere est ex voluntate divina absque alia ratione determinante ex parte eorum." (Codices A [f. 174va] & S [f. 215ra]; cf. Vivès n. 6 15:433)

from his divine will apart from any other determining reason on the part of the objects themselves.

In answering an objection that God's charitable love cannot extend to inanimate or irrational creatures Scotus gives this answer:[43]

> If inanimate things are not properly speaking able to be loved out of charity, since charity is friendship love and one cannot have such objects as friends, nevertheless one may have such a charitable love towards them as is possible, for I can love out of charity that a tree exists insofar as it enables me to love God more in himself. Now in this manner it can be admitted that God loves all things out of charity, not by a volition that is friendship love, but by such a friendship love as it is possible for him to have in their regard.

II. How God's love relates to Christ

What needs to be added to this, of course, is what Scotus said earlier in the *Ordinatio* about the predestination of Christ,[44] since the whole of God's creation, according to Scotus, is Christocentric. Not only is Christ's human nature a natural microcosm of the rest of God's creation,[45] but by reason of its hypostatic union with the

---

[43]*Ibid.*: "Ad secundum dico quod si proprie inanimata non sint diligibilia ex caritate, quia caritas est amicitia, et ad ista non est amicitia proprie habenda, tamen possum ex caritate ad ista habere aliquod velle quale habendum est ad ea ex caritate; possum enim ex caritate velle arborem esse, et arborem mihi servire ad talem actum, in quantum talis actus iuvat me ulterius ad diligendum Deum in se; et hoc modo potest concedi quod Deus ex caritate diligit omnia, non volitione amicitiae, sed volitione tali qualis est habenda respectu eorum." (Codices A [f. 174va] & S [f. 215ra]; cf. Vivès n. 6 15:434)

[44]See *Ordinatio* III, dist. 7, q. 3 in the critical edition by C. Balic, O.F.M. *Ioannis Duns Scoti, Doctor Mariani, Theologiae Marianae Elementa* (Sibenik: Kacic, 1933), pp 1-10. Hereafter this work is referred to as *Theologiae Marianae Elementa*.

[45]The ancient Greek notion of man as a microscom played an important role in medieval conception of human nature, especially in the humanistic thought of the School of St. Victor. Godfrey's masterword, *Microcosmos*, for example, presents an allegorical account of the Hexaemeron or six days of creation, the first three of which correspond to the nature God gives to humankind, and the last three days to the crowning of that nature; in the second portion he indicates how the gifts of grace

Word it also was destined to become the perfect link between creation and its creator. For Scotus believed it could receive, and indeed was given, the greatest possible sanctifying grace (*gratia gratificans*) any created co-lover could receive.[46] And since this graced-nature could be assumed by a divine person, it was fittingly united with the Word, thus linking the Trinitarian family with the human family created in its image and likeness.

Since I have treated elsewhere[47] the *Ordinatio* version of the questions where Scotus dealt with Christ's predestination and the grace he received,[48] let me turn to the refinements Scotus added when he touched on the same topic in Paris in distinction 7 of Bk. III, question 4. Fortunately we have a critical edition of this lecture by Carl Balic.[49] In translation it reads as follows: "*It is asked whether Christ is predestined to be the Son of God.*[50] I will limit myself what is contained in the body of the question which he articulates as follows:[51]

> To the question: First, how does this union fall under predestination? Second, in what way was Christ predestined? Third, what is the way this predestination is ordered to the other predestinations?

---

are added to and perfect this nature. Though his particular work itself does not seem to have been widely read, his distinction of grace and nature and the integral positive role both play in the life of a Christian continued to be reaffirmed throughout the period of high scholasticism.

[46]Since grace is identified with charity (see note 39 above) and charity as an infused virtue was regarded by Scotus's contemporaries as a quality that could exist in various degrees of intensity, Scotus's argued that an absolutely highest degree of grace is possible, and that it could be created at a single stroke and given to a rational creature. Furthermore, he believed such grace was actually given to the created soul of Christ; see *Ordinatio* III, dist. 13, q. 1. For a biligual edition of the relevant passages, see *infra*, note 48.

[47]See my article "John Duns Scotus on the Primacy and Personality of Christ" in *Franciscan Christology*, ed. Damian McElrath (St. Bonaventure, NY: Franciscan Institute, 1980), p. 146-153. Hereafter referred to as *Franciscan Christology*.

[48]See *Ordinatio*, Bk. III dist. 13, q. 1-4: For my bilingual edition of the relevant passages see *Franciscan Christology*, 158-167.

[49]*Theologiae Marianae Elementa*, 11-16.

[50] *Ibid.*, 11: "Quaeritur, utrum Christus sit praedestinatus esse Filius Dei."

[51] *Ibid.*, 11-12: "Ad quaestionum: Primo quomodo ista unio potest cadere sub praedestinatione? Secundo, qualiter Christus sit praedestinatus? Tertio, quis sit ordo huius praedestinationis ad alias praedestinationes?"

Article 1. Predestination and the Incarnation

To the first question, "How does the hypostatic union fall under predestination?" Scotus gives this explanation:[52]

> About the first. Predestination is the prior ordering of some individual to glory, and to what is ordered [as a means] to such glory. But something able to be glorified can be ordered to glory and to those things that are ordered [as a means] to glory. And something is able to be ordered to such glory as it would not be fitting to order a pure creature. For to what subsists in the Word it was fitting to order a greater glory than to any pure creature existing in itself, and such glory could not fall under merit. Therefore, such a nature can be ordered to such a union as is that of the human nature with the Word. Such a nature is first [predestined] to such glory as has been given to Christ, and then there is some congruence as to why some glory can fall under merit of a creature and why some cannot. And here it is fitting to preordain a union which is first [ordered as a means] to such glory as could not fall under the merit of a pure creature.

Let us unpack the several statements Scotus makes in this paragraph. The first concerns the nature of predestination itself, which he defines as 'the prior ordering of some individual to glory.' Earlier Scotus already admitted that where predestination is concerned we are in the area of the mysterious and inexplicable.[53]

---

[52] *Ibid.*, 12: "De primo. Praedestinatio est praeordinatio alicuius glorificabilis ad gloriam et ad ordinata ad gloriam; nunc autem aliquod glorificabile potest ordinari ad gloriam et ad ea quae sunt ordinata ad ipsam, et aliquid est ordinabile ad tantam gloriam, quantam non decet ordinare purae creaturae. Subsistenti enim in Verbo decet ordinare maiorem gloriam quam alicui purae creaturae existenti in se, et talis gloria non potest cadere sub merito, ideo talis natura potest ordinari ad talem unionem, quae est naturae humanae ad Verbum, quae est prima ad tantam gloriam, quanta est collata Christo, et tunc est congruentia aliqua, quare aliqua gloria potest cadere sub merito creaturae, et aliqua non potest, et ibi decens est praeordinare unionem, quae est prima ad tantam gloriam, quanta non potest cadere sub merito purae creaturae."

[53] See his lengthy discussion in distinction 41 of Bk. I of the *Ordinatio*. The sole question in this distinction reads: *Utrum sit aliquod meritum praedestinationis vel reprobationis*. Scotus evaluates the merits and weaknesses of five answers to the question and fails to find any of them completely satisfactory. He accepts the fifth opinion as least objectionable, since it admits there is an antecedent reason that

For as he interprets this, predestination represents a free and apparently arbitrary, decision on the part of our triune God to glorify some individual rational creature by gratuitously allowing it to share with the three divine persons forever their enjoyment as co-lovers of their infinitely lovable divine nature. Such a glorified share in the divine life God clearly owes to no one distinct from himself and no purely natural causality or meritorious action on the part of a creature or creatures can bring this about. Yet paradoxically God has created rational[54] creatures with this as their proper destiny and ultimate end. For all have a congenital inclination and unconscious 'desire' for such happiness as well as a capacity to receive and be perfected by such a life.[55] To put it

---

justifies reprobation. Where predestination is concerned, however, no antecedent reason can be given for God's election, since he owes such a gratuitous gift as a share in his inner love life to no one, and hence in not giving it to some, does them no more injustice than a human lover does in not sharing his love equally with all. Scotus concludes his analysis with this advice: "De istis opinionibus omnibus: quia Apostolus videtur, disputare de materia ista ad Romanos in fine, quasi totum inscrutabile relinquere (*O altitudo divitiarum sapientiae et scientiae Dei*, et *quis novit sensum Domini, aut quis consiliarius eius fuit?*), ideo ne scrutando de profundo – secundum sententiam Magistri—eatur in profundum, eligatur quae magis placet, dum tamen salvatur libertas divina (sine aliqua iniustitia) et alia quae salvanda sunt circa Deum ut liberaliter eligentem; et qui aliquam opinionem tenuerit, respondeat ad illa quae tacta sunt contra eum" (*Ordinatio* I, dist. 41, n. 52 Vat. ed. 6:336-337).

[54]Following Anselm of Canterbury, Scotus distinguishes a purely intellectual creature with a corresponding intelligent appetite but lacking free will, from a rational creature endowed with such a will. It is the latter faculty, not the intellect, that is truly rational. See my essay "Duns Scotus on the Will as a Rational Potency" in *Philosophical Theology*, 163-80.

[55]Scotus did not accept the two level teleological theory of human nature advanced a decade later by Thomas Cajetan to highlight the supernatural character of grace and glory, namely that we can distinguish in man a purely natural end of self-fulfilment apart from the supernatural end he can enjoy by reason of the supernatural gifts that elevate that nature. Scotus insists no accidental additions can supernaturally elevate our humanity unless it already has an innate capacity to be perfected by such supernatural additions. We have but one true end and it is paradoxically in some sense both natural and supernatural. As the lowest created nature that is still *capax Dei*, our intellect as part of our spiritual soul has a natural ability to intuit created things directly when no longer confined to the body and constrained to work with the senses. It is this natural intuitive ability that is in obediential potency to receive the beatific vision of God as a gratuitous or voluntary gift, for God relates to creatures only contingently and hence not by reason of his divine nature as such but rather by means of his will. Our intellect has a natural capacity to be perfected by this beatific vision God gives of himself,

another way, all have a natural desire for the supernatural, and herein lies the mystery of predestination, for with injustice towards none and with the offering of supernatural assistance to all, some are foreseen by God to achieve their goal, others to be forever excluded from such.

Second, Scotus declares that some created *thing*, able to be glorified, can be predestined to such glory and the means whereby it can be obtained. He uses here the neuter impersonal adjective *'aliquod'* to indicate he is not talking about a created person but some created spiritual substance, such as a human soul or an angelic nature.

Third, he indicates that this impersonal created thing (*aliquid*) can be ordered to such glory as would be unfitting for a pure creature existing in itself to possess. And he gives this reason why such is so. To a human nature that has been hypostatically assumed by the Word a higher degree of glory is appropriate than it is fitting to give to any created person. And he adds the further claim, that such glory could not be in any way merited.

This third statement is rather involved, since it seems to have some puzzling implications, if we keep in mind what Scotus meant specifically by the following particular expressions. First is the meaning of 'such glory.' Recall what Scotus held about an absolutely highest degree of grace being something God could create at a single stroke.[56] It is to this that 'such glory' refers. 'Pure creature' is another expression with particular meaning for Scotus in view of his preferred theory of what constitutes human

---

whereas the will, by reason of its natural affection for justice, can be elevated by the supernatural gifts of grace and glory. Since everything is said to naturally desire what fulfils and perfects its nature, paradoxically we can be said to have a natural desire for the supernatural, as Scotus makes clear in the opening question of his *Ordinatio*. Without supernatural revelation, however, we remain unaware of this eschatological truth, for we have no natural experiential knowledge of anything supernatural within us. See my article, "Duns Scotus on the Natural Desire for the Supernatural," *New Scholasticism* 23 (1949): 281-317, reprinted in a shortened form in *Philosophical Theology*, 125-147; and my translation and commentary entitled "Duns Scotus on the Necessity of Revealed Knowledge," *Franciscan Studies* 11 (1951): [231]-[272].

[56] See note 46 above.

personality.[57] For this refers to an individual human or angelic being 'existing in itself' and not 'in the Word' or in some other divine person or persons.[58] Such an individual would automatically be a created *person* and not just a created *nature*. Third, there is the distinction between *glory* that Scotus believes can fall in some sense under 'merit'[59] and that which cannot.[60] The latter he claimed

---

[57] See *Franciscan Christology*, 166-181. Richard of St. Victor, Scotus tells us, corrected Boethius's definition of a person as 'an individual substance of an intellectual nature,' since this would have made the divine nature that the three persons share in common, a fourth person in its own right. Since the divine nature is communicable, whereas paternity, filiation and passive spiration are not, Richard defined a person as 'the incommunicable existence of an intellectual nature.' Scotus argues that where a divine person is concerned there is some positive incommunicable entity that represents this unique subjectivity, whereas where created persons are concerned "we find no positive entity in addition to singularity which makes a singular nature incommunicable." What constitutes a created person, in addition to its positive individuality is that it has no need to be communicated to be an autonomous person, nor has it been actually assumed by a divine person. This double negation of 'communicated' if added to the Boethian definition makes every complete individual human being incommunicable in a qualified sense and hence a human person in its own right. For a more nuanced account of the opinion he preferred (*non asserendo*) see the text of *Ordinatio* III, dist. 1, q. 1, n. 44 (Codex A, f. 139 bis ra) in the above article, 168-169.

[58] Scotus asserted that other forms of divine assumption were possible than what had occurred in the incarnation of the Son of God. See his discussion of *Ordinatio* III, dist. 1, qq. 1 & 2.

[59] See *Will and Morality*, 218-221. Scotus distinguishes three grades of moral goodness. The first is generic, based on the fact that a voluntary act is generically good because the object intended apart from any circumstances or end is in accord with right reason. A generically good action has the quasi-potential of becoming specifically a good act if in addition to the moral nature of the act, it is performed under such circumstances and for a purpose in accord with right reason. The third grade of goodness is a meritorious act which is prompted by grace or charity. As Scotus explains in *Ordinatio* II, dist. 7, n. 31: "Tertia bonitas competit actui ex hoc quod, praesupposita duplici bonitate iam dicta, ipsa elicitur conformiter principio merendi (quod est caritas vel gratia) sive secundum inclinationem caritatis." Because God wills to accept certain morally good actions as meritorius, they are meritorius; it is not because they are meritorius, that God accepts them as such. It is in this connection that he writes in the supplement to Bk. III of the *Ordinatio*, dist. 19: "Dico quod sicut omne aliud a Deo ideo bonum est quia a Deo est volitum, et non e converso, similiter meritum illud ita tantum bonum erat pro quanto acceptabatur, et ideo meritum quia acceptatum et non e converso quia meritum et bonum, ideo acceptatum." (Codices A [f. 161vb] & S [f. 198vb]; cf. Vivès n. 7 14:718)

[60] Actions in this life performed in accord with the virtue of charity are meritorius in the sense that they bring as their reward an increased degree of charitable grace. Since Christ had the maximum degree of grace or charity to begin

cannot be given appropriately to a creature that has not been assumed by a divine person. Here the incarnation takes the place of merit as the rationale for God giving the degree of glory he does to a creature hypostatically united to divinity.

It is not clear to me from what Scotus says here as to just why he considered God could not give the highest degree of glory to a pure creature. This needs to be discussed more fully elsewhere[61] in the light of his statements in Bk. III of the *Ordinatio*, distinction 7, question 3 as well as in several other hitherto unedited *reportata* that Balic has fortunately given us in his *Theologiae Marianae Elementa.*[62]

For the moment, however, let us continue with Scotus's analysis of what he believed God's priorities must be in regard to the incarnation.[63]

---

with, he could not merit with respect to himself, but as head of the Church he merited grace for the rest of elect.

[61]I plan to do a more extensive study as to how Scotus changed his views regarding whether personality should be considered to be essentially something absolute or wholly relative.

[62] Confer *Theologiae Marianae Elementa*, 175-189. There is also the interesting question of how far the theory Scotus accepted tentatively would fit in with the problem contemporary theologians raise. How much did Jesus, as the son of Mary, know of the hypostatic union before the resurrection, and could a complete and perfect individual human being have in some measure have played an active role as Pannenberg suggests?: "According to Duns Scotus, there resides in created personality the possibility of becoming a person either in dedication to God or in rendering oneself independent. While the latter possibility is realized in all other men, Jesus actualized being a person in dedication to God so that the divine person became the element of his existence which was constitutive of his person. This solution retains a shadow of disjunctive Christology only because it understands dedication to God not as the dedication of Jesus to the Father, but in the pattern of the two natures doctrine as dedication of Jesus' human will to the divine will of the Logos . . . instead of recognizing Jesus' dedication to the Father as the basis for his identity with the Son or the Logos." See Wolfhart Pannenberg, *Jesus—God and Man* (Philadelphia: Westminster Press, 1974) 296. See also See Heribert Mühlen, *Sein und Person nach Johannes Duns Scotus* (Werl Westf.: Dietrich-Coelde-Verlag, 1954).

[63] *Theologiae Marianae Elementa*, p. 12-13: "Ex isto patet quod primo praeordinatur finis a sapiente, et secundo alia, quae sunt ad finem; et sic primo praeordinatur gloria summa Christo, deinde unio naturae ad Verbum, per quam potest attingere ad tantam gloriam, quia universaliter primum in intentione est ultimum in executione in omnibus exequendis; ideo in executione prius fuit unio ad Verbum, quam summa gloria collata Christo, et sic prius praedestinatio ad unionem quam ad gloriam.

And from this it is evident that one who is wise intends first the end and second other things which are means to that end. And so the highest glory is first preordained to Christ, and then the union of his [human] nature to the Word, through which it can attain to such glory. For generally what is first in intention is last in implementation as to everything that must follow later. Therefore in the implementation there was first the [hypostatic] union with the Word, before the highest glory was given to Christ, and thus he was first predestined to union before being predestined to glory.

You may say: it is necessary that predestination first refers to a person before it does to a nature, for it cannot primarily refer to a nature. I say that although in other predestinations it does refer precisely to a person, it is not necessary that it always do so. For God can accept the goodness of a nature qua nature, before accepting the goodness of a person qua person. But the reason why in other predestinations, the predestination refers primarily to the person is because to that nature existing in itself there is a prior ordination which may not exist in another person.[64]

"Dices: oportet quod praedestinatio respiciat personam prius quam naturam; non enim potest primo respicere naturam. Dico quod quamquam in aliis praedestinatio respiciat praecise primo personam, non tamen est necesse quod semper respiciat primo personam. Potest enim Deus acceptare bonum naturae, ut natura, prius quam personae, ut persona. Ratio autem, quare in aliis praedestinationibus praeordinatio primo respicit personam, est quia illi naturae subsistenti in se est praeordinatio quod non existat in alia persona, sed isti naturae subsistenti in Verbo convenit primo praedestinatio; ideo ista praedestinatio est naturae, ut natura, in primo instanti naturae; in secundo instanti naturae est praedestinatio ad unionem, vel ad alia sequentia."

[64]Though God by reason of his absolute power could have ordained otherwise, no other nature received a grace equal to Christ's. "For according to the laws divine wisdom has set up, there will be but one head in the Church," Scotus tells us, "from whom graces flow to its members." See *Ordinatio* III, dist. 13, q. 1: "Hic posset dici quod, licet Deus de potentia Dei absoluta posset tantam gratiam conferre alii naturae, sive assumptae *sive forte non assumptae*, non tamen de potentia ordinata, quia secundum leges iam positas a sapientia divina, non erit nisi unum caput in Ecclesia a quo sit influentia gratiarum in membris." (Codices A [f. 153va] & S [f. 188va]; cf. Vivès n. 8 14:447-477) Scotus might have had Paul's letter to the Ephesians, ch. 1 in mind" "God chose us in him before the world began . . . he likewise predestined us through Christ to be his adopted sons . . . God has given us the wisdom to understand fully the mystery, the plan he was pleased to decree in

But to this nature subsisting in the Word pertains the first predestination. And therefore this predestination is of a nature qua nature in the first instance of nature. In the second instant of nature there is a predestination to union, or to other things that follow.

Article 2. The Unique Way Christ Was Predestined.

To the second question—'In what way was Christ predestined?' —Scotus gives this answer:[65]

To the second, I say that the ordering that refers to the person of the Word and this man is unique, as was stated earlier. Just as there is one unique fact which refers to many items, so too what is predestined and ordered beforehand refers to many things. Therefore the Son of God is predestined to be man; secondly, the converse, this man is predestined to be the Son of God; then there is a union of the [human] nature to the Word, and then the merit of the elect, and then the fall of the wicked, and then mediation and redemption.

You may say:[66] a person, not only a nature must necessarily precede the predestination. I say: it is not necessary that only a person precede what may be ordered [for it] beforehand, although what was ordered beforehand may precede the subject for which it was ordered, as is the case if some [priest] orders something beforehand for himself by celebrating a mass beforehand. It is not necessary

---

Christ, to be carried out in the fulness of time, namely, to bring all things in the heaven and on earth into one under Christ's headship."

[65]*Theologiae Marianae Elementa*, p. 13 "Secundo dico quod unica est ordinatio, qua denominatur suppositum Verbi, et ille homo, sicut prius dictum est, quod unica est passio, qua multa denominantur in factione passiva, ita quod praeordinari et praeordinare multa denominant. Ideo Filius Dei primo est praedestinatus esse homo; secundo econtra, ille homo praedestinatus est esse Filius Dei; deinde unio naturae ad Verbum; deinde merita electorum: deinde casus malorum; deinde mediatio et redemptio.

[66]*ibid.*: "Dices: oportet quod praedestinationem praecedat suppositum, et non solum natura. Dico quod non oportet, quod illud quod praeordinatur praecedat suppositum, licet illud cui praeordinatur praecedat praeordinatum, sicut si aliquis praeordinat sibi aliquod bonum, ut de celebrando iam missam, non oportet quod illud bonum praecedat illud cui praeordinatur; ideo primo Filius Dei est praedestinatus esse homo, et secundo ille homo econtra."

that the recipient of what was preordered exist before the good [to be received] exists. Therefore primarily the Son of God has been predestined to be man, and second, this man to be the Son of God.

Article 3. The Incarnation and Redemption.

In the Paris lecture, Scotus's third question was: How is Christ's predestination ordered to the other predestinations? At Oxford he dealt with much of what he treats here in distinction 19 of Bk. III[67] where he indicates how Christ merited grace and glory for the human race initially as well as redeeming its sin and taking on himself the punishment due to its fall from grace. This did not imply in any way that the incarnation itself was occasioned by sin. Rather it was a good intended primarily for its own sake as contributing most directly to God's ultimate purpose in creating. In fact as Scotus explained earlier,[68] "No one is predestined to grace and glory simply because God foresaw another would fall, lest anyone have reason to rejoice at the misfortune of another."

---

[67]*Ordinatio* III (suppl.), dist. 19: "Dico quod incarnatio Christi non fuit occasionaliter praevisa, sed sicut finis immediate videbatur a Deo ab aeterno, ita Christus in natura humana, cum sit propinquior fini, caeteris prius praedestinatur, loquendo de his qui praedestinantur, quia cuicumque alius et quilibet alius prius ordinatur ad gratiam et gloriam quam praevidebatur eius casus, ut patet superius; et tunc iste fuit ordo in praevisione divina; quod primo Deus intellexit se sub ratione summi boni; in secundo signo intellexit omnes creaturas; in tertio praedestinavit aliquod ad gloriam et gratiam, et circa aliquod habuit actum negativum, non praedestinando; et in quarto praevidit omnes istos et illos casuros in Adam; in quinto praeordinavit et praevidit de remedio quomodo redimerentur per passionem Filii sui, ita quod Christus in carne, sicut onmes electi, prius praevideretur passio Christi ut medicina contra lapsum, sicut medicus prius vult sanitatem hominis, quam vult de medicina ad sanandum hominem. Ergo sicut prius praedestinantur electi, quam passio praevidebatur ut remedium contra lapsum eorum, ita tota Trinitas prius praeordinavit praedestinatos et electos ad gratiam et gloriam finalem, quantum ad efficaciam, quam praevidit Christi passionem tamquam medicinam acceptandam pro electis cadentibus in Adam. Et sicut Verbum praevidit passionem Patri offerendam pro praedestinatis et electis, et eam sic efficaciter obtulit in effectu, ita tota Trinitas passionem efficaciter acceptavit, et quia pro nullis fuit efficaciter oblata, nec ab aeterno acceptata, ideo tantum meruit eis gratiam primam ordinantem ad gloriam consequentem; hoc quantum ad efficaciam meriti eius. (Codices A [f. 174ra-va] & S [f. 198vb]; cf. Vivès n. 7 14:714)

[68]See my bilingual edition of *Ordinatio* III, dist. 7, q. 3 in *Franciscan Christology*, 146-153.

Rather[69] "we can say that God selected for his heavenly choir all
the angels and men he wished to have with their varied degrees of
perfection, and all this before considering either the sin or the
punishment of the sinner." These same ideas are expressed in this
portion of the Paris lecture. It begins with a rejection of the common
Anselmian answer to the third question.[70]

> As for the third question, one needs to show how this
> predestination is related to other predestinations. —And it
> is said that the fall of man is the necessary reason for this
> predestination. From the fact that God foresaw the fall of
> man he saw him as redeemed by this way, and therefore he
> foresaw that human nature would be assumed and be
> glorified by such glory.

His frank declaration in refutation reads as follow:[71]

> *I say*, however, that the fall of man was not the cause of
> Christ's predestination. Indeed if neither man nor an angel
> had fallen, nor several men were created besides Christ,
> Christ still would have been predestined in this way. I

---

[69]*Ibid.*, 151.

[70]*Theologiae Marianae Elementa*, p. 13: "Tertio ostendendum est, quis sit ordo
huius praedestinationis ad alias praedestinationes? Et dicitur, quod lapsus hominis
est ratio necessaria huius praedestinationis. Ex hoc quod Deus vidit hominem
casurum, vidit eum per hanc viam redempturum, et ideo praevidit naturam
humanam assumendam, et tanta gloria glorificandam."

[71]*Ibid.*, p. 14: "Dico tamen quod lapsus non fuit causa praedestinationis Christi.
Immo etsi nec homo nec angelus fuisset lapsus, nec plures homines creandi quam solus
Christus, adhuc fuisset Christus praedestinatus sic. Istud probo: quia omnis ordinate
volens primo vult finem, deinde immediatius illa quae sunt fini immediatiora; sed
Deus est ordinatissime volens: ergo sic vult. Primo ergo vult se; et post se immediate,
quantum ad extrinseca, est anima Christi: ergo primum post velle intrinseca, voluit
gloriam istam Christo; ergo ante quodcumque meritum et ante quodcumque
demeritum praevidit Christum sibi esse uniendum in unitate suppositi.

"Item, ut declaratum est in primo libro, in materia de praedestinatione, prius
est praeordinatio et praedestinatio completa circa electos quam aliquid fiat circa
reprobos in actu secundo, ne aliquis gaudeat ex perditione alterius quod sibi sit
lucrum: ergo ante lapsum praevisum et ante omne demeritum fuit totus processus
praevisus circa Christum.

"Item, si lapsus esset ratio praedestinationis Christi, sequeretur quod summum
opus Dei esset maxime occasionatum, quia gloria omnium non est tanta intensive,
quanta fuit Christi et quod tantum opus dimisisset Deus per bonum factum Adae,
puta si non peccasset, videtur valde irrationabile."

prove this: everyone willing in an orderly fashion first wills the end, then immediately that which attains the end more directly. But God wills in a most orderly way; therefore he wills in this fashion. First he wills himself, and then after himself immediately—so far as things extrinsic to himself are concerned, is the soul of Christ. Therefore first of all, after willing what is intrinsic to himself, he wills this glory to Christ. Therefore, before any merit and before any sin whatsoever he foresees Christ as united to himself in a hypostatic or personal unity

Also, as was declared in the first book, in matters of predestination, there is first of all a complete preordering and predestination in regard to the elect before anything occurs in regard to the reprobates in a second act, lest anyone rejoice at the perdition of another which would seem to be for such a [predestined] one a matter of gain. Therefore before the fall was foreseen or before all demerit, the entire process as regards Christ was foreseen.

Also, if the fall were the reason why Christ was predestined, it would follow that the supreme work of God was a matter of the purest chance, because the glory of all combined is not as intensive as was that of Christ and the idea that God would have put off performing such a work because of a good Adam might have performed had he not sinned seems exceedingly irrational.

Once again Scotus sets forth the orderly way in which Christ's predestination fits into God's plan of creation as a manifestation of his love for the divine nature.[72]

Therefore, I declare it was this way: God first loves himself. Secondly he loves himself in others and this is a chaste love; thirdly he wills to be loved by that which can love him most of all, speaking of the love of someone outside; and fourth he provides the [hypostatic] union of this nature which owes him the supreme love even had there never been a fall.

---

[72]*Ibid.*, 14-15: "Dico ergo sic: Primo Deus diligit se, secundo diligit se aliis et iste est amor castus; tertio vult se diligi ab illo qui potest eum summe diligere, loquendo de amore alicuius extrinseci; et quarto praevidit unionem illius naturae, quae debet eum summe diligere etsi nullus cecidisset."

And he shows how given the actual nature of God's creative plan, the immediate glorification of Christ's body was a lesser good considered in itself than the glory that would come to it by the role it played in our redemption.[73]

> How, therefore, are we to understand the authoritative statements of the saints that God would not have become a mediator had no one become a sinner, and many other such statements which seem to assert the contrary? I say that glory is ordered to the soul of Christ and to his flesh as well, so far as this can share in such, and in the measure glory was given to the soul by being assumed [hypostatically]. Therefore it would have been given immediately to his flesh had it not its postponement been a greater good which could have come to it and ought to have come to it by being the redeemer who would reclaim his race from the power of the devil. For the glory of the blessed to be redeemed through the suffering of his body was a greater good than the glory of the flesh of Christ. And therefore, in the fifth place God foresaw a suffering mediator coming to redeem his people; and he would not have come *qua mediator* as one who would suffer and would redeem unless someone had not first sinned. Neither would the future glory of the body have been delayed were it not for those who were to be redeemed, but the entire Christ would have been at once glorified.

Note here that though the perdition of no one became the occasion of the predestination of another, sin does play a secondary

---

[73]*Ibid.*, 15: "Quomodo ergo sunt intelligendae auctoritates sanctorum ponentium, quod Deus non fuisset mediator, nisi aliquis fuisset peccator, et multae aliae auctoritates, quae videntur sonare in contrarium? Dico, quod gloria est ordinata animae Christi et carni, sicut potest carni competere, et sicut fuit collata animae in assumptione; ideo statim fuisset collata carni, nisi quod propter maius bonum fuit istud dilatum, ut per mediatorem, qui potuit et debuit, redimeretur gens a potestate diaboli, quia maius bonum fuit gloria beatorum redimendorum per passionem carnis, quam gloria carnis Christi; et ideo in quinto instanti vidit Deus mediatorem venientem passurum, redempturum populum suum; et non venisset, ut mediator, ut passurus et redempturus, nisi aliquis prius peccasset, neque fuisset gloria carnis dilata, nisi fuissent redimendi, sed statim fuisset totus Christus glorificatus."

causal role, according to Scotus, in the overall plan of God's creation. Its existence as an evil to be overcome by virtue provides both the challenge and the opportunity to prove one's love of God and so merit a greater good and glory than if it did not exist at all. This is meant to provide a partial answer at least to the vexing problem as to why God did not create a sinless universe from the outset. As Paul assured the Corinthians (II Cor. 12:9): "Power is made perfect in weakness."

This same curious relationship seems to run through the whole of salvation history.[74] "God's folly is wiser than men, and his weakness more powerful than men" (I Cor. 1: 25). For God often seems to choose the most unlikely means to achieve marvelous results. And this brings us consider two other aspects of the means God chooses to achieve his ends. First, it is tailored to the individual (for where higher creatures are concerned it is the individual rather than the species that God is most interested in)[75] and second, God seems to prefer an historical scenario where the perfect evolves from the imperfect. Scotus gives as an example, the orderly way God went about revealing his supernatural law.[76]

> In the course of human generation the knowledge of truth always increases, as is evident from Gregory's *Homily on*

---

[74]See I Cor. 1:18-25.

[75]In answer to an objection that individuals do not pertain to the order of the universe, since order is based on priority and posteriority whereas all individuals are on a par with one another, Scotus replies that where angels and human beings are concerned "it is the individual that is primarily intended by God." See *Ordinatio* II, dist. 3, n. 251 (Vat. 7: 513-514): "In toto universo, licet principaliter ordo attendatur secundum distinctionem specierum, in quibus est imparitas, pertinens ad ordinem,—tamen, quia secundum Augustinum, *De civitate* libro XIX cap. 13, 'ordo est parium impariumque, unicuique sua loca tribuens, congrua dispositio,' —ab illo agente qui principaliter intendit ordinem universi (sicut bonum, intrinsecum sibi), non tantum intenditur ista imparitas, quae est 'unum requisitum' ad ordinem (scilicet specierum), sed etiam paritas individuorum (scilicet in eadem specie) quae est 'aliud concurrens' ad ordinem. Et simpliciter individua intenduntur ab ipso Primo prout ipsum intendit aliquid 'aliud a se' non ut finem, sed ut aliquid aliud ad finem; unde propter bonitatem suam communicandam, ut propter suam beatitudinem, plura in eadem specie produxit. In principalissimis autem entibus est a Deo principaliter intentum individuum."

[76]*Ordinatio* IV, dist. 1, q. 3: "In processu generationis humanae, semper crevit notitia veritatis, ut patet per Gregorium *Super Ezechielem*. . . . Lex autem posterior semper fuit perfectior, quia Deus ordinate agens procedit de imperfecto ad perfectum." (Codices A [f. 188ra] & M [f. 127ra]; cf. Vivès n. 8 16:136)

Ezechiel.[77]. . . The later law, however, was always more perfect, because God acting in an orderly way proceeds from the imperfect to the perfect.

Like Pope Gregory, the Great, whom he quotes, Scotus believed that the human race was given sufficient knowledge[78] at any stage of its history to be saved.[79] How it was handed on in each age may

---

[77]St. Gregory the Great, *Homilarium in Ezechielem Prophetam libi duo*, lib. II, hom. 4, vers. 11, n. 12 (PL 76, 980-981): "Qua in re hoc quoque nobis sciendum est quia et per incrementa temporum crevit scientia spiritalium patrum. Plus namque Moyses quam Abraham, plus prophetae quam Moyses, plus apostoli quam prophetae in omnipotentis Dei scientia eruditi sunt. Fallor si haec ipsa Scriptura non loquitur: *Pertransibunt*, inquit, *plurimi, et multiplex erit scientia (Dan.* xii, 4). Sed haec eadem quae de Abraham, Moyse, prophetis et apostolis diximus, ex eiusdem Scripturae verbis, si possumus, ostendamus. Quis enim nesciat quia Abraham cum Deo locutus est (*Genes.* xii, *seq.*)? et tamen ad Moysen Dominus dicit: *Ego sum Deus Abraham, Deus Isaac, et Deus Jacob, et nomen meum Adonai non indicavi eis (Exod.* vi, 5; *Ibid.*, iii, 6)? Ergo plus quam Abrahae innotuerat, qui illud de se Moysi indicat quod se Abrahae non indicasse narrabat. Sed videamus si prophetae plus quam Moyses divinam scientiam apprehendere potuerunt. Certe Psalmista dicit: "*Quomodo dilexi legem tuam, Domine? tota die meditatio mea est (Psal.* cxviii, 97). Atque subjunxit: *Super omnes docentes me intellexi; quia testimonia tua meditatio mea est (Ibid.*, 99). Et iterum: *Super seniores intellexi (Ibid.*, 100). Qui ergo legem meditari se memorat et super omnes docentes se ac super seniores intellexisse testatur, quia divinam scientiam plus quam Moyses acceperat manifestat. Quomodo autem ostensuri sumus quia plus sancti apostoli edocti sunt quam prophetae? Certe Veritas dicit: *Multi reges et prophetae voluerunt videre quae videtis, et audire quae auditis, sed non viderunt (Luc.* x, 24) Plus ergo quam prophetae de divina scientia noverunt, quia quod illi solo spiritu viderunt, isti etiam corporaliter viderunt."

[78]Though God could have required more of mankind, he made the observation of the decalog alone a necessary requirement. *Ordinatio* IV, dist. 26: "Licet homo ex creatione Deo teneatur in omnibus quae potest, tamen Deus non tantum exigit ab homine, immo dimittit liberum eum sibi, solummodo exigens quod servet praecepta decalogi." (Codex A f. 249ra; cf. Vivès n. 10 19:160) In its general outlines, at least, this law is written into the heart of man. *Ordinatio* prol. (n. 108): "In omnibus videtur esse quasi quaedam explicatio legis naturae, quae *scripta est in cordibus nostris*." (Vat. 1:70)

[79] Scotus admits that by reason of what is written in our hearts we only know the general outlines of natural law, not its finer details. See for example, *Ordinatio* IV, dist. 26: "Sed lex naturae etsi obliget ad indissolubilitatem vinculi praedicti [i.e., matrimonii], praemisso tali contractu, non tamen lex naturae evidentissima, sed secundo modo dicta. Illud autem quod non erit de lege naturae nisi secundo modo, non est omnibus manifestum; ergo expedit necessitatem illius praecepti a lege positiva divina determinari." (Codex A f. 248vb; cf. Vivès, n.9 19, 160). In addition to this general knowledge of the decalogue, sufficient grace is given for its observation. *Ordinatio* II, dist. 28: "Si non erant obligati ad legem Moysi nisi filii Israel, alii Gentiles potuerunt iuste vivere servando legem naturae, et tunc ipsi facti

have differed,[80] but each individual is only bound to use those means right reason indicates are necessary. He makes this clear in his explanation of why moral goodness is not simply tailoring or conforming our will to God's will, but rather of willing what God wills us to will.[81] For only God knows specifically what means we are to use to attain our end.[82]

> Our will, however, as it exists in this life is not so obliged to that end that it be in all things conformed to it, for just as our intellect does not comprehend all that is ordered to that end so that it could be conformed to it in every detail, so neither does our will comprehend all that is ordered to that end so that there would always be in it a conformity of rectitude as regards that end. And because it does not comprehend everything, therefore it is not obligated to everything ordered to that end. But it pertains only to the divine will to comprehend its end which is its beatitude, to

---

sunt suiipsius lex id est per legem naturae scriptam interius in cordibus eorum direxerunt se recte vivendo, sicut Iudaei per legem scriptam; sed isti non bene vixerunt sine omni gratia, quia gratia potuit esse in eis hypothesi supposita absque observatione legis Mosaicae." Codices A [f. 134va]; P [f. 191va]; S [f. [139vb]; & V [f. 215rb]; cf. Vivès n. 8 (13:262); *Lectura* II, dist. 28, n. 22: "Sed credibile est quod ante legem multi habuerunt gratiam . . . tunc fecerunt sibi gentes legem in mente, et habuerunt gratiam tales, bene viventes secundum legem naturae et secundum dictamen rationis rectae naturalis." (Vat. 19:279-280). See also the interesting note Scotus added in revising the first question in his *Ordinatio* prol. (n. 54-55; Vat. 1:33-35).

[80]*Ordinatio* III, suppl. d. 37: "In statu etiam innocentiae tenebantur omnes ad ista praecepta, quae erant praescripta interius in corde cuiuslibet, vel forte per aliquam doctrinam exteriorem datam a Deo, quam descenderunt a patribus ad filios, licet non essent tunc scripta in libro. Nec oportuit, quia potuerunt illa faciliter memoraliter retinere, et populus illius temporis erat maioris vitae, et dispositionis melioris in naturalibus quam populus temporis posterioris, quo tempore infirmitas populi rogabat legam dari et scribi." (Codices A [f. 180rb] & S [f. 222rb]; cf. Vivès, n. 14 15, 851)

[81]See *Will and Morality*, 234-237.

[82]*Reportatio* IA, dist. 48: "Voluntas autem nostra, ut est in via, non obligatur ad illum finem, ut sit in omnibus ei conformis, quia sicut intellectus noster non comprehendit omnia ordinata ad illum finem, ut possit ei esse conformis in omni veritate, sic nec voluntas nostra comprehendi omnia ordinata ad illum finem, ut semper sit in ea conformitas rectitudinis per respectum ad illum finem. Et quia non comprehendit, ideo non obligatur ad omnia ordinata ad illum finem. Sed hoc pertinet tantum ad voluntatem divinam comprehendere finem suum, qui est beatitudo sua, ad quam nos perducat qui est benedictus in saecula saeculorum. Amen. Amen.Amen."

which it leads us and is blessed for endless ages. Amen. Amen. Amen.

III. Scotus's Eschatological Vision

Such was the grand eschatological conception Scotus had of God's creation. It came forth from a triune God of co-lovers in love with their divine being "lacking no entity it is possible for anything to have." Because love is a sharing of one's goodness with another, this triune God, that is "essentially love," chose to "communicate the rays of its goodness most liberally" in the form of a Christocentric universe of co-lovers "knit together in a far more excellent way" than any "aggregation of citizens." Governed by laws where justice is tempered with mercy, this *ecclesia* has but one head, a God-man whose soul is endowed with the highest grace, whose life, passion and death, has made him the font "from whom all graces flow to its members." Since grace entails an indwelling of the Trinity, its presence in the souls of the elect becomes the means whereby "every single being in its own way is brought back to God as its ultimate end."

These are all theological views that flesh out what Scotus believed we can know philosophically from natural reason alone. Students of Scotus expanded his Christocentrism explicitly integrating it with his views on the role of Mary as the immaculate recipient of Christ's greatest mediation.

Seven centuries have passed since Scotus, against the overwhelming theological opposition of his contemporaries first proposed his belief in Mary's Immaculate Conception. Scarcely less accepted was his contention that the incarnation represented the supreme work of God and that it was Christ who was our Creator's intended 'firstborn.' Today theologians recognize one as a defined dogma, the other as a necessary premise, as did Scotus, to their eschatological conviction that ours is indeed a Christocentric universe and we have no purely natural destiny where grace plays no constitutive role.[83] Scotus himself is now recognized officially by

---

[83]Summing up the Pauline and Johannine epistles, Richard McBrian writes: "All creation is oriented towards the Covenant between God and the People of God, and the Covenant, in turn, towards the New Covenant grounded in the incarnation of the Son of God in Jesus Christ. The human community and entire world in which the

the Church as blessed[84] and a medal struck to honor the fact
commemorates these two cardinal tenets. It carries the facial
inscription: "B. Ioannes Duns Scotus. 1265-1308. Immaculatae
Conceptionis Dei Vindex" and on the reverse side "Incarnatio
Summum Opus Dei."

IV. Some Contemporary Considerations

In addition to these two cardinal tenets that could make him
eligible in the unforeseeable future to become another Doctor of the
Church there are undoubtedly a number of other tenets that should
interest contemporary theologians. For one of the refreshing aspects
of Scotus's philosophical theology is its open-endedness. He never
lived long enough to fully solve to his own satisfaction all the
questions he raised in his masterwork. He generally sought to
present a mediating position between rival theories and the acute
analysis he gave to many problems of contemporary interest often
suggests new ways of solving old riddles. I could show that several
of these Scotistic tenets are relevant to problems raised by modern
science, but, because of their complexity, I reluctantly leave that
for another day and another study.[85]

---

human community exists is oriented towards Christ and is sustained by him.
Although hypothetically it could have been otherwise, in fact it has not been
otherwise. There is no creation except in view of Christ. There is no Covenant except
in view of Christ. There is no human existence, therefore, except in view of Christ
and of our New Covenant in Christ. This intrinsic orientation of the human person
and of the entire human community in Christ radically excludes any dualism, or
sharp separation, between nature and grace. Although in principle we could know
God apart from revelation and apart specifically from revelation of God in Christ,
in fact we cannot and do not know God apart from this revelation (Romans 1:18-28;
Acts of the Apostles 17:24-27)." *Catholicism*, new ed. (San Francisco: Harper-
SanFrancisco, 1994) 181-182.

[84] Pope John Paul II in conferring liturgical honors on Duns Scotus at the
Saturday Vespers service, March 20, 1993 reminded his audience that "John Duns
Scotus was called 'blessed' almost immediately after his death . . . and . . . for
centuries public veneration has been offered to him which the Church solemnly
recognized on 6 July 1991 (cf. *Acta Apostolica Sedis* 84 [1992], 396-399) and confirms
today." See *L'OSSERVATORE ROMANO* (Weekly Edition in English, 24 March
1993) 1.

[85] Present day science indicates the nature of the physical universe is not only
vastly different from what Scotus believed it to be, but even from what it was
thought to be at the beginning of this century. (See e.g. the essays edited by Noriss
S. Hetherington in *COSMOLOGY: Historical, Literary, Philosophical, Religious,*

There is one, however, that I would like to mention here because of its eschatological nature, and that is Scotus's conception of our body/soul relationship. As he pointed out in his discussion of the resurrection of the dead,[86] the substantial subject of our intellectual and volitional acts must be an immaterial simple entity.[87] However, the more one proves this to be the substantial form of a mortal body, the less one can assume it to be immortal and capable of existence apart from the body.[88] If we view this

---

and Scientific Perspectives [New York/London: Garland, 1993].) Velocity of stars in the outer regions of galaxies appear to be moving far more rapidly than can be explained on the basis of the scientifically measurable amount of matter they seem to contain. It has been suggested that what is presently detectable represents only a small fraction of what constitutes the total matter of the universe. Although discontinuities beginning with the big-bang expansion on one end and black holes on the other indicate the time-continuum open to scientific investigation is relatively limited, the new sciences of chaos and complexity extend the boundaries of what is ruled by law into what was once believed to be purely random behavior and happenstance. (See e.g. James Gleick, *Chaos: Making a New Science*. New York: Penguin Books, 1987; M. Mitchell Waldrop, *Complexity*. New York: Simon & Schuster, 1992). Interesting EPR experiments fail to disprove the claims of quantum-mechanics and indicate that at a very fundamental physical level the whole material universe is interconnected in a mysterious fashion reminiscent more of Leibniz's monadology than Aristotle's insensitive primary matter. (See e.g. Nick Herbert, *Quantum Reality*. New York: Anchor Books, 1985). Even our planet earth, if not a living organism as the gaia hypothesis suggests, is continually renewing itself in surprising ways. (See e.g. Thomas Berry, *The Dream of the Earth*, San Francisco: Sierra Club, 1988; Rupert Sheldrake, *The Rebirth of Nature*. New York: Bantam Books, 1991). And neurological discoveries indicate our spiritual self may be more loosely connected to an organic body than traditionally believed. (See for example, Oliver Sacks, *The Man who Mistook His Wife for a Hat and Other Clinical Tales* New York: Harper Perennial, 1990; see also E. P. Pollen, *Critique of the Psycho-physical Identity Theory* The Hague/Paris: Moutin, 1973).

[86]For the bilingual edition of *Ordinatio* IV, dist. 43, q. 2 based on Codex A see my *Duns Scotus: Philosophical Writings*, 2ed. (Indianapolis/Cambridge: Hackett Publishing Co., 1987) 134-162.

[87]*Ibid.*, 139-145.

[88]*Ibid.*, 147: "Ergo si concessit animam intellectivam esse formam hominis, ut patet ex probatione propositionis praecedentis, non ponit eam manere separatum a materia, toto non manente" (Codex A f. 260va; cf. Vivès n. 15, 20: 45). In the parallel passage from his Paris lecture, Scotus indicates that although Aristotle earlier followed Plato in his belief that the intellectual part of the soul was incorruptible, in virtue of his later contention that it was the substantial form of the body he would have had to admit it was also corruptible. "Item 12 *Metaphy*. dicit quod forte non est tota anima, sed pars, quae manet post corpus; igitur ubique loquitur incerte et dubitative de perpetuitate eius. Si enim posuisset eam simpliciter incorruptibilem omnia principia sua de naturalibus essent destructa. . . . Ideo credo

relationship conversely, however, it seems to have a surprising consequence. For if we have proof from revelation that the portion of the soul that thinks and wills and is aware of its own identity is immortal,[89] the less one can prove it is the exclusively limited to its tenure as the substantial form of our present mortal body.

Here it is intriguing to review what Scotus wrote about what our intellect's *natural powers* as a faculty must be if God can supernaturally enlighten it with the intuitive vision of his divine nature.[90] Scotus tells us the human intellect is capable of far greater intellectual activity than we would dream of if we merely analyzed its functions in our present state of existence. If man's soul is not a fallen angel as some platonists suggest, at least his intellect is not essentially inferior to that of the angel.[91] Though this was

---

quod magis convenienter dixisset animam intellectivam esse corrputibilem, posito quod sit propria forma corporis et non totius." (*Reportata parisiensia* IV, q. 2, n. 13. Vivès 24, 494b)

[89]Though we have probable reasons to believe our existence is not limited to the present life, it is our faith that assures us it is not an idle dream. Hence Scotus writes: "Ex his apparet quantae sunt gratiae referendae nostrae Creatori qui nos per fidem certissimos reddidit in his, quae pertinent ad finem nostrum, et ad perpetuitatem sempiternam ad quae ingeniosissimi et eruditissimi per rationem naturalem quasi nihil poterant attingere . . . Si fides adsit quae est in eis quibus dedit filios Dei fieri, nulla quaestio est quia ipse suos credentes in hoc certissimos reddit." (*Ordinatio* IV, dist. 43, q. 2. Codex A f. 261rb; cf. Vivès 20:59).

[90]Recall that for Aristotle the possible intellect was not an active but a passive potency and the process of the soul coming to knowledge was primarily one of receiving an impression from without. Among Scotus's contemporaries Godfrey of Fontaine, the Parisian master under whom Scotus disputed as a bachelor, had perhaps the purest form of this intellectual passivism, whereas Henry of Ghent was the chief representative of Augustinian intellectual activism. Scotus's position represented a mean between these two extremes. Neither the object alone (whether in itself or in an intelligible species), nor the soul alone is the complete cause of actual knowledge. The two are partial, but essentially ordered efficient causes of the effect we know as intellection. (*Ordinatio* I, dist. 3, n. 495-500. [Vat. 4: 293-297]). This partial concession to the Aristotelian position was theologically important, for it enabled Scotus to distinguish between an object that is by nature ordained to act as a partial cause in producing knowledge and one which is not so ordained but, nevertheless, does move the intellect as he believed God does in the beatific vision.

[91]*Ordinatio* II, dist. 1, n. 319 (Vat. 7:155): "Potest enim addi. . . intellectualitas angeli, in quantum intellectualitas, non differt specie ab intellectualitate animae in quantum intellectualitas, − hoc est quod licet iste actus primus et ille differant specie ut considerantur absolute in se, non tamen secundum illam perfectionem quam virtualiter continent secundum quam sunt principia actuum secundorum." *Quodlibet*, q. 14, n. 12 (Vivès 26:46): "Objectum adaequatum intellectui nostro ex natura potentiae non est aliquid specialius objecto intellectui angelici."

not a philosophical but a theological conclusion, so far as its demonstrability was concerned, Scotus believed we did have probable plausible arguments to suspect it might be the case.[92] Its certainty, Scotus argued could be inferred from the promise of a face-to-face vision of God in the afterlife or such as was granted perhaps temporarily to St. Paul when "snatched up to the third heaven."[93] For the beatific vision, at least, represents an immediate intuition of the divine essence on the part of a created intellect.

This implies that the intellect as such must be capable of intuitive knowledge.[94] For there seems to be no intrinsic reason why an intellectual power rooted in a spiritual nature should not extend to whatever is intelligible in nature. Any limitation must come from a special ordination on the part of God because of the state in which it exists. That is why Scotus distinguishes between (a) what is natural to the intellect as a *faculty* or *power* and (b) what is natural to it in *some particular state*. In the first instance, we abstract from the limitations associated with any particular state and consider the intellect under the best possible conditions. In the second instance, we consider the intellect from the viewpoint of the limitations God has associated with a given state, a state being here understood in Augustinian fashion as a relatively stable or

---

[92]Scotus cites several: one is the fact that we can form an abstract concept of being qua being. If the natural adequate object of our intellect were material or sensible quiddity, how come we can form a more universal concept than that of material quiddity? No cognitive faculty should have knowledge of any subject that does not fall under its adequate object. A second clue from natural reason is the fact that the soul intuits its own intellectual, volitional, and sense activity. We are certain that we think, doubt, are alive, etc. We can only be certain of such contingent propositions, however, if we intuit the situation that justifies them. What is capable of the least degree of intuitive knowledge, Scotus argues, is capable of intuition in general. See note 94 infra.

[93]II Cor. 12:2.

[94]We might ask: why is it necessary to assume that the intellect as such must be capable of intuitive knowledge? Could not God infuse some intellectual habit or accidental quality which would transform the intellect, making it capable of intuition? Scotus says No! A *habitus* or quality of this kind never actually confers the basic active potentiality to perform a specific kind of action. It only perfects what is already there. Furthermore, man is not beatified by reason of something accidental to his soul. It is the human intellect itself and not merely its habit of vision that sees God, just as it is the human will and not the habit of charity that loves God.

permanent condition established by the laws of divine wisdom.[95] The fact that man's intellect at present is limited to abstracting its primary data from the phantasm, or that its intuitive powers are restricted to the knowledge of our conscious acts,[96] is the outcome of such a positive ordination on the part of divine wisdom. Consequently, the possibility of other states is not excluded. And some of these possible states Scotus believed we could infer from revelation will be actually realized. Such for instance is the state of the separated soul. In such a state, the reason for the ligation of the intellectual faculty to the internal senses no longer exists. As a result, man's intellect becomes like unto that of the angelic intellect itself. It will be intuitively aware of its soul-substance, and not just of its mental thoughts, feelings or sensations. It will be able to know immediately other created beings, both spiritual and corporeal, and all this by reason of its own native powers and not by reason of any infused species as St. Thomas suggests.

Scotus believed that in the glorified body, the human intellect would retain this natural intuitive awareness of any creature it might encounter.[97] Hence, in the afterlife whether separated from

---

[95]*Ordinatio* I, dist. 3, n. 187 (Vat. 3:113-114): "Status non videtur esse nisi 'stabilis permanentia,' firmata legibus sapientiae. Firmatum est autem illis legibus, quod intellectus noster non intelligat pro statu isto nisi illa quorum species relucent in phantasmate, et hoc sive propter poenam peccati originalis, sive propter naturalem concordantiam potentiarum animae in operando, secundum quod videmus quod potentia superior operatur circa idem circa quod inferior, si utraque habebit operationem perfectam. Et de facto ita est in nobis, quod quodcumque universale intelligimus, eius singulare actu phantsiamur. Ista tamen concordantia, quae est de facto pro statu isto, *non est de natura intellectus ut intellectus est.,—nec etiam unde in corpore*, quia tunc in corpore glorioso necessario haberet similem concordantiam, quod falsum est. Undecumque ergo sit iste status, sive ex mera voluntate Dei, sive ex iustitia puniente (quam causam innuit Augustinus XV *De Trinitate* cap. ultimo: 'Quae causa' —inquit— 'cur ipsam lucem acie fixa videre non possis, nisi utique infirmitas? et quis eam tibi fecit, nisi utique iniquitas?') sive—inquam—haec sit tota causa, sive aliqua alia, saltem non est primum obiectum intelllectus *unde potentia est et natura*, nisi aliquid commune ad omnia intelligibilia, licet primum obiectum, adaequatum sibi in movendo, pro statu isto sit quidtas rei sensibilis."

[96]According to Scotus, object and intellect are partial co-causes of knowledge. Where the knowledge is abstractive, the intelligible species substitutes causally for the object. Where this knowledge is intuitive it is the actual presence of the object that exercises this co-causality. See my article on how Scotus's conception of intuition developed in "Duns Scotus on Intuition, Memory and Knowledge of Individuals" reprinted in *Philosophical Theology.* 98-122.

[97]See note 95 above.

its mortal body, or in its glorified body, the rational soul could directly study and investigate the whole of God's marvelous material creation. And our wonder at its splendor would prompt our will to praise its creator in a way impossible in the present life when so much of the material universe and how it functions modern scientists recognize is still veiled in mystery.

Some contemporary scientists are all too ready to write off human evolution as a happy accident rather than the result of any planned design of an infinitely wise creator. But as my former teacher and colleague Father Philotheus Boehner, loved to remind us, God is an artist, not an economist. Quoting that line from Proverbs 8:31, *ludens in orbe terrarum*, he would emphasize God's wisdom is *at play* in the universe. The theory of evolution, he would explain, is intimately connected with the problem of the species and their almost unbelievable multitude. By faith we know that this prodigious abundance and wealth goes back ultimately to the Creator of heaven and earth. Why all these forms? Evolution can explain them only in part. Many have no particular worth or special values in the struggle of life; they are useless in this sense, and yet for that reason they are beautiful. Beauty is a factor that is not necessitated by lower needs, but is something that presupposes the liberty and freedom to create artistically. When we look in fascination at all these forms and their loveliness, are we not led back in admiration to the ingenuity and wisdom of their Creator. God himself has spread out before our gaze this mighty work of art, the result of divine wisdom at play. But this is not a static picture. For each of these various forms has a special history of its own. Paleontological discoveries indicate evolution has not occurred as a continuous process, but rather in series of jumps. Surprisingly a new species makes a tentative appearance, feeling its way as it were in a strange environment. Then it learns to adapt, grows stronger and suddenly burst forth in a vast variety of forms. Eventually, however, the development slows down and degeneration sets in until only a few forms remain or the species dies out, leaving only its remains as fossilized rock. Here again, we are watching the great Artist of the Universe, the Wisdom of God *ludens in orbe terrarum*. But now in a dynamic piece of art, in a real dramatic stage-play. St. Augustine, Boehner would remind us, first conceived of history as a *pulcherimum carmen* and Bonaventure repeated the idea. Here in evolution, with its various periods, its acts and scenes, its individual actors, we enjoy an enchanting poetic production (*carmen*) which has been staged by the divine Wisdom since the first organisms were called into existence, and of which our present forms are but a single scene.

Boehner suffered from *angina pectoris* and died relatively young in his sleep after returning from a biological field trip. If he found so much to admire on this earth which scientists tell us is just one planet of a lonely sun in a relatively vacant arm of our local galaxy, what must he be finding to praise God about in the afterlife when the whole of God's material creation is spread out for his scientific investigation? For if God's wisdom is only "playing in the universe, it delights to be with the children of men."[98]

If Scotus is right, I think it is still important to recognize that the whole of the universe as modern science conceives of it today is destined to be brought back to God through the appreciation and praise of human beings.[99] This spiritual substance we call our self—destined, if it leaves this life in a state of grace, to co-love God in glory—is admittedly incomplete as a ghost or purely spiritual substance. It requires a material complement, a glorified 'body' which Christ assured us will be like the angels, and Paul insists will be incorruptible.[100] Contemporary theologians and philosophers of religion over the years have expressed varying conflicting views on the subject.[101] One theological view that seems to have

---

[98](Prov. 8: 31): "Ludens in orbe terrarum; et delicae meae esse cum filiis hominum."

[99]See for example, Denis Edwards, *Jesus and the Cosmos* (New York: Paulist Press, 1991); Brian Swimme & Thomas Berry, *The Universe Story* (San Francisco: HarperSanfrancisco, 1992); John F. Haught, *The Promise of Nature* (New York: Paulist Press, 1993).

[100]I Cor. 15:53.

[101]See for example, Lynn E. Boliek, *The Resurrection of the Flesh* (Grand Rapids: Wm. B. Eerdmans, 1962); C. F. F. Moule, "St. Paul and Dualism: The Pauline Concept of the Resurrection," *New Testament Studies* 12 (Jan., 1966): 106-123; Peter T. Geach, *God and the Soul* (New York: Schocken Books, 1969); Ronald J. Sider, "The Pauline Conception of the Resurrection Body in I Corinthians xv, 35-54," *New Testament Studies* 21 (April, 1975): 428-439; Paul Badham, *Christian Beliefs About Life After Death* (London: Macmillan, 1976); Paul Helm, "A Theory of Diembodied Survivial and Re-embodied Existence," *Religious Studies* 14 (March 1978): 15-26;

become rather widely accepted is that we will be given a new and different body, but expressing basically within its new material environment its distinctive personality.[102] It is not my role to suggest where the answer may lie,[103] but it seems to me that as Christians what we may look forward to is a new superior relationship of our spirit to the material world. As the adopted brothers and sisters of God's firstborn, we are to be an integral part of the "the new heavens and a new earth."[104] And for this we may well echo Scotus's prayer of gratitude:[105]

From this it is apparent how much thanks must be given to our Creator, who through faith has made us most certain of those things which pertain to our end and to eternal life— things about which the most learned and ingenious men can know almost nothing according to Augustine's statement in

---

Bruce R. Reichenbach, "Monism and Possibility of Life After Death," *Religious Studies* 14 (March 1978), 27-34; Frank Dilley, "Resurrection and the 'Replica' Objection," in *Religious Studies* 19 (1983): 459-474; B. R. Reichenbach, *Is Man the Phoenix?: A Study in Immortality* (Washington, D.C.: University Press of America, 1983); Stephen T.Davis, "Is Personal Identity Retained in the Resurrection?," *Modern Theology* 2 (1986): 328-340.

[102]See for example John Hick, *Death and Eternal Life* (New York: Harper and Row, 1976), p. 186. Frequently associated with this view is the claim that St. Paul did not mean simply by 'body' the physical organism we now possess, but rather the person who will be raised. Others, however, insist that Paul's use of *soma* and his notion of our present body as the seed that is sown and the resurrected body its new form implies some bodily continuity. See e.g. Robert H. Gundry, *Soma in Biblical Theology: With Emphasis on Pauline Anthropology* (New York: Cambridge Univ. Press, 1976) 186; R. J. Sider, *op. cit.*, 429-438; Bruce R. Reichenbach, "On Disembodied Resurrection Persons: A Reply," *Religious Studies* 18 (1982): 227. S. T. Davis continues to defend this patristic and scholastic view as an alternative in "Traditional Christian Belief in the Resurrection of the Body," *New Scholasticism* 62 (Winter, 1988): 72-97.

[103]Especially not to one who has written so extensively and with a perfectly balanced view on *De novissimis* as has Zachary Hayes. See, for example, his *What Are They Saying About the End of the World* (New York/Ramsey: Paulist Press, 1983); "Fundamentalist Escatology, *New Theological Reviewo* 1 (May, 1988): 21-25, or *Visions of the Future: A Study of Christian Eschatology* (Wilmington, DE: Michael Glazier, 1989).

[104]Rom. 8: 19-23; Revelation 21:1-3. See also Ted Peters, *God as Trinity*, (Louisville, KY: Westminster/John Knox Press, 1993), esp. ch. 4 entitled "The Temporal and Eternal Trinity."

[105]Cf. my *Duns Scotus: Philosophical Writings*, 162.

De Trinitate, Bk. XIII, c. 9.[106] "But if faith be there—that faith which is to be found in those whom [Jesus] has given the power to become the sons of God—there is no question about it," for this He has made those who believe in him most certain.

---

[106]Augustine, *De Trinitate* XIII, cap. 9 (PL 42, 1023): "Sed si fides adsit, quae inest eis quibus dedit potestatem Jesus filios Dei fieri, nulla quaestio est. Humanis quippe argumentationibus haec invenire conantes, vix pauci magno praediti ingenio, abundantes otio, doctrinisque subtibilissimis eruditi, ad indagandam solius animae immortalitatem pervenire potuerunt."